EUROPE 2020:
Competitive or Complacent?

Daniel S. Hamilton

Austrian Marshall Plan Foundation Professor
Executive Director
Center for Transatlantic Relations
American Consortium on EU Studies
Paul H. Nitze School of Advanced International Studies
Johns Hopkins University

Hamilton, Daniel S., *Europe 2020: Competitive or Complacent?*

Washington, DC: Center for Transatlantic Relations, 2011

Center for Transatlantic Relations
American Consortium on EU Studies
EU Center of Excellence Washington, DC
The Paul H. Nitze School of Advanced International Studies
The Johns Hopkins University
1717 Massachusetts Ave., NW, Suite 525
Washington, DC 20036
Tel: (202) 663-5880
Fax (202) 663-5879
Email: transatlantic@jhu.edu
http://transatlantic.sais-jhu.edu

ISBN 978-0-9841341-6-8
ISBN 0-9841341-6-6

Cover photo: Bill Frymire/Masterfile

Table of Contents

Section I: Goods, Services, Money, Energy, People and Ideas

Section II: Partners and Competitors: The EU and Other World Regions

Section III: Europe 2020: Competitive or Complacent?

Figures, Maps, and Tables

Chapter 4: Energy

Maps

Chapter 7: The EU and North America: Deep Integration

Chapter 8: The EU and Wider Europe

Chapter 10: The EU and China

Chapter 19: Creating a Competitive Europe

Preface and Acknowledgements

A new world is rising, one powered by multiple centers of economic dynamism and growth. As Europeans cope with the lingering consequences of the Great Recession, other continents roar on. How is Europe dealing with these changes? Is it positioning itself to be competitive in this new world? Or is it complacent, failing to meet its challenges while a world of opportunities passes it by? How are the European Union (EU) and its member states linked to other established and emerging economies? Where are those links thick, where are they thin, how have they been changing? What does this tell us about the EU's position in the global economy and prospects for the future?

This study tries to answer these questions. It examines how the EU is connected to other continents, and what it means for its competitiveness in a G20 world. It looks at the EU's global links in goods, services, money, energy, people and ideas. It maps each of these flows and describes how they affect relations between the EU and other world regions. It assesses the EU's strengths and weaknesses, and offers four scenarios for the EU's future.

I want to thank the Executive Council of the American Chamber of Commerce to the European Union for their support of this project and to thank AmCham EU and its member companies for their continuing support of the Center for Transatlantic Relations at Johns Hopkins University SAIS.

This study would not have been possible without the stellar efforts of my research team, led by Nikolas Foster, Grant Long and Michael Stanton-Geddes. I am extremely grateful to them for their diligence and good humor as I asked them to track down and make sense of often obscure and seemingly unrelated data.

I would also like to thank my colleagues Kurt Volker, Michael Haltzel, Gretchen Losee and Katrien Maes for their help and good cheer throughout this project, and for ensuring that the Center for Transatlantic Relations continued to thrive as I focused on writing; and Peggy Irvine and colleagues at AGS for working with me on the many details related to the production of the book. My colleague and co-author on many other endeavors, Joe Quinlan, is always a great source of wisdom on the issues covered in this book.

I am particularly grateful to Heidi, Siri and Sean Hamilton for bearing with my preoccupations and mental absences as I worked on this book.

The views expressed here are my own, as are any errors. Other views and data sources have been cited, and are appreciated.

Daniel S. Hamilton

Executive Summary

Rising powers are resetting the global economy. But they haven't done so yet. The European Union has a decade to position itself to prosper in an increasingly competitive and connected world. If it does not, the resulting strains could challenge Europe's very construction. The lingering economic crisis could be a watershed moment, either as the spur to a more competitive continent, or the time when Europe lost out decisively to more vigorous challengers.

The EU brings considerable strengths.[1] It is a world-class trader and investor. Five of the top ten and ten of the top twenty most competitive countries in the world are EU member states. The EU is among the most networked regions in the world, with deep financial assets and many pockets of innovation and high skilled talent. It is either the most important economic partner, or among the most important economic partners, for almost all other regions. But in the G20 world it is losing ground or has failed to reposition itself in some key markets, has suffered major financial shocks, is plagued by persistently low growth, has a high degree of energy dependence, and is a magnet for the unskilled at a time when its aging and shrinking population acutely needs a steady stream of high-skilled migration. By and large EU leaders have failed to convey the relevance of the European project to rising generations in a new world. In the words of former Hungarian Prime Minister Gordon Bajnai, many Europeans still view European integration as "half-finished, half-explained, half-considered, and half-hearted."[2] Perhaps most importantly, the EU itself is not a coherent competitor, but rather an often-ragged community of solidarity composed of an ever more disparate group of European countries. Too often its sum is less than its parts.

The EU's future economic performance depends on its ability and its propensity to utilize its extensive networks to leverage global growth, human talent and innovation while consolidating public finances, exploiting its considerable strengths and generating greater coherence and competitiveness among its constituent members.

Eight Priorities

8 priorities deserve immediate and sustained attention:

First things first. Get the recovery right. Policymakers urgently need to fix the financial system and advance fiscal austerity without undermining the EU's fragile return to growth. Fundamental reforms are needed, including a permanent crisis resolution mechanism to replace the temporary European Financial Stability Facility; fiscal and financial reforms that actually support—and enforce—growth and stability pact targets; and related efforts to improve economic performance.

Boost productivity to drive overall growth. The EU must raise its productivity if it is to deal with its demographic challenges and sustain its social welfare model. Failure to do so will mean a period of low or no growth, which is likely to generate greater domestic and intra-EU conflicts while leaving the EU behind in a world of high-growth competitors.

Complete the Single Market. The Single Market is the bedrock of European integration and the EU's most potent instrument to address the challenges of the G20 world. Completing the Single Market could produce growth of about 4% of GDP over the next ten years. It would provide EU countries and companies with a stronger geo-economic base in a world of continental-sized players.

Awaken Europe's sleeping giant: services—the EU's biggest untapped source of jobs and economic growth. Services account for 70% of Europe's output but just 23% of Europe's trade: there is room to grow. If the EU Services Directive were fully implemented, it could deliver more than 600,000 new jobs and economic gains ranging between €60-140 billion, representing an annual growth potential of at least 0.6-1.5% of GDP. It should also be extended to financial services, health, employment and social services. The EU should do more to capitalize fully on it strengths in trade and foreign direct investment in services.

Break the link between the production of wealth and the consumption of resources. The EU should lead in the transition to a low-carbon economy and promote itself as a showcase of energy efficiency and innovation. This will be neither quick nor easy. Fossil fuels are convenient, versatile, and in many cases cheaper than many renewables. But the EU has the capacity and the propensity to lead the great escape from fossil fuels.

Innovate. The EU's competitive advantage is increasingly as a knowledge economy. It must encourage entrepreneurs; focus on innovation outputs, not just inputs like R&D; pay more attention to social innovation, process innovation, services innovation, and user innovation; boost possibilities for continuous development of skills; introduce a unified EU patent system; protect intellectual property rights; and strengthen its innovation networks around the globe.

Power to the people. The EU must tap the potential of its people to manage demographic challenges, sustain social models, and develop skills for a knowledge-based economy. A pan-European talent strategy must attract skilled foreign labor; ensure free movement of people; facilitate business-education links; improve labor market access; promote education in key technologies; and boost overall skills training.

Become a critical hub in the G20 world. The EU should make itself a focal point for the intercontinental exchange of ideas, people, capital, goods, services and energy innovation. The more connected the EU is, the more competitive it is likely to be. It needs to complete the Single Market and extend its competitive networks throughout Wider Europe; create an open Transatlantic Marketplace; leverage high-growth opportunities in emerging markets; and reengage in neglected markets such as Turkey, Africa and Latin America.

Critical Connections

This study tracks the EU's competitive position in the world through six critical interdependencies: goods, services, money, energy, people and ideas. It maps the EU's connections in each of these areas with 12 other world regions: North America, Wider Europe, Japan, China, Rising Asia, India, Russia, the Middle East, Africa, Latin America, the Caribbean and Oceania. In each case we ask two questions: How connected is the EU? How competitive is the EU?

Goods

- The EU is the world's largest exporting entity and the world's largest trader in goods. It is the top supplier of goods to developing countries and is the largest trading partner of each of the BRICs.

- The EU has maintained world export share over the past 15 years; has gained market share in both high-tech and upmarket goods; and has withstood the competitive pressures of rising trading powers better than the U.S. and Japan, which have lost ground.

- The EU ranks #1 in export market share in 9 of 20 different product categories. Many emerging economies are demanding goods in which European companies specialize and in which the EU's comparative advantage is expected to continue.

- Two-thirds of EU goods trade is conducted with other EU member states.

- North America is the #1 regional market for EU goods (23% of EU total). The U.S. is the #1 country market (19%) for EU goods, but its share has declined 9% over the past decade.

- Wider Europe is the #2 regional market for EU goods, accounting for 21% of EU goods exports. EU goods exports to Wider Europe in 2009 were almost 3 times the value of EU goods exports to China.

- Between 1999 and 2008 total EU export shares to the old member states, the advanced OECD countries and Asia declined, while total EU export shares increased to the new member states, the BRICs and to the rest of the world outside the advanced countries and Asia.

- EU exports to China, Japan and India are strikingly low, and the EU has lost considerable ground in Africa to Asian competitors.

- EU goods exports to China are increasing 30% annually and China's share of EU goods exports has increased from 2.7% to 8%. But the EU exports more to Switzerland than to China.

- EU export growth rates are not keeping pace with some key emerging economies.

- Many EU companies are "overweight" in their export presence in developed countries and "underweight" in their exports to high growth developing markets. The key is to expand in new markets without relinquishing critical market presence in the EU itself, Wider Europe and North America, which still provide the primary base for EU export competitiveness.

- The EU is the world's largest importing entity. In 2009 China was the #1 source of EU goods imports (18.2%), followed by Wider Europe (18%), North America (16%) and Rising Asia (12%).

- The EU is challenged by China's rise as a high-tech exporter; the share of technology-driven industries in EU imports from China is higher than in intra-EU imports. Yet a good share of these imports are produced or assembled by European and other foreign companies in China: "Made in China" does not necessarily mean "Made by China." Germany is poised to continue as a formidable manufacturing competitor, and France and Poland stand to gain as well. But other EU member states face sobering challenges to their manufacturing base as other powers rise.

Services

- The services sector is the sleeping giant of the European economy—its greatest source of untapped growth and the source of all net job growth in the EU.

- Services account for over 70% of EU GDP but only 23% of global exports: there is room to grow.

- The EU is the world's largest regional trader in services. The EU15 almost quadrupled their services trade balance over the past decade; the EU in 2009 had a trade surplus in services with every world region except North America and the Caribbean.

- Europe registered 10% annual average growth in commercial services exports between 2000 and 2009, 1% more than the global average, 1% less than Asia, but 4% more than North America.

- 18 EU member states ranked among the top 40 exporters of services in 2009, accounting for 43.4% of world market share. The EU ranked #1 in the world in 8 of 11 categories.

- Two-thirds of EU services trade is conducted among EU member states. The EU Single Market has boosted intra-EU services trade by 35%.

- The most important external services partner for the EU by far is North America, and in particular the United States, accounting for roughly a third of all EU services exports and imports.

- Wider Europe accounted for 19% of extra-EU services exports and 17% of EU services imports from outside the Union in 2009—the second most important services trading partner for the EU.

- EU services trade is quite important for each of the BRICs, but less significant to the EU. The BRICS in 2009 accounted for less than 12% of EU services exports and 10.3% of EU services imports.

- FDI, not exports, is the main means for EU services companies to access BRIC markets. Services account for about 60% of total EU FDI stocks in the BRICs, manufacturing only 33%.

- Overall the EU is failing to capitalize on its strength in services, and lagging services productivity is the primary source of the EU's gap in GDP and productivity gap with the U.S. EU15 productivity could be boosted 3% by improved services sector productivity, and by 20% by reaching European best-practice levels per sector.

- Full implementation of the EU Services Directive could deliver more than 600,000 new jobs and economic gains ranging between €60-140 billion, representing an annual growth potential of at least 0.6-1.5% of GDP. And if competition in the eurozone was raised to U.S. levels, service sector output could be increased by 12%.

- EU decision-makers must avoid a false choice between services and manufacturing. The two sectors are increasingly symbiotic; if services win, so does manufacturing.

Money

- Europe is the largest provider and recipient of FDI among all world regions. EU countries accounted for 51% of global FDI outflows and nearly 40% of global FDI inflows between 2005 and 2009.

- The EU is the largest source of FDI in the United States as well as in the BRICs, and its position as an investor in these countries is even stronger than as a trader.

- 55 of the 100 largest non-financial multinational corporations are domiciled on EU territory.

- 62% of EU FDI outflows in 2008 remained within the EU, 2.5% more than in 2000. Intra-EU investments have increased much more rapidly than outward FDI – further evidence of the importance of a larger Single Market.

- The EU invested 35% more in the rest of the world than vice versa 2000-2009. The EU records net positive income from FDI with the rest of the world of around €75 billion a year.

- Outward FDI boosted EU GDP by more than €20 billion between 2001 and 2006; EU workers increased their income by almost €13 billion.

- 38% of EU FDI went to North America (32.5% to the U.S.). EU FDI outflows to the U.S. were more than the next 6 destinations combined.

- 22.5% of EU FDI went to Wider Europe—almost 6% more than in 2001.

- EU FDI to developing nations has accelerated, but from a very low base. Still, the EU provides more FDI than North America or Japan in each of the BRIC countries. EU FDI outflows to the BRICs are directed primarily to Russia and Brazil, rather than China or India.

- Almost half of FDI into the EU came from North America. The U.S. remains the principal source (44.4%) of FDI in the EU; the EU is the top destination of U.S. global FDI. In 2008 U.S. FDI in the EU totaled €1.05 trillion, more than the next 20 investors combined.

- About 63% of corporate America's total foreign assets is in Europe. U.S. companies in Europe employ millions of European workers and are the largest source of onshored jobs throughout the EU.

- Switzerland is a distant 2nd as an investor in the EU, with 29% of the U.S. total. Japan ranks 3rd.

- FDI by the BRICs in the EU is miniscule, accounting only 3.5% of EU FDI inflows 2002-2007—about the same as Norwegian FDI in the EU, and only about 9% of U.S. FDI in the EU.

- In 2008 the EU was the largest portfolio investor in North America, Wider Europe, Russia, India and Oceania; the second largest portfolio investor after North America in Africa, the Caribbean, Rising Asia, Japan, Latin America, and the Middle East; and the third largest portfolio investor in China, behind North America and Rising Asia.

- 68% of the $15.28 trillion in outward EU private portfolio investment in 2008 remained in the EU.

- 55% of outward extra-EU portfolio investment in 2008 went to North America (U.S.: 51%), compared with 20% to all of the Asia-Pacific and 11% each to the Caribbean and to Wider Europe.

- EU private portfolio investment in North America was 50 times that in China, and more than 65 times that in Russia.

- North America accounted for 45% of all portfolio investment into the EU in 2008, compared to 27% from the entire Asia-Pacific region and 24% from Wider Europe.

- Although EU private portfolio investment flows to China increased from only $4.5 billion in 2001 to $53.1 billion in 2008, they still remained miniscule, going from one-hundredth of 1% of the EU total in 2001 to one-third of 1% in 2008.

- Even following the financial crisis, U.S. and EU financial markets continue to account for well over two-thirds of global banking assets; three-quarters of global financial services; more than 70% of all private and public debt securities; almost 80% of all interest-rate derivatives; almost 75% of all new international debt securities; and 70% of all foreign exchange derivatives transactions.

- Nonetheless, over the past decade Asia's share of investment banking revenues has risen from 13% to more than 20%. The transatlantic share in global stock market capitalization has declined substantially from 78% to just over 50% today, and its share in stock trading has fallen from 86% to just over 70%. BRIC stock markets grew more than 40% per year in the past decade, while EU and U.S. markets contracted. The BRIC share of listed companies worldwide has jumped from just over 2% in 2000 to 22% today. More than half of the world's IPOs in 2009 were listed in China alone.

- Secondary European financial centers are losing ground to other advanced and emerging financial centers. The EU has only 4 of the top 20 financial centers worldwide.

- Despite the euro's woes, it has increased its role as a legitimate alternative to the dollar. In mid-2010 the euro accounted for 26.5% of total allocated global foreign exchange holdings, up from 18.3% at the end of 2000. Sterling's share increased from 2.8% to 4.2%, while the dollar's share declined from 71.1% to 62.1% and Japanese yen's share declined from 6.1% to 3.3%. Developing country demand for the euro and pound sterling is even higher.

Energy

- The EU holds about 0.6% of the world's oil reserves, 2% of its natural gas reserves, and 4% of coal reserves; and accounts for 18% of electricity generation capacity and 17% of total world energy consumption.

- Oil accounts for 40% of total EU energy consumption, natural gas 24%, nuclear 14%, coal 13%, hydroelectric power 4%, and other renewables 2%.

- EU dependency on foreign sources of energy rose from 46.8% in 2000 to 53.8% in 2008, and could rise to 70% over the next 20–30 years. Except for Denmark, all EU member states are net importers of energy; some are extremely dependent on foreign sources of energy.

- The EU is one of the most energy efficient economies. The EU15 needs only half as much energy per unit of economic output as the U.S., and 20% less than Japan. Europe is better positioned than most to break the link between the production of wealth and the consumption of resources.

- EU companies account for 13 of the world's top 15 R&D companies dedicated to clean energy technological development, and the EU leads all world regions in patents for air and water pollution control, renewable energy and solid waste management.

- Russia has displaced the Middle East as the EU's #1 regional oil supplier, followed by Wider Europe. Russia is also the EU's major supplier of coal, followed by Latin America. Africa is the EU's largest regional supplier of natural gas, followed by Wider Europe and Russia.

- EU imports of solar power parts grew from €1.4 billion in 2000 to over €10 billion in 2009—a 65% average annual growth rate, and over 7 times more than EU solar exports. Asian countries, led by China, account for almost all EU solar imports.

- EU solar exports are starting from a relatively low base but grew to €1.25 billion in 2009. The EU's main regional solar customer is Rising Asia.

- EU windpower imports are still relatively small, but with a high growth rate. China has become the EU's largest regional windpower parts provider, supplying over half of EU total imports, followed by Rising Asia and Latin America.

- EU windpower exports rose seven times from 2000-2006, but have fallen since. Top 3 EU exporting countries: Denmark, Germany and Spain. Biggest clients: North America, Middle East, and Japan.

- The EU is the #1 biodiesel producer in the world, accounting for about 95% of global production, and the #3 bioethanol producer (after the U.S. and Brazil), but with only 4% of production.

- EU biofuels exports posted average annual growth of 5.3% since 2000, but crashed after 2006. Primary customer: Wider Europe. Top supplier: Brazil.

- Germany is the world's leading exporter of environmental goods, ahead of the U.S., Japan and China. But nearly 60% of Germany's exports of environmental goods go to other EU member states.

People

- In 2009, 31.9 million foreign citizens lived in the EU, of which 11.9 million (37%) were citizens of another EU country. The remaining (63%) were citizens of countries outside the EU, in particular from Wider Europe (7.2 million), Africa (4.9 million), Asia (4.0 million) and North, South and Central America (3.3 million). Foreign citizens accounted for 6.4% of the total EU population.

- Of the 164 million migrants in the world, the largest number is in Europe—69.8 million, or about 42.6% of the total. More than half of the migrants coming to the EU in 2006 were from Wider Europe (27%) and Africa (26%), followed by Latin America (14%), North America (7%), and China (7%).

- Migrants also leave the EU for other world regions, particularly Oceania (33%), North America (32%) and Wider Europe (26%).

- The EU's labor force comprises 235 million people; 21 million (about 9%) are foreign-born. Between 1995 and the eve of the financial crisis, migrants filled 1/3 to 2/3 of all new jobs in the EU.

- The EU has rich human resources; compared with most other world regions, its citizens are well-educated and its workforce well-trained. Yet the EU is aging, shrinking, and has become a net importer of labor. Europe will lose 60 million workers over the next decade. Absent structural reforms, aging populations alone could reduce EU output growth by nearly half by 2040.

- Europe needs to double current net immigration to halt its population decline, triple it to maintain the size of its working-age population, and quintuple it to keep worker/elderly ratios at today's levels.

- Europe needs a large influx of skilled immigrants to help fill holes in the job market, maintain European living standards and the continent's economic well-being, and support its aging population. Yet Europe has become a magnet for the unskilled.

- Highly skilled foreign workers account for only 1.7% of all workers in the EU, compared with 9.9% in Australia, 7.3% in Canada and 3.5% in the United States.

- 85% of unskilled labor goes to the EU and 5% to the U.S., whereas 55% of skilled labor goes to the U.S and only 5% to the EU.

Innovation and Ideas

- Innovation is essential to Europe's ability to recover from the economic crisis and to prosper in today's highly competitive and connected global economy. EU prosperity will also be increasingly dependent on the strength of its knowledge links to other global hubs of innovation and ideas.

- Foreign R&D sources doubled their share of EU15 GDP from about 4% in 1981 to close to 9% in 2007; for the UK the share climbed to 18%. In Hungary, Belgium, the Czech Republic and Austria foreign affiliates accounted for over half of R&D investments by enterprises.

- The U.S. continues as the leading non-EU R&D investor in the EU; U.S. affiliates accounted for 71% of all industrial R&D in the EU by non-EU actors in 2007.

- EU-based companies account for 30.6% of the top R&D companies in the world, compared to 34.3% for the U.S. and 22% for Japan.

- The EU accounted for over 75% of all foreign R&D investment in the U.S. in 2007.

- California shared 64% of its foreign co-inventions with Europe and only 16% with other non-U.S. regions in North America in 2005.

- The Southeast of England, the Southern and Eastern region of Ireland, Lisbon, Portugal and the western Netherlands each share 40-50% of their foreign co-inventions with regions in North America.

- Globally, EU research networks are less thick or productive than U.S. networks: in Canada, China, India, Israel, Korea, Mexico and Taiwan the share of patents co-invented with the U.S. is at least twice as high as the share co-invented with the EU.

- The share of the BRICs in all patented inventions of the EU is just 1%, but rising fast, mainly because of China. Russian, Indian and Brazilian shares remain marginal.

- The EU is home to some of the most competitive knowledge-based economies in the world, including Denmark, Finland, Germany, Sweden and the UK. Yet there are great discrepancies within the Union, both among countries and among sub-regions within countries.

- Overall the EU risks being squeezed between high-performance innovation economies, such as the U.S. and Japan, and rising innovation performers from other world regions.

- Inadequate attention has been paid to social innovation and services innovation.

- EU innovators are relatively less effective than Americans at taking their ideas to market.

- The U.S. performs better than the EU in 11 innovation performance indicators, while the EU performs better than the U.S. in 6 areas.

- Japan performs better in 12 indicators; the EU performs better in 5 indicators.

- EU innovation performance growth, however, is growing faster than that of either the U.S. or Japan.

- The EU has a strong lead in innovation performance compared to each of the BRIC countries. But growth performance by China and India is 5 times better than that of the EU.

- The EU has failed to increase R&D investments as a share of GDP to catch up with the U.S., has fallen behind other key countries, and now could be eclipsed by China.

- Meeting the EU's target of boosting R&D investment to 3% of GDP from its 2008 level of 1.87% could create 3.75 million jobs and increase annual EU GDP by up to €795 billion by 2025.

- European metro areas lag significantly behind their U.S. counterparts as competitive world knowledge regions, as well as in per capita R&D expenditures and labor productivity.

- In 2007, one out of every two tertiary-level students studying in another country went to only four countries: the U.S. (19.7% of all foreign students worldwide); UK (11.6%); Germany (8.6%); and France (8.2%).

Partners and Competitors: The EU and Other World Regions

The EU and North America: Deep Integration

- The EU and North America are more deeply integrated across more economically relevant areas than any other two regions of the world. Ties are particular thick in foreign direct investment, portfolio investment, banking claims, trade in goods and services, and flows of ideas in terms of mutual R&D investment; patent cooperation; technology flows; and sales of knowledge-intensive services.

- North America is the largest regional destination of EU FDI and the largest regional source of FDI in the EU. The EU is the top destination of U.S. FDI around the world. In 2008 U.S. FDI in the EU totaled over €1 trillion, more than the next 20 investors combined.

- The EU had a total of €1.25 trillion in FDI in North America in 2008, more than the next 6 destinations combined, and 1.7 times more than in Wider Europe; 4½ times more than in Rising Asia; 5 times more than in Latin America; over 9 times more than in Africa; over 13 times more than in Russia; 16 times more than in Japan; 18 times more than in the Middle East; over 26 times more than in China; and 65 times more than in India.

- EU firms are the largest foreign employers of U.S. workers, and U.S. firms are the largest foreign employers of EU citizens, accounting together in the transatlantic economy for 14 million jobs.

- 92.8% of global foreign exchange holdings are in dollars (62.1%), euros (26.5%) or sterling (4.2%).

- The two regions account for 65% of global banking assets, three-quarters of global financial services, 77% of equity-linked derivatives, more than 70% of all private and public debt securities, almost 80% of all interest-rate derivatives, almost three-quarters of all new international debt securities, 70% of all foreign exchange derivatives transactions, 65% of the top R&D companies and 56% of all global R&D, and 18 of the top 20 knowledge regions in the world.

- North America is the largest regional destination of EU portfolio investment and the largest regional source of portfolio investment in the EU. 50% of overall foreign portfolio investment in North America in 2008 came from the EU, and another 15% came from Japan.

- EU portfolio investment in North America in 2008 was 5 times more than in the Caribbean and in Wider Europe; 6.5 times more than in Japan; 11 times more than in Rising Asia; 28 times more than in Latin America; 50 times more than in China; 54 times more than in India; 68 times more than in Russia; 74 times more than in the Middle East; and 78 times more than in Africa..

- European capital accounted for 71% of total U.S. inflows in Q1 2010.

- North American private portfolio investment in the EU in 2008 of almost $2 trillion was about double that from Wider Europe; 2.3 times more than from Japan; 8 times more than from Rising Asia; 20 times more than from the Caribbean; 85 times more than from Latin America; and 115 times more than from Russia.

- North America was the largest destination for EU goods exports (23%) in 2009. EU goods exports to North America were about 7% more than to Wider Europe; 2½ times more than to Africa; 2.2 times more than to Rising Asia; about 3 times more than to China (U.S. share 2.4 times more than to China); almost 4 times more than to Russia; almost 7 times more than to Japan; almost 9 times more than to India.

- The EU exports about the same amount of goods to North America as to the entire Asia-Pacific region, with each region accounting for about 23% of EU exports.

- North America was the #3 source of EU goods imports (15.9%), behind Wider Europe and China. EU goods imports from North America were 87% of EU goods imports from China (U.S. share 70% of that coming from China) and 88% of EU goods imports from Wider Europe; 40% more than from Russia; 74% more than from Rising Asia; almost 2 times more than from Africa, over 3 times more than from Japan; and over 7 times more than from India.

- The EU has withstood trade competition by emerging countries better than the U.S. The EU has maintained its 19% world export share of world exports over 15 years; the U.S. lost around 6% and now accounts for 12.5%.

- The EU registered close to a 1% gain in global market share in high-tech products between 1994 and the onset of the recession; the U.S. recorded an 11% loss.

- Between 2000 and 2007 the EU gained market shares in "upmarket" goods; the U.S. lost shares.

- North America was the largest destination for EU services exports (30%) and the largest source of EU services imports (37%) in 2009.

- EU services exports to North America were in 2009 were 31% higher than to Wider Europe; over 3.5 times more than to Rising Asia and Latin America; 4 times more than to the Middle East and to Africa; almost 5 times more than to Oceania; over 7 times more to Russia, China and Japan; almost 15 times more than to India; and 29 times more than to the Caribbean.

- EU services imports from North America in 2009 were 43% more than from Wider Europe; over 4.5 times from Rising Asia; over 5 times from Africa; over 6 times from the Middle East; over 9 times more than from Oceania, China and Latin America; over 12 times more than from Japan and Russia; over 18 times more than from India; and 37 times more than from the Caribbean.

- The EU was #1 in the world in 8 of 11 categories of services exports; the U.S. leads in the other 3.

- Leading EU services exporters such as the UK, Germany and France lag the U.S. when it comes to key markets such as Japan, India, China and Rising Asia.

- The EU15's per capita GDP lags that of the United States by about 24%—$4.5 trillion in total, or about $11,250 per inhabitant—reflecting lower labor utilization and lower hourly productivity.

- The core of the U.S. competitive advantage is a large pan-continental market, flexible labor markets, and strong innovation. The EU trails in all three.

- The U.S. performs better than the EU in 11 of 17 indicators of innovation performance and the R&D intensity of U.S. companies is larger than that of EU companies in 9 of 15 sectors.

- U.S. companies invest nearly five times more than EU companies in semiconductors, four times more in software and eight times more in biotechnology.

- North America accounts for 13 of the top knowledge regions in the world, compared to only 5 in the EU, and 53 of the 100 most competitive cities, compared to 30 for the EU.

- The EU has failed in its goal to catch up to the U.S. in the share of GDP it devotes to R&D, and continues to lag in labor productivity, particularly in services.

- Younger EU companies also tend to be less R&D intensive than their U.S. counterparts; this difference alone accounts for over half of the EU-U.S. R&D intensity gap.

- North America is the EU's largest export market for windpower parts and oil, and is the EU's third largest solar client, fourth largest solar provider, and fourth largest source of coal.

- North America received one-third of all emigrants from the EU; 7.2% of all emigrants from North America go to the EU.

- The EU is Canada's second largest investment partner after the U.S., and Canada is the fourth largest country investment partner for the EU.

- The EU is Canada's second most important trading partner, after the U.S., with a 10.5% share of its total external trade. Canada is currently the EU's 11th most important trading partner, accounting for 1.8% of the EU's total external trade in 2009.

- A U.S.-EU zero-tariff agreement on trade in goods alone could boost annual EU GDP by up to .48% and 1.48% for the U.S.; generate welfare gains of up to $89 billion for the EU and $87 billion for the U.S.; and increase EU exports to the U.S. by up to 18% and U.S. exports to the EU by up to 17%.

- A 75% reduction of U.S.-EU services tariffs would yield almost $13.9 billion annually for the EU and $5.6 billion for the U.S.

- Aligning half of relevant U.S.-EU non-tariff barriers and regulatory differences would push EU GDP .7% higher in 2018 (€122 billion/yr) and EU exports 2.1%; and boost U.S. GDP .3% in 2018 (€41 billion/yr) and U.S. exports 6.1%.

- An EU-Canada economic agreement promises to boost EU exports to Canada by 24.3% and Canadian exports to the EU by 20.6% by 2014. Annual real income gain would be approximately €11.6 billion for the EU and €8.2 billion for Canada.

The EU and Wider Europe: The China Next Door?

- Wider Europe was the second largest regional destination for EU goods exports (21%) and the second largest source of EU goods imports (18%) in 2009. The EU exported €226.4 billion of goods to Wider Europe, 93% as much as to North America but more than twice as much as to Rising Asia and to Africa; 2.8 times more than to China; over 3 times more than to Russia; over 6 times more than to Japan; and over 8 times more than to India.

- The EU imported €213.1 billion of goods from Wider Europe in 2009, marginally less than from China, but 12% more than from North America; over 1½ times more than from Rising Asia; almost twice as much as from Russia and from Africa; almost 4 times more than from Japan; and over 8 times more than from India.

- Wider Europe was the second largest regional destination for EU services exports (19%) and second largest source of EU services imports (17%) in 2009.

- EU services exports to Wider Europe in 2009 were 69% of its services exports to North America, but 2.5 times more than to Rising Asia and to Latin America; almost 3 times more than to the Middle East and to Africa; over 3 times more than to Oceania; 5 times more than to China, Russia and Japan; 10 times more than to India; and 20 times more than to the Caribbean.

- EU services imports from Wider Europe in 2009 were 57% of EU services imports from North America, but over 2.5 times more than from Rising Asia; 3 times more than from Africa; 3.5 times more than from the Middle East; over 5 times more than from Oceania, China and Latin America; 7 times more than from Japan and Russia; over 10 times more than from India; and 21 times more than from the Caribbean.

- Wider Europe is the second largest regional destination for FDI from the EU. The EU had a total of €732 billion in foreign direct investment in Wider Europe in 2008, only about 60% of EU FDI in North America, but almost 3 times more than in Rising Asia; over 3 times more than in Latin America and the Caribbean; over 5 times more than in Africa; 8 times more than in Russia; over 9 times more than in Japan; over 10 times more than in the Middle East; over 15 times more than in China; and 38 times more than in India.

- Wider Europe is also the second largest regional source of foreign direct investment in the EU. Wider Europe had a total of €464 billion in foreign direct investment in the EU in 2008, only 40% of FDI coming into the EU from North America, but 69% more than from the Caribbean, 4 times more than from Japan; over 6 times more than from Rising Asia; 6½ times more than from Latin America; over 9 times more from the Middle East; over 16 times more than from Russia; 22 times more than from Africa; 33 times more than from China; and 66 times more than from India.

- 52% of overall foreign portfolio investment in Wider Europe came from the EU. Another 30% came from the United States, and 7% came from Japan.

- The EU had a total of $543 billion in portfolio investment in Wider Europe in 2008, slightly more than in the Caribbean and 25% more than in Japan; over twice as much as in Rising Asia; almost 6 times more than in Latin America; over 10 times more than in China; 11 times more than in India; 14 times more than in Russia; 15 times more than in the Middle East; and 16 times more than in Africa.

- Wider Europe had a total of $1.034 trillion in private portfolio investment in the EU in 2008, only slightly more than half that from North America, but 82% more than from Japan; 4 times more than from Rising Asia; over 10 times more than from the Caribbean; 45 times more than from Latin America; 60 times more than from Russia; and 64 times more than from the Middle East.

- Wider Europe is the EU's second largest regional source and buyer of natural gas; the second largest buyer of EU oil and third largest source of oil; and largest buyer of coal and seventh largest source.

- Wider Europe is the EU's #1 regional purchaser of biofuels and #3 provider; and second largest buyer of windpower parts and fourth largest provider.

- Wider Europe is the largest regional source of both refugees (39.7%) and migrants (28.1%) into the EU, and the third largest regional destination of EU emigrants (26.3%).

The EU and Japan: Fading Ties?

- The EU and the Japan are major exporters of goods and competitors in a range of products, particularly upmarket, manufacturing and capital-intensive goods.

- The EU accounted for 15.2% of world market share in automotive parts, compared to Japan's 13.9% share.

- The EU has withstood competitive pressures from rapidly emerging economies better than Japan. The EU has maintained its 19% market share of world exports over 15 years; Japan lost around 6%, and now accounts for 8.6% of world market share.

- The EU registered close to a 1% gain in global market share in high-tech products between 1994 and the onset of the recession; Japan recorded a 13% loss.

- The EU enjoys significant advantages over Japan in services, with much higher market shares across every commercial sector.

- The EU also leads Japan in energy efficiency and sustainability: the EU15 need only 80% as much energy per unit of economic output as Japan, and rival Japanese companies in terms of patents in renewables and environmental goods.

- The EU compares favorably to Japan when it comes to young innovative companies.

- Bilateral trade in goods and services has weakened in recent decades. EU imports of goods from Japan fell 40% and the EU trade deficit with Japan fell 57% this past decade. Much intermediate trade in goods has shifted from Japan to China.

- With a share of 3.3% of EU exports in 2009, Japan is the EU's seventh largest regional export market. With a 4.6% (2009) share of the EU import market, Japan is the sixth largest source of imports into the EU. The EU trades more with Norway than with Japan.

- Japan accounted for 3.6% of EU FDI inflows in 2008 and 4.51% of the stock of EU inward FDI.

- Japan had a total of €117 billion in foreign direct investment in the EU in 2008, only 10% of that from North America, 4 times less than that from Wider Europe and almost 3 times less than from the Caribbean, but 38% more than from Rising Asia; 39% more than from

Latin America; 58% more than from the Middle East; 76% more than from Russia; 82% more than from Africa; 88% more than from China; and 17 times more than from India.

- Only 1.7% of the EU FDI outflow went to Japan in 2008, and Japan accounted for only 2.36% of the stock of EU outward FDI, less than in Russia, about half of that in Africa, around a third of that in the Caribbean and in Latin America, a fourth of that in Rising Asia, a tenth of that in Wider Europe and 16 times less than EU FDI in North America.

- Even at low levels, the EU has been the largest source of FDI into Japan in recent years.

- The EU accounted for 43% of overall foreign portfolio investment in Japan, slightly more than the U.S. investment share of 41%.

- Japanese private portfolio investment in the EU is 2.3 times less than from North America and 82% less than from Wider Europe, but over 3 times more than from Rising Asia; almost 9 times more than from the Caribbean; 37 times more than from Latin America; 50 times more than from Russia; 53 times more than from the Middle East; and 60 times more than from China.

- EU-Japan connections in the realm of innovation and ideas are stronger than between most regions, but still pale in comparison with those between the EU and North America.

- The EU consistently lags Japan in terms of innovation performance, but registers better growth rates.

- In terms of global foreign exchange holdings, over the past ten years there has been a boost in the role of the euro (26.5%) and pound sterling (4.2%) whereas the yen's position has slipped (3.3%).

The EU and China: Shaping the Future?

- EU ties to China are weak in terms of services, investment, energy, people and ideas, but strong in terms of Chinese exports of goods.

- China is the EU's #1 goods supplier, accounting for 17.9% of EU imports in 2009. The EU is China's single most important export market: 20.4% of Chinese exports, slightly more than the U.S.

- EU goods imports from China of €214.7 billion in 2009 were slightly greater than good imports from Wider Europe of €213.1 billion and 13% greater than goods imports from North America, but 1.5 times more than from Rising Asia; almost double goods imports from Russia, and more than double goods imports from Africa.

- The EU is challenged by China's faster export growth rates and the growing share of technology-driven industries in Chinese exports to the EU.

- China is only the sixth largest regional destination for EU goods exports; the EU exports more to Switzerland.

- EU goods exports of €81.6 billion to China in 2009 were only one-third EU good exports to North America, 36% of good exports to Wider Europe; 75% of EU goods exports to Rising Asia, and slightly less than EU goods exports to Africa. Still, the EU has a 13.4% export market share in China, ahead of the United States, Japan and South Korea.

- The EU has a large and chronic trade deficit with China.

- EU goods exports to China have been growing at a 30% annual average growth rate over the course of the past decade—faster than any other goods export destination, but still relatively low.

- Accounting for purchasing power, China's GDP per capita was 11% of that of the EU in 2009. 150 million Chinese still live on less than €2 a day.

- European companies lose out on an estimated €20 billion a year due to China's many non-tariff barriers and regulatory discrimination, its preferential treatment of Chinese companies and indigenous technology for government procurement, its undervalued currency, its weak enforcement or implementation of existing regulations in many areas, and its lack of protections for intellectual property rights. Roughly 50% of counterfeit goods in the EU come directly from China.

- China accounts for only 4% of both EU services exports and imports. The EU tripled its services trade surplus with China over the past five years.

- EU services exports to China in 2009 were 7 times less than those to North America; 5 times less than to Wider Europe; half of EU services exports to Latin America, and slightly less than EU services exports to Russia.

- EU services imports from China were 9 times less than from North America; 5 times less than from Wider Europe; half from Rising Asia, but more than from Russia and from India.

- The EU's FDI links to China are also weak, due in particular to Chinese barriers. EU FDI in China in 2008 was 26 times less than in North America; over 15 times less than in Wider Europe; almost 6 times less than in Rising Asia; almost 5 times less than in the Caribbean and in Latin America; almost 3 times less than in Africa; and half of EU FDI in Russia.

- Chinese FDI in the EU is also miniscule, less than 1% of all foreign FDI in the EU.

- China accounted for only 1% of EU portfolio outflows; EU portfolio investment accounted for 22% of overall foreign portfolio investment in China.

- The EU accounted for 24% of global R&D in 2007, China for 9%.

- China's share of global R&D is less than half that of the EU. But China accounted for almost a third of the global increase in R&D between 2001 and 2006, as much as Japan and the EU combined.

- China accounts for only 1.3% of the top R&D companies in the world, compared to 30.6% for EU companies.

- The EU outperforms China in all innovation indicators except ICT expenditures and high-tech exports. Of the top 100 most competitive cities, 30 were from the EU; none from China.

- International use of China's currency, the renminbi, is still marginal, but growing.

- China accounts for less of global clean tech investment than the EU as a whole, but spent four times more than EU leader Germany and surpassed the United States for the first time in 2008.

- China offers the world's largest solar manufacturing capacity and a leading wind manufacturing industry. It is the EU's largest supplier of wind and solar components and the 2nd largest buyer.

The EU and Rising Asia: Opportunity Knocks

- Rising Asia was the fourth largest regional destination of EU goods exports (10%) and is a larger export market for the EU than China. Rising Asia was also the fourth largest source of EU goods imports (11.7%) in 2009.

- Overall goods trade with Rising Asia has been growing only slowly over the past decade. This has sliced the EU's goods trade deficit with the region by 42%, and is another reflection of the shift in inter-Asian production patterns from Rising Asia and Japan to China.

- Rising Asia was the third largest destination for EU services exports (8%) and the third largest source of EU services imports (8%) in 2009. The EU has a services trade surplus with Rising Asia.

- The 2010 EU-South Korea trade agreement promises to create about €19 billion of new exports for EU producers and about €12 billion of new exports for South Korean companies.

- The EU had a total of €270 billion in foreign direct investment in Rising Asia in 2008, making the region the third largest regional destination for FDI from the EU—4.6 times less than FDI in North America and 2.7 times less than in Wider Europe, but slightly more than in Latin America and in the Caribbean, twice as much as in Africa, 3 times more than in Russia, in Japan and in the Middle East, and almost 6 times more than in China.

- Rising Asia's €73 billion in FDI in the EU in 2008 made it the fifth largest source of FDI in the EU—but 16 times less than from North America, 6 times less than from Wider Europe, over 4 times less than from the Caribbean, and 63% of FDI from Japan; but about the same as from Latin America, 67% more than from the Middle East, 38% more than from Russia, and over 3 times more than from Africa, 5 times more than from China, and 10 times more than from India.

- 33% of overall foreign portfolio investment in Rising Asia came from the EU. Another 33% came from the United States, and 6% came from Japan.

- Rising Asia was the #1 purchaser of EU solar parts and second largest seller in 2009; the EU's number two provider of windpower parts and fifth largest windpower client in 2009.

- Rising Asia is the second largest regional source of EU biofuel imports in 2009 and fifth largest destination for EU biofuels—although imports from Rising Asia have declined 50% and exports have suffered a 99% decline since 2004, and overall totals are but a fraction of those from Brazil.

- The EU has fallen further behind South Korea and Singapore in terms of the share of GDP devoted to R&D.

- Rising Asia has a much larger share of young firms than the EU, and companies from Rising Asia have increased their share of high- and medium-high R&D intensive sectors.

The EU and India: Surprisingly Weak Links

- The EU's economically relevant links to India are relatively thin in most areas.

- The EU is India's largest trade partner, accounting for 21.1% of Indian exports and 17% of Indian imports. But India accounted for only 3% of overall EU goods exports and 2.1% of EU goods imports in 2009. EU trade with China is 6 times greater than with India.

- India is the only BRIC country with which the EU has a trade surplus.

- India's rapid development has been essentially service-led and supported by services exports. India has become the world's top country exporter in computer and information services, but the EU fares better in all other services categories.

- India's direct services ties to the EU are extremely weak; India accounts for only 2% of EU services exports and imports. Essentially, India is building its growing prowess in computers, information and communication services in third markets rather than in the EU, and competing with EU companies in those third markets.

- India ranks 11th of 12 regions both as a destination and source for EU FDI and as a source of FDI into the EU. The EU total of €19 billion in FDI in India in 2008 was 40% of its FDI in China; 28% of its FDI in the Middle East; 25% of its FDI in Japan; about 20% of its FDI in Russia; 14% of its FDI in Africa; 8% of its FDI in Latin America and in the Caribbean; 7% of its FDI in Rising Asia; less than 3% of its FDI in Wider Europe; and less than 2% of its FDI in North America.

- 44% of the foreign portfolio investment in India came from the EU in 2008. Another 29% came from the U.S., and 3% came from Japan. The EU total of $49 billion in private portfolio investment was 73% more than in the Middle East and 69% more than in Africa, 35% more than in Russia and roughly the same as in China, but only 53% of its investment in Latin America; 21% of that in Rising Asia; 12% of that in Japan; 9% of that in the Caribbean and in Wider Europe; and less than 2% of that in North America. India had only $1 billion in private portfolio investment in the EU in 2008.

- EU-India energy ties in traditional energy sources are marginal. India's solar trade with the EU has grown quickly, but from very low levels.

- The EU far outperforms India in all indicators of innovation performance except ICT expenditures and knowledge-intensive services exports, but India's innovation growth performance is more than 5 times better than that of the EU.

- Despite its surging prowess in a select number of services, essentially India has failed to improve significantly on most basic drivers of its competitiveness.

The EU and Russia: Stormy Weather

- The EU's economically relevant ties to Russia center on Russian energy flows of oil, gas and coal. There is also considerable trade in capital-intensive goods.

- Russia holds around 6.4% of the world's oil reserves and around 25% of the world's gas reserves. It is also the world's biggest gas producer and the second biggest oil producer.

- Russia is the EU's #1 supplier of oil and coal, and its third largest regional provider of natural gas. A number of EU member states rely on Russian energy imports, and some are critically dependent on such flows.

- Russia is not a significant partner for the EU in renewables.

- The EU's ties to Russia are relatively thin in terms of mutual portfolio flows, FDI, services, people and ideas, even though the EU is Russia's largest trading partner and leading source of FDI and portfolio investment.

- The EU is by far Russia's major commercial partner, accounting for 52.3% of its overall trade turnover in 2008. It is also by far the most important investor in Russia, accounting for up to 75% of FDI stocks in Russia.

- The EU accounted for just over half of foreign portfolio investment in Russia in 2008, compared with 32% from the U.S. and 2% from Japan. The EU total of $39 billion was 13% more than its investment in Africa and 8% more than in the Middle East, but only 80% of that in India; 74% of that in China; 42% of that in Latin America; 17% of that in Rising Asia; only 9% of that in Japan; 7% of that in the Caribbean and in Wider Europe, and 1% of that in North America.

- Russia had a total of $17 billion in private portfolio investment in the EU in 2008, 74% of that coming from Latin America and about the same as from the Middle East, but only 17% of that from the Caribbean; 7% of that from Rising Asia; 2% of that from Japan; less than 2% of that from Wider Europe, and less than 1% of that from North America.

- Russia was the seventh largest regional destination for EU goods exports (6%) and fifth largest source of EU goods imports (9.8%) in 2009. EU exports to Russia roughly tripled over the course of the past decade, but fell 37.6% between 2008 and 2009.

- Traditionally the EU's main export destination among the BRICs, Russia has now lost that distinction to China. But Russia remains the EU's third largest country trading partner, after China and the U.S.

- Medium-skill industries, particularly refined petroleum, dominate EU imports from Russia.

- Russia was the eighth largest regional destination for EU services exports (4%) and the tenth largest source of EU services imports (3%) in 2009. The EU's services trade surplus with Russia increased six-fold between 2004 and 2008.

- Russia is the seventh largest regional destination for of FDI from the EU and the eighth largest source of FDI into the EU. EU FDI of €92 billion in Russia in 2008 was almost 5 times more than in India; about double that in China; a quarter more than in the Middle East; 18% more than in Japan; but only 60% of EU FDI in Africa; 40% of that in Latin America and in the Caribbean; 34% of that in Rising Asia; 8 times less than in Wider Europe; and 13 times less than in North America.

- Russian FDI of €28 billion in the EU in 2008 was four times more than Indian FDI in the EU, double China's FDI in the EU, and a quarter more than FDI from Africa; but only 57% of that from the Middle East; 40% of that from Latin America; 38% of that from Rising Asia; 24% of that from Japan; 11 times less than from the Caribbean; 16 times less than from Wider Europe; and 41 times less than from North America.

- Migrant flows from Russia accounted for 4.6% of the total migrant flows to the EU in 2006, making it the seventh largest of the ten regions for which data is available, although migrant flows from Russia decreased by 22.1% from 2000 to 2006.

- Russia's competitiveness continues to worsen, and it faces considerable hurdles in terms of keeping up with other rapidly developing economies.

The EU and the Middle East: Energy and People

- The Middle East was the third largest regional destination of EU goods exports (10%) and the ninth largest regional source of EU goods imports (4.6%) in 2009. The EU has run large trade surpluses in goods every year since 2000 with the Middle East, despite EU energy needs.

- The Middle East was the fifth largest regional destination for EU services exports (7%) and the fifth largest source of EU services imports (6%) in 2009.

- The Middle East is the ninth largest regional destination for FDI from the EU, and the seventh largest regional source of FDI in the EU.

- Although the Middle East has been the EU's second largest regional source of oil since 2000, oil exports from the region to the EU have declined by 44% over the last ten years.

- The Middle East was the EU's third largest regional destination for natural gas and fourth largest source of natural gas.

- Refugees from the Middle East accounted for 18.3% of the total refugees in the EU, making it the second largest contributing region of the twelve regions examined.

- Migrant flows from the Middle East accounted for 3.8% of total migrant flows to the EU in 2006.

The EU and Africa: Energy, People, and Neglected Opportunities

- Africa was both Europe's largest regional source of and destination for natural gas and Europe's second largest source of and destination for oil in 2009. It is growing as a partner for the EU in renewables.

- Africa accounted for 26.8% of the total migrant flows to the EU in 2006, making it the second largest contributing region, sending slightly less than Wider Europe, but accounting for 6 times more migrants to the EU than the Middle East.

- Refugees from Africa accounted for 17.6% of the total refugees in the EU, making it the third largest contributing region of the eleven regions examined, sending less than half of those coming from Wider Europe, slightly less than those from the Middle East, and slightly more than Rising Asia.

- Africa was the fifth largest regional destination for EU goods exports (9%) in 2009 and the sixth largest source of EU goods imports (8.5%). EU goods exports to Africa exceed EU goods exports to Russia, Japan and China, but EU goods imports from Africa are less than half of EU goods imports from China and slightly less than from Russia.

- EU goods trade with Africa is nearly double its trade with Latin America.

- The EU is losing ground in Africa; between 1990 and 2008 its share of Africa's trade shrank to 28%, from 51%, while Asia's share doubled to equal the EU share at 28%.

- The EU is South Africa's most important economic trade partner, accounting for over 40% of its imports and exports, as well as for 70% of foreign direct investment. Yet China has become South Africa's #1 country trading partner.

- EU FDI in Africa is also of only medium importance, although larger than some other major world regions. The flow of ideas between the EU and Africa is weak. EU R&D expenditure in Africa is negligible in all countries except South Africa. The EU is the largest aid donor to African countries.

The EU and Latin America: Commodities, Services, Energy, and People

- The EU is Latin America's leading regional trade partner and largest regional source of FDI. Latin America is the 3rd largest source of migrants into the EU, a relatively important supplier of coal, and Brazil is the EU's primary supplier of biofuels. Other flows are of less significance.

- Latin America was the eighth largest destination for EU goods exports (4%) and the seventh largest source of EU goods imports (5.1%) in 2009. Brazil accounted for 47% of EU goods exports to the region and 42% of EU goods imports from the region. EU exports to Latin America averaged only 1.6% annual growth over the course of the past decade.

- The EU mainly imports primary products (70%) from Latin America, while it exports machinery and transport equipment (85%).

- Brazil is the EU's largest trading partner in Latin America, and the EU is Brazil's largest regional trading partner, accounting for 22.5% of Brazil's external trade. Brazil is the single biggest exporter of agricultural products to the EU, accounting for 12.4% of total EU imports in 2009, and ranks as the EU's 10th country trading partner.

- Latin America was the fourth largest destination for EU services exports (8%) and the eighth largest source of EU services imports (4%) in 2009.

- The EU has neglected Latin America and is losing ground as a trade partner. By 2014, China alone could displace the EU as a market for Latin American exports and by 2020 could account for more than 19% of Latin American exports, versus a EU share of less than 14%.

- Latin America is the fourth largest regional destination for FDI from the EU. The EU's €228 billion in FDI in Latin America in 2008 was 12 times more than its FDI in India, almost 5 times more than in China, over 3 times more than in the Middle East and 3 times more than in Japan; almost 2½ times more than in Russia; twice that in Africa; and about the same as in the Caribbean; but only 84% of EU FDI in Rising Asia; 3 times less than in Wider Europe and 5 times less than in North America.

- Latin America is the sixth largest regional source of FDI into the EU. Latin America's €71 billion in FDI in the EU in 2008 was 10 times more than that from India; 5 times more than that from China; over 3 times more than that from Africa; 2.5 times more than that from Russia; 31% more than that from the Middle East; and about the same as from Rising Asia; but only 60% of that from Japan; 4.5 times less than from the Caribbean; 6.5 times less than from Wider Europe; 16 times less than from North America.

- 31% of overall foreign portfolio investment in Latin America came from the EU, compared with 46% from the United States and 4% from Japan.

- Latin America accounted for 14.2% of the total migrant flows to the EU in 2006, making it the third largest of the ten regions for which data is available.

The EU and the Caribbean: Follow the Money

- The EU's financial ties to the Caribbean are extremely strong, reflecting the region's role as a money center. 75% of the world's hedge funds are in the Caribbean. Links are particularly intensive with the UK. New EU rules may hamper bilateral financial flows.

- The Caribbean was the EU's 3rd most important regional source of FDI in the world in 2008, accounting for €321 billion in foreign direct investment in the EU. Until the recession, Caribbean investment in the EU grew at an annual average of about 19% over the past decade. Caribbean FDI in the EU in 2008 was almost 1/3 of that coming from North America and 70% of that from Wider Europe. Yet it was about 3 times more than from Japan, 4½ times more than from Latin America and 6½ times more than from the Middle East, and more than from the entire Asia-Pacific region (China, Rising Asia, India, Japan, Oceania).

- The Caribbean is the fifth largest regional destination for EU FDI. Before the recession, EU investment in the Caribbean grew 32% on average annually over the past decade. The EU had a total of €226 billion in foreign direct investment in the Caribbean in 2008, almost 12 times more than in India, 5 times more than in China, 3 times more than in Japan and in the Middle East, 2½ times more than in Russia, roughly the same as in Latin America, about 40% more than in Africa, and about 90% more than in Rising Asia, but only 31% of that in Wider Europe and 18% of that in North America.

- 30% of overall foreign portfolio investment in the Caribbean came from the EU. Another 30% came from the United States, and 22% came from Japan.

- The EU had a total of $532 billion in private portfolio investment in the Caribbean in 2008, more than in any other region except North America, which held 5 times that amount, and Wider Europe ($543 billion).

- EU private portfolio investment in the Caribbean was 23% more than EU portfolio investments in Japan; almost 2½ times more than in Rising Asia; almost 6 times more than in Latin America; over 10 times more than in China and in India; over 13 times more than in Russia; and almost 15 times more than in the Middle East or in Africa.

- The Caribbean had a total of $97 billion in private portfolio investment in the EU in 2008—5th among regions, behind North America, Wider Europe, Japan and Rising Asia but far ahead of Latin America, Russia, China, India and Africa.

- The Caribbean has also become a growing source of natural gas for Europe. All other links are rather weak. Of the 12 regions surveyed, the Caribbean ranks as the EU's least important trading partner. The Caribbean accounted for 1% of EU exports and a negligible amount of EU imports.

The EU and Oceania: Distant Cousins

- Oceania is the largest regional destination for European emigrants leaving the EU (32.4%).

- Oceania is among the smallest goods trade partners for the EU, accounting for only 2% of EU goods exports and just 1% of EU goods imports in 2009.

- Australia and New Zealand constitute 90-95% of Oceania's goods trade with the EU.

- The EU exported €26 billion of goods to Oceania, about a third of EU goods exports to China, about the same as to India, and about three-quarters of EU goods exports to Japan, but only one-quarter of that to Rising Asia, 27% of that to Africa.

- Oceania was also a small services trade partner for the EU, accounting for 6% of EU services exports and 4% of EU services imports in 2009.

- Oceania's FDI links with the EU are also quite thin. The EU had a total of only €67 billion in foreign direct investment in Oceania in 2008, but still about 72% more than in India and 30% more than in China; about the same as in the Middle East.

- Oceania had a total of €22 billion in foreign direct investment in the EU in 2008, about one-third more than Chinese FDI in the EU; about the same as FDI from Africa; 78% less than FDI from Russia; and slightly less than half of FDI from the Middle East.

Four Scenarios

Europe's future economic performance depends on its ability and its propensity to leverage global growth, human talent and innovation while exploiting European strengths and consolidating public finances. These external and internal drivers define four possible scenarios for Europe's future:

- ***Competitive Europe.*** If the EU is to maintain and even advance its competitive position, it must not only build on its strengths and address its weaknesses, it must bolster its capacity to leverage the dynamism of other key regions and to absorb innovation and talent from beyond its borders. In the scenario dubbed *Competitive Europe*, the EU and its member states are successful in doing these things in a high-growth global environment.

- ***Losing Steam.*** Under this scenario the EU and its member states agree on ways to improve their competitiveness, but the promise dissipates due to persistently low European and global growth as the recovery from the financial crisis stutters. Opportunities falter in emerging markets, and EU integration itself comes under greater pressure as the divergences widen between high-performing member states and others who fall further behind. The EU fails to attract or nurture high-skilled labor as populations age and shrink, adding to pressures on workers, migrants, companies and governments.

- ***Europe Unhooked.*** Under this scenario the EU fails to leverage high global growth, the recovery is weakened, and confidence erodes in the euro and in sterling. Faster-growing and more innovative competitors capture market share in a variety of goods and services, and investment shrivels as high-growth opportunities beckon elsewhere. Divergences widen even further among member states, and social tensions rise.

- ***Europe Adrift.*** Under this scenario there is low global and European growth and the EU and its member states fail to advance efforts to advance their competitiveness. Debt levels remain stubbornly high and continual crisis management erodes the credibility of European integration and the European model, diminishing European influence in the world, prompting intense debate about the nature and relevance of the EU itself. Innovation and productivity flag. The EU loses critical market share both in goods and services to faster-growing, more innovative competitors. Social divisions are exacerbated and the welfare state provisions of EU member states simply become unsustainable as a smaller workforce proves unable to support aging populations. Workers suffer, wages decline, and anti-migrant forces gain ground.

Introduction

Rising powers are resetting the global economy. But this transformation is neither complete nor pre-ordained. And a different world economy is not necessarily a worse one for Europe—if Europeans seize the moment to leverage global growth, human talent and innovation while exploiting European strengths and tackling related challenges of deficits and debt.

Given the trends outlined in this study, the European Union has a closing window of a decade's time to position itself as a world-class player in an increasingly competitive and connected world. If it does not, the resulting strains and stresses could challenge Europe's very construction. In this regard, the lingering economic crisis could be a watershed moment: either the spur to a more competitive continent, or the time when Europe lost out decisively to more vigorous powers.

The New Landscape

Over the past two decades walls have fallen and borders have been erased. Billions of workers and consumers around the world have fully joined the global economy, and hundreds of millions of people have been lifted from poverty.[1] The communications and computing revolutions have transformed both the nature of work and the nature of competition. New centers of innovation are emerging. Companies have moved from their home bases to establish geographically dispersed networks. Continents are connecting as never before. Rapid technological diffusion, greater economic opportunities, lower barriers to investment, higher resource needs, and policy reforms at home are generating dynamic cross-border flows of goods, services, money, energy, people and ideas between established and emerging economies.

On balance, these dynamics have benefited the people living in the 27 member states of the European Union (EU).[2] Yet the economic crisis that swept through Europe and across the globe in 2008 and 2009 demonstrated forcefully that the very connections that generate economic opportunity in good times can be transmission belts for economic turmoil in bad times. The same interlinked monetary system that exerts downward pressure on inflation and interest rates can transmit financial insecurity at the click of a mouse. The same global demand that fuels European exports can also boost prices for many daily needs.

The Great Recession hit the EU hard, plunging the continent into its deepest downturn in the postwar period.[3] Unemployment rose by more than 7 million; almost €150 billion was erased from EU output; and average EU debt levels jumped to almost 80% of gross domestic product (GDP).[4] In the two years since early 2008, the eurozone lost about 2.5% in per capita GDP relative to the United States and barely kept par with Japan, even though Japan's recession was more severe.[5] Most of the EU's old member states, already plagued by low growth, have struggled to reestablish their footing. Many of the EU's new member states, which until the crisis had been doing better than many non-European emerging economies, fell further. As all scramble to recover, divergent policies could undermine European solidarity.[6]

Dangers on the Periphery

Rapidly unraveling debt and banking crises in Greece and Ireland in 2010 offer stark evidence that the 2008 financial meltdown continues to reverberate and will take years to play out.[7] Only months after committing to bail out near-bankrupt Greece, the eurozone plunged back into crisis as the EU and the IMF were forced to provide a multibillion euro rescue package for Ireland, even as Greece's budget deficit continued to grow despite its own rescue package and severe budget cuts.

There are important differences between Greece's woes and Ireland's challenges. Greece buckled under the weight of government overspending, mismanagement and corruption. Ireland's crisis stemmed from deeply troubled banks riddled with bad loans from a massive real estate bust.[8] In response the Irish government nationalized three banks, backing them with a €50 billion euro bailout. This unaffordable expenditure of taxpayer funds, combined with a severe 7.6% contraction of the economy in 2009, pushed the Irish government's fiscal deficit to 32% of GDP and its public debt to 100% of GDP. Massive cuts in budgets, wages and prices failed to staunch the bleeding. Loans outstanding at Irish banks were more than 11 times the size of the economy. European banks had half a trillion dollars in outstanding loans in Ireland, nearly more than 3 times European exposure in Greece.[9]

Despite the different nature of the two crises, their combined effect has been to impose severe pain on each economy and to expose fundamental weaknesses in the mechanisms governing the eurozone, testing European unity. Despite massive fiscal cuts and several years of deep recession, Greece and Ireland will accumulate 150% of GDP in debt by 2014. Failure to contain the Irish and Greek crises could undermine Portugal, which has done even less to deal with its economic woes, and even extend to much larger debt-wracked economies such as Spain, or to Italy, where public debt at the end of 2010 stood at $2.3 trillion, or about 115% of GDP. EU leaders have endorsed plans for a permanent crisis management fund to rescue indebted euro-zone countries. Yet successive crises are tearing European solidarity, as angry German taxpayers rebel against paying for what they believe to be Greek corruption and Irish greed.[10]

In short, Europe's recovery from the Great Recession remains tentative. Financial reforms are lagging and sovereign risks linger. Europe must steel itself for an inevitable string of bank restructurings. EU member states need to fix the conditions that gave rise to big budget deficits. New mechanisms are needed at EU level and within the eurozone to deal with future defaults.[11] Recovery will take time and require painful adjustments, as households and creditors work through the overhang of excessive borrowing and lending, and the associated decline in asset prices and job opportunities; and as financial institutions work to strengthen their balance sheets to meet higher standards for capital and liquidity.[12] The challenge will be to implement fiscal adjustments without undermining the frail economic recovery.

These troubles will plague the EU for at least the initial years of the coming decade. GDP in the eurozone is projected to grow at a meager 1.5% in 2011, down from 1.7% in 2010. While countries such as Germany may expand more quickly, the economies of Ireland, Greece and Spain will be stagnant or could shrink, underscoring the uneven and prolonged nature of the recovery, as concerns linger about fiscal sustainability.[13]

Europe's recovery, however fragile, has been boosted by the resurgence of the world economy. Global GDP is approaching pre-crisis growth rates (4.8% in 2010 and 4.2% in 2011), and European exports are benefiting. Global trade plunged 12.2% in 2009, but was projected to climb even more sharply by 13.5% in 2010. Global foreign direct investment (FDI) was expected to recover to $1.2 trillion in 2010 after plunging from $2 trillion in 2007 to $1 trillion in 2009. Financial markets have rebounded, and cross-border flows are recovering.[14]

The EU in a G20 World

Behind the headline stories of financial meltdown, recession and skyrocketing debt in Europe and the United States lies a more fundamental trend. Even as the world becomes increasingly interlinked and interdependent, the balance of economic power is shifting away from the traditional "West" towards countries such as China, India and Brazil. Ten years ago rich countries dominated the world economy, contributing about two-thirds of global GDP after allowing for differences in purchasing power. Since then that share has fallen to just over half. By 2020 it could be down to 40%. The bulk of global output will be produced in the emerging world.[15]

The financial crisis has exacerbated these trends and damaged the developed world's ability to cope with them. The debt-to-GDP ratio of G7 economies is expected to exceed 100% in 2011, dampening their future growth rates. Reinhardt and Rogoff estimate[16] that median GDP growth rates in developed economies fall by about 1% a year once a debt-to-GDP ratio of 90% is reached. To maintain macroeconomic stability and competitiveness, fiscal policies will have to be put on a sounder footing. G20 leaders have agreed to cut fiscal deficits in half by 2013 and to stabilize the debt-to-GDP ratio by 2016. But the financial and fiscal crises have sliced years off the EU's ability to respond to the challenges of the new world rising.

The rise of developing countries represents an historic shift in global economic relations. The increasing integration of emerging economies into the world economy has opened robust markets to European products and services and has provided European companies with new opportunities to expand international production chains. High growth in developing economies could offset the impact of Europe's slow growth and graying populations. Yet European manufacturers and service providers are also confronted with fresh sources of competition. As rapidly developing economies integrate further into the world economy, there is more scope in Europe for structural changes, job losses, uneven income growth, and other painful developments. In short, even as the EU and its member states grapple with the lingering recession and its aftermath, they must also address the rise of the G20 world.

EU leaders are thus challenged to find ways to recover from the crisis in the short-term while laying the foundation for a more competitive Europe over the medium-term—all while ensuring that Europe's diversity does not challenge the achievements of European integration. The early years of the next decade will be devoted to recovery from the crisis and to efforts to restore confidence in the EU's economic policy system. But EU leaders cannot afford to focus only on crisis management. They must also lay the groundwork for a more competitive Europe.

This Study

Today's global economy is highly competitive and increasingly connected. In *The Lexus and the Olive Tree*, journalist Thomas Friedman suggests that a defining question of our age is no longer "whose side are you on," but rather "to what extent are you connected?"[17] This study tries to answer this question for Europe. It examines how the European Union is connected to other world regions, and what it means for its competitiveness. It looks at the EU's strengths and challenges in this G20 world—a world economy powered by multiple engines and multiple centers of demand and liquidity.

In Chapters 1 through 6 we map the EU's ties to other world regions in terms of flows of goods, services, money, energy, people and ideas. These six areas allow us to gain an understanding of how deeply linked Europe is to other world regions, and of the EU's most important partners and competitors. In Chapters 7 through 18 we describe how these flows affect relations between the EU and 12 other world regions: North America, Wider Europe, Japan, China, Rising Asia, India, Russia, the Middle East, Africa, Latin America, the Caribbean, and Oceania.[18] In the final chapter we discuss the competitiveness of individual EU member states; offer a "SWOT" analysis of the EU's strengths, weaknesses, opportunities and threats; and offer four scenarios for the EU's future.

This mapping exercise gives us visual evidence of a fundamental reality often lost in accounts of the new world rising before us. Interactions among world regions may be accelerating, but the breadth, depth and speed of those interactions vary considerably. Most discussion of a "multipolar" world or the supposed rise of a new "G2" between the U.S. and China ignores the fact that each "pole" is bound to the others in very different ways.[19] The Italian scholar Giovanni Grevi posits that multipolarity is a less apt description of what is going on than "interpolarity," which he defines as multipolarity in the age of interdependence.[20] Deepening interdependence among the major world regions provides an important context in which to consider power relations between established and emerging countries. Power may be shifting, but it is doing so unevenly across different dimensions. In short, it is not enough to look at the redistribution of power: the effects of globalization have to be factored in too.[21]

A good place to begin to understand the EU's competitive position, therefore, is to look at how it is connected to other G20 countries and to other world regions; how such evolving interdependencies are re-drawing the map of the EU's traditional relationships; and how they could affect the EU's prospects over the next decade.[22] We thus conducted our mapping exercise with the following questions in mind: How are the EU and its member states linked to the rest of the world? Where are those links thick, where are they thin, how have they been changing, and what does this tell us about the EU's position in the global economy and prospects for the future?

One important basis for comprehending the EU's competitive strengths and weaknesses is to understand its interdependencies. Another is to understand how well the EU is harnessing the power of its linkages—its networks—to advance its economic standing. Robert Huggins and Hiro Izushi argue[23] that network capital—the ability to access and link different connections, sources and forms of knowledge—can be as important as physical or human capital. They show how companies that invest in the relationships and networks they need to meet their economic expectations can generate significant advantages in their innovation perform-

Defining Competitiveness

The term "competitiveness" is used often in public debate, yet there is no agreed way to define and measure it. Major institutions such as the OECD define competitiveness as all those factors that impact on the ability of an economy to compete in international markets. Jean-Claude Trichet, president of the European Central Bank, has used the term in a broad sense to mean "the ability of economies to thrive in an increasingly integrated international economy and to embark on a sustained path of high output growth that enhances people's wealth."[28] The European Commission defines competitiveness as "a sustained rise in the standards of living of a nation or region and as low a level of involuntary unemployment as possible."[29]

One must be cautious when discussing competitiveness in terms of countries, as it suggests a false analogy with companies. The public debate is often reduced to the question of how to boost export shares to achieve cost and price advantages against other countries. But imports can also improve welfare by giving consumers greater choice at lower prices; stimulating competition; reducing intermediate costs for companies; and putting downward pressure on inflation and interest rates. Countries do not compete with other countries in the same way as companies do.[30] Commerce among countries is not about profit but about the international division of labor and can benefit all by raising productivity and increasing overall economic well-being.

A more meaningful concept of competitiveness at the national level would focus on the ability of the EU and its member states to provide their citizens with high and rising standards of living, which depends in turn on the quality of economic and political institutions, the strength of their relationships, the ability to export in order to afford imports, and the extent to which such factors are supportive of employment, productivity growth, innovation and the ability to adjust to changing circumstances. That is the approach taken in this study.[31]

---

ance. Network capital, they assert, provides the glue necessary to maximize the effectiveness of other endowments, such as human capital, financial capital, physical and knowledge capital.[24]

This study seeks to understand what the multifarious efforts of thousands of EU-based firms to build their network capital means for the collective capacity of the EU to harness its own network capital. In other words, to extrapolate the network capital of European firms to say something about the network capital of the European Union itself.

Network capital is not only about reaching out to establish new links or to strengthen old ones in terms of boosting outward flows of goods, services, money, energy, people and ideas; it is also about the ability to absorb and access such flows to benefit one's own economy. The more connected a place is, the greater its chances of securing critical resources and tapping into new markets and new sources of innovation. Whether it will make best use of these connections, however, depends not only on its ability and propensity to access ideas and concepts generated elsewhere, but also its absorptive capacity—its ability and propensity to assimilate and exploit new sources of innovation. The more connected a place is, the greater its ability to attract global ideas; and the greater its absorptive capacity, the greater its ability to reap the benefits of such ideas at home.[25] This need is particularly strong at the frontier of new knowledge, and as other countries develop comparative advantages in labor- and capital-intensive products, the EU—as a knowledge economy—is increasingly reliant on its capacity to generate innovative products and services that can keep it competitive.[26]

The second aspect of the study, then, is to look at how the EU's connectedness and absorptive capacity contribute to its competitiveness; the nature of its strengths and challenges as the G20 world unfolds; and how it may harness those strengths and best address its challenges looking out to the year 2020.

Competitive—or Complacent?

Has the EU positioned itself to be competitive in this new world? Or is it complacent, failing to meet its challenges while a world of opportunities passes it by?

Overall, our mapping exercise allows us to reach some basic conclusions. The European Union is a major hub in the multi-continental flows of goods, services, money, energy, people and ideas that are driving the new dynamics of the G20 world. On the whole, these connections have fostered large gains for Europe: robust growth in exports and imports of goods and services; strong outflows and inflows of investment; diversified energy sources; greater stimuli to innovation; net inflows of labor; net downward pressure on inflation and interest rates; more jobs, higher incomes, modest increases in wages; and higher GDP growth than if Europe was less connected to other world regions. These benefits have not been evenly shared, however, and for many Europeans the redeployment of labor, capital, goods and services production across firms, industries, and communities has meant disruption and uncertainty. There have been winners and losers. Moreover, some connections to other world regions are weaker than they could be, depriving the EU of the full potential of its network capital.[27]

Goods

The EU is the top supplier of goods to the developing nations and is a more significant trading partner for the BRICs than either the U.S. or Japan. EU goods exporters have also withstood the challenge of rising economies better than Japan or the United States; rapidly emerging economies are registering high demand in the types of products in which many European exporters specialize. Nonetheless, the EU trade balance has been consistently negative through past decade, and the EU has trade deficits with all BRICs except India. In addition, China has achieved a small comparative advantage over the EU as a whole in research-intensive goods and technology-driven industries, which increasingly dominate EU imports from China. Overall, EU goods exporters have gained greater market share by boosting the value of existing products to traditional trade partners rather than by introducing new products or gaining new partners. The challenge is to leverage new markets without neglecting larger, higher value legacy markets. This includes creating greater opportunities at home, since two-thirds of all EU exports go to other EU member states. Completing the Single Market promises to boost goods trade considerably and would strengthen EU competitiveness in manufacturing, which is under growing pressure from rising powers.

Services

The services sector is the sleeping giant of the European economy—its greatest source of untapped growth. Services are the source of all net job growth in the EU. The EU is the world's largest regional trader in services, with dominant global shares in both traditional and non-traditional services activities. The EU ranks #1 in the world in 8 of 11 categories of services exports. It enjoys a services trade surplus with every other world region except North America and the Caribbean, and in the past decade the EU15 almost quadrupled their services trade balance. Services account for over 70% of EU GDP but only 23% of global exports: there is room to grow. Yet the EU's failure to capitalize fully on its strength in services is the single most important cause of the gap between the EU and the U.S. in both GDP and productivity growth. Moreover, the EU's home base is just as critical to services trade as it is for goods: two-thirds of all EU services exports go to other EU member states. If the EU is to create jobs and build upon its comparative advantage in services, it needs to implement and extend the EU's Services Directive to complete the Single Market in Services; spur services innovation and productivity; build on its IT capabilities; stop posing false choices between services and manufacturing; and adequately educate and train its workforce.

Money

The EU is the world's largest regional source and destination of foreign direct investment. It is the largest source of FDI in the United States as well as in the BRICs, and its position as an investor in these countries is even stronger than as a trader. The EU also has higher ratios of inward and outward investments to GDP than the U.S. and most other developed countries, which means that the EU is comparatively more open to foreign investments and more willing to invest abroad than either the United States or Japan. 55 of the 100 largest non-financial multinational corporations are domiciled on EU territory. Europe's expanding inward stock of FDI has added to the employment ranks of many European countries, increased the level of productive capacity, and helped promote the technological advancement of the region through greater expenditures on research and development. The EU is reliant on inward flows of FDI and must maintain its attractiveness as a place in which to invest. EU outward FDI boosted EU GDP by more than €20 billion and the income of EU workers by almost €13 billion between 2001 and 2006. Yet many developing economies impose restrictions on such investments. Working to open non-tariff barriers in such areas as public procurement and services could open considerable new opportunities to EU companies.

The EU is a critical source of capital for other world regions. In 2008 the EU was the largest portfolio investor in North America, Wider Europe, Russia, India and Oceania; the second largest portfolio investor after North America in Africa, the Caribbean, Rising Asia, Japan, Latin America, and the Middle East; and the third largest portfolio investor in China, behind North America and Rising Asia. The EU accounted for 50% of all foreign portfolio investment in North America, Russia and Wider Europe; for over 40% of all foreign portfolio investment in Africa, India, and Japan; and for roughly 30% or more in the Caribbean, Developing Asia, Latin America, the Middle East and Oceania. Even following the financial crisis, EU and U.S. financial markets continue to account for well over two-thirds of global banking assets and provide around three-quarters of global financial services, although at substantially lower overall levels of market activity in many market segments.

Despite its current woes, the creation of the euro has given Europe a global currency that is a legitimate and favorable alternative to the U.S. dollar. Of total global foreign exchange holdings in the second quarter of 2007, the euro accounted for 25.6% of the total, compared with just 18.3% in 2000. Among developing nations, demand for the euro is slightly higher — the euro accounted for nearly 29% of developing nation global reserves in mid-2007. The attractiveness of the euro as a world reserve currency has allowed eurozone countries to attract more of the world's excess savings and deepen their capital markets. One result of this dynamic is a more competitive financial sector in Europe and more low-cost capital available for capital investment and consumer spending with the region. Enabling capital to flow from one member state to another without exchange rate risk is a key advantage of the euro.

Nonetheless, many eurozone members must tackle big government deficits and mounting debt. The eurozone's Stability and Growth Pact proved grossly inadequate during the single currency's first ten years. The travails of Greece and Ireland in 2010 have demonstrated the need for a more permanent facility to ensure financial stability in the eurozone. And the euro's fundamental contradiction remains unresolved—the lack of a common economic policy to go with the common currency.

The EU was hit hardest among world regions by the financial crisis, stoking fears that it is less financially competitive than before. The EU has only 4 of the top 20 financial centers worldwide. While EU financial centers account for 10 of the 20 best performers, they also account for 8 of the 20 worst performers. Secondary European financial market places, such as Paris, Madrid, Milan, Frankfurt, and Amsterdam, are losing ground to other advanced and emerging financial centers.

Energy

Europe is pioneering alternative energies and critical strategies of energy efficiency and sustainability, a field that could offer major opportunities over coming decades. Clean technology solutions are expected to develop a global market potential of around €2 trillion in 2020, growing at an average 13% per annum. The EU leads both the U.S. and Japan in energy efficiency and sustainability. EU companies lead the global clean energy sector, which is growing rapidly in number of companies and size. EU companies account for 13 of the world's top 15 R&D companies dedicated to clean energy technological development, and the EU leads all world regions in patents for air and water pollution control, renewable energy and solid waste management.

Despite the EU's renewable energy success story, significant barriers remain to the widespread commercialization of clean energy technologies. European companies will be challenged by the vast investments being made in China, the single-minded determination of countries such as South Korea, and competition from the U.S. and Japan. In addition, renewables are simply not big enough to make a significant difference to the EU's overall energy picture in the short term, nor are they likely to be consistently cheaper than dirty sources of energy anytime soon. The EU will continue to rely on traditional sources of energy and depend on foreign sources for over half of its energy supply, with many EU member states critically dependent on a handful of foreign sources. Moreover, the ravenous and ultimately unsustainable resource and energy needs of rapidly developing countries are adding significant pressure to Europe's energy picture.

People

The European Union has rich human resources; overall, its citizens are well-educated and its workforce well-trained. The EU commitment to the free flow of labor within its borders has been a boon to sending and receiving countries alike. Most EU countries have undertaken steps in recent years to change immigration rules in order to better target highly skilled migrants, which has resulted in a growing share of high-skilled migrants settling in the EU. Initiatives that enable migrants to work within the entire EU and which focus on the highly skilled, such as the EU's Blue Card, could provide substantial benefits.

Nonetheless, the EU is aging and shrinking, has become a net importer of labor, and is grappling with considerable mismatches in demand and supply of labor. It has also become a magnet for the unskilled, receiving many poorly educated immigrants with relatively low levels of training without receiving as many well educated, high skilled immigrants as it needs. Highly skilled foreign workers account for only 1.7% of all workers in the EU, compared with 9.9% in Australia, 7.3% in Canada and 3.5% in the United States. 85% of unskilled labor goes to the EU and 5% to the U.S., whereas 55% of skilled labor goes to the U.S and only 5% to the EU. Highly skilled migrants have lower labor market participation rates, higher unemployment rates and lower employment rates than natives with comparable qualifications, and face a substantially higher risk of being employed in jobs that do not fit their skill profiles. The EU would have to double its net immigration rate to 2 million per year to offset the trends. EU migration policy will have to be much more effective in making the EU and its member states a more attractive destination for qualified and highly motivated potential immigrants and their families. And despite progress in intra-EU mobility, labor markets remain fragmented.

Ideas

The EU is home to some of the most competitive knowledge-based economies in the world. Countries such as Denmark, Finland, Germany, Sweden and the UK are among the world's most innovative. The EU's overall innovation performance is better than both the U.S. and Japan in terms of private credit, trademarks, technology balance of payments flows and knowledge-intensive services. The R&D intensity of EU companies is greater than that of the U.S. and Japan in software and computers, services, technology, hardware & equipment, and automobiles and parts. EU-based companies account for 30.6% of the top R&D companies in the world, compared to 34.3% for the U.S. and 22% for Japan. European-based affiliates of non-European countries, particularly from the U.S., are prime motors of R&D investment in the EU. The EU has a strong lead in innovation performance compared to each of the BRIC countries. Nine EU countries rank among the top 20 in terms of Network Readiness. The EU accounted for slightly more than 25% of scientific publications in 2007, the highest share of any region. The top 20 knowledge regions include 13 U.S. regions, 5 European regions, and 2 Japanese regions. Reallocating one-third of the subsidies currently spent on agriculture to R&D would vault the EU's government-financed R&D spending as a percent of GDP to the U.S. level. Meeting the EU's 2020 target of boosting R&D investment to 3% of GDP from its 2008 level of 1.87% could create 3.7 million jobs and increase annual EU GDP by up to €795 billion by 2025.

Overall, the European Union remains a competitive and highly connected innovation economy. But it risks being squeezed between high-performance innovation economies, such as the U.S. and Japan, and rising innovation performers from other world regions. In terms of R&D investments the EU has failed to catch up with the U.S., has fallen behind other key countries, and now could be eclipsed by China. U.S. companies invested nearly five times more than EU companies in semiconductors, four times more in software and eight times more in biotechnology. The EU's share of young, innovative firms is lower than other key countries. EU R&D companies are facing growing competitive pressures from companies from Rising Asia and China in a range of medium-high R&D intensity sectors. The EU is also hobbled by great discrepancies in innovation performance, both among countries and among sub-regions within countries.

Moreover, inadequate attention has been paid to demand-driven innovation, including social innovation; and to innovation in services, a sector of competitive strength for the EU yet one which has failed to keep pace in productivity with the U.S. and has failed to reap the full benefits that could come from the EU's large Single Market. A stronger focus is needed on user needs, demand and market opportunities and more effective connections are required between innovation, research, education and job creation.

Significant barriers also persist with regard to the circulation of highly-skilled individuals both within the EU and between the EU and other world regions. The EU's fragmented patent system and many organizational, human capital and cultural barriers have hampered research and innovation activities. EU innovators are also relatively less effective than those in the United States at taking their ideas to market, commercializing innovation so that it results in products, processes or new ways of organizing that generate jobs and growth.

In sum, the EU and its member states are slipping in their efforts to promote themselves as world-class knowledge economies. More effective cooperation among member states and greater attention to the innovation needs and potential of sub-regions within member states are required if the EU is truly to become an Innovation Union.

Critical Connections

Across the different flows, three key themes emerge with regard to the EU's economic relations with other world regions. The first is the continuing—and in some cases, growing—

significance of the EU's base on the European continent. The second is the deep integration between the EU and North America, particularly the United States. The third is the EU's rapidly expanding yet uneven links with rising emerging markets, often from very low levels.

The EU's home base is dynamic and significant: two-thirds of EU goods and services, portfolio investments and FDI are transferred among EU member states. EU countries are becoming more deeply integrated with each other at the same time as they all are becoming more integrated into the global economy outside of Europe. EU enlargement has enabled EU companies to invest in a larger Single Market to extend their production networks and improve their respective comparative advantage. The structural adjustment that is occurring within the EU's relatively integrated economic space is generating opportunities for advanced and less advanced member state economies alike. Both types of economies are benefiting from new pan-European structures of specialization and integration. In this regard, Europeanization may be understood for some companies and countries as a "first-stage globalization," which in fact may better prepare them for the full force of globalization. Yet the EU has failed to take full advantage of the potential of its home base. Completing the Single Market would be a significant contribution to the EU's competitive position in the G20 world, giving it more robust scale and scope in a world of continental-sized players.

The linkages between the EU and two other regions—Wider Europe and North America—are so deep and critical that they are essentially organic, and provide the EU with an extended geo-economic base. The challenge is to make this base more vibrant while taking advantage of higher-growth opportunities elsewhere.

The nature of EU economic ties to other world regions varies considerably. In this regard, as we shall see, terms such as BRICs—a common label for Brazil, Russia, India and China—are not particularly useful, since each of these countries has a distinct relationship with the EU, and each presents its own opportunities and challenges. Given the relative popularity of the term, we have included references to the BRICs in this study. More often than not, however, such references tend to underscore the very different relationship each of the BRIC countries has with the EU.

Eight Priorities

This study reveals considerable EU strengths and some serious weaknesses. After carefully examining the EU's connections and its competitiveness, we conclude that the EU is more competitive in some key areas than many critics are prepared to acknowledge, yet also faces more profound challenges than some policymakers are prepared to admit. The EU's diversity argues against a one-size-fits-all strategy. Yet common themes emerge. In fact, a key test of the EU's ability to prosper in the G20 world will be whether its member states regain the sense of shared purpose that has always been at the core of an "ever closer Union," but which has been sorely missing of late. Eight priorities loom large:

1. Get the recovery right. EU leaders urgently need to fix the financial system and tackle burgeoning deficits and debt without undermining Europe's fragile return to growth. Case-by-case crisis management isn't working. More fundamental reforms are needed, including a permanent crisis resolution mechanism to replace the temporary European Financial Stability Facility established in 2010; fiscal and financial reforms that actually support—and enforce—the growth and stability pact targets that have been ignored for many years; and related efforts to improve economic performance.

2. Boost productivity. The EU must boost its productivity if it is to deal with its demographic challenges and sustain its social welfare model. Stagnant or flagging productivity will mean a period of low or no growth, which is likely to generate greater domestic and intra-EU conflicts while leaving the EU behind in a world or high-growth competitors.

3. Complete the Single Market. A true EU Single Market could produce growth of about 4% of GDP over the next ten years. It would create jobs and boost trade, investment and productivity. It would enhance EU manufacturing competitiveness, which is under growing pressure from rising powers. A more complete and vibrant Single Market would provide EU countries and companies with a stronger geo-economic base in a world of continental-sized players.

4. Awaken Europe's sleeping giant: services. Services are the EU's biggest untapped source of jobs and economic growth. Yet services account for just 23% of Europe's trade, even though they account for 70% of Europe's output. If the EU-wide Services Directive were fully implemented, it could deliver more than 600,000 new jobs and economic gains ranging between €60-140 billion, representing a growth potential of at least 0.6-1.5% of GDP.[32] It should also be extended to include such critical areas of potential innovation and productivity growth as financial services, health, employment and social services. In addition, the EU should do more to capitalize fully on it strengths in services trade and foreign direct investment. EU decision-makers should avoid the false choice between services and manufacturing, which are increasingly symbiotic. If services win, so does manufacturing.

5. Lead the global effort to break the link between the production of wealth and the consumption of resources. The EU should lead in the transition to a low-carbon economy and promote itself as a showcase of energy efficiency and innovation. This will be neither quick nor easy, but the EU has both the capacity and the propensity to lead the great escape from fossil fuels.

6. Innovate. Innovation drives economic growth and has become even more important as Europe's native population ages and shrinks, and as the EU's competitive advantage lies increasingly in its capacities as a knowledge economy. The EU must offer greater opportunities to young start-ups and entrepreneurs; focus on innovation outputs, not just inputs like R&D; pay more attention to social innovation, process innovation, services innovation, and user innovation; boost possibilities for continuous development of skills; introduce a unified EU patent system; protect intellectual property rights; and strengthen its innovation networks around the globe.

7. Power to the people. The EU and its member states must tap the potential of their people if they are to manage demographic challenges, sustain their social model, develop the skills needed in a knowledge-based economy, and prosper in the G20 world. A pan-European talent strategy must attract skilled foreign labor; ensure free movement of people among member states; facilitate better links between business and education; improve access to the labor market; promote education in key enabling technologies; and boost overall skills training and re-skilling across the Union.

8. Become a critical hub in the G20 world. The EU is well placed to be a key hub of an interpolar world in which new centers of economic and political power have emerged. The EU should use its network capital to make itself a focal point for the intercontinental exchange of ideas, people, capital, goods, services and energy innovation. The more connected the EU is, the more competitive it is likely to be. The EU needs to solidify its base by completing the Single Market and extending its competitive networks throughout Wider Europe; build on its deep ties to North America to create an open Transatlantic Marketplace; overcome the relative inertia evident in the export orientation of EU companies to leverage high-growth opportunities in emerging markets; and reengage in markets it has neglected, such as Turkey, Africa and Latin America.

Europe 2020: Four Scenarios

The European Union and its member states have a window of opportunity to reposition themselves for the challenges of a vastly different world. The EU's future economic performance depends on its ability and its propensity to leverage global growth, human talent and innovation while exploiting European strengths and consolidating public finances. Based on these external and internal drivers, we define four possible scenarios for Europe's future.

In the scenario dubbed *Competitive Europe*, the EU and its member states are successful in advancing these priorities in a high-growth global environment. They tackle their fiscal problems and inject new vibrancy into the Single Market. They leverage higher growth to seek greater economic convergence among EU member states at levels of high competitiveness across the board. They supplement these initiatives with efforts to infuse additional dynamism into their broader geo-economic base in Wider Europe, and to invigorate the EU's deep economic connections to North America, in particular by knocking down non-tariff barriers to transatlantic commerce, fueling greater innovation linkages, and opening up the transatlantic services economy. These initiatives proceed in tandem with more effective efforts to capture greater market share in new markets, particularly in China and Rising Asia, and renewed attention to Africa. EU firms capitalize on their advantages in services and in high-tech, upmarket and environmental goods across all markets; as well as the opportunities offered by rapidly rising economies to EU medium-tech capital goods industries and those engaged in infrastructure development. Activist policies address aging and shrinking populations, boost integration levels and advance skills and training across the board. They promote innovation and knowledge-based investments, particularly in energy sustainability.

The *Europe Adrift* scenario offers an alternative future of low global and European growth. The EU and its member states fail to advance their competitiveness. Debt levels remain stubbornly high and further debt crises erupt in various EU member states, triggering a crisis of confidence in the euro and sterling. Continual crisis management erodes the credibility of European integration and the European model, diminishing European influence in the world, prompting intense debate about the nature and relevance of the EU itself. Innovation and productivity flag. The EU loses critical market share both in goods and services to faster-growing, more innovative competitors. Social divisions are exacerbated and the welfare state provisions of EU member states simply become unsustainable as a smaller workforce proves unable to support aging populations. The lack of energy innovation and internal EU disputes limit the possibilities for coherent EU energy policies, deepening energy dependencies among a greater number of EU member states. Consumers are confronted with less choice at higher prices. Workers suffer, wages decline, and anti-migrant forces gain ground.

Two other scenarios paint other less-than-optimal futures. In the end, much depends on the choices Europeans make and the trade-offs they are prepared to accept to obtain a better life in a more competitive and highly connected world. And time is not standing still.

Section I

Goods, Services, Money, Energy, People and Ideas

Chapter 1
Goods

The Changing Nature of Trade

Until the financial crisis hit global markets in 2008, world trade had been expanding at a healthy average rate of 6.7% a year for about 20 years. The financial crisis and attendant recession, however, then triggered the greatest drop in global trade on record—deeper even than during the Great Depression. While global GDP fell by roughly one-half of 1% in 2009, the volume of world exports fell by over 12%.[1] Trade has since recovered from the deepest trough of the Great Recession. But the recovery is uneven and will take time.

The particularly sharp and abrupt nature of the dive in global trade was due in part to the manner in which trade itself has changed. Perhaps 30-40% of overall trade today consists of units within companies transferring materials, component parts and finished goods to other units within the same firm. This cross-border trade in intermediate parts and components has been growing even faster than trade in finished goods. In fact, by 2006 more than half of global goods trade and three-quarters of global services trade were in intermediate goods. Two-way trade in intermediates accounts for more than 50% of overall trade for Germany and for France.[2]

Production processes have become increasingly fragmented as goods are produced in stages in different countries in intra-regional or even global value chains. Firms seek to optimize the production process by situating intermediate production stages in different locations, often across a number of countries, depending on the comparative advantage such sites offer. Intermediate inputs such as parts and components are produced in one country and then exported to others for further production and/or assembly in final products. A Nokia cell phone, for example, contains more than nine hundred components sourced in more than forty countries, and is then sold in over eighty markets around the world. Components for Apple's iPod are produced in Japan, Korea and the United States, assembled in China and then exported to the United States.[3]

This phenomenon is not limited to Asia, even though China's participation in Asian production chains gives them a quality all their own. Intra-regional trade in intermediate parts and components can also be found in the EU: around 70% of the intermediates embodied in exports and imports from EU member states come from other EU member states.[4] Ireland, in comparison, has been more deeply tied to trade in intermediates across the Atlantic. North America and Europe trade a considerable amount of intermediate goods with each other, and in fact trade more services inputs with each other than all Asian countries do amongst themselves. And while Europe exports more intermediate goods to North America, it imports more intermediate services.[5]

These value chains have increased the economic interdependence of EU member states with each other, and with other world regions. Trade in intermediates fueled the overall rapid expansion of trade over the past 15 years, but also served as a powerful transmission and amplification channel for the downturn in global demand. Overall, trade in intermediates, and espe-

Figure 1A. Intra- and Inter-Regional Imports of Intermediate Goods, by Region
($ billions, 2005)

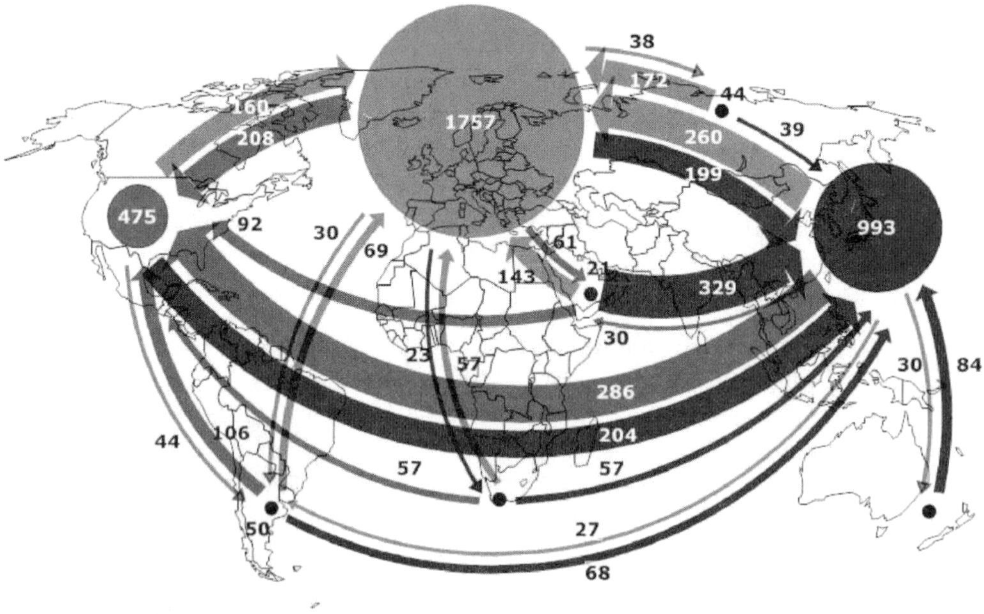

Source: OECD, Measuring Globalisation: OECD Economic Globalisation Indicators, 2010

cially in parts and components, was hit particularly hard by the crisis. Trading volumes of parts and components slumped by some 38% compared to pre-crisis levels.[6]

Just as the EU was a primary beneficiary of the rise in global trade in recent decades, it was hit particularly hard by the steep decline in global trade during the recession. Eurozone exports of capital goods to destinations outside the eurozone declined by approximately 26% between September 2008 and March 2009, and exports of intermediate goods declined by almost 17%.[7] This led to a 60% reduction in the EU's overall trade deficit to €105.3 billion in 2009.

The recovery of global trade from the severe contraction of 2008/09 has been remarkable. The upturn that started to take hold in the second half of 2009 continued into 2010, with export growth in many countries well above the average over the last two decades. By mid-2010, international merchandise trade flows had almost fully recovered to the levels seen just before the collapse of Lehman Brothers. The WTO projected that trade was likely to grow by 13.5% in 2010.[8]

Nevertheless, while the downturn was highly synchronized, affecting all major world regions in some way, the recovery has been quite uneven. On the whole, emerging and developing countries have recovered faster than developed countries. EU goods exports have picked up, but at a slower pace than those of many other countries. Extra-euro area exports grew by almost 21% relative to their trough in May 2009, slightly lower than the 24% in overall global growth but marginally higher than the 20% growth recorded by advanced economies. EU goods exporters have recovered, but have not yet made up all the ground lost since the recession began.[9] Moreover, within the EU the recovery has been quite patchy, with countries such as Germany rebounding well and some southern European countries recovering slowly.

The uneven nature of the global economic recovery and global economic growth means that the performance of the EU's goods export sector will be determined in part by the geographical orientation of its markets. The EU is the world's major trading region, but two-thirds of that trade is intra-regional. In fact, intra-regional trade among the EU27 represents more than 25% of world merchandise trade. This share has fluctuated over the past decade, with a downward trend after 2003.[10] The following section "maps" the EU's goods trade with other world regions.

How Connected is the EU in Trade in Goods?

Exports

Most EU trade consists of goods rather than services, and about 90% of overall EU exports of goods is comprised of manufacturing products. When it comes to trade in goods, EU member states are heavily intertwined with each other. In 2008, 67.4% of overall EU merchandise exports was comprised of intra-EU exports. That figure remained relatively constant throughout the past decade. For example, UK exports to the 4.5 million people in neighboring Ireland are three times greater than UK exports to the 1.3 billion people in China and more than combined UK exports to the BRICs.[11] In short, EU member states are their own most important trading partners. Higher growth in the EU would benefit EU member states above all, whereas a downturn, such as the Irish banking and debt crisis, can hurt EU neighbors considerably.

Intermediate goods account for 53.7% of EU exports, while exports of consumer goods and capital goods account for 22.6% and 17.6%, respectively.[12]

The geographical pattern of EU exports of goods has changed over the past decade. If intra-EU exports are included, then between 1999 and 2008 total EU export shares to the old member states, the advanced OECD countries and Asia declined, while total EU export shares increased to the new member states, the BRICs and to the rest of the world outside the advanced countries and Asia. This also holds true for most individual EU member states.[13]

Outside the EU itself, North America is the #1 regional market for EU goods in the world, accounting for 23% of EU goods exports in 2009. The U.S. remains the #1 country market for EU goods, accounting for 19% of total EU goods exports outside the EU in 2009. But the U.S. share has declined by 9% over the course of the past decade, and the EU now exports more to developing countries rather than developed markets. Over the past decade, for instance, China's share of EU goods exports increased from 2.7% to 8% and that of the Russian Federation from 2.2% to 6%.

Wider Europe is the #2 regional market for EU goods, accounting for 21% of EU goods exports. Wider European demand for EU exports is far more significant than Chinese demand, which is growing rapidly but from a low base. In fact, the EU exports less to China than to Switzerland. EU goods exports to Wider Europe in 2009 were almost 3 times the value of EU goods exports to China. On the other hand, Chinese demand for EU goods is growing faster than from any other world region and far outpaces demand from Wider Europe: EU goods exports to China grew 30% on average per annum over the past decade, compared to 4.3% average annual growth in Wider European demand for EU goods. In other words, EU goods exports to China grew 7 times faster than to Wider Europe over the past decade. Moreover, China's consumption base is expanding rapidly: by 2030 China's middle class will swell to over 360 million people, comprising one of the largest consumer markets in the world, including for the EU.[14]

The Middle East and Rising Asia each accounted for 10% of EU goods exports in 2009. The BRICs accounted for about 19% of EU goods exports. The EU exports about the same amount of goods to North America as to the entire Asia-Pacific region, with each region accounting for about 23% of EU exports. And while much attention is focused on the rise of the Asia-Pacific region, Atlantic Basin countries outside of Europe are more important customers for the EU, accounting for 36% of EU goods exports.

Imports

The EU is the world's largest importing entity. Excluding intra-EU trade, the EU accounted for 17.4% of all global imports in 2009, just ahead of the U.S. share of 16.7%.[15] Moreover, intra-EU trade is huge, accounting for 63.5% of overall EU merchandise imports, only 1% less than in 2000. The EU's size and wealth make it an important market for almost every other world region.

Intermediate inputs account for 53.7% of all EU imports. Consumer goods account for 22.6% of EU imports, followed by capital goods, with a 17.6% share of EU imports.[16]

A noticeable shift is underway in terms of EU import sources. If one includes intra-EU imports, over the period 1999-2008 the EU15 and the advanced OECD countries lost 4.6% and 5.3% market share, respectively, of total EU imports, whereas the new EU member states and the BRIC countries gained 3.9% and 4.9% market share, respectively, of total EU imports. In short, there has been a significant shift from imports sourced from old member states towards imports sourced from new member states, and from imports sourced from advanced countries towards imports sourced from rising economies. In both cases the shift has been particularly pronounced in capital goods.[17]

China has become the most important source of goods imported by the EU. Between 2000 and 2009, China's share of EU goods imports grew to 18.2% from 7.7%, while North America's share shrank to 15.9% from 23.9%.

China's large and growing share of global goods exports to Europe over the past decade has been mirrored by a decline in goods exports to the EU from Rising Asia and from Japan. This reflects in part Japan's "lost decade," but the more important overall trend has been a shift in intra-Asian production networks. Revolutions in transportation, communications and computing, together with China's decision to reengage in the global economy, have driven companies

Figure 1B. EU Goods Exports by Region 2009

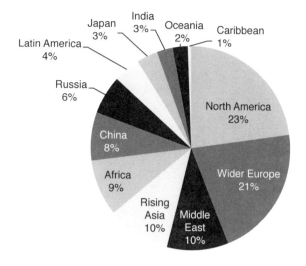

Source: Eurostat

to slice up their production chains. Many intermediate parts and components produced in Japan, Taiwan and South Korea are exported to emerging Asian economies, particularly China, where they are assembled into finished products and then exported to Europe and other destinations.

More than half of China's exports to the EU flows from these processing and assembling operations. In fact, almost all of China's top three export categories to the EU—office machinery, computers and telecommunications equipment—can be traced to these activities.

Figure 1C. EU Goods Exports by Region 2000-2009

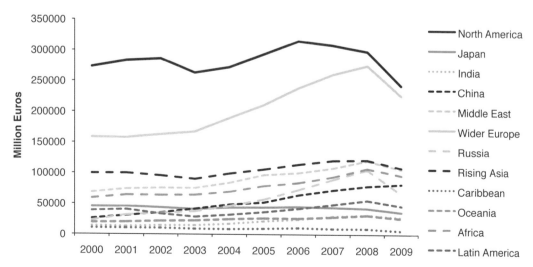

Source: Eurostat

Figure 1D. EU Goods Imports by Region 2009

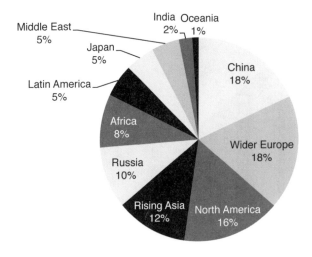

Source: Eurostat

One consequence of this development is that the EU's goods trade deficit with China has soared, even though its overall goods trade deficit with Asia has not. In fact, in 2009, China alone accounted for 80% of the EU's goods trade deficit with Asia. In short, simple bilateral statistics are misleading, since they reflect only trade stemming from the final assembly point—often China—rather than the more complex nexus of trade and investment that now characterizes international commerce. European companies are part of this phenomenon: a significant portion of EU goods imports from China is actually produced by European compa-

Figure 1E. EU Goods Imports by Region 2000-2009

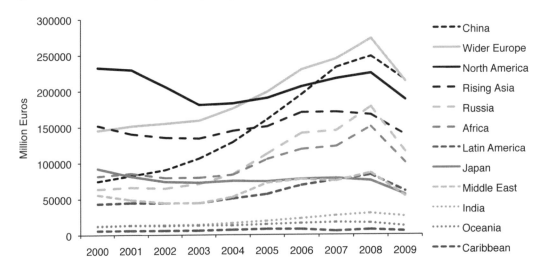

Source: Eurostat

Figure 1F. EU Goods Trade Balance by Region 2009

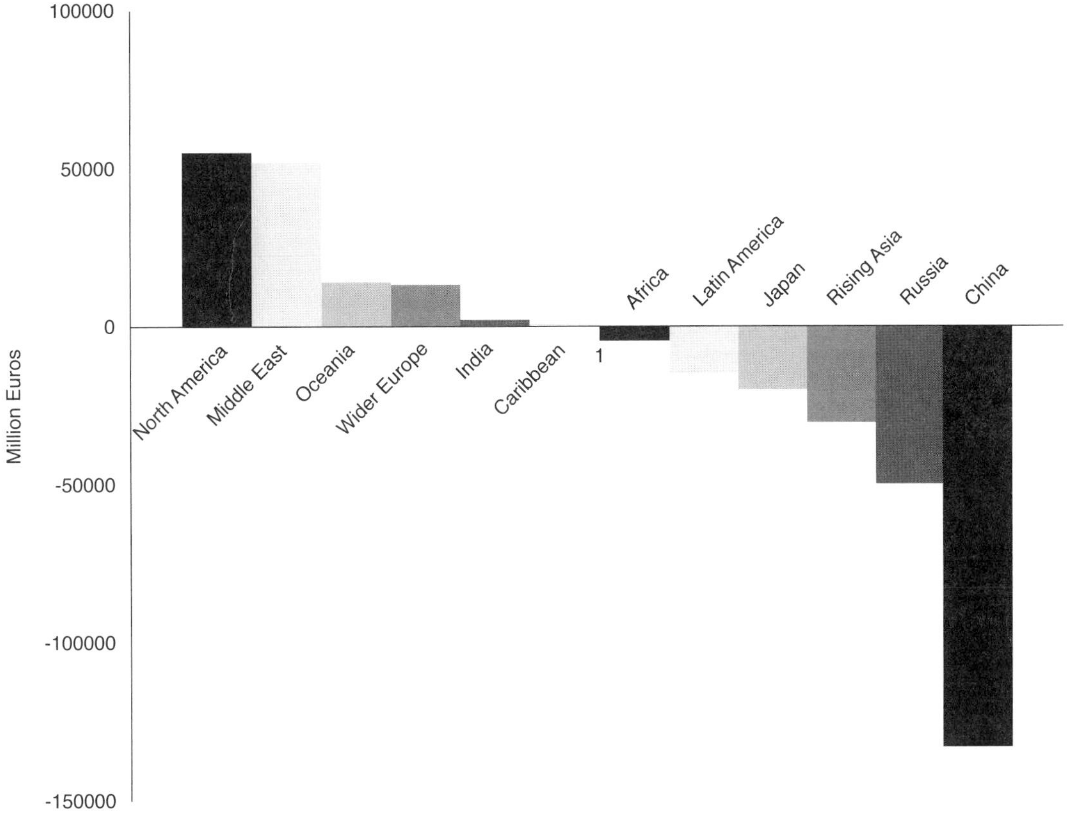

Source: Eurostat; IMF; WTO.

nies based in China, rather than by Chinese companies themselves. So "Made *in* China" is not necessarily "Made *by* China."[18]

Wider Europe was the #2 regional source of EU goods imports (18%), followed by North America (16%) and Rising Asia (12%). The entire Asia-Pacific region accounted for 36% of EU goods imports, compared to 29% for Atlantic Basin countries outside of Europe.

Considerable attention focuses on the EU's commercial relations with the BRICs. Although as a group the BRICs accounted for 18.8% of EU exports (excluding intra-EU trade) in 2009—less than EU exports to the U.S. (19.9%)— their share has doubled since 2000. The growing importance of the BRICs is even more visible in EU imports (33.2% of total EU imports in 2009, excluding intra-EU imports), largely due to China (18.7%).[19] Conversely, the EU is the most important trading partner for the BRICs—especially for Russia, Brazil and India.

A closer look, however, reveals that EU goods trade with the BRICs is very diverse; the BRIC label obscures significant aspects of EU goods trade with each individual country. For

Figure 1G. EU Goods Trade Balance by Region 2000–2009

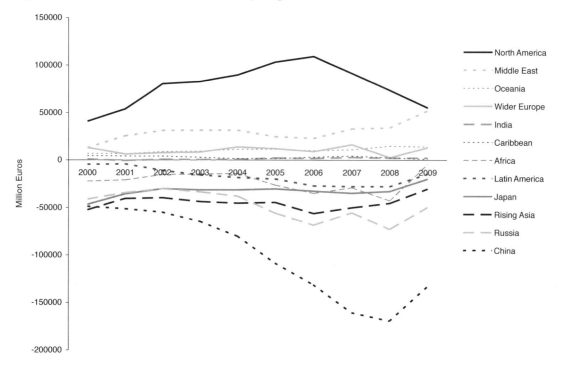

Source: Eurostat; IMF; WTO.

instance, for most of the past decade Russia, not China, has been the EU's most important BRIC market for goods. EU goods imports from Russia roughly doubled, and EU exports to Russia roughly tripled, over the course of the past decade. The recession hit EU trade with Russia particularly hard, however. EU goods exports to Russia fell by more than a third in 2009, and it is an open question when EU-Russian goods trade will rebound and whether it will resume its previous pattern. In 2009 Russia accounted for 6% of EU global exports and 10% of EU global imports. Neither Brazil nor India, in contrast, have developed their goods trade relationship with the EU to any significant extent.[20]

EU imports from the BRICs are also quite diverse. Technology-driven industries are increasingly important in EU goods imports from China, whereas capital-intensive industries prevail in EU imports from Russia and Brazil and labor-intensive industries characterize EU goods imports from India.[21]

Similarly, low-skill industries dominate in EU imports from Brazil and India, and medium-skill industries (i.e. refined petroleum) in imports from Russia. The share of EU imports from China provided by these two types of skills, on the other hand, declined over the course of the past decade, while the share provided by high-skill industries rose rapidly—an important sign of China's technological development. In fact, the labor skills structure of EU imports from China is becoming increasingly like the structure of intra-EU trade itself.[22]

How Competitive is the EU in Trade in Goods?

The European Union is the world's largest exporting entity and the world's largest trader in goods. It has maintained its share of world exports despite the rise of other trading powers. In 2009, extra-EU exports comprised the same share of world exports as they did in 1994.[23] The EU's goods exports to the world expanded by 7.7% on an annual basis over the past decade until the recession. If the recession year 2009 is included, then EU goods exports to the world expanded 5.3% on an annual basis from 2000 to 2009.

The EU's share of global imports has remained steady, accounting for 19.3% of world imports in 2000 and 19.1% in 2008. However, in 2009, the EU's share of global goods imports decreased to 17.6%. EU goods imports from the world grew 5.9% on an annual basis from 2000 to 2009. Leaving aside the severe 23.4% fall in EU global imports from 2008 to 2009, the EU's global goods imports grew 9.1% on annual basis from 2000 to 2008.

EU Strengths

The EU exhibits a number of strengths as a global exporter of goods. First, the EU is a more significant trading partner for the BRICs than either the U.S. or Japan. Of the major developed economies, the EU is the top supplier of goods to the developing nations—by a significant margin—and has enjoyed far greater growth rates than either Japan or the United States.[24]

Second, the EU is well positioned in a range of different products. In general, the EU remains a global market leader in medium-technology and capital-intensive exports.[25] It ranks #1 in export market share in 9 of 20 different product categories. Between 2000 and 2008, the EU's share of world exports of automotive parts rose from 49.8% to 53.1%; excluding intra-EU trade the EU had the largest share (15.2%), ahead of Japan (13.9%). The EU's share of world chemical exports (53.4%) is still dominant; excluding intra-EU trade it is the leading exporter, with a world market share of 17.7%, considerably ahead of the United States, which registered a 10.5% share. The EU's share of global manufactures exports even increased over the course of the past decade until the recession, rising from a 42.8% share in 2000 to 44.1% in 2008. Excluding intra-EU trade, the EU still ranks first, with a 15.0% share, compared to China's share of 12.7%.[26]

Third, between 1994 and the onset of the recession the EU25 withstood the competition of emerging countries better than the U.S. and Japan. During the past 15 years there has been a major redistribution of market share between emerging and developed countries. Yet research by Angela Cheptea, Lionel Fontagné and Soledad Zignago offers evidence that the EU essentially maintained its 19% market share of world exports over this period, despite the rise of China, which tripled its performance and on the eve of the recession accounted for 16.1% of world market shares.[27] In contrast, Japan and the U.S. each lost around 6% in market shares, so that the U.S. accounted for 12.5% and Japan 8.6% of world market shares in 2007.

Overall, the EU lost market share in the 1990s but rebounded to recover its losses over the past decade, whereas Japan lost market share over the entire period and U.S. losses were concentrated in the past decade rather than in the 1990s.

Figure 1H. Shares of the Triad in Brazil's Imports

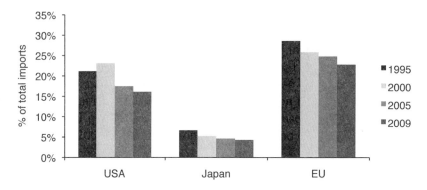

Sources: IMF; WTO; European Competitiveness Report 2009.

Figure 1I. Shares of the Triad in Russia's Imports

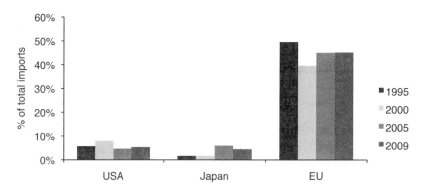

Sources: IMF; WTO; European Competitiveness Report 2009.

Figure 1J. Share of the Triad in India's Imports

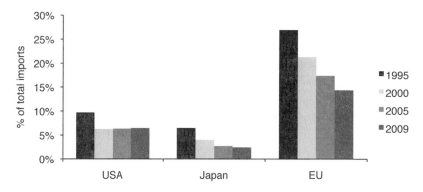

Sources: IMF; WTO; European Competitiveness Report 2009.

Figure 1K. Share of the Triad in China's Imports

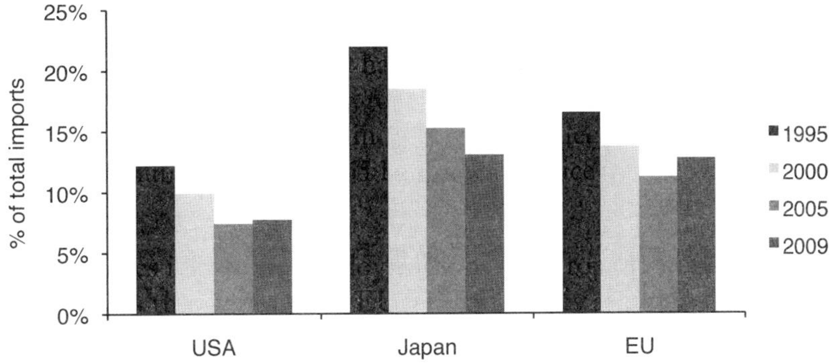

Sources: IMF; WTO; European Competitiveness Report 2009.

The resilience of EU market share was due in part to the rebound of the EU's export powerhouse Germany. But it was also due to the competitiveness of new member states and the shift of production processes from old to new member states: while the EU15 market share in third markets was virtually unchanged, new member states almost doubled their market shares over the decade. Exports derived from foreign direct investment also played a role. Ireland, for instance, topped the charts of EU member state performers, doubling its market share. A good deal of this success stemmed from Irish affiliates of U.S. multinationals, which invested heavily in Ireland as a base for exports. Poland, Hungary, Belgium, Austria, and the Czech Republic also recorded large gains in market shares, while the UK, France, and Italy registered the greatest relative losses.

Fourth, Cheptea, Fontagné and Zignago demonstrate that the EU continues to maintain its position in high-tech exports, and has fared better than either the U.S. or Japan in this area. While the EU registered close to a 1% gain in global market share in high-tech products between 1994 and the onset of the recession, the United States and Japan recorded significant losses of 11% and 13% respectively.[28]

Table 1.1. Changes in World Market Shares 1994–2007 for Largest World Exporters, in Value (current US$) Terms

Exporter	Market Share, %			% Change in Market Share		
	1994	2000	2007	94-07	94-00	00-07
EU 25	**19.7**	**18.1**	**19.3**	**-0.34**	**-1.58**	**1.23**
EU 15	**19.1**	**17.5**	**18.0**	**-1.06**	**-1.62**	**0.56**
NMS 10	**0.6**	**0.6**	**1.3**	**0.71**	**0.04**	**0.67**
USA	18.5	18.3	12.5	-5.97	-0.23	-5.74
Japan	14.8	11.7	8.6	-6.23	-3.12	-3.11
China	5.8	8.0	16.1	10.26	2.17	8.09
India	1.0	1.1	1.7	0.61	0.09	0.51
Russia	0.9	1.3	1.5	0.62	0.37	0.25
Brazil	1.5	1.3	1.6	0.10	-0.27	0.37

Source: Angela Cheptea, Lionel Fontagné, Soledad Zignago, "European Export Performance," Document de Travail, No. 2010 – 12, Centre d'Etudes Prospectives et d' Informations Internationales (CEPII).

Table 1.2. EU25 Member States: Changes in World Market Shares 1994–2007

Exporter	Market Share, %			% Change in Market Share		
	1994	2000	2007	94-07	94-00	00-07
EU 25	19.70	18.10	19.30	-0.34	-1.58	1.23
Germany	5.50	4.67	5.52	0.02	-0.82	0.85
Italy	2.65	2.23	2.34	-0.31	-0.42	0.11
France	2.77	2.41	2.29	-0.49	-0.36	-0.12
UK	2.85	2.57	1.95	-0.89	-0.28	-0.61
Netherlands	1.07	0.95	1.05	-0.02	-0.12	0.10
Belgium-Luxembourg	0.81	0.98	0.98	0.18	0.17	0.01
Spain	0.75	0.71	0.79	0.04	-0.04	0.09
Sweden	0.83	0.84	0.76	-0.08	0.00	-0.08
Ireland	0.34	0.76	0.67	0.33	0.42	-0.08
Austria	0.44	0.38	0.58	0.14	-0.06	0.21
Finland	0.40	0.42	0.48	0.07	0.02	0.05
Poland	0.15	0.15	0.38	0.22	0.00	0.22
Denmark	0.46	0.36	0.36	-0.10	-0.11	0.01
Hungary	0.11	0.16	0.29	0.19	0.06	0.13
Czech Rep.	0.12	0.12	0.25	0.14	0.00	0.14
Portugal	0.12	0.11	0.14	0.02	-0.01	0.02
Slovakia	0.05	0.04	0.13	0.08	-0.01	0.09
Greece	0.10	0.09	0.11	0.01	0.00	0.01
Slovenia	0.07	0.06	0.10	0.03	-0.01	0.04
Lithuania	0.04	0.02	0.06	0.02	-0.01	0.04
Estonia	0.00	0.02	0.03	0.03	0.02	0.01
Malta	0.02	0.04	0.03	0.01	0.02	-0.01
Latvia	0.02	0.01	0.03	0.00	-0.01	0.01
Cyprus	0.02	0.01	0.01	-0.01	-0.01	0.00

Source: Angela Cheptea, Lionel Fontagné, Soledad Zignago, "European Export Performance," Document de Travail, No. 2010 – 12, Centre d'Etudes Prospectives et d' Informations Internationales (CEPII)

Figure 1L. World Market Shares 1994-2007 for Largest World Exporters, in Value (Current US$) Terms

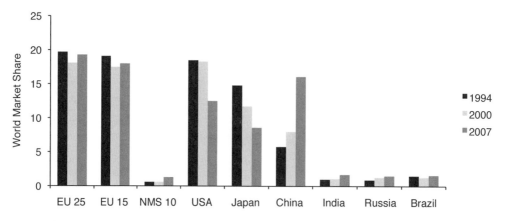

Sources: IMF; WTO; European Competitiveness Report 2009.

Figure 1M. EU25 Member States: Share of World Exports 1994-2007

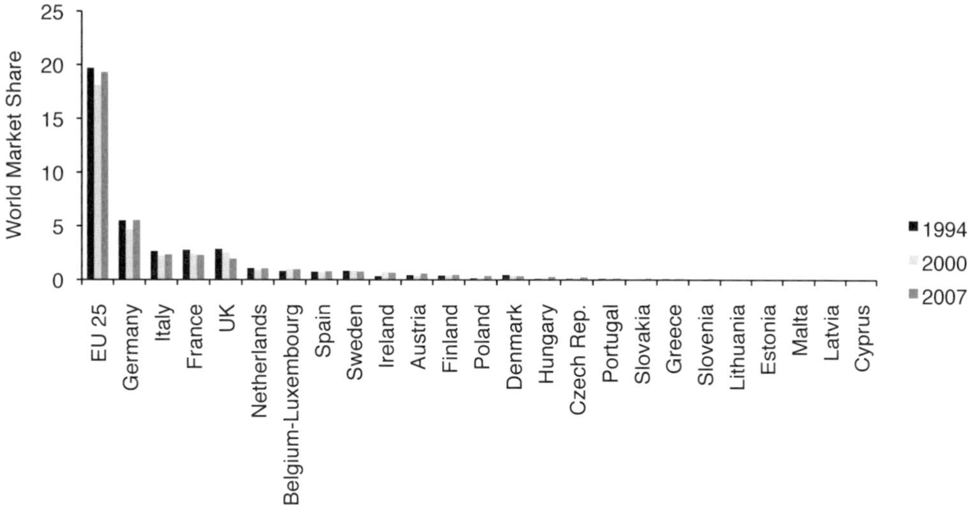

Sources: IMF; WTO; European Competitiveness Report 2009.

High- and medium-high-technology goods account for about 80% of Japanese manufacturing exports and 73% of U.S. manufacturing exports, slightly more than Germany and the UK, which are at the same level as Korea. The EU19 share is about 62%; China's share is about 57%; Brazil's share is less than 40%; India's share is about 25% and Russia's share only 19%.[29]

Fifth, between 2000 and 2007 the EU25 managed to gain market shares in "upmarket," high-quality goods, while Japan and in particular the U.S. lost shares. The EU's good performance compared to the United States or Japan is due to an upgrading of the quality of its products, combined with the ability of EU companies to sell products at premium price because of quality, branding and related services. According to Cheptea, Fontagné and Zignago, these upmarket products now account for a third of world demand and represent half of EU exports,

Table 1.3. Change in World Market Shares for High-Tech Products and by Market Segment: EU25 and Main Competitors

Exporter	High-tech products		Up-market		Mid-market		Low-market	
	2007 Market Share %	94-07 % Change	2007 Market Share %	94-07 % Change	2007 Market Share %	94-07 % Change	2007 Market Share %	94-07 % Change
EU 25	**16.9**	**0.81**	**28.8**	**0.83**	**16.8**	**-1.51**	**16.1**	**0.25**
EU 15	**15.7**	**-0.02**	**27.5**	**-0.16**	**15.6**	**-2.18**	**14.6**	**-0.24**
NMS 10	**1.2**	**0.83**	**1.3**	**0.99**	**1.2**	**0.68**	**1.5**	**0.49**
USA	13.7	-11.15	13.5	-6.00	13.5	-3.20	10.5	-5.39
Japan	8.0	-12.68	9.8	-9.76	8.0	-10.79	8.5	-1.34
China	21.2	17.79	7.6	5.94	15.5	11.37	22.9	10.67
India	0.6	0.39	1.0	0.52	1.9	1.00	1.9	0.50
Russia	0.4	0.14	0.9	0.59	2.0	0.90	1.5	0.22
Brazil	0.6	0.32	0.9	0.12	2.1	-0.20	1.7	-0.19

Source: Angela Cheptea, Lionel Fontagné, Soledad Zignago, "European Export Performance," Document de Travail, No. 2010 – 12, Centre d'Etudes Prospectives et d' Informations Internationales (CEPII)

Table 1.4. Change in World Market Shares for High-Tech Products and by Market Segment: EU25 Member States

Exporter	High-tech products		Up-market		Mid-market		Low-market	
	2007 Market Share %	94-07 % Change	2007 Market Share %	94-07 % Change	2007 Market Share %	94-07 % Change	2007 Market Share %	94-07 % Change
EU 25	16.9	0.81	28.8	0.83	16.8	-1.51	16.1	0.25
EU 15	15.7	-0.02	27.5	-0.16	15.6	-2.18	14.6	-0.24
NMS 10	1.20	0.83	1.30	0.99	1.20	0.68	1.50	0.49
Germany	4.49	0.53	7.71	-1.93	5.14	0.02	4.59	1.32
France	2.88	-0.25	3.69	-0.43	1.91	-0.71	1.75	-0.40
UK	1.98	-1.18	3.10	-0.70	1.65	-0.95	1.55	-0.71
Ireland	1.08	0.56	1.92	1.30	0.26	0.05	0.28	0.04
Italy	1.05	-0.18	3.26	0.23	1.99	-0.40	2.17	-0.68
Netherlands	0.95	-0.06	1.61	0.24	0.92	-0.28	0.82	-0.07
Sweden	0.75	-0.14	1.20	-0.02	0.65	-0.17	0.58	0.00
Belgium-Luxembourg	0.58	0.14	1.41	0.50	1.01	0.43	0.69	0.26
Finland	0.54	0.23	0.70	0.23	0.45	-0.03	0.36	0.02
Hungary	0.53	0.46	0.31	0.23	0.27	0.18	0.32	0.15
Spain	0.46	0.01	1.03	0.23	0.66	-0.14	0.81	-0.02
Austria	0.44	0.17	0.97	0.24	0.46	0.11	0.47	0.13
Denmark	0.40	0.05	0.60	-0.09	0.30	-0.11	0.28	-0.13
Czech Rep.	0.22	0.18	0.30	0.23	0.21	0.11	0.28	0.08
Portugal	0.12	0.08	0.18	0.02	0.11	-0.02	0.14	0.04
Poland	0.11	0.06	0.32	0.26	0.33	0.20	0.47	0.18
Slovenia	0.09	0.04	0.10	0.04	0.08	0.01	0.13	0.02
Malta	0.08	0.03	0.04	0.03	0.01	0.01	0.04	0.04
Slovakia	0.07	0.06	0.12	0.11	0.14	0.11	0.13	0.02
Greece	0.03	0.01	0.11	0.03	0.11	0.01	0.11	-0.03
Lithuania	0.03	0.00	0.05	0.03	0.05	0.03	0.08	0.01
Latvia	0.01	0.00	0.02	0.02	0.02	0.01	0.03	-0.02
Cyprus	0.01	0.00	0.01	0.00	0.01	-0.01	0.02	-0.02
Estonia	0.01	0.01	0.04	0.04	0.03	0.02	0.03	0.03

Source: Angela Cheptea, Lionel Fontagné, Soledad Zignago, "European Export Performance," Document de Travail, No. 2010 – 12, Centre d'Etudes Prospectives et d' Informations Internationales (CEPII)

not only in luxury consumer goods, but across the whole range of products, including intermediate goods, machinery and transport equipment. The EU ranks second in world market share in such products, just behind Japan but ahead of the U.S.[30] Moreover, the EU's market share for upmarket products is almost twice as high as its share of middle- to lower-range products. It has managed to increase its market share in such products while managing to maintain a stable or slightly declining share in other products. Japan and the U.S., in contrast, are losing ground in all product ranges. Although Chinese gains are concentrated in the middle and the bottom segments of the market, Chinese exporters (actually mostly foreign firms assembling in China) have also started to gain market shares in upmarket goods.

One reason why the EU has better resisted the competition of emerging big traders is that rapidly emerging economies are registering high demand in the types of products in which many European exporters specialize. As China and Rising Asia in particular restructure their economies and upgrade their technological capabilities, they will continue to absorb a large amount of investment goods, where the EU's comparative advantage is expected to continue.[31]

Germany, the EU's export engine, seems particularly well placed to meet demand from emerging markets. Manufacturing industries account for almost double the share of GDP in Germany than they do in the U.S., for instance, and the bulk of German exports are capital goods, for which demand is especially strong from emerging economies.[32]

In addition, as these countries continue to rise, private consumption will presumably increase, to the benefit of EU export industries. Greater demand for more upmarket, high-quality consumer goods is likely to provide ample opportunities for EU exports and market-seeking FDI in these fields. Over time, the EU is likely to achieve a greater balance between consumer goods and exports of investment goods and intermediates, which currently dominate. China intends to boost private consumption. The rising Chinese middle class, for instance, is larger than most countries in the world yet the current share of consumption in Chinese GDP is less than 40% (by comparison, Germany's share is nearly 60% and the U.S. share is more than 70%). Moreover, many key rapidly developing countries have ambitious plans to increase infrastructure investment—such as for transport infrastructure in Brazil, Russia and India; for increasing energy efficiency and protecting the environment in China; and for power generation and telecommunications in India. This will open up many new opportunities for EU suppliers specialized in these fields. Some EU member states, however, still mostly rely on exports of low-tech goods that tend to encounter less dynamic world demand, hampering gains in market share, and also more intense competition from low-cost countries.[33]

One other area of EU export strength is that of environmental goods. Over the last four years, trade in environmental goods has grown dynamically, increasing faster than total merchandise trade, particularly in the BRICS, where exports have grown at an annual average rate of 35%. The leading world exporters of environmental goods are Germany, the United States, Japan and China. These four countries together account for more than half of the total exports of environmental goods from OECD countries and the BRICS. They also benefit from the highest levels of public R&D budgets for environmental protection.[34]

Challenges

The EU also faces some challenges. One is China's rise as a high-tech exporter. China registered an 18% gain on the world high-tech market between 1994 and the onset of the recession. By 2007 the share of technology-driven industries in EU imports from China was already higher than in intra-EU imports. In EDP and office equipment, for instance, China now accounts for 32.2% of the global market, compared to 6.8% for the EU. In office and telecom equipment, China now accounts for 24.5% of the world market, compared to 7.7% for the EU. In telecommunications equipment China accounts for a 27.1% share and the EU for 9.3%.

China has achieved a small comparative advantage over the EU as a whole in technology-driven industries, which increasingly dominate EU imports from China. In fact, the share of these industries in EU imports from China is higher than in intra-EU imports.[35] China's global market share of manufacturing of advanced machinery could climb from 8% today to 30% of global exports within the decade.[36]

Figure 1N. Revealed Comparative Advantage by Factor Intensity—Euro Area vs. China

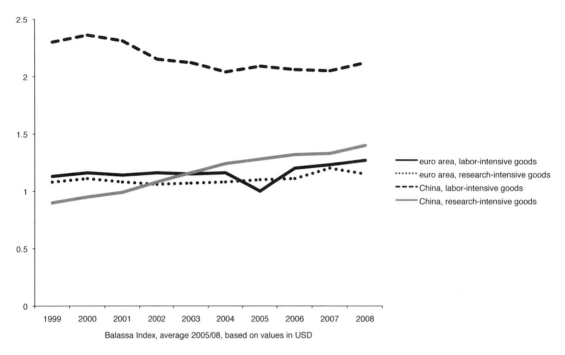

Balassa Index, average 2005/08, based on values in USD

Source: Filippo Di Mauro, Katrin Forster, Ana Lima, "The global downturn and its impact on euro area exports and competitiveness," ECB Occasional Paper 119, Frankfurt, October 2010, p. 22.

A related measure of comparative advantage is in research-intensive goods. While China has long held an advantage in labor-intensive goods, it is also now demonstrating a comparative advantage in research-intensive goods.

A third comparative frame related to China is the extent to which the export orientation of individual EU member states overlaps with that of China. Countries such as Portugal, Spain, Italy, Greece and Austria each overlap more with China than the EU average, while Finland, Germany, Ireland, Belgium, the Netherlands and France have less overlap than the EU average.

These trends can be worrying for the EU. Yet the challenge is not a straightforward case of skyrocketing Chinese indigenous technological prowess, as some pundits claim. A significant share of these imports are produced or assembled by European and other foreign companies in China. As we discussed earlier, "Made in China" does not necessarily mean "Made by China." Yet while intra-company imports of such products can give European consumers more choices at lower prices and keep European companies competitive, they can also challenge European-based high-tech production. To stay ahead, EU companies have to accelerate indigenous tech-nological development, particularly since competition from other rapidly developing countries in high value-added and technology-driven products will increase on the EU market and on third markets, in particular in other emerging economies.[37] While a significant part of the shift in R&D activities to China and other emerging economies is still largely focused on more rou-tinized "D" (for development) activities rather than more sophisticated, value-added "R"

Figure 1O. Degree of Overlap in Export Specialization between Selected Economies and China

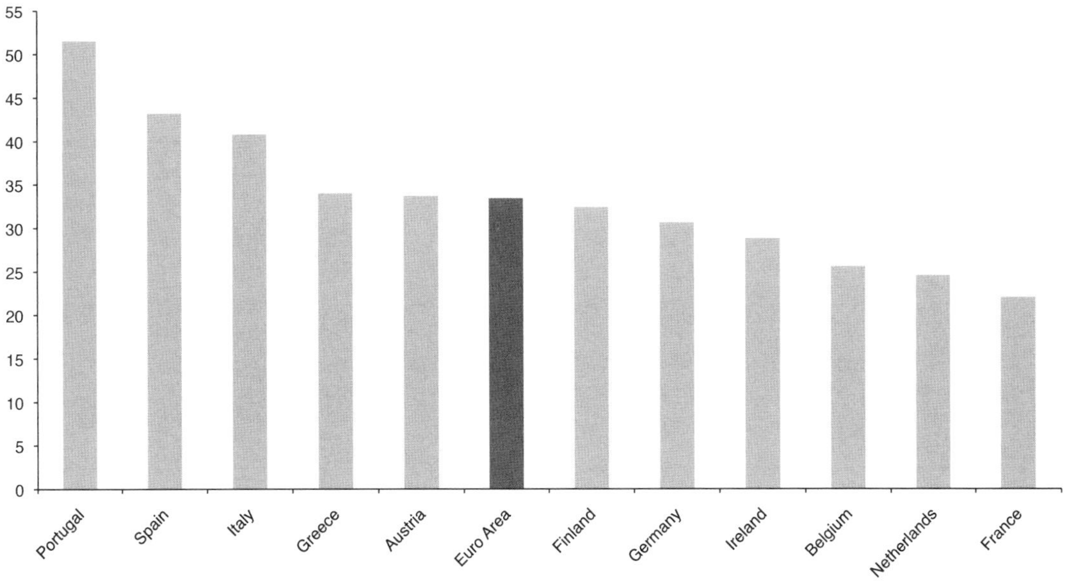

Note: Average overlap 2005/2008; percentages. Source: Filippo Di Mauro, Katrin Forster, Ana Lima, "The global downturn and its impact on euro area exports and competitiveness," ECB Occasional Paper 119, Frankfurt, October 2010, p. 22.

(research) activities, there is no reason to assume that this will remain the case over time. More likely is that such "D" activities will result in spillover to higher-value "R" activities, spurred by more open forms of innovation.[38]

EU and other Western countries are particularly challenged by the rise in manufacturing competitiveness by a number of rising powers, led by China, India and South Korea. The U.S. still boasts high labor productivity and is the largest manufacturing economy, with 20% of the world's manufactured outputs. Japan remains a formidable competitor, despite growing challenges. And German manufacturers continue as world-class leaders in "mechatronics"—the ability to integrate information technology, electronics, and old-fashioned mechanics. Yet China is not just a hub for foreign outsourced production; it continues to develop a highly-skilled talent base while retaining low-cost advantages, and now accounts for 12% of the world's manufactured outputs. India is also developing a core of talent, and boosting its manufacturing competence by using its strengths in services, including engineering and software inputs, which are integral to many modern manufactured products. South Korea remains persistent in injecting value-added to its formidable manufacturing base. Brazil has become one of the world's major steel producers and car manufacturers. And Mexico is building out its manufacturing base considerably.[39]

Germany seems poised to maintain its competitive position in manufacturing. The 2010 Global Manufacturing Competitive Index also gives positive marks to France and to Poland,

Table 1.5. Extensive and Intensive Trade Margins, 1994–2007: EU25 Member States,%

	Intensive Margin (larger value of already traded products between same partners)	Net Extensive Margin (increased number of involved countries and/or exchanged products; new flows – disappearing flows)
EU25	**96.9**	**3.1**
Germany	93.3	6.7
United Kingdom	93.2	6.8
Ireland	90.7	9.3
Italy	88.4	11.6
France	87.0	13.0
Netherlands	86.4	13.6
Denmark	82.1	17.9
Sweden	81.7	17.3
Finland	81.2	18.8
Austria	77.1	22.9
Spain	70.6	29.4
Portugal	67.3	32.7
Malta	57.3	42.7
Hungary	55.8	44.2
Czech Republic	53.6	46.4
Belgium-Luxembourg	50.2	49.8
Slovenia	47.7	52.3
Greece	47.2	52.8
Lithuania	46.0	54.0
Latvia	41.9	58.1
Poland	39.4	60.6
Slovakia	32.7	67.3
Estonia	11.9	88.1
Cyprus	0.9	99.1

Source: Angela Cheptea, Lionel Fontagné, Soledad Zignago, "European Export Performance," Document de Travail, No. 2010 – 12, Centre d'Etudes Prospectives et d' Informations Internationales (CEPII).

each of which could actually improve its relative position over the next five years. But the Netherlands, the UK, Italy, Belgium and a number of new member states all face more sobering challenges.[40]

A vital manufacturing sector is essential to EU prosperity. While this book underscores the importance of the EU capitalizing on its relatively untapped strength in services, it is important that EU decision-makers avoid the false choice between services and manufacturing. In today's increasingly sophisticated world of global products, there is an important and growing symbiosis between the two sectors: each must be developed, and particular attention must be paid to ways each can enhance the competitiveness of the other. Japan offers a cautionary tale: in the 1980s, Japan was heralded by many as the epicenter of manufacturing best practices. Today, Japan is facing formidable competitive pressures due to a declining workforce, an aging population, the "loss of a manufacturing culture,"[41] and failure to build a competitive services economy, which has become critical also to manufacturing competitiveness.

Beyond issues related to China, the EU faces another challenge: considerable inertia in its export orientation. While the EU has maintained its overall global market share over the past 15 years, the biggest export share gains were recorded in existing markets, particularly the

U.S., while market share losses were recorded in Japan and in some of the most dynamic emerging markets. This points to considerable inertia in EU15 export orientation.[42]

Trade can increase either by exchanging a larger value of already traded products between the same partners (the intensive margin of trade), or by increasing the number of involved countries and/or exchanged products (the extensive margin of trade). The former refers to the change in the value of existing trade flows, while the latter refers to the change in the composition of trade flows. Cheptea, Fontagné and Zignagno demonstrate that trade growth of the EU, the U.S. and Japan is mainly due to expansion in existing markets (96.9%, 97.5% and 101.9%, respectively). Among the Triad, Japan has lost more products and markets to other competitors, while the EU has fared better than either the U.S. or Japan.

Within the EU, old members states have tended to boost exports mainly among established trade relationships. Germany, the UK and Ireland each record an intensive margin of trade of over 90%, meaning that their export gains are overwhelmingly in traditional products and traditional markets, rather than in new products or new markets. This reflects a particular knack by German companies to infuse innovation and upgraded technologies within existing products, rather than to come up with completely different products.[43] New member states, on the other hand, have grown their exports mainly by developing new trade relationships. The new member states doubled their market shares in third markets since 2001, whereas the EU15's share remained essentially steady.

One caveat is important when discussing the relative importance of intensive vs. extensive margins of trade. While exports of new products to previously unexploited markets can be critical to new growth, they represented less than 15% of the increase in global trade in value between 1994 and 2007.[44] The contribution of the intensive margin—higher value of existing products or greater shares in traditional markets—remains substantial and is critical to the EU's export position.

In sum, even though the overall balance of EU exports has shifted from developed to developing countries, the EU is still "overweight" in its trade ties to developed countries, where demand is relatively static or growing slowly, and "underweight" in its trade ties with rapidly growing developing markets. The EU has lost market share in some of the fast-growing emerging markets, particularly in Asia. This underperformance could undermine the EU's trade position.[45] At the same time, its traditional markets provide a large and important base for the EU's overall position, and it would be unwise to abandon key market shares in established, high-value markets in favor of those that may be growing more quickly but are far smaller. EU goods exporters need to do a better job in both areas: they must boost shares in fast-growing new markets, rather than overly rely on marginal increases in slower-growing "legacy" markets; without at the same time relinquishing those core markets, which in many areas still provide the foundation for the EU's competitive position.

While the EU had been faring relatively better than either the U.S. or Japan before the recession, the EU recorded bigger losses in market share during the recession than the U.S. and Japan, and may have greater difficulty rebounding. The prospects for such a rebound are tied closely to the EU's geographic links. Emerging Asia, for instance, accounts for about 27% of total world imports (excluding the euro area), but only about 11% of euro-area foreign

Figure 1P. Exports 1999-2009

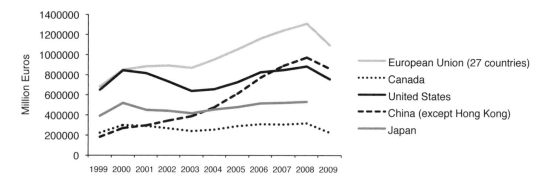

Source: OECD, WTO.

Figure 1Q. Imports 1999-2009

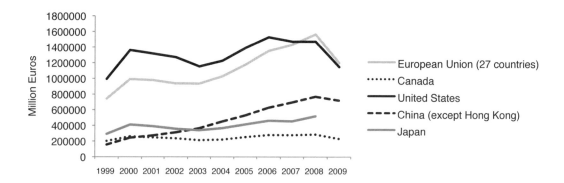

Source: OECD, WTO.

demand. At the same time, more traditional markets (such as other EU member states), which represent about 20% of euro area export markets, are experiencing relatively sluggish growth, weighing down the recovery.[46]

A related challenge is that some emerging countries are developing their competitive capabilities at a faster rate than some key EU industries and economies. Average annual growth of EU15 exports and imports of goods and services of 9-14% between 2000 and 2008 were far outpaced by Chinese export growth of 26% and import growth of 23%; Indian rates of 20% and 21%; Brazilian rates of 17% and 13%; South African rates of 13% and 17%; Turkish rates of 15% and 16%; and Russian rates of 19% and 24%. Most new EU member states fared better, with growth rates ranging from 16-24%. While the recession has dampened growth rates across the board, should such relative growth rates reestablish themselves, then by 2020 a number of emerging markets, and some new EU member states, will be have gained considerable ground on old EU member states in terms of exports, even as they provide potentially lucrative markets in terms of imports.

Comparative growth rates for medium- and high-tech exports offer another indication of relative competitiveness, and demonstrate the gap in growth between the EU and major emerging economies. The EU19 recorded 10% average annual growth rates in these areas between 1997 and 2007, ahead of the U.S. (5%) and Japan (6%) but considerably less than China (26%), Turkey (23%), India (18%), South Africa and Indonesia (15%).

The EU is also characterized by its relative success in keeping high market shares, despite its consistently negative trade balance through the past decade. It has trade deficits with all BRICs except India—although not as large as the deficits the U.S. has with these countries. One result of the recession was a reduction in the EU's trade deficit by more than half in 2009 to €105 billion, as imports fell by 23% and exports fell by 16.5%. But the trade deficit with China in particular is likely to rise again, barring appreciation of the Chinese renminbi against the euro. Only Japan has succeeded in aligning its exports on its imports from China and thus in limiting its trade deficit or generating a trade surplus.[47]

Rapidly developing economies are also developing their own comparative advantages in some key areas. The European Competitiveness Report 2009 shows that all BRICs have revealed comparative advantages (RCAs) in trade with the EU, the U.S. and Japan in labor-intensive industries. They also have positive RCAs in marketing-driven industries (except for Russia in trade with the EU and the U.S., and for Brazil in trade with Japan).[48] The trade specialization patterns of the BRICs are far from identical: Brazil has positive RCAs in marketing-driven (food processing) and in labor-intensive (textiles) industries. Russia has positive RCAs only in capital-intensive industries, mostly due to strong exports of refined petroleum and diverse metal products. Russia is an exception among the BRICs in this respect, since it has a comparative disadvantage in labor-intensive industries in trade with the EU and the United States. India's distribution of RCAs is very similar to those of Brazil. From the EU point of view, the RCA patterns in trade with the BRICs are also rather diverse. The EU exhibited positive RCAs in mainstream and technology-driven trade with Brazil and India both in 2000 and in 2007. It exhibited positive RCAs in all industry groupings except capital-intensive industries in its trade with Russia. It recorded negative RCAs, however, in both labor-intensive and marketing-driven industries in its trade with China between 2000 and 2007.

Chapter 2
Services

Trade in services is much less important than trade in goods, as measured by both absolute volumes and shares in GDP. Services account for only about one-fifth of global trade. In the EU, trade in services accounts on average for less than 10% of GDP, compared to 32% for goods trade. Many service activities require a local presence and do not lend themselves to being traded internationally. Moreover, services that can be exported or imported are still subject to numerous restrictions, since the Doha Round accords of the General Agreement on Trade in Services (GATS) have yet to be ratified.[1]

Nonetheless, trade in services has intensified and is poised to expand rapidly. In fact, while the services sector accounts for only 23% of global exports, it accounts for over 70% of GDP in advanced economies.[2] Bradford Jensen and Lori Kletzer have estimated that the share of services that is tradable is comparable with manufactured goods.[3] Computerization and digitalization have allowed for greater global trade in such services as advertising, education, medicine, data processing, consulting, legal services, engineering and a host of other functions. The internet is to trade in services what the advent of container shipping was to trade in goods—a transforming capability that enables faster, cross-border delivery of a variety of activities that were once consider non-tradable. This global sourcing of services does not just include call centers and other low-skill functions; high-skilled activities are also involved. Greater openness to foreign direct investment has also contributed to this process.

How Connected is the EU in Services?

Trade in services is critical to the long-term prosperity and competitiveness of the European Union. Services already account for roughly 72% of the EU25's gross domestic product and around 70% of total employment, compared to 25% in industry and 5% in agriculture. The services sector provided for all net job growth in the EU over the past decade. The services sector also proved more resilient than the goods sector in the 2008-9 recession; the decline in services trade was far less severe than the contraction in goods trade.

The EU Single Market has been an important stimulus to intra-EU services trade. The revised Services Directive, which was ratified by EU member states at the end of 2009, eases procedures to establish new businesses or trading services across the EU in most commercial services sectors. Intra-EU trade in services is 35% higher than would otherwise be expected in the absence of the EU's moves towards a Single Market.[4]

The EU is a global leader in services exports. While the U.S. remains the world's top national exporter of commercial services, with a global export share of 14.1% in 2009, the U.K. ranks second (7%), followed by Germany (6.8%) and France (4.3%).[5]

European regionalization is significant for services trade, just as it is for trade in goods. Intra-EU services trade is larger than EU services trade with the rest of the world. Intra-EU25 services exports topped $2 trillion for the first time in 2006. Imports totaled $1.96 trillion. The EU's neighbors in Wider Europe accounted for 19% of extra-EU services exports and 17% of

EU services imports from outside the Union in 2009—the second most important services trading partner for the EU after North America.

Despite the EU's regional orientation in services trade, extra-EU services trade is still quite significant. Extra-EU exports of services in 2009 totaled $652 billion, accounting for 26.3% of world services exports; extra-EU imports of services totaled $620.7 billion, accounting for 23% of world services imports.[6]

Beyond European shores, the EU's interconnections in its services trade are different than in its goods trade. The most important services partner for the EU by far is North America, and in particular the United States. North America was the largest destination for extra-EU services exports (29.6%) and the largest source of extra-EU services imports (36.9%) even in recession year 2009 (down from 32% of exports and 39% of exports in 2008). Transatlantic services trade is critical to the prosperity of both North America and Europe, and reflects their role as services economies. Services is an area ripe with opportunities to strengthen and deepen transatlantic commercial ties.[7]

EU services exports to North America totaled €133 billion in recession year 2009 and imports totaled €135.7 billion, for a deficit of €2.7 billion, compared to €150.8 billion in exports and €145.6 billion in imports in 2008—a surplus of €5.2 billion. Thanks to a variety of factors—stronger growth, the weaker dollar, EU enlargement, industry reform and deregulation—U.S. services exports to Europe more than doubled between 1998 and 2008, rising from around $99 billion to nearly $230 billion in 2008. The bulk of these gains were in exports of "other private services," or in such value-added activities like computer processing, engineering, advertising and related activities. In this category, the U.S. posted a $51 billion trade surplus with Europe in 2008.

U.S. services imports from Europe, meanwhile, expanded just as fast as exports in the last decade. Imports doubled between 1998 and 2008, climbing from $79 billion to $133 billion in 2007. The U.S. and EU each owe a good part of their competitive position in services globally to deep transatlantic connections in services industries provided by mutual investment flows. A good share of U.S. services exports to the world are generated by U.S. affiliates of European multinationals, just as a good share of EU services exports to the world are generated by European affiliates of U.S. multinationals.

On a regional basis, Europe accounted for 41% of total U.S. services exports and for 43% of total U.S. services imports in 2009. Five of the top ten export markets for U.S. services in 2009 were in Europe. The UK ranked #1, followed by Ireland (4th), Germany (5th), Switzerland (7th), and France (8th). Similarly, the same five nations ranked among the top ten service providers to the U.S.[8] The U.S. enjoyed a $54 billion trade surplus in services with Europe in 2009, compared with its $120 trade deficit in goods with Europe. New York and London rank as the "most connected" global cities in advanced producer services.[9]

While transatlantic trade in services is important, the delivery of transatlantic services by U.S. and European foreign affiliates has exploded on both sides of the Atlantic over the past decade. In fact, affiliate sales of services have not only supplemented trade in services but also become the overwhelming mode of delivery in a rather short period of time.

Figure 2A. EU Services Exports by Region, 2009

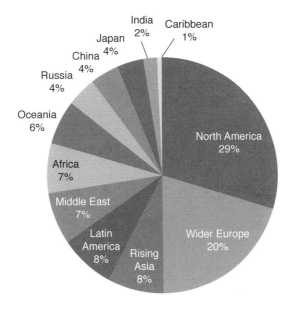

Source: Eurostat.

Figure 2B. EU Services Exports by Region, 2004–2009

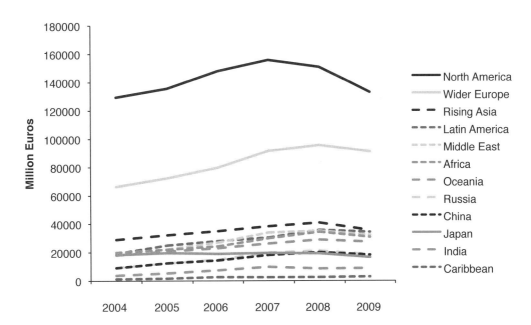

Source: Eurostat.

Figure 2C. EU Services Imports by Region, 2009

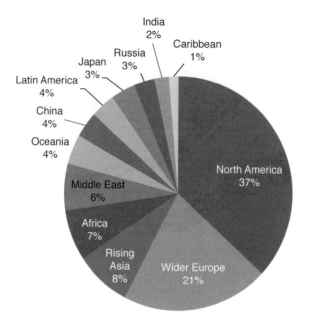

Source: Eurostat.

Figure 2D. EU Services Imports by Region, 2004–2009

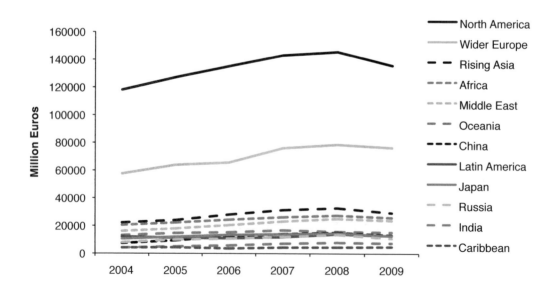

Source: Eurostat.

Figure 2E. EU Services Trade Balance by Region, 2009

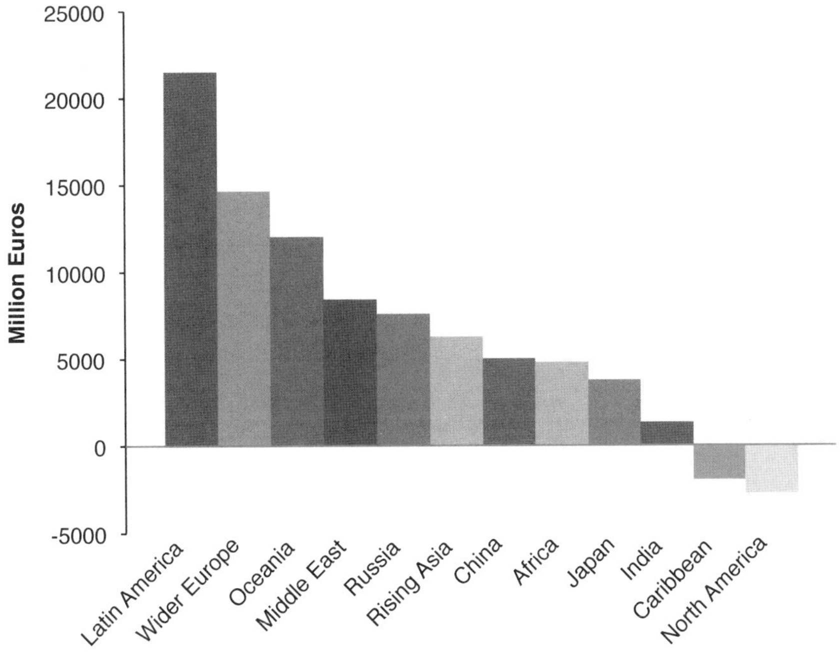

Source: Eurostat.

Sales of services of U.S. foreign affiliates in the European Union rose to a record $3.1 trillion in 2008, more than double the level in 2002. Meanwhile, services sales were nearly triple U.S. service exports to Europe in the same year. The United Kingdom accounts for the bulk of U.S. services sales in Europe. In 2007, the UK accounted for around 38% of all U.S. affiliate sales of services in Europe. On a global basis, Europe accounted for 55% of total U.S. services sales.

European affiliates in the United States were also major purveyors of services. European affiliate sales of services in the U.S. were nearly triple EU services exports to the U.S.—a fact that underscores the ever widening presence of European services leaders in the U.S. economy.

The BRICs are far less important in EU services trade than China and Russia are in EU goods trade. As a group, the BRICs in 2009 accounted for about 12% of extra-EU services exports and 10.3% of extra-EU services imports, with the new member states importing relatively more services from the BRICs than the old member states. In contrast to its role as the EU's top source for goods imports, China was only the seventh largest regional source of EU services imports (4.1%) and the ninth largest regional destination for EU services exports (3%) in 2008. Russia was the eighth largest regional destination for EU services exports (4.1%) and the ninth largest regional source of EU services imports (3%) in 2009. All of Latin America was only the fourth largest regional destination for EU services exports (7.6%) and the eighth

Figure 2F. EU Services Trade Balance by Region, 2004–2009

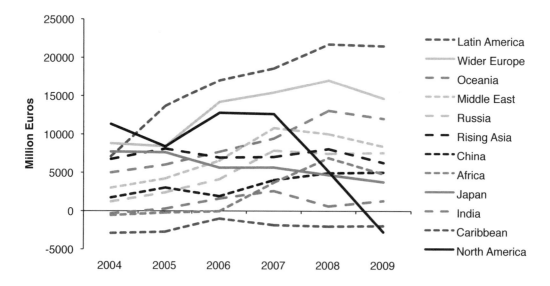

Source: Eurostat.

largest regional source of EU services imports (3.5%) in 2009. And despite India's burgeoning role as a services economy, it ranked eleventh as a regional destination for EU services exports (2%) and eleventh as a source of EU services imports (2%) in 2009—less than Oceania and only slightly more than the Caribbean.

From the BRICs' perspective, on the other hand, the EU is quite an important market for service exporters. The shares of the EU in services exports range from 13% for Hong Kong to over 40% for Russia, and in the case of China and Hong Kong the EU's share has been growing.[10]

How Competitive is the EU in Services?

Services are a competitive strength for the EU, even though services markets in the EU are less integrated and competitive than goods markets. The EU is the world's largest regional trader in services, with dominant global shares in both traditional and non-traditional services activities. In the past decade the EU15 almost quadrupled their services trade balance. While the U.S. remains the world's top national exporter of commercial services, with a global export share of 14.1% in 2009, the United Kingdom ranks second in the world in exports of services after the U.S. and third in imports after the U.S. and Germany. Between 2005 and 2008, UK trade in services generated a surplus of $69 billion, compared with a $155 billion deficit in trade in goods. Germany ranked as the third-largest exporter of services between 2005 and 2008, recording a deficit of $37.4 billion, which was amply offset by its $232 billion surplus in trade in goods.[11]

Other key EU services traders include France, Spain, Italy, Ireland, the Netherlands, Belgium, Sweden, Luxembourg, Denmark and Austria. 7 EU member states ranked among the

Table 2.1. Leading Exporters and Importers in World Trade in Commercial Services, 2009

(Billion $ and percentage)

Rank	Exporter	Value	Share	Rank	Importer	Value	Share
1	U.S.	474	14.1	1	U.S.	331	10.5
2	**UK**	**233**	**7.0**	2	**Germany**	**253**	**8.1**
3	**Germany**	**227**	**6.8**	3	**UK**	**161**	**5.1**
4	**France**	**143**	**4.3**	4	China	158	5.0
5	China	129	3.8	5	Japan	147	4.7
6	Japan	126	3.8	6	**France**	**126**	**4.0**
7	**Spain**	**122**	**3.6**	7	**Italy**	**115**	**3.6**
8	**Italy**	**101**	**3.0**	8	**Ireland**	**103**	**3.3**
9	**Ireland**	97	2.9	9	**Spain**	87	2.8
10	**Netherlands**	91	2.7	10	**Netherlands**	85	2.7
11	Singapore	88	2.6	11	Singapore	81	2.6
12	India	87	2.6	12	India	80	2.5
13	Hong Kong	86	2.6	13	Canada	78	2.5
14	**Belgium**	**79**	**2.4**	14	South Korea	75	2.4
15	Switzerland	69	2.1	15	**Belgium**	**74**	**2.4**
16	**Sweden**	**61**	**1.8**	16	Russia	59	1.9
17	**Luxembourg**	**61**	**1.8**	17	**Denmark**	**51**	**1.6**
18	Canada	58	1.7	18	**Sweden**	**46**	**1.5**
19	South Korea	57	1.7	19	Saudi Arabia	46	1.4
20	**Denmark**	**55**	**1.6**	20	Hong Kong	44	1.4
21	**Austria**	**53**	**1.6**	21	Brazil	44	1.4
22	Australia	41	1.2	22	Australia	41	1.3
23	Russia	41	1.2	23	Thailand	38	1.2
24	Norway	38	1.1	24	Norway	38	1.2
25	**Greece**	**38**	**1.1**	25	**Austria**	**37**	**1.2**
26	Turkey	33	1.0	26	UAE	37	1.2
27	Taiwan	31	0.9	27	**Luxembourg**	**36**	**1.1**
28	Thailand	30	0.9	28	Switzerland	36	1.1
29	**Poland**	**29**	**0.9**	29	Taiwan	29	0.9
30	Malaysia	28	0.8	30	Indonesia	28	0.9
31	Brazil	26	0.8	31	Malaysia	27	0.9
32	**Finland**	**25**	**0.7**	32	**Poland**	**24**	**0.8**
33	**Portugal**	**23**	**0.7**	33	**Finland**	**23**	**0.7**
34	Israel	22	0.6	34	Mexico	21	0.7
35	Egypt	21	0.6	35	**Greece**	**20**	**0.6**
36	**Czech Rep.**	**20**	**0.6**	36	**Czech Rep.**	**19**	**0.6**
37	Macao, China	19	0.6	37	Israel	17	0.5
38	**Hungary**	**18**	**0.5**	38	Iran[a]	16	0.5
39	Lebanon	17	0.5	39	**Hungary**	**16**	**0.5**
40	Mexico	15	0.5	40	Turkey	16	0.5

[a]WTO Secretariat estimate.

Note: Figures for a number of countries and territories have been estimated by the WTP Secretariat. Annual percentage changes and rankings are affected by continuity breaks in the series for a large number of economies, and by limitations in cross-country comparability.

Source: WTO, International Trade Statistics, 2010.

top 10 exporters of services in 2009 and 18 ranked among the top 40, accounting for 43.4% of world market share. Moreover, the EU has sustained or expanded its share of world trade in most broad service categories except transport services, in contrast to the United States. In 2009 the EU registered a surplus of nearly $104.3 billion in commercial services and a $29.6

billion surplus in transportation services, easily enough to cover its $25.1 billion deficit in travel.[12] The EU enjoys a services trade surplus with every other world region except the Caribbean.

Regarding services exports, the EU ranked #1 in the world in 8 of 11 categories, and in fact boosted its position between 2005 and 2008 in communications, telecommunications, construction, computer and information services. In the three remaining categories, the U.S. has the lead: royalties and license fees; personal, cultural and recreational services; and audiovisual services.

Europe registered 10% annual average growth in commercial services exports between 2000 and 2009, 1% more than the global average, 1% less than Asia, but 4% more than North America.[13]

The EU boosted its world market share in exports of transportation services from 42.5% to 45.2% between 2000 and 2009 (extra-EU exports share: 21.9%), largely at the expense of North America, whose share dropped dramatically from 17.1% in 2000 to 11.7% in 2009 (the U.S. share declined from 14.5% to 10.2%). Japan's share also declined from 7.4% to 4.5%, whereas Korea increased its share slightly from 3.9% to 4.1% and China from 1.1% to 3.4%. EU imports, in turn, declined from 35.6% to 33.5% (extra-EU imports share: 14.8%), expanding the EU's trade surplus in this area. U.S. and Japanese imports also fell to 9.7% and 4.9%, respectively, while the share of China and India grew to 5.6% and 4.2%, respectively.[14]

The EU is the world's largest trader in travel. It trails the U.S. in export share but has a greater import share. Its export share decreased from 42% in 2000 to 39.2% in 2009 (extra-EU export share:10.9%) and its annual average growth of 6% during this period trailed the world average by 1%. The U.S. share dropped significantly, however, during this period, from 20.7% to 14.2%. China's share, the world's third largest, grew slightly from 3.4% to 4.3%. North America's share dropped significantly from 24.6% to 16.7%, whereas Asia's share grew from 17.5% to 22.8%. Asia's share of travel imports increased from 20.9% to 22.2%, whereas the EU's share decreased from 45.3% to 42.3% (extra-EU import share: 15.3%) and North America's share declined from 19.6% to 14%. China's share increased from 3% to 5.5%.[15]

The EU has a particular comparative advantage in exports of "other commercial services." It boosted its world market share in this category from 45.1% in 2000 to 48.8% in 2009 (extra-EU export share: 22.7%). North America's share declined from 23.4% to 18.0% (U.S. share: 15.9%); Asia's share increased from 20.2% to 21.9% (China's share: 3.7%). Other world regions registered only marginal changes. EU imports also increased slightly from 46.0% to 47.1% (extra-EU import share: 19.7%), whereas the U.S. share declined to 11.2%, the Japanese share declined to 5.3%, and the Chinese share increased to 4.5%.[16]

The EU is the world's largest trader in communications services, registering 59.2% market share (extra-EU export share: 20.4%) of the 15 largest trading countries in 2008, the last year of available data, compared to a 15.3% share for the U.S. and Canada together (U.S. 12.2%, Canada 3.1%); 3.1% for India; 2.1% for Egypt; 2.0% for China; 1.9% for Russia; 1.6% for Switzerland; and 1.5% for Singapore. The EU import share of 64.3% (extra-EU share: 23.6%) was far higher than the 14.6% recorded by the U.S. and Canada together (U.S. 11.7%, Canada

Table 2.2. Extra-EU Share of World Imports/Exports by Service 2009/2008 (%)**

Share of exports	Service	Share of imports
21.9	Transportation	14.8
10.9	Travel	15.3
22.7	Other Commercial Services	19.7
20.4	Communications*	23.6
20.3	Telecommunications*	24.8
30.0	Construction*	17.7
29.0	Insurance*	8.5
25.6	Financial*	23.6
22.8	Computer and Information*	18.7
17.1	Royalties and License Fees*	13.1
24.9	Other Business Services*	23.3
18.3	Personal, Cultural, Recreational*	25.8
14.0	Audiovisual*	8.1

*2008.
**Share of top 15 exporters and importers.
Source: WTO.

2.9%); 2.8% for Russia; 2.3% for China; 2.2% for Singapore; 1.9% for Saudi Arabia, 1.8% for Hong Kong, and 1.7% for South Korea.[17]

The EU is the world's largest trader in telecommunications services, registering a 61.1% market share (extra-EU export share: 20.3%) of the 15 largest trading countries in 2008, the last year of available data, compared to 17.1% for the U.S. and Canada together (U.S. 14.7%, Canada 2.4%); 2.3% for Russia; 1.9% for India; 1.2% for Turkey, and negligible amounts for other major economies. The EU import share of 69.8% (extra-EU share: 24.8%) was significantly larger than the 16.4% recorded by the U.S. and Canada together (U.S.14.3%, Canada 2.1%), with most other economies quite marginal.[18]

The EU is the world's largest trader in construction services, registering a 54% market share (extra-EU export share: 30%) of the 15 largest trading countries in 2008, the last year of available data, compared to Japan (16%), China (12%), Russia (5.4%), and the United States (1.9%). The EU import share of 42% (extra-EU import share: 17.7%), was larger than that of Japan (14.3%), Russia (11.1%), Saudi Arabia (5.7%), China (5.5%) and the United States (1.0%).[19]

The EU is the world's largest trader in insurance services, accounting for a 57.5% market share (extra-EU export share: 29%) of the top 15 trading economies in 2008, compared to North America's share of 21.9% (U.S. 13.9%, Canada 5.4%, Mexico 2.6) and Switzerland accounting for 7.4%, with most other economies registering only small shares. The EU import share of 24.7% (extra-EU import share: 8.5%) trails those of the U.S. (33.2%), China (9.8%) and Mexico (9.5%), with most other countries registering only small shares.[20]

The EU is the world's largest trader in financial services, accounting for 57.5% market share of the top 15 economies (extra-EU export share: 25.6%) in 2008, compared to the U.S. (21.1%), Switzerland (6.8%), Hong Kong (4.2%), Singapore (2.3%), Japan (1.9%) and all others quite marginal. The EU import share of 60% (extra-EU import share: 23.6%), was larger than those of the U.S. (16.5%), Canada and Japan (each 3.4%), India (3.1%), and Hong Kong (2.7%), with all others marginal.[21]

The EU is the world's largest trader in computer and information services, accounting for a 58.3% market share of the top 15 economies (extra-EU export share: 22.8%) in 2008, compared to India (19.4%), U.S. (6.8%), Israel (3.7%), China (3.4%) and Canada (2.6%), with the rest marginal. The EU registered an import share of 55.5% (extra-EU import share: 18.7%) compared with 17.9% for the U.S., 4.4% for Japan, 3.8% for India, 3.5% for China, 3.1% for Brazil, and 2.8% for Canada.[22]

The EU is the world's largest trader in royalties and license fees. It trails the U.S. (43.7%) as an exporter, with 32.6% market share of the top 15 trading economies in 2008 (extra-EU export share: 17.1%), but ahead of Japan (12.2%), Switzerland (5.9%), Canada (1.7%) and all others. And the EU import share of 44.7% (extra-EU import share: 26.9%), is significantly larger than that of the U.S. (13.1%), Japan (9.0%), Singapore (6%), Switzerland (5.7%), China (5.1%) and Canada (4.2%).[23]

The EU is the world's largest trader in other business services,[24] registering a 54.7% market share of the top 15 economies (extra-EU export share: 24.9%) in 2008, compared to the U.S. (10.4%), China (5.2%), Japan (4.6%), Singapore (4.2%), India (3.8%), and Hong Kong (3.7%). The EU import share of 59% (extra-EU import share: 23.3%) was far larger than those of the U.S. (8%), Japan (5.6%), China (5.3%), South Korea (3.7%), India (2.9%), Singapore (2.9%), Russia (2.2%) and Canada (2%).[25]

A large share of EU services exports and imports are linked to North America, and particularly the United States. Over the course of the past decade the UK, Ireland, Germany, Norway and Denmark improved their relative export shares of services to the U.S., while the relative shares of Canada and France declined.

Leading EU services exporters such as the UK, Germany and France lag the U.S., however, when it comes to key markets such as Japan (U.S. share 56%), India (U.S. share 41.3%), and China (U.S. share 27.9%), and Rising Asia, although U.S. shares of services export markets in India, China and Rising Asia have fallen relative to EU shares.

In sum, the EU enjoys a strong position as a services exporter and is well positioned to take further advantage of the globalization of services. Services account for over 70% of EU GDP but only 23% of global exports: there is room to grow. Moreover, the supposed trade-off between services and manufacturing is a false choice: manufacturing "pulls" on average 17% of its total production from services and "pushes" an average 8% of its total supply into the services sector.[26] If services win, so does manufacturing.

That said, the benefits are more diffuse when one looks at specific EU member states. In general, the UK, Ireland, and the Nordic nations are well positioned to benefit, as are certain sectors of Germany and France. Owing largely to their underdeveloped IT infrastructures, however, the countries of southern and central Europe could find themselves at a competitive disadvantage in trade in global services.

Many service companies tend to use high technology intensively. They need relatively highly skilled workers if they are to benefit from technological innovation. The EU's standing as a services economy, therefore, depends on the ability of all 27 member states to harness high technology and adequately educate and train their workforce.

World-class education and skills training has never been more urgent for the EU if it is to maintain its dominant position as a knowledge-intensive services economy. Although the BRICs' share in global services trade is much lower than that of the EU, all BRICs have been increasing their services exports much faster than the EU, the U.S. or Japan. India is the absolute leader in terms of growth rates—its annual services exports grew more than five-fold during 2000-2007. Services exports by China and Russia increased four-fold during that period.

The EU has a strong services economy, yet is failing to capitalize on this strength, and its relative weakness in services compared to the United States is a major cause of the gap in both its absolute productivity and productivity growth vis-a-vis the United States. McKinsey concludes that services sectors are the primary source of the GDP and productivity growth gap between the EU15 and the United States. Between 1995 and 2005, for example, services contributed 1.8% to GDP growth in the U.S. (overall GDP growth 2.9%) compared to 1.1% in the EU (overall GDP growth 2.2%), and 1% to productivity growth in the U.S. (overall 2%) and only 0.4% in the EU (overall 1.4%).[27] McKinsey calculates that the EU15 need to find 0.4% of incremental productivity growth throughout the next 20 years if they are to match their economic growth rate of the past 20 years. Services productivity growth will be critical to this.

Reforms to stimulate services sectors across the broad range of EU member state economies would boost growth and create jobs. Free movement of services would reduce the fragmentation of EU services sectors and increase competition, boosting productivity. McKinsey estimates that boosting services sector productivity to the EU15 average or to European best-practice levels per sector could add around 3 or 20%, respectively, to the EU's productivity.[28]

Chapter 3
Money

Beyond trade in goods and services, nothing better captures the EU's economic interlinkages in the G20 world than the movement of money—whether portfolio investments, banking claims, or foreign direct investment.

Foreign Direct Investment

Europe is the world's most dynamic region for foreign direct investment (FDI). The EU is the largest provider and recipient of FDI among all world regions. FDI flows have significantly deepened Europe's linkages with the rest of the world. According to the United Nations, EU countries accounted for roughly 51% of global FDI outflows and for nearly 40% of global FDI inflows between 2005 and 2009.

Companies invest abroad for various reasons. They may want to make a strategic investment, for instance to introduce a new product or service. They may seek resources, such as acquiring access to specialized knowledge or particular technologies. They may want to win share in new markets, or they may want to achieve greater efficiencies by gaining access to cheap factors of production.[12]

The stock of foreign direct investment totaled nearly $18 trillion in 2009, over seven times more than in 1990, and equivalent to roughly 31% of world GDP. This was accompanied by a spike in foreign affiliate sales, which exceeded world exports by nearly 80%. This gap between foreign affiliate sales and exports underscores a basic point: global production by affiliates, not exports, is the primary mode by which multinationals deliver goods and services to foreign customers.

On the eve of the global financial crisis nearly half of world FDI inflows went to developing countries, compared with only 20% in 1990. Even excluding China, the share doubled to 32%. New actors—private equity, hedge funds, sovereign wealth funds, and state-controlled companies—played a significant role in driving these flows.[3]

Globalization entails the heightened mobility of capital and greater access to cross-border resources, twin factors that have enabled European firms to invest in virtually any place in the world. Many companies did just that; the aggregate level of outward foreign direct investment stocks of EU countries rose roughly eleven-fold between 1990 and 2009. The level of outward extra-EU FDI stock totaled €3.2 trillion in 2008, roughly 35% larger than the level of FDI inward stock. In other words, by the start of 2009, Europe had invested 35% more in the rest of the world than the rest of the world had invested in Europe.

Overall, the EU's expanding inward stock of FDI has created jobs in many EU member states, increased the level of productive capacity, and helped promote the technological advancement of the Union through greater expenditures on research and development. Inward FDI in such strategic industries as finance, chemicals, pharmaceuticals, and automobiles has sustained and embellished the global competitiveness of these sectors. Many EU member states have profited. Between 2005 and 2009, for instance, Belgium received €255 billion in foreign direct investment, the UK received €497 billion, France €312 billion and Germany €165 billion. In short, virtually all of Europe's primary stakeholders have benefited from this dynamic.

How Connected is the EU in Foreign Direct Investment?

The European Dynamic

If one examines the EU's global links through foreign direct investment, the same basic patterns appear as with trade in goods and services: the significance of its base on the European continent; the deep integration between the EU and North America, particularly the U.S.; and rapidly expanding links with rising emerging markets.

EU FDI outflows in 2008 amounted to €8.57 trillion, more than twice the amount of EU FDI outflows in 2000. 62% of the total remained within the EU, a 2.5% increase from 2000, further evidence of the importance of EU enlargement and broader European regionalization. FDI inflows into the EU in 2008 totaled €7.51 trillion, twice the level of 2000. They exhibit the same dynamic: 68.3% of the total circulated within the EU, about 4% more than in 2000. Intra-EU investments have increased much more rapidly than outward FDI. Between 1994 and 2007 the intra-EU FDI stock increased 9 times from €500 billion to more than €4.5 trillion. As a result, the intra-EU FDI stock in 2007 was more than double the EU outward FDI stock even though they started out at almost the same level in 1994. Investments across borders within the EU have grown much faster than investments by EU firms out of the EU, and cross-border investments internally in the EU have reached a much higher level than outward FDI.[4]

While popular depictions often equate such investments with the export of jobs, know-how and capital, most empirical research suggests that outward FDI does not have a detrimental effect on the home economy. This may be particularly true for Europe, since the bulk of the outward stock of EU nations is in the EU itself. More than half the FDI outflows from all major European countries except the UK goes to other European countries. Moreover, for most European countries this regional orientation has actually increased.

As with trade, outward-bound FDI by European companies has been sparked by the enlargement of the European Union. Central Europe has emerged as a primary destination for French, German and Dutch firms in particular. The EBRD estimates that FDI into central and southeastern Europe in 2007 totaled €30 billion. Yet even though FDI inflows increased sharply in Hungary, Poland and the Czech Republic over the past decade, rising inflows have not been at the expense at the 15 older members. EU enlargement has not led diverted foreign direct investment within the EU from high-cost nations like Germany and France to low-cost producers like Hungary and the Czech Republic. Between 2005 and 2008, Luxembourg continuously ranked second, in absolute value, as both host and investor of FDI. This is due to the presence in Luxembourg of foreign financial holding companies that channel their investment through that country. In Europe, over the period, Luxembourg was the leading host country

Figure 3A. Outgoing EU FDI in million Euro (€) (2008)

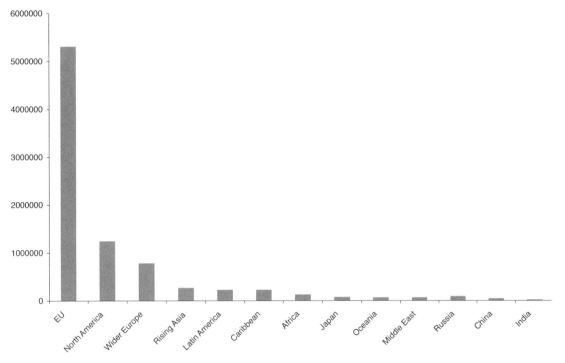

Source: International Monetary Fund (IMF).

Figure 3B. Outgoing EU FDI w/o EU in million Euro (€) (2008)

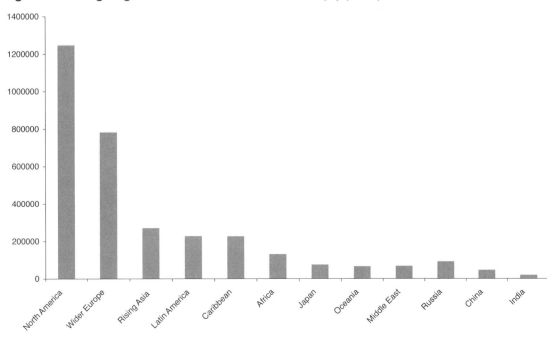

Source: IMF

Figure 3C. Outgoing EU FDI by Region in million Euro (€), 2000-2008

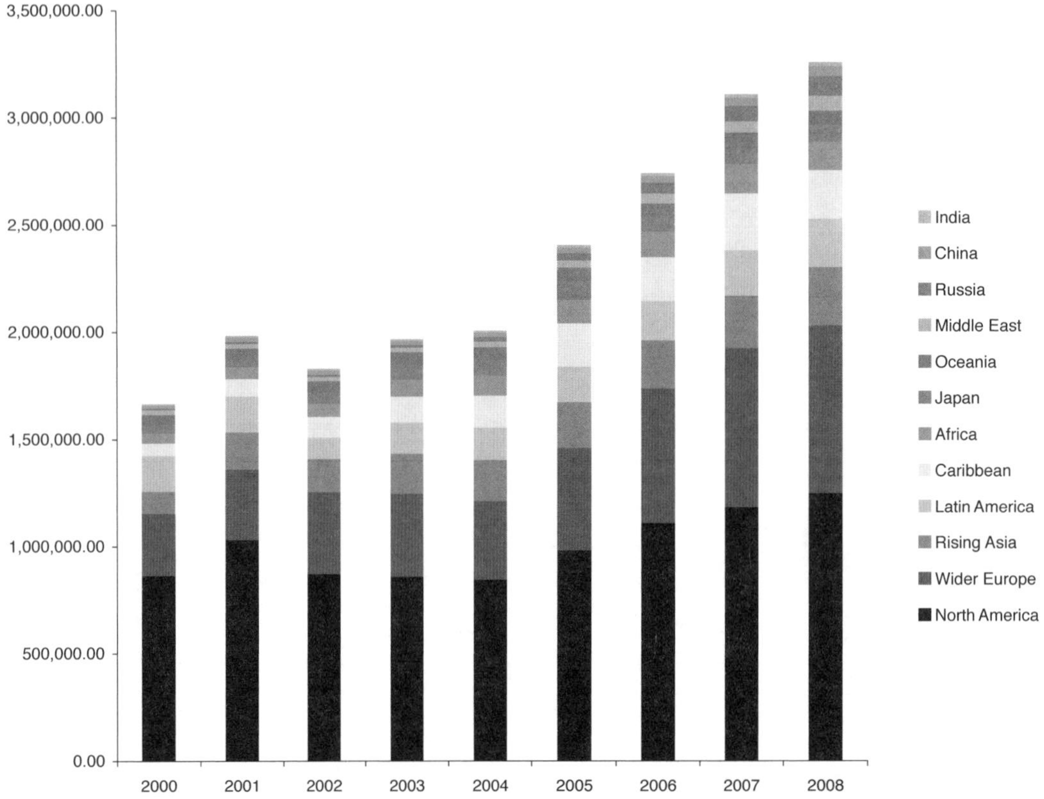

Source: IMF

for foreign direct investment, followed by the United Kingdom and France.[5] Combined inflows to the accession nations totaled roughly $40 billion in 2006, half the level of inflows to France and roughly 30% of inflows to the UK. FDI inflows into the accession members have been a fraction of total EU inflows, totaling just 7.3% in 2006, down from a high of 11% in 1995.[6]

Deep Integration Across the Atlantic

If one excludes intra-EU FDI, then in 2008 EU FDI abroad totaled €3.258 trillion, double the level of 2001. 38% of the total—€1.06 billion—went to North America (32.5% to the U.S.), still considerably more than to other world regions, but a decline of 14% from 2001. 22.5% went to Wider Europe—almost 6% more than in 2001. 8.3% went to Rising Asia, about 2% more than in 2001. 7% went to Latin America, a decline of more than 3% from 2001. 6.9% went to the Caribbean, twice the level of 2001. 4% went to Africa, about 1.3% more than in 2001; and 3.7% to the Middle East, more than twice the amount of 2001. EU FDI to Russia increased 12.5 times over this period, but still accounted for only 2.8% of the total. Only 2.3% went to Japan and 2% to Oceania. EU FDI to China tripled between 2000

Table 3.1. Top Country Destinations for EU FDI, 2008

Million Euro (€)

	Destination Country	Amount
1	United States	1,058,052
2	Switzerland	453,696
3	Canada	139,903
4	Brazil	112,520
5	Russia	91,955
6	Hong Kong	88,864
7	Singapore	80,898
8	Japan	76,069
9	Norway	67,127
10	Australia	58,742
11	Turkey	51,660
12	Mexico	49,048
13	China	47,285
14	South Africa	46,345
15	Argentina	44,103
16	South Korea	28,888
17	Nigeria	25,595
18	Egypt	20,933
19	India	19,362
20	Venezuela	15,293

Source: Eurostat

and 2008, but remained miniscule at only 1.5% of the total. And only one-half of 1% went to India.

The United States is the top recipient country of FDI from the European Union. In fact, in 2008 the amount of EU FDI flowing to the U.S. was more than to the next 6 destinations combined. Switzerland ranked 2nd, registering about 43% of the amount going to the United States. Canada was 3rd and Mexico 12th, bolstering the importance of North America as the EU's preferred FDI destination. Of the BRICs, Brazil ranked 4th, Russia 5th, China 13th and India 19th. EU FDI in the United States in 2008 was 9 times more than in Brazil, 11 times more than in Russia, 22 times more than in China and 55 times more than in India.

These deep transatlantic investment bonds underscore a fundamental point. While exports and imports have become the most common measurement of cross-border business between nations, trade alone is a misleading benchmark of international commerce. This is particularly important when it comes to commercial ties between the EU and the United States. The unappreciated, invisible and little understood activities of foreign affiliates that represent the real backbone of the transatlantic economy. Taken together U.S. and European exports to the world accounted for only 27.1% of global exports in 2008; and combined U.S. and European imports accounted for 34.6% of global imports. But the U.S. and Europe together accounted for 61.7% of the inward stock of foreign direct investment (FDI), and a whopping 74.9% of outward stock of FDI. Moreover, each partner has built up the great majority of that stock in the other economy.

The United States remains the primary destination of EU investment in terms of FDI flows and outward stock.[7] In the United States, European affiliates are major economic producers in

Figure 3D. FDI into the EU in million Euro (€) (2008)

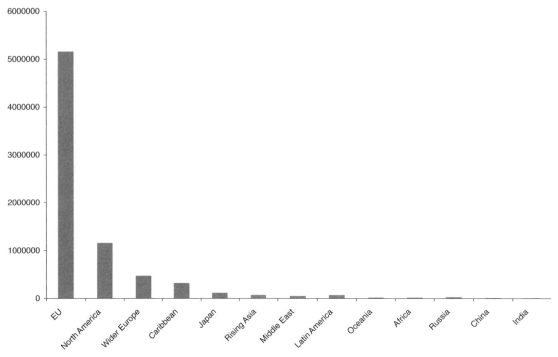

Source: Eurostat

Figure 3E. FDI into the EU w/o EU in million Euro (€) (2008)

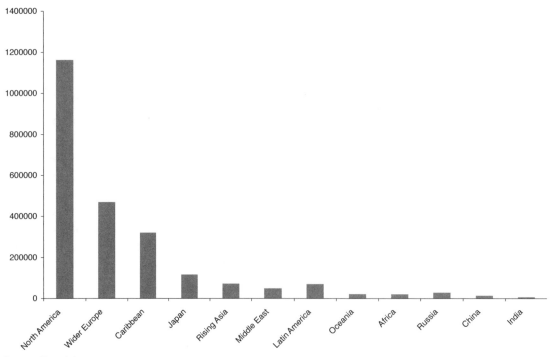

Source: Eurostat

Figure 3F. Top Direct Investors in the EU by Region in million Euro (€), 2000-2008

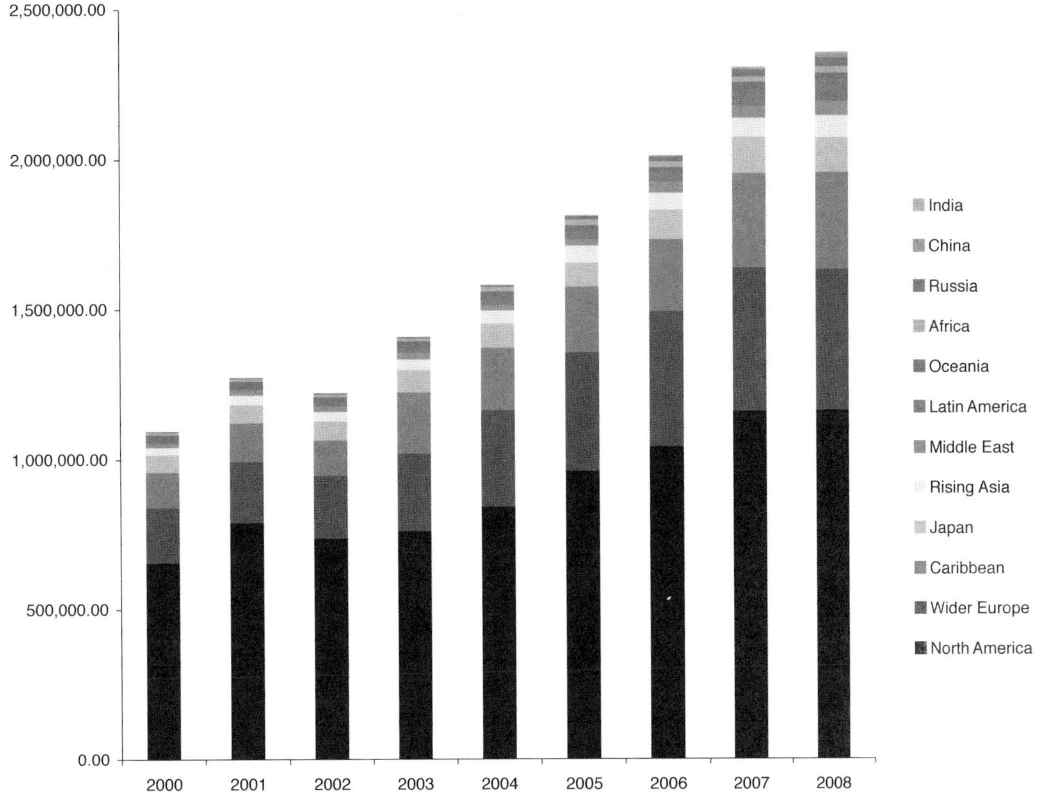

Source: Eurostat

their own right, with British firms of notable importance. Their U.S. output reached nearly $118 billion in 2007, or nearly 30% of the total. Output from German affiliates operating in the U.S. totaled $86 billion, up nearly 20% from a year earlier, while output from French affiliates rose nearly 5% to $61 billion in 2007. Beyond European affiliates, only Corporate Japan has any real economic presence in the United States—Japanese affiliate output totaled $81.4 billion in 2007, well below output from British affiliates and to a lesser degree, output from German affiliates. Overall, foreign affiliates contributed nearly $658 billion to U.S. aggregate production in 2007, with European affiliates accounting for nearly two-thirds of the total.

The EU's investment stock in the United States rose by 43% between 2000 and 2008, with the U.S. accounting for roughly one-third of extra-EU FDI stock abroad. European firms accounted for roughly 72% of total inward investment stock in the U.S. in 2008—about $9.1 trillion in U.S. assets.[8] The United Kingdom ranked first as the largest holder of U.S. assets in 2008 ($2.3 trillion), followed closely behind by Swiss firms ($1.7 trillion). Germany and France ranked third and fourth, respectively, in 2008. Affiliate sales are also the primary means by which European firms deliver goods and services to consumers in the United States. In 2007, for instance, majority-owned nonbank European affiliate sales in the U.S. ($1.8 trillion) were roughly three times larger than U.S. imports from Europe ($577 billion). In the case of Ger-

Table 3.2. Top Direct Investors in the EU in million of Euro (€), 2008

	Investing Country	Amount
1	United States	1,046,157
2	Switzerland	306,199
3	Japan	116,927
4	Canada	105,054
5	Norway	88,993
6	Brazil	42,101
7	Singapore	41,046
8	Russia	28,423
9	Australia	20,657
10	Hong Kong	19,108
11	China	13,862
12	Mexico	11,366
13	South Korea	7,401
14	India	6,958
15	Iceland	6,531
16	Israel	6,493
17	Liechtenstein	5,948
18	South Africa	5,911
19	Turkey	5,339
20	Nigeria	4,675

Source: Eurostat

many, foreign affiliate sales in the United States totaled $383 billion in 2007, nearly three times U.S. imports of goods and services from Germany the same year. For virtually all nations in Europe, foreign affiliate sales were easily in excess of their U.S. imports in 2007.[9]

The United States remains the most important market in the world in terms of earnings for many European multinationals. Profits of European foreign affiliates in the United States actually rose by 19% in 2008, but fell by almost the same amount in 2009.

North America, particularly the U.S., is also the primary investor in the European Union. 49.4% of FDI inflows into the EU from non-EU countries came from North America (44.4% from the U.S. alone). 19.7% came from Wider Europe (85% of which came from Switzerland and Norway). 13.6% came from the Caribbean. 5% from Japan, 3.1% from Rising Asia; 3% from Latin America (60% of which from Brazil); 2.3% from the Middle East; 1.2% from Russia, and less than 1% each from Oceania, India and China.

The U.S. is by far the most important source country of foreign direct investment in the European Union. In 2008 U.S. FDI in the EU totaled €1.05 trillion, more than the next 20 investors combined. Switzerland ranked a distant 2nd, with FDI of €306,199—29% of the U.S. total. Japan ranked 3rd. Of the BRICs, Brazil ranked 6th, Russia 8th, China 11th, and India 14th. Combined FDI in the EU by the BRICs amounted to about the same as Norwegian FDI in the EU, and only about 9% of U.S. FDI in the EU.

The EU is the top destination of U.S. FDI around the world. Corporate America's aggregate foreign assets totaled $13 trillion in 2007, and the bulk of these assets—roughly 63%—were located in Europe. The largest share, by far, was in the United Kingdom. U.S. assets in the UK totaled $3.5 trillion in 2007, roughly one-quarter of the global total, and an amount greater than total combined U.S. assets in South America, Africa and the Middle East.

U.S. assets in the Netherlands ($1.3 trillion) were the second largest in the world in 2007 (after the UK). America's sizable asset base in the Netherlands reflects the host nation's strategic role as an export platform/distribution hub for U.S. firms doing business in the rest of the European Union. To this point, more than half of U.S. affiliate sales in the Netherlands are for export, namely within the EU. Meanwhile, America's asset base in Germany ($613 billion) was nearly double the base of South America in 2006. The collective asset base in Poland, Hungary, and the Czech Republic (roughly $65 billion) was twice the size of corporate America's assets in India.

U.S. corporate affiliates in Europe employ millions of European workers and are the largest source of onshored jobs throughout the EU. U.S. affiliates accounted for 21% of Ireland's aggregate output in 2007, 6.7% of Switzerland's, 6.2% of the United Kingdom's, and 5.2% of Belgium's total output. U.S. foreign affiliate output in Belgium in 2007 ($23.7 billion) was some 6% larger than U.S. foreign affiliate output in China in 2007 ($22.4 billion) and more than three times as large as affiliate output in India ($7.32 billion). Reflecting the rising presence of U.S. affiliates in Hungary, U.S. affiliate output accounted for 3.6% of the host nation's GDP in 2007, up from 3% the prior year. U.S. affiliate output in Poland, meanwhile, jumped 29% in 2007, to $8.5 billion, after rising 12% in 2006, to $6.4 billion, exceeding U.S. output in more developed markets like Austria, Portugal, and Denmark.

Europe accounted for more than half of total U.S. global foreign affiliate sales in 2007, and double comparable sales in the entire Asia/Pacific region. U.S. affiliate sales in the United Kingdom alone ($672 billion) exceeded aggregate sales in Latin America. While U.S. affiliate sales in China have soared over the past decade, they do so from a low base, and still remain well below comparable sales in Europe. For instance, U.S. affiliate sales of $146 billion in China in 2007 were slightly below sales to Italy ($155 billion) and well below those in Germany ($357 billion) or France ($228 billion).

In sum, mutual investment in the North Atlantic space is very large, dwarfs trade, and has become essential to U.S. and European jobs and prosperity. While the Great Recession has taken its toll on both the European and American economies, there has been no significant shift in FDI away from each other to other destinations. European affiliates in the United States employ millions of American workers and are the largest source of onshored jobs in America. Similarly, the European affiliates of U.S. companies employ millions of European workers and are the largest source of onshored jobs in the European Union. While transatlantic trade in goods and services remains important, transatlantic investment now accounts for three-quarters of the total $4.3 trillion transatlantic economic relationship.[10]

EU FDI and Other World Regions

European FDI to developing nations has accelerated over the past decade, but from a very low base. Despite Asia's economic rise, the EU invested just €413 billion there in 2008, about 15% of the EU's global total and just slightly over one third of what it invested in North America. Central America and the Caribbean and South America are the third and fourth largest destinations for EU foreign direct investment outside Europe, accounting for €297 billion and €206 billion in 2008, respectively (9% and 6% of all non-EU outward FDI stocks, respectively)

Figure 3G. EU FDI Outflows (Billion of Euros)

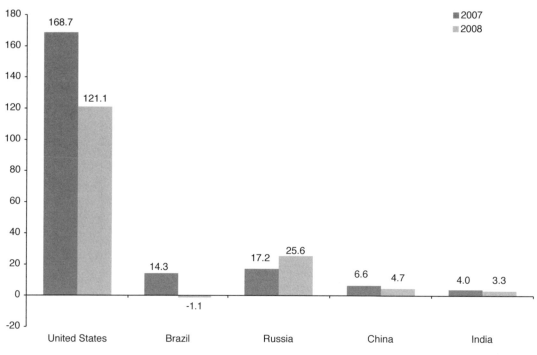

Source: Eurostat
Data for 2008 preliminary

In terms of FDI into the EU, other world regions also account for only a fraction of that supplied by North America. Central America and the Caribbean account for €345 billion (14%) of FDI into the EU, and Asia accounts for €255 billion (11%). The Caribbean figures are high because of the Caribbean's role as an offshore financial center, with particularly close ties to UK financial institutions.

Although the share of EU FDI going to the BRICs still remains small—and has increased only moderately since 2002—overall the EU is the largest provider of FDI to the BRICs. EU FDI outflows to the BRICs are focused primarily on Russia, and then Brazil, rather than China or India. EU FDI outflows to Russia in 2007 and 2008 totaled €42.8 billion, roughly three times EU FDI to Brazil, four times EU FDI to China and six times EU FDI to India. Yet EU FDI outflows to Russia in 2007-2008 represented only about one-seventh the value of EU FDI outflows to the United States. Although these figures are comparatively low, the EU is by far the most important investor in Russia and Brazil, accounting on average for 57% and 53%, respectively, of the total FDI in the period 2004-2007. The amount invested by EU firms in Russia and Brazil on average between 2005 and 2007 was 7-8 times the amount of U.S. FDI in these countries.

The share of the EU in total FDI in India and China is much lower—31% in India and only 10% in China. Nonetheless, the average annual FDI flow from the EU to China between 2005 and 2007 amounted to €6.6 billion, more than twice the amount of U.S. FDI into China, and

Table 3.3. FDI flows from the EU in the BRICs

Destination Country	FDI flows from the EU-27 to the BRICs (in € billion)					Share in the total extra-EU outward FDI stocks		EU share in total FDI flows to the BRICs (in %) average
	2003	2004	2005	2006	2007	2003	2007	2005-2007
Brazil	2.1	5.7	8.4	6.5	15.3	2.9	3.1	53.2
Russia	7.7	6.0	9.7	10.8	16.7	0.7	2.3	56.9
India	0.8	1.6	2.5	2.5	5.4	0.3	0.6	30.9
China	3.2	3.9	6.1	6.7	7.1	0.9	1.2	10.4
Hong Kong	3.8	11.3	3.8	3.6	7.2	4.2	2.8	20.5
BRICs	**17.6**	**28.5**	**30.6**	**30.0**	**51.7**	**9.2**	**10.1**	

Destination Country	EU-15 investment projects in the BRICs (Number of projects)						EU Share of total projects in the BRICS (in %)			
	2003	2004	2005	2006	2007	2008	2003	2007	2007	average 2005-2007
Brazil	140	115	66	57	58	107	48.4	38.2	43.7	38.2
Russia	216	217	270	212	211	303	50.6	57.3	54.0	57.3
India	139	202	160	346	264	358	30.8	38.3	37.4	38.3
China	298	367	371	435	427	481	22.5	35.9	32.4	35.9
Hong Kong	35	36	38	60	56	62	38.5	38.4	32.4	38.4
BRICs	**828**	**937**	**905**	**1,110**	**1,016**	**1,311**	**32.1**	**39.9**	**38.0**	**39.9**

Remark: EU is EU-25 for 2001-2003 and EU-27 for 2004-2007 in Eurostat; EU is EU-15 in fDi database. China excludes Hong Kong. BRICs in the this table includes Hong Kong.

Source: Eurostat; UNCTAD; US Bureau of Economic Analysis; FDI Intelligence from the Financial Times Ltd.; European Commission, *European Competitiveness Report 2009*.

even more than average Japanese FDI flows of €4.9 billion. FDI flows from the EU and the U.S. into Hong Kong are more similar, amounting to €4.9 billion and €3.7 billion respectively.[11]

Germany and the United Kingdom are the EU's main FDI investors in the BRICs, followed by France and the Netherlands. In terms of the amounts invested, Spain also ranks among the top five investors. The strong presence of EU firms in Brazil mainly reflects FDI from Spain and Germany. When looking at the number of projects, Italy also emerges as an important investor for the BRICs. Portugal, the former colonial power in Brazil, is not a major investor in terms of value, but has the highest number of investment projects. In addition to the activities of the top EU investors, Austrian, Belgian and Swedish companies also are responsible for relatively significant FDI in Russia.[12]

Despite low overall FDI in the BRICS, for some EU firms FDI can be an important mode of entry and vehicle for production in BRIC markets. In fact, for several EU member states, sales by foreign affiliates of manufacturing firms in some BRIC markets already surpass their exports. For example, the sales of German manufacturing affiliates in Brazil (€23 billion in 2006) exceed by far German merchandise exports to Brazil (€6 billion in 2006).

In terms of overall EU FDI assets in each country, however, the gap between EU investment assets in the U.S. and the BRICs is huge. EU investment assets in the U.S. are nearly 33% of extra-EU investment stock. EU investment assets in Brazil were roughly one-tenth of those in the United States in 2008. EU investment assets in Russia were about 8% of those in the U.S. EU investment assets in China were less than 5% of EU investment stock in the

Table 3.4. EU FDI Assets, Billions of Euros

	2000	2001	2002	2003	2004	2005	2006	2007	2008
United States	752	915	760	748	732	845	949	1,006	1,075
Brazil	75	73	44	59	70	74	92	114	111
Russia	7	11	10	15	21	33	51	70	91
China*	15	19	20	19	21	28	33	40	47
India	6	6	6	7	8	11	12	16	19
BRICs	**104**	**110**	**81**	**99**	**121**	**145**	**188**	**241**	**269**

Source: Eurostat
*China does not include Hong Kong

Table 3.5. FDI Assets, Percent of Extra-EU27 Total

	2004	2005	2006	2007	2008
United States	36.2%	34.8%	34.6%	31.9%	32.5%
Brazil	3.5%	3.1%	3.4%	3.6%	3.4%
Russia	1.0%	1.4%	1.8%	2.2%	2.8%
China	1.1%	1.1%	1.2%	1.3%	1.4%
India	0.4%	0.4%	0.5%	0.5%	0.6%
BRICs	**6.0%**	**6.0%**	**6.8%**	**7.7%**	**8.1%**

Source: Eurostat

United States. India's total was even smaller, representing less than 1% of extra-EU investment stock in 2008. All told, EU investment assets in the BRICs are one-quarter of EU investment assets in the United States.

As with the EU's overall outward FDI, EU FDI stocks owned in the BRICs are skewed to the services sector.[13] Services account for about 60% of EU projects and accumulated FDI stocks in the BRICS, compared to about 33% for manufacturing. EU FDI in manufacturing plays more of a role in China and India. The dominance of services over manufacturing is in line with the structure of the EU economy, but in stark contrast with the relative importance of these two broad sectors in international trade, confirming the importance of direct investment in the internationalization of services. Indeed, as services are typically more difficult to trade across borders, settling in BRICs through FDI is the main means for EU service companies to get access to BRIC markets.

The bottom line is that European and U.S. multinationals continue to show a strong preference for each other's market when it comes to investing overseas. The notion that the U.S. and Europe are decamping from each other's markets for the low-cost destinations of China and India is wide of the mark. Between 2001 and 2008 EU FDI outflows to the BRICS represented only 8.3% of global EU FDI outflows outside the EU, and most of that was to Russia, not China and India. U.S. FDI outflows to the BRICS during this same period accounted for only 4.5% of global U.S. FDI outflows.[14]

One important question following the Great Recession is whether EU FDI flows will continue to reflect the patterns of the past or shift to new patterns. One indicator could be return on investment. FDI is driven to some extent by returns on investment, and the BRICs are very attractive in this respect. Hunya and Stöllinger used as a crude measure for returns on FDI the

Figure 3H. EU-U.S. FDI Outflows to the BRICs[1] 2001-2008 (Percent of total[2])

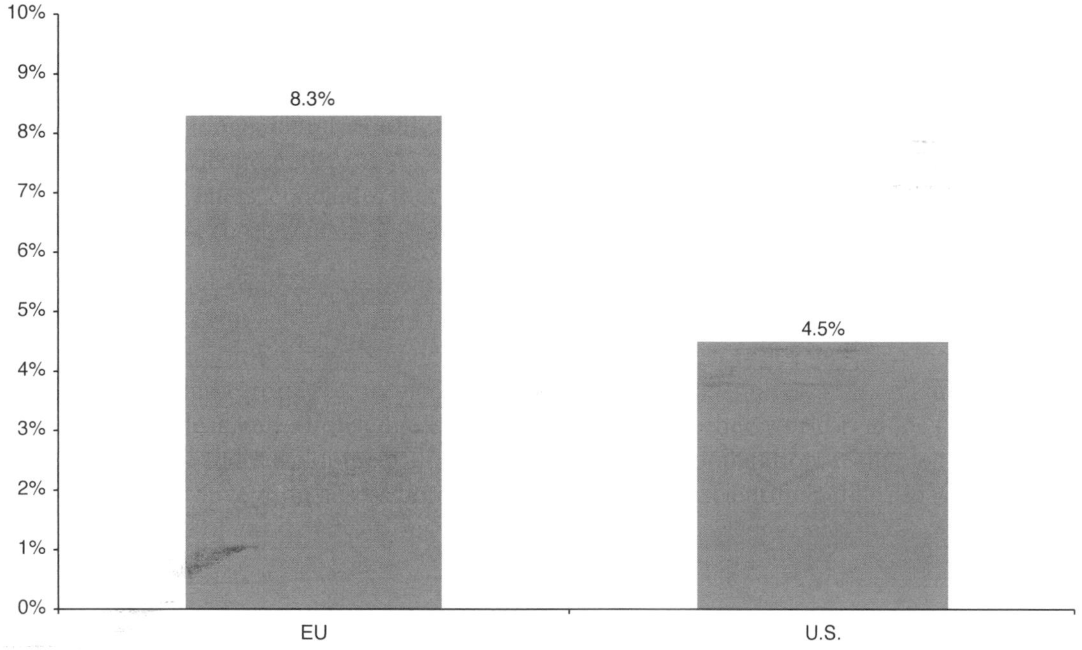

Source: Eurostat, Bureau of Economic Analysis
[1]China does not include Hong Kong.
[2]2008 data for EU preliminary, percent of extra-EU27 outflows.

ratio of income earned on EU FDI abroad in 2007 to accumulated stocks until the end of 2006. They found that FDI in the BRICs appears to be more profitable than FDI in the new EU member states. In 2007 EU firms in China and Hong Kong earned returns on their FDI of more than 13%, well above the average of EU-extra FDI but also above the returns achieved in the most profitable new member states, Bulgaria and Slovakia. Profitability of EU FDI in Russia and Brazil is somewhat lower, 11.3% and 11.8% respectively—similar to the returns on FDI in the most profitable new member states, but well above their average. With returns on FDI exceeding 18%, India emerges as the most profitable location by far among the BRICs for EU firms, although from a very low base.[15]

Returns on investment may be counterbalanced, however, by perceptions of risk. Some commentators suggest that after adjusting for risk several EU firms have considered returns on FDI to be higher in the new EU member states than in the BRICs. Geographical proximity and compatible industry structure also play a role. Other negative considerations dampening EU FDI to the BRICS are more specific to individual countries. For example, inefficient bureaucracy and a poorly developed infrastructure figure among the most important barriers for FDI in India. In China, investor concerns about property rights, intellectual property and remaining restrictions and caps on foreign ownership in the service sectors limit EU investment.[16]

The BRICs are only a minor source of FDI into the EU. Flows from the BRICs and Hong Kong, taken together, accounted on average for only 5.5% of extra-EU inward FDI flows

Table 3.6. Major EU Investor Countries in the BRICs

Average annual outflow (2004-2007) and outflows in 2007 (€ million)

Brazil				Russia			
2004-2007		2007		2004-2007		2007	
Spain	2946	Spain	6201	Germany	2190	Germany	6699
France	1331	France	1760	Netherlands	2075	Austria	2597
Germany	1102	Germany	1146	United Kingdom	1287	United Kingdom	1958
United Kingdom	553	United Kingdom	1054	Austria	985	Belgium	1231
Belgium	502	Netherlands	559	Sweden	804	Sweden	1084
Share in EU total	*83%*			*Share in EU total*	*76%*		

India				China			
2004-2007		2007		2004-2007		2007	
Germany	883	Germany	1721	Germany	1934	United Kingdom	1669
United Kingdom	608	United Kingdom	975	United Kingdom	972	Germany	1531
France	281	Netherlands	495	France	758	France	1433
Netherlands	276	France	366	Denmark	434	Denmark	752
Sweden	102	Sweden	192	Netherlands	395	Finland	499
Share in EU total	*86%*			*Share in EU total*	*82%*		

Hong Kong				BRIC (including Hong Kong)			
2004-2007		2007		2004-2007		2007	
United Kingdom	3770	United Kingdom	2548	United Kingdom	7190	Germany	11813
France	650	Netherlands	1823	Germany	6684	United Kingdom	8204
Netherlands	581	France	937	Spain	3879	Spain	7150
Germany	575	Germany	716	Netherlands	3730	France	5214
Spain	567	Spain	567	France	3604	Austria	2769
Share in EU total	*94%*			*Share in EU total*	*78%*		

Remark: EU is EU27. China excludes Hong Kong. BRIC includes Hong Kong in this table.
Source: Gabor Hunya and Roman Stöllinger, "Foreign Direct Investment Flows between the EU and the BRICs," The Vienna Institute for International Economic Studies, Research Report No. 358, December 2009; Eurostat.

between 2002 and 2007, with most coming from Russia. Moreover, their share is not really increasing, mainly because of falling flows from Hong Kong. If Hong Kong is excluded, FDI flows from the BRICs accounted for only 3.5% of extra-EU inflows into the EU over the 2002-2007 period, with no clear upward trend. This makes the BRIC countries underrepresented in the EU market in terms of FDI flows when compared to their share in global FDI, which stood at 7.1% in 2007.

Despite isolated examples that capture the headlines, relatively few multinationals from the BRICs have established subsidiaries in the EU. Foreign affiliates of BRIC manufacturing multinationals register very low sales volumes in the EU. Competition from the BRICs on the EU market is much fiercer via trade than foreign direct investment. Announcements in 2010 of new investments by Chinese companies in Greece attracted considerable attention, and can be important for Greek ports and shipping, but overall the volume of investment is quite low.[17]

How Competitive is the EU with regard to Foreign Direct Investment?

The EU is the largest provider and destination of FDI among all world regions. It owns 33% and hosts 29% of extra-EU world investment stocks. In 2008, the stock of EU outward

FDI in non-EU countries amounted to €3.3 trillion, whereas the stock of FDI into the EU by non-EU investors amounted to €2.4 trillion, meaning that the EU is a net capital exporter vis-à-vis the rest of the world. The EU had a net asset position of €0.9 trillion in 2008, up from €0.4 trillion in 2004.[18] EU outward FDI increased five-fold in the 15 years before the onset of the recession. In 2007 extra-EU FDI by EU firms increased to €484 billion (in comparison, U.S. and Japanese FDI amounted to €229 billion and €54 billion, respectively). 55 of the 100 largest non-financial multinational corporations are domiciled on EU territory.[19]

The EU has also been the largest recipient of FDI, attracting €360 billion from outside the EU in 2007, more than twice the amount of the inflows into the U.S. economy. The recession took a toll on FDI, however: overall global FDI flows fell from their peak of 2007 to $1.8 trillion in 2008, and FDI in the EU fell by around 43%.[20]

In addition, the EU has higher ratios of inward and outward investments to GDP than the U.S. and most other developed countries, which means that the EU is comparatively more open to foreign investments and more willing to invest abroad than countries of a similar level of development, in particular the United States.[21] While the U.S. is the largest host and investor country, foreign investment in the U.S. represented only 18% and its outward investments 24% of GDP, whereas German FDI stocks represent more than 30% of GDP.

Since the competitiveness of the EU as a whole depends on the competitiveness of both domestic and foreign firms operating in the EU, there is a positive relationship between inward FDI and the EU competitiveness. Foreign affiliates contribute to a host country's international competitiveness through several channels. They generate jobs and provide access to new markets and new technologies for domestic suppliers and buyers along the value chain; they generate knowledge spillovers to domestic firms; and they invest a higher share of their revenue in research and development (R&D).[22]

Leading EU member states exhibit relatively more important outward investments than inward investments. For the UK, France, and Italy the difference between the relative size of outward and inward investments in 2007 was 20%, 13%, and 7%, respectively. Outward investments of northern EU member states countries were also relatively more important in 2007 than their inward investment stocks. For some smaller EU member states such as Belgium, Luxembourg, Ireland and the Netherlands, maintaining inward FDI is critical, as it is for central European member states. FDI as a percentage of GDP is particularly high for Hungary (72%), the Czech Republic (65%), the Slovak Republic (54%) and Poland (41%).[23]

Rising levels of outward FDI concern many policy makers and some parts of the European public. These concerns stem from the perception that the foreign activities of European multinational firms might take jobs away from EU workers and divert investment that could have been deployed within the EU. Yet in a July 2010 study Copenhagen Economics estimated that outward FDI contributed to an increase in EU GDP of more than €20 billion over the period 2001-2006, and helped boost EU worker income by almost €13 billion. The study finds that EU outward FDI has made a positive and significant contribution to EU firms' competitiveness in the form of higher productivity, and has had no measurable negative impact on aggregate employment, although transitional costs for lower-skill workers have been higher than the net benefits accruing to high-skilled workers.[24]

In short, the popular notion that European firms are abandoning Europe for low-wage locales like China and India is not supported by any factual evidence. In fact, most FDI by European companies occurs within the borders of the EU, and 55% of EU outward FDI stock is invested in other high-wage advanced economies in Wider Europe, North America and Oceania. EU outward investment to countries like India and China is growing rapidly, but the stock of EU FDI in these economies accounts for only 2% of total EU outward FDI stock. Moreover, empirical research[25] demonstrates that firms who invest abroad have higher productivity than comparable firms who have not established foreign affiliates; with positive scale effects and demand for headquarter services that trickle back to home country employment.

European firms operating abroad also appear to earn a higher return (around 8.7%) than what is earned by foreign firms operating in the EU (6.8%). The return on the EU's outward FDI generated more than €200 billion in 2006, compared to a return on FDI in the EU made by non-EU companies of only €125 billion. The EU thus receives a net positive income from FDI with the rest of the world of around €75 billion per year. The positive net income creates demand for European labor across all sectors in the economy.[26]

In terms of outward FDI, European companies are relatively well placed to invest in some of the high-growth sectors of rapidly rising economies, such as infrastructure development, services and more technologically-intensive products—although restrictions on FDI still persist in a number of emerging markets.[27] The EU provides more FDI than North America or Japan in each of the BRICs. In Russia and Brazil, the amounts invested by EU firms between 2005 and 2007 were on average seven to eight times the amount of FDI undertaken by U.S. firms in these countries. The average flows from the EU to China over the same period amounted to €6.6 billion, more than twice the amount from the United States. Japan, which has a strong Asian focus in its outward FDI, recorded average FDI flows of €4.9 billion to China during the same period. It is interesting to note that the EU has a stronger position as an investor in the BRICs than as an exporter.[28] While the strong FDI links between the EU and Russia are to be expected due to the proximity of the two markets (and is also found in trade in goods and services), EU firms also compare favorably to U.S. firms in Brazil.

In terms of inward FDI, the EU remains an attractive location for investors, but it faces considerable and growing competition from rapidly emerging markets and other advanced economies such as the United States.[29]

Services have come to dominate global foreign direct investment over the past decade, with Europe at the forefront, driving this process. Today, services represent nearly two-thirds of global FDI stock, up from a 49% share in 1990. Extra-EU outward investment is dominated by service activities—roughly 70% of the EU outward stock was in services at the end of 2004, up from 62% at the end of 2001.

Meanwhile, intra-EU investment in services, bolstered by single market initiatives, has remained quite strong, centering on financial services and service investment in such infrastructure-related activities as water, electricity, and energy. Because of rising levels of investment in services, FDI-intensity within Europe remains strong. Indeed, according to the UN, of the top 50 pairs of nations with the strongest FDI links in terms of bilateral inward FDI stock in 2005, 22 were from Europe, compared to 17 in 1995.

Whereas services FDI used to be strongly related to trade and trade-supporting services for manufacturing multinationals, over the past decade more services FDI has been directed at such activities as hotels, restaurants, and financial services. Electricity, water, telecommunications and other infrastructure-related activities have also been receiving more foreign direct investment.[30]

A number of factors have lead to a rise in services FDI. The first has to do with the ascendancy of the services economy, not only in the EU but around the world. Second, since many services are not tradable, cross-border investment is the only way to bring services to foreign customers. In addition, services FDI has expanded as more European firms seek out new markets and new resources outside the European Union. Finally, more Free Trade Agreements (FTAs) are centered on services, promoting greater cross-border investment in various service activities. Until 1999, there were only 11 FTAs that included services. Since 2000 that number has increased to 42.[31]

Portfolio Investments[32]

In 1900, private capital flows could be measured in the hundreds of millions of dollars, and involved relatively few countries.[33] Today, they are measured in the hundreds of billions of dollars, and many, many countries are involved. Money is traded around the clock, with more and more of the world's financial markets electronically connected and linked.

Most investment during those early days of globalization was limited largely to portfolio investment in railroads, municipal and national bonds, and a few other types of assets in the newly emerging markets of the time. Lending focused on governmental authorities. Foreign direct investment played a smaller role, and production processes were not as highly integrated as they are now. In recent decades, however, the breadth and depth of international capital investments grew rapidly. Firms used their investments to form alliances and extend value chains internationally in very complex networks. Industry, finance, and the services sector in emerging markets became important candidates for foreign portfolio investments.

The result was a significant boost in capital flows around the world. From 1980 through 2007, the world's financial assets—including equities, private and public debt, and bank deposits—nearly quadrupled in size relative to global GDP. Global capital flows similarly surged. Between 1990 and 2006, cross-border capital flows grew more than 10% annually. Over this period, capital flows to emerging markets grew twice as fast as inflows to developed countries.[34] In the wake of the Great Recession, as the EU, the U.S. and Japan record low growth and struggle with debt and challenges to their still-fragile financial systems, the flow of capital to emerging markets has accelerated, prompting some capitals to adopt controls on the inflow.

Daily turnover in the foreign exchange markets totaled $3.2 trillion on the eve of the recession in early 2007, an increase of over 70% from 2004 and nearly four times that of two decades earlier. The euro was at the cutting edge of this trend; by 2007 Europe's single currency accounted for 37% of daily global turnover, second only to the U.S. dollar. The velocity of capital also spawned more of a global equity culture, evident by the fact that at the end of

2006, the world's stock market capitalization represented 99.2% of world output, up from a 36.2% share in 1990.

As capital became more mobile, Europe deepened its financial integration with the rest of the world. The level of foreign ownership and participation in Europe's capital markets soared, expanding and enhancing the capital efficiency of the region's financial infrastructure. Europe's primary banks began to shed their home bias, becoming more pan-European on the one hand and more global on the other by expanding their presence in the United States, Latin America and Asia.

At the same time, however, credit bubbles grew both in the United States and Europe. Contrary to popular perceptions, credit in Europe grew larger as a percent of GDP than in the United States. Total U.S. credit outstanding rose from 221% of GDP in 2000 to 291% in 2008, reaching $42 trillion. Eurozone indebtedness rose even higher, to 304% of GDP by the end of 2008, while UK borrowing climbed even higher, to 320%.[35]

Finally, the bubble burst. The global economic crisis was triggered by the deteriorating quality of U.S. subprime mortgages—housing loans offered to homebuyers at below prime rates. Although this device was invented and offered widely in the United States, these mortgages were packaged or securitized, then given top-rate credit ratings, and sold all over the world. Many European banks and investors snapped up these mortgage-related instruments, such as collateralized debt obligations, credit default swaps and structured investment vehicles (SIVs). In addition, many European banks were eager lenders to construction firms and households, given low global interest rates and abundant levels of global capital. When falling home prices and a series of defaults turned into a major subprime meltdown in the U.S. in 2007, Europe was also engulfed in a global credit crisis.

The global financial crisis and worldwide recession abruptly halted nearly three decades of expansion for international capital markets. It has raised widespread concerns about the volatility of capital flows and generated a greater sense of vulnerability among stakeholders to such flows. The total value of the world's financial assets fell by $16 trillion in 2008, to $178 trillion, the largest setback on record.[36] Declines in equity and real estate wiped out $28.8 trillion of global wealth in 2008 and the first half of 2009. Cross-border capital flows[37] fell 82% from $10.5 trillion in 2007 to just $1.9 trillion in 2008. Relative to GDP, the 2008 level of cross-border capital flows was the lowest since 1991. Cross-border lending fell from $4.9 trillion in 2007 to minus $1.3 trillion in 2008, meaning that lenders cancelled more cross-border loans than they made. In the worst-hit countries, foreign bank credit contracted by as much as 67%. Flows of foreign deposits also reversed course, as investors withdrew $400 billion of deposits from foreign financial centers in 2008.[38]

Across world regions, the UK and the eurozone experienced the largest declines in cross-border capital flows. In 2008 foreign investors withdrew more money from the UK than they put in. The fall-off in capital flows in western Europe— equivalent to 21% of collective GDP—reflected the reversal of lending flows between the UK and the eurozone, a decline in flows between individual eurozone countries, and the plunge of flows between European countries and the United States.

It is unclear how quickly capital flows will revive, or the pace and manner in which financial markets will integrate. It is likely that mature financial markets in Europe and North America will grow more slowly in coming years while fiscal deficits cause government debt to soar. According to the McKinsey Global Institute, "2008 may have marked an inflection point in the growth trajectory of financial markets in North America, Europe, and Japan. Financial assets in those regions more than tripled from 1990 through 2007, to $158 trillion, or 403 percent of GDP. But the circumstances that fueled the rapid increases of past years, particularly in equities and private debt, have changed, making it likely that total financial assets will grow more in line with GDP in coming years."[39]

The crisis is likely to have been no more than a temporary interruption in the financial market development of emerging markets, however, because their underlying sources of growth remain strong. For investors and financial intermediaries alike, emerging markets will become more important as their share of global capital markets continues to expand.[40]

A key question, then, is how the EU is linked to other key regions in terms of private portfolio investments and banking claims. In the following section we "map" the EU's ties in each of these areas.

Portfolio Investment and the Deepening of Europe's Capital Markets

Overall EU private outward portfolio investment increased almost 2½ times between 2001 and 2008. Extra-EU flows increased 1.8 times. Of the total $15.28 trillion in outward EU private portfolio investment in 2008, 68% remained within the EU. Beyond EU borders the EU's key financial interlinkage remains that with North America, and particularly the United States. If intra-EU flows are removed from the equation, then in 2008 North America accounted for 54.7% (U.S. 51.4%) of EU outflows, followed by 10.8% to the Caribbean and 10.4% to Wider Europe; 8.4% to Japan; 4.7% to Rising Asia; 1.9% to Latin America; 1.4% to the Middle East; 1% each to China and India; and less than 1% to Russia and Africa. EU private portfolio investment in North America was 50 times that in China, and more than 65 times that in Russia. EU private portfolio investment in Latin America was also twice than in Russia, but both at comparatively low levels. While EU portfolio investment in India and Russia is miniscule, it is still larger than that of the United States and Japan combined.

Of total inward private portfolio investment into the EU in 2008, 70.7% consisted of intra-EU flows, an increase of 10% from 2001 and another sign of European regionalization. If one excludes intra-EU flows, then in 2008 North America accounted for 45.3% of all inward private portfolio investment into the EU—more than the rest of the world combined except Norway and Switzerland and over 100 times greater than Russian investment in the EU. 20% came from Japan, 5.7% from Rising Asia; 2.2% from the Caribbean; 1.7% from Oceania; and less than ½ of 1% each from the Middle East, Latin America and Russia. Compared with 2001, North America's share increased 10%, whereas Wider Europe's share declined by roughly 6%. Rising Asia increased its share by 2%.

These figures once again underscore the importance to the EU of European regionalization. In 2001 62.8% of EU outward private portfolio investment stayed within the EU. By

Figure 3l. EU Private Portfolio Investment Abroad in million $

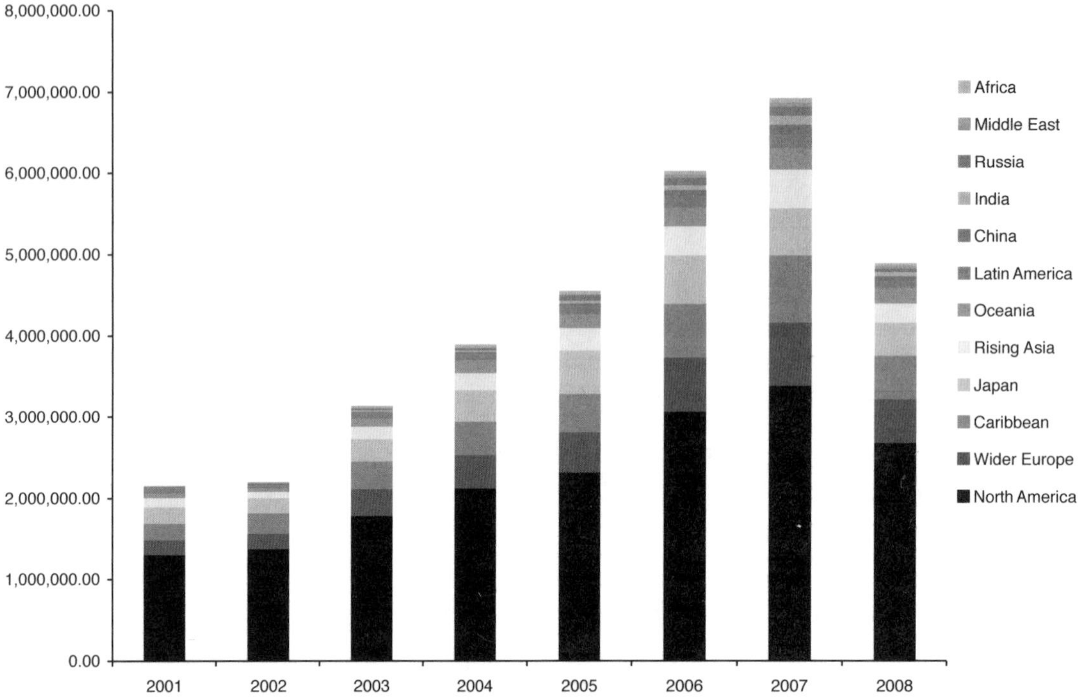

Source: CPIS, http://www.imf.org/external/np/sta/pi/datarsl.htm

Table 3.7. Top Country Destinations for EU Portfolio Investment in 2008

	Destination Country	Amount
1	United States	2,516,141
2	Japan	410,385
3	Cayman Islands	382,068
4	International Organizations	207,963
5	Switzerland	193,938
6	Australia	185,695
7	Jersey	154,119
8	Canada	128,273
9	Norway	100,695
10	Netherlands Antilles	73,361
11	Korea, Republic of	66,605
12	Brazil	62,886
13	Hong Kong	58,984
14	China	53,138
15	India	49,198
16	Bermuda	46,278
17	Russian Federation	39,095
18	Turkey	33,131
19	Mexico	32,460
20	Guernsey	32,225

Source: CPIS, http://www.imf.org/external/np/sta/pi/datarsl.htm

Figure 3J. Private Portfolio Investment in the EU in million $

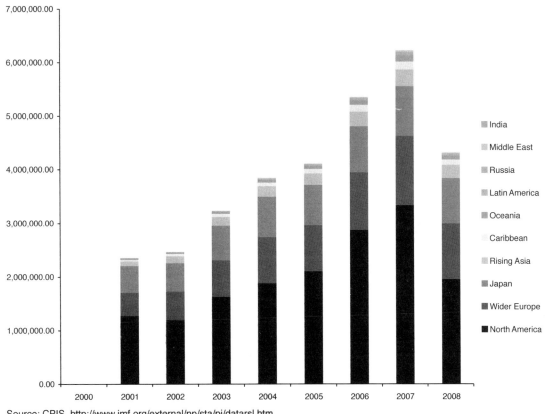

Source: CPIS, http://www.imf.org/external/np/sta/pi/datarsl.htm

2008 the intra-EU share had climbed to 68%. If one adds portfolio investment in Wider Europe of 3.6%, then Europe accounts for 71.6% of the EU's private portfolio investment.

When considering the EU's financial links to other world regions beyond Europe, the key interlinkage remains that with North America, and particularly the United States. In terms of general portfolio investment, 54% of all reported outward EU portfolio investment in 2008 went to North America, compared to 15% to Asia and 11% each to the Caribbean and to Wider Europe. In return, 45% of all reported inward EU portfolio investment in 2008 came from North America, compared to 25% from Asia and 24% from Wider Europe. While these numbers are significant, over the course of the past decade an extra 5% of EU outward private portfolio investment stayed within the EU rather than being invested in North America. The share of EU outward private portfolio investment going to all other regions remained fairly similar over the course of the decade.[41]

The financial ties between the UK and the U.S. are particularly strong. While China and Japan have most recently been and continue to be the largest holders of U.S. Treasury securities (with $916 billion and $708 billion, respectively), during the peak of the financial crisis the UK was the dominant net purchaser of Treasuries, with $15.9 billion in net purchases during the fourth quarter of 2008, more than China and Japan combined. This was also true in the

Table 3.8   Top Portfolio Investors in the EU in 2008

	Investing Country	Amount
1	United States	1,821,341
2	Japan	847,537
3	Switzerland	450,727
4	Norway	315,346
5	Jersey	142,882
6	Canada	132,625
7	Hong Kong	130,851
8	Guernsey	88,742
9	Singapore	85,401
10	Bermuda	81,566
11	Australia	72,028
12	South Africa	41,888
13	Isle of Man	24,736
14	Russian Federation	17,498
15	Chile	12,903
16	Korea, Republic of	12,796
17	Kazakhstan	8,862
18	Iceland	8,275
19	Israel	5,944
20	Netherlands Antilles	5,813

Source: CPIS, http://www.imf.org/external/np/sta/pi/datarsl.htm

second and fourth quarters of 2009, and most prominently in the first quarter of 2010, when UK-based investors purchased on net $96 billion in U.S. Treasuries, compared to $29 billion by those in China and $27 billion by those in Japan.[42]

The UK's role is amplified if one includes other EU member states. Although media and political attention focuses on the fact that China and Japan hold such large shares of U.S. securities, in fact the EU also holds considerable long-term and short-term U.S. debt, comparable to and at times greater than that held by China or Japan. The EU held $2.91 trillion in U.S. long-term and short-term debt as of June 2009, for instance, during the recession, while China held $1.46 trillion and Japan $1.27 trillion. In terms of individual countries, the UK was the third largest holder of U.S. long-term and short-term debt ($787.9 billion).

Although EU private portfolio investment flows to China increased from only $4.5 billion in 2001 to $53.1 billion in 2008, they still remained miniscule, going from one-hundredth of 1% of the EU total in 2001 to one-third of 1% in 2008. And while the EU invests nearly as much in China as does the United States, the number is a small fraction of what the EU and the U.S. invest in each other.

One result of the financial crisis, however, was to create closer financial bonds between the EU and Japan and South Korea. In 2008, the EU had $20 billion more invested in Japan than did the United States, even though the two were nearly even during 2007. The EU has other strong financial bonds—for instance the EU has more invested with India and Russia than do the United States and Japan combined.

The EU is a critical investment partner for other world regions. In 2008 the EU was the largest portfolio investor in North America, Wider Europe, Russia, India and Oceania; the second largest portfolio investor after North America in Africa, the Caribbean, Rising Asia, Japan, Latin America, and the Middle East; and the third largest portfolio investor in China, behind North America and Rising Asia. The EU accounted for 50% of all foreign portfolio investment in North America, Russia and Wider Europe; for over 40% of all foreign portfolio investment in Africa, India, and Japan; and for roughly 30% or more in the Caribbean, Developing Asia, Latin America, the Middle East and Oceania.

Bank Claims

Claims of European banks in other countries in 2009 totaled $19.39 trillion, 3 times the level at the beginning of the decade. 55.4% of these claims was within the EU itself, about 7% more than in 2000, another sign of EU enlargement and broader European regionalization. 20.8% of the total was in North America (18.8% in the U.S.)—a 5.4% decline from 2000. 5.1% in Wider Europe, about 2% more than in 2000. 4.5% was in Rising Asia, a 1% decline from 2000. 2.7% was in the Caribbean; 2.5% in Latin America (of which 58% was in Brazil), a drop of 1.3%; 2.4% in Japan, only about half as much as in 2000; 2.1% in Oceania; 1.3% in the Middle East; 1.2% in Africa; and less than 1% in Russia, China and India.

If intra-EU bank claims are excluded, then 46.6% of all claims of European banks outside the EU are in North America; 11.4% in Wider Europe; 10% in Developing Asia; 6% in the

Figure 3K. EU Portfolio Debt Held Abroad in million $

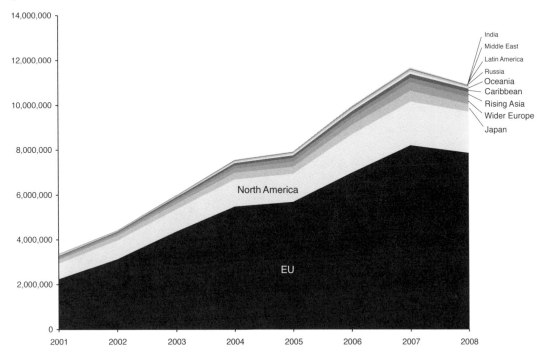

Source: IMF

Figure 3L. EU Portfolio Debt Held Abroad w/o EU in million $

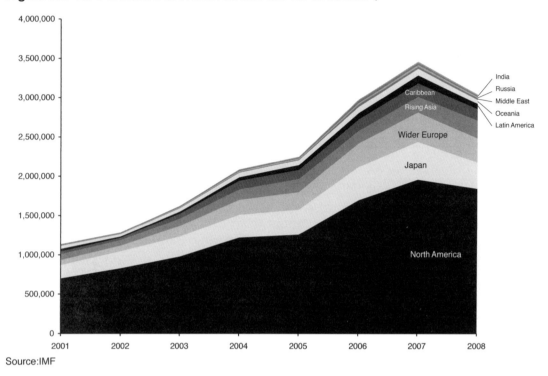

Source:IMF

Figure 3M. EU Portfolio Equity Held Abroad in million $

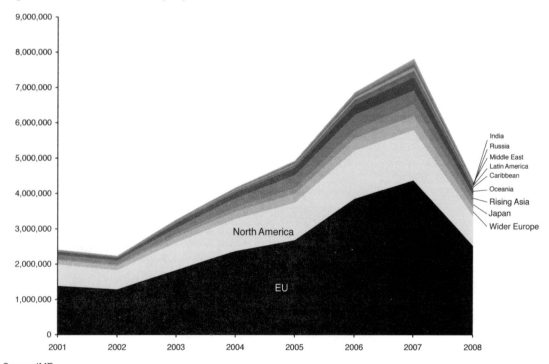

Source:IMF

Figure 3N. EU Portfolio Equity Held Abroad w/o EU in million $

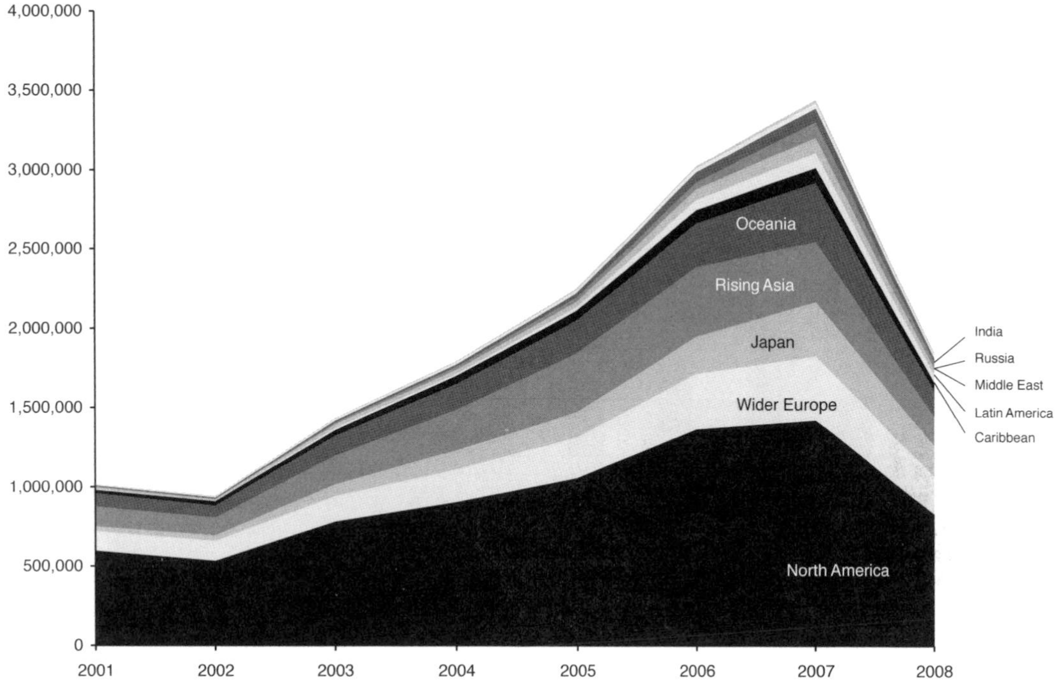

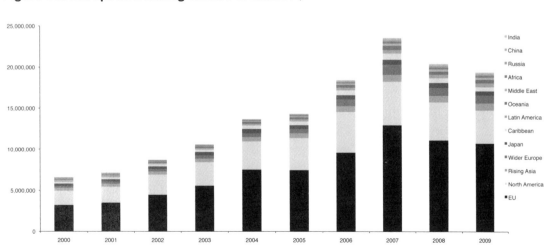

Source:IMF

Figure 3O. European Banking Claims in million $

Note: These are European Banks, as defined by the BIS, which includes: Austria, Belgium, Finland, France, Germany, Greece, Ireland, Italy, Netherlands, Portugal, Spain, and the UK as well as Switzerland, Norway, and Turkey.
Source: BIS Consolidated Banking Statistics, Immediate Borrower Basis.

Figure 3P. European Banking Claims w/o EU in million $

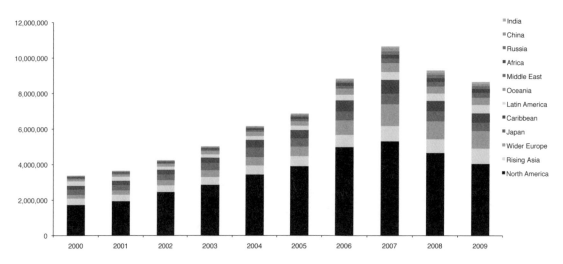

Note: These are European Banks, as defined by the BIS, which includes: Austria, Belgium, Finland, France, Germany, Greece, Ireland, Italy, Netherlands, Portugal, Spain, and the UK as well as Switzerland, Norway, and Turkey.
Source: BIS Consolidated Banking Statistics, Immediate Borrower Basis.

Caribbean; 5.5% in Latin America and in Japan; 4.8% in Oceania; 3.0% in the Middle East; 2.6% in Africa; 1.6% in Russia; 1.4% in China; and 1.3% in India.

The U.S. is the #1 destination of European bank claims—more than the next 18 destinations combined. Japan ranks a distant 2nd, registering only 12% of EU bank claims on the U.S. Of the BRICs, Brazil ranks 6th, followed by Russia (13th), China (14th) and India (15th).

Table 3.9. Top European Banking Claim Destinations, Q1 2010 (million $)

	Destination Country	Amount
1	United States	3,648,186
2	Japan	439,505
3	Cayman Islands	355,627
4	Australia	335,049
5	Hong Kong	307,804
6	Brazil	278,470
7	Canada	247,972
8	Norway	243,638
9	Mexico	205,656
10	Switzerland	204,707
11	South Korea	180,608
12	Singapore	157,311
13	Russia	149,892
14	China	143,703
15	India	126,312
16	Turkey	117,604
17	Jersey	108,519
18	South Africa	107,654
19	United Arab Emirates	91,180
20	West Indies UK	78,095

Source: BIS Consolidated Banking Statistics, Immediate Borrower Basis.

Is Europe Financially Competitive?

A healthy financial services sector is critical to European prosperity. The financial services sector generates 6% of EU economic output and fuels many other sectors of the economy.[43] Yet the financial crisis and continuing European debt crises have stoked fears that the EU has become less financially competitive; prompted questions about the viability of the eurozone's economic governance; raised public concerns about the volatility of capital flows; generated a greater sense of vulnerability among stakeholders to such flows; and exacerbated worries that the center of gravity of global finance is shifting eastward toward Asia.[44]

Challenges linger from the recession. The IMF has called the financial sector the "Achilles Heel "of the stuttering economic recovery, due to rising public debt burdens, unfinished financial reforms and continued funding challenges for banks. Yet the financial crisis itself did not cause any immediate tectonic shift among the world's major financial centers. Even following the financial crisis, U.S. and EU financial markets continue to account for well over two-thirds of global banking assets and provide around three-quarters of global financial services, although at substantially lower overall levels of activity in many areas.[45]

Nonetheless, the financial ground is shifting. London and New York remain the world's leading financial centers. But Hong Kong and Singapore, which hold the third and fourth spots, are gaining ground. Tokyo takes the fifth place and Shanghai has surged to sixth, giving Asia four of the top six spots overall.[46] Over the course of the past decade Asia's share of investment banking revenues has risen from 13% to more than 20%.[47]

Secondary European financial market places, such as Paris, Madrid, Milan, Frankfurt and Amsterdam, are clearly losing ground to other advanced and emerging financial centers. Nearly all of the top 20 European financial centers declined in the ratings between 2009 and 2010, with the exception of Madrid and Glasgow. Emerging financial centers such as Beijing, Seoul, Shenzhen, Shanghai, and Dubai have improved their competitiveness ratings strongly since 2007. They and others are likely to assume strong regional and possibly also global positions within the next decade, particularly as higher growth rates outside of Europe generate strong financing needs. Since financial flows from advanced to emerging economies are projected to remain behind pre-crisis levels, a good deal of the financing needed by rapidly growing emerging markets is likely to be met by domestic markets.[48]

China's domestic needs are certain to fuel the growth of China's financial industry. Goldman Sachs estimates the traded value of equities and futures in Shanghai alone could exceed $350 billion a day by 2020, up from $47 billion now, representing more than 75% of Chinese liquidity and as much as 53% of regional liquidity, meaning that Chinese markets could provide 70% of regional liquidity.[49]

In light of these long-term trends, it is evident that traditional financial centers, including New York, London, Paris, and Zurich, but also Hong Kong and Singapore, are under greater pressure. The EU has only 4 of the top 20 financial centers worldwide. While EU financial centers accounted for 10 of the 20 best performers, they also accounted for 8 of the 20 worst performers.

Table 3.10. Ranking of Top Financial Centers Worldwide

1. London	**11. Frankfurt**	21. Vancouver	32. Isle of Man*
2. New York	12. Toronto	22. Jersey*	**33. Amsterdam**
3. Hong Kong	13. Boston	23. Melbourne	34. Qatar
4. Singapore	14. Shenzhen	25. Montreal	34. Hamilton
5. Tokyo	14. San Francisco	26. Guernsey*	34. Cayman Islands
6. Shanghai	16. Beijing	**27. Munich**	**37. Stockholm**
7. Chicago	17. Washington D.C.	28. Dubai	38. Wellington
8. Zurich	**18. Paris**	**29. Dublin**	**39. Madrid**
9. Geneva	19. Taipei	30. Osaka	40. British Virgin Islands
10. Sydney	**20. Luxembourg**	**31. Edinburgh**	**40. Brussels**

Note: EU-based centers in bold.

*These British Crown Dependencies have a special relationship with the EU. They are exempt from certain areas of EU jurisdiction, but included in others.

Source: *The Global Financial Centres Index 8*, September 2010, Z/Yen 24. SeoulGroup Limited, available at http://www.zyen.com/GFCI/GFCI%208.pdf

Table 3.11. Financial Competitiveness Rankings: Top and Bottom Performers

Top 20		Bottom 20	
Seoul 42	**Budapest 13**	Geneva 6.8	**Madrid 4.1**
Beijing 27	**Warsaw 13**	**Helsinki 6.7**	Zurich 3.2
Moscow 23	**Luxembourg 13**	**Stockholm 6.6**	**Paris 2.7**
Mumbai 22	**Vienna 13**	Chicago 6.6	Melbourne 2.3
Athens 22	**Copenhagen 12**	San Francisco 6.5	**Frankfurt 2.0**
Rome 21	Vancouver 12	Montreal 6.4	New York 2.0
Prague 20	Singapore 11	**Milan 6.0**	Cayman Islands 1.8
Lisbon 17	Oslo 10	**Dublin 5.7**	Edinburgh 1.7
Shanghai 16	Tokyo 9	Sydney 4.9	Hamilton 1.5
Wellington 15	**Brussels 9**	**Amsterdam 4.7**	**London 1.3**

Note: Top-20 and bottom-20 performers in GFCI competitiveness rating progress, % change in ratings between 2007 and 2010. EU-based centers in bold.

Sources: *The Global Financial Centres Index 8*, September 2010, Z/Yen Group Limited, available at http://www.zyen.com/GFCI/GFCI%208.pdf; City of London; DB Research

In many ways the transatlantic financial industry remains at the heart of global finance. More than 70% of all private and public debt securities and almost 80% of all interest-rate derivatives outstanding are registered in traditional financial centers in the U.S. and the EU.[50] Almost 75% of all new international debt securities are issued in New York or the major financial centers in Europe.[51] Foreign exchange trading remains highly concentrated in London and Chicago, with the UK and the U.S. capturing a combined 50% share in global trading. 70% of all foreign exchange derivatives transactions are undertaken in the U.S. and the EU.[52]

Traditional stock exchanges in the U.S., the EU, Japan, Hong Kong, and Singapore still account for almost two-thirds of global stock market capitalization. But this is considerably lower than their 90% share in 2000. They still maintain a 79% share in global equity trading, however, and U.S. and EU equity-linked derivatives make up more than three-quarters of the global total.[53] Nonetheless, the historic position of traditional financial centers in Europe and America is increasingly being challenged by emerging competitors. The transatlantic share in global stock market capitalization has declined substantially from its 78% peak in 2001 to just

Figure 3Q. Domestic Stock Market Capitalization, 2009

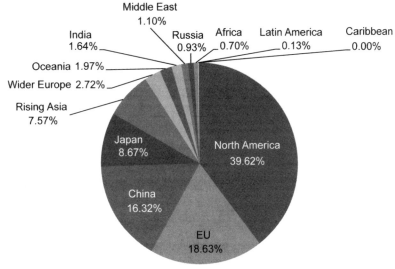

over 50% today, while its share in stock trading has fallen from 86% to just over 70% in the same period. BRIC stock markets have been growing by a whopping 40% per year, while EU and U.S. markets have actually contracted. Likewise, the share of the BRIC countries in the number of listed companies worldwide has jumped from just over 2% in 2000 to 22% today. More than half of the world's IPOs in 2009 were listed in China alone.[54]

These changes are reflected in relative shares of domestic stock market capitalization. In 2009 North America accounted for 34.8% of overall stock market capitalization, followed by the EU (21.3%), Rising Asia (10.3%), China (7.3%) and Japan (7.2%). North America also

Figure 3R. Total Value of Shares Traded, 2009

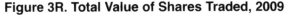

Figure 3S. Market Capitalization of New Listings, 2009

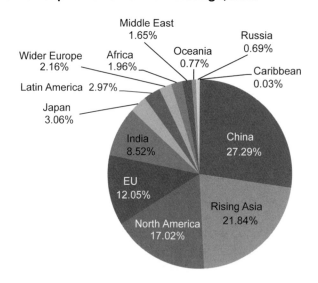

accounted for the largest share of shares traded in terms of value with 39.62% of the total, followed by the EU (18.63%), China (16.32%), Japan (8.67%), and Rising Asia (7.57%). But in terms of the market capitalization of new listings in 2009, China ranked first with a 27.29% share, followed by Rising Asia (21.84%). North America ranked only third (17.02%) and the EU a distant fourth (12.05%), followed by India (8.52%) and Japan (3.06%).

In sum, established financial centers in Europe and the U.S. have maintained their dominant positions even in the face of recent turmoil. But their credibility was damaged considerably by the financial crisis. As Chinese Deputy Premier Wang Qishan reportedly noted, "the teachers now have some problems." At the same time, emerging financial markets emerged from the crisis with their reputations as dynamic and reliable markets enhanced, are growing fast, and are capturing increasing shares of local and regional businesses. European financial centers that are complacent about their position, or that lack critical mass either in terms of underlying economic growth or concentration of financial activity, will find it harder to compete in the long run.[55]

The Euro and Sterling

These challenges are all aggravated by continuing uncertainty over the euro. Martin Wolf notes that the failings of the eurozone have not been fiscal irresponsibility, but rather macroeconomic divergence, financial irresponsibility, asset price bubbles, and shifts in competitiveness. If the eurozone is to function more effectively, it must manage these disorders.[56]

Despite its current woes, the euro has given Europe a global currency that is a legitimate and favorable alternative to the U.S. dollar. The greenback remains the world's reserve currency, but the euro has gained traction as a possible alternative since its introduction more than a decade ago. Despite the global financial crisis and the Greek and Irish dramas of 2010, the euro held its own. According to the IMF, the euro accounted for 26.5% of total allocated global foreign exchange holdings at mid-year 2010, significantly higher than its 18.3% share at the end of 2000. The pound sterling also increased its share, from 2.8% to 4.2%, while the dollar's share declined from 71.1% at the end of 2000 to 62.1% at mid-year 2010. The Japanese yen's share also declined during this period from 6.1% to 3.3%.

Among developing nations, demand for the euro is slightly higher—the euro accounted for 28.3% percent of allocated reserves by emerging and developing countries at mid-year 2010, compared with just 18.1% in 2000. The pound sterling also boosted its share from 2.6% to 6.3%. The dollar's share during this period declined from 74.8% to 58.4%; the yen's share also declined from 2.7% to 2.4%.

Global claims in all other currencies amounted to only 3.9%. International use of China's currency, the renminbi, is still marginal. Chinese authorities have started to allow certain investors to buy renminbi bonds issued in the domestic capital market. Some Asian central banks have started now to buy such instruments, and some Western multinationals are experimenting with using the renminbi in trade deals. But China maintains capital controls and does not seem keen on making its currency convertible. Major questions remain regarding the rule of law and information flows with regard to financial transactions. And the Chinese financial industry remains relatively immature, quite opaque, and difficult for foreigners to access. All of these factors will limit the international use of the Chinese currency and ultimately constrain the international role of China's financial centers.[57] The IMF has resisted China's interest in including the renminbi in the IMF's basket of main currencies—so-called Special Drawing Rights—because it does not pass the test of being "freely usable."[58] The renminbi's trajectory to become a significant part of central bank foreign reserves will take years, yet could reshape global trade and finance. Initially, however, it is more likely to be used in China's trade with developing countries.

The euro has allowed the EU to attract more of the word's excess savings. Europe's capital markets have deepened and become more globally competitive on account of the attractiveness of the euro as a world reserve currency. The result has been a more competitive financial sector in Europe, more low-cost capital available for capital investment and consumer spending within the region, and greater intra- and extra-euro area trade in goods and services.[59]

But the euro area's Stability and Growth pact and no-bailout clause proved grossly inadequate during the single currency's first ten years. Its strictures on budget deficits were ignored by Germany, France and Greece, and proved irrelevant to Spain and Ireland, whose problems centered not on public finances but on private sector debt and asset bubbles.[60]

The Greek crisis prompted lenders, especially from Germany, to call for more fiscal discipline by member states, leading to agreement among the EU members to consider ways to rewrite parts of the EU treaties to ensure the euro's stability, by establishing permanent bailout procedures for future Greece-like crises to replace the current European Financial Stability Facility, a temporary €440 billion rescue fund, which expires in 2013. Yet this will take time, there is no agreement on how to pay for such a fund or whether private investors should bear more of the costs of future rescues, and the fundamental contradiction at the heart of the euro—the lack of a common economic policy to go with the common currency—remains unresolved. Uncertainty about the euro, at a time of skyrocketing debts, deficits and sluggish growth, is something the EU simply cannot afford. And as goes the euro, so goes the EU itself.

Chapter 4
Energy

The EU holds approximately 0.6% of the world's proven oil reserves, 2% of the world's proven natural gas reserves, 4% of proven coal reserves, and 18% of the world's electricity generating capacity. The EU accounts for 17% of the world's total energy consumption (in comparison, the United States accounts for 23%). The EU's dominant fuel is oil, accounting for 40% of total EU energy consumption, followed by natural gas at 24%, nuclear at 14%, coal at 13%, hydroelectric power at 4% and other "renewables"(geothermal, biomass, solar and wind) at 2%.[1]

According to the European Commission, the EU's overall dependence on energy imports will rise from 50% in 2000 to 70% in 2030.[2] At present, all member states, with the exception of Denmark, are net importers of energy, and some individual member states are extremely dependent on foreign sources of energy. EU member states with the highest energy dependency include Ireland (90.9% dependent), Italy (86.8%), Portugal (83.1%), Spain (81.4%) and Belgium (77.9%).

The EU's demand for energy is projected to grow by less than 1% a year over the next quarter century.[3] Yet the EU's energy dependency, together with the tension between rapidly rising resource consumption and environmental sustainability, and the fact that the energy sector is a central element of economic growth and competitiveness, underscores the importance of the EU's energy links with other world regions for the EU's economic future. Failure to secure sufficient energy supplies would be devastating.

Ravenous resource and energy needs of rapidly developing countries are adding significant pressure to Europe's ability to access energy and resources, even if they may also offer opportunities. As China and India grow they will inevitably claim something closer to their fair share of the world's resources—representing a scale of consumption the planet has never seen before.[4] China's total energy consumption, for instance, rose by 103% over the past decade (2000-2009), compared to a 4.3% increase in the EU (2000-2008) and a 4.4% decline in the United States (2000-2009). In 2000, China consumed only half the energy consumed by the United States. But by 2009 it had became the world's leading energy consumer, surpassing the United States, which held that position since the beginning of the 20th century. And prospects for continuing consumption growth are high, given that China's per-capita consumption is only one-third of the OECD average. China's primary energy demand is projected to rise 75% by 2035. By then, it will use 22% of world energy, compared to 17% today.[5]

China not only needs considerable energy to fuel its growth, it also wastes a lot of energy, and things are getting worse, not better. China requires 4.3 times as much energy as the United States, for instance, to produce one unit of GDP, up from 3.4 times in 2002. China consumed 15% more energy per unit of GDP in 2005 than it did in 2002. India consumes only 61% as much energy as China per unit of GDP.[6]

Even the most conservative projections for global economic growth over the next decade suggest that demand for oil, coal, iron ore, and other natural resources will rise by at least a

Figure 4A. EU Energy Mix, 1990-2005

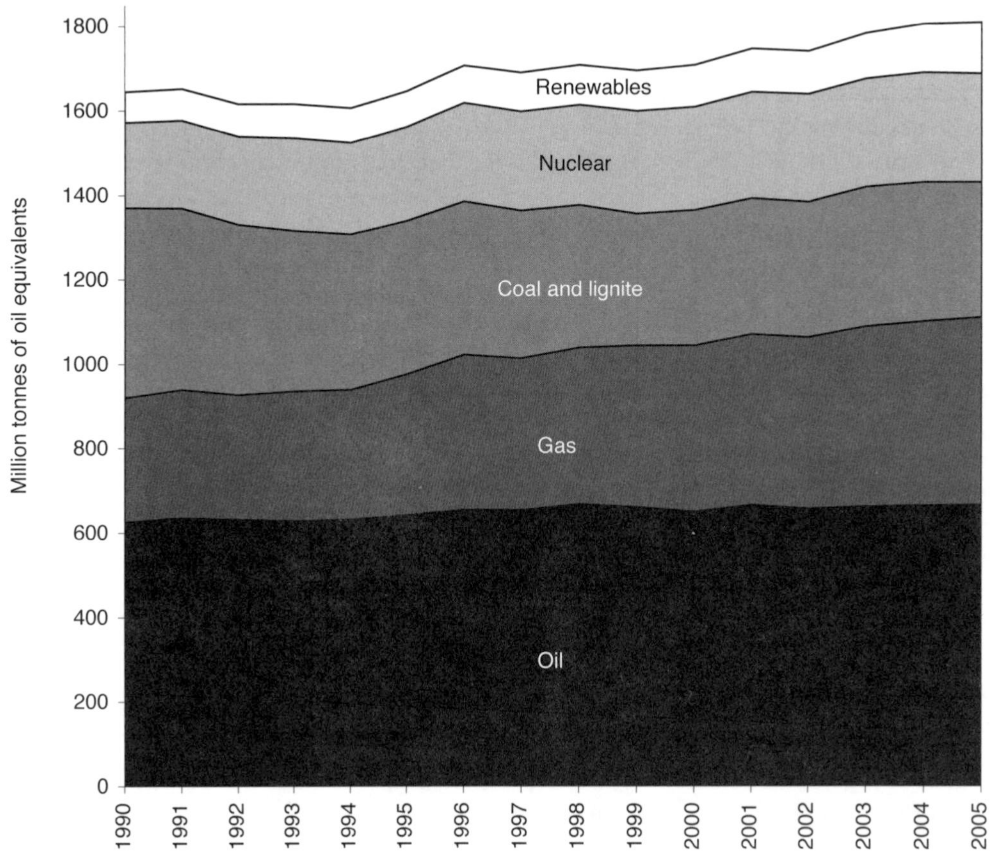

Source: European Environment Agency and Eurostat

third. About 90% of that increase will come from growth in emerging markets. In addition, as easy-to-tap and high-quality reserves are depleted, supply will come from harder-to-access, more costly, and more politically unstable environments.

China and India are projected to account for 40% of the increase in global energy demand by 2035 and, together with the Middle East, for 75% of the growth in CO_2 emissions. In 2035 energy-related emissions from non-OECD countries are expected to be nearly two-and-a-half times those of the OECD. Emissions from China alone will exceed those of the entire OECD. There is widespread consensus that these growth rates are unsustainable. The consequences of this rapid and wasteful rise in demand will also be felt ecologically from wind-borne particulates, river basin pollution flows and demand on the world's forests. While the world's energy resources are adequate to meet the projected demand increase through to 2035 and well beyond, these trends have profound implications for environmental protection, energy security and economic development and dire consequences for climate change—all further elements of pressure on Europe.[7]

Furthermore, China's growing global economic and financial networks and its mounting dependencies have expanded its reach to such areas as Africa, Central Asia, the Middle East and Latin America—with uncertain implications, not only for Western economic policies but such issues as human rights and peacekeeping. China's rise could trigger geopolitical rivalries in various regions of the world with historic ties to either Europe or the United States.[8]

The situation is acute because both the largest and the fastest growing economies are extremely dependent on a relatively limited number of countries to fuel their economies. The 12 most energy-rich countries control over 80% of the world's proven oil and gas reserves yet produce only 6.5% of global GDP, whereas all OECD countries combined, together with China and India, control only 10% of the world's oil and gas reserves yet produce over 75% of global wealth. Both the dependency of major economies on energy imports and the concentration of energy production in a handful of countries is growing, as are wealth transfers from the former to the latter. While coal resources are more evenly distributed, oil and gas are concentrated in a few geopolitically critical countries. The largest oil reserves are located, in decreasing order of magnitude, in Saudi Arabia, Iran, Iraq, Kuwait, the United Arab Emirates (UAE), Venezuela and Russia. The largest gas reserves, by the same criterion, are in Russia, Iran, Qatar, Saudi Arabia, UAE, the United States, and Nigeria.[9]

In sum, the EU's energy and resource needs require it to adopt a differentiated approach to other competitors and partners. In this context, for instance, the BRIC label is not particularly useful. While the EU faces rising and potentially competing demand from China and India, especially for oil and to a much lesser extent for gas, it can look to Russia and Brazil as suppliers of energy. Support for energy efficiency and the use of renewable energy sources will be important with regard to China and India. In the case of Russia, energy security in connection with the EU's internal energy market regulations and energy transit represent the major challenges. With respect to Brazil, important issues include agreement on biofuels standards, subsidies and trade barriers.[10]

Figure 4A depicts the EU's basic energy picture. Despite huge investments in clean energy, in 2020 the ratio of fossil fuel consumption to renewable and nuclear power will remain largely as it is today—roughly 80%. No effort to develop alternatives, no matter how promising, will change this situation fundamentally in the short- or medium-term. The embedded resource infrastructure is so large that any transition away from fossil fuels will take decades. Marginal gains can be made, however, and Europe is as well positioned as any regional economy to make progress in the effort to break the link between the production of wealth and the consumption of resources.

The EU leads both the U.S. and Japan in energy efficiency and sustainability. The EU15 need only half as much energy per unit of economic output as the U.S., and 20% less than Japan.[11] Energy sustainability is critical to the EU's position in the world, not only as an input in the production and consumption of goods and services and as an important consideration with regards to security of EU energy supplies, but also as a potentially lucrative source of future EU competitiveness, given the growing need to reduce energy and carbon intensities due to rising global energy demand, climate change and other unsustainable environmental trends.

Figure 4B. World Primary Energy Demand by Fuel, 1980-2035

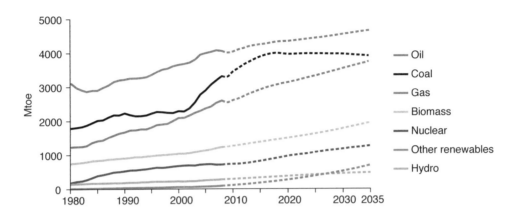

Source: *World Energy Outlook 2010*, © OECD/IEA, figure 2.4, p. 84.

In this chapter we look first at the EU's links and position with regard to traditional energy sources, then turn to the EU's links and its competitive position in nuclear, renewables, and environmental goods.

Traditional Energy: Coal, Oil, Gas

Global demand for oil, gas and coal is forecast to continue to rise over the next few decades. The IEA envisages a 38% rise in world primary energy demand between 2008 and 2035, assuming no change in government policies. If governments implement commitments they have made to phase out fossil-fuel subsidies and to restrain greenhouse gas emissions, the projected increase in demand falls to 36%, or about 1.2% average annual growth in demand, compared with 2% over the previous 27 years. Emerging and developing countries are likely to account for over 90% of the increase. Under this scenario, China would overtake the U.S. soon after 2025 to become the world's biggest importer of oil and gas, while India would surpass Japan soon after 2020 to take third place. Strong growth from ASEAN would further shift the focus of the global energy landscape toward Asia. Outside of Asia, the Middle East is slated to register the fastest rate of increase, contributing 10% to incremental demand. In all, the economic rise of China and India is leading to a substantial re-distribution in relative market shares more for oil than for gas. But China has also shifted from being a net exporter of coal to a net importer, helping to push up prices and to squeeze supplies.[12]

Oil

Fossil fuels will remain the dominant sources of energy worldwide, accounting for 77% of demand increase between 2007 and 2030. The recession caused oil demand to drop in 2008 and 2009, and primary oil demand is projected to decline 21% from 2008 to 2035—on average

Figure 4C. World Net Oil Import Dependence In Main Importing Countries/Regions, 2007-2030

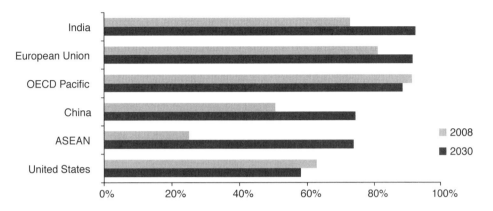

Source: *World Energy Outlook 2010*, © OECD/IEA, figure 3.8, p. 110.

about 0.9% a year. Decreases are forecast for both the EU and the U.S. and increases for both China and India. And as non-OPEC conventional oil production peaks before 2015, most additional oil production is slated to come from OPEC countries.[13]

The EU's oil imports have grown only slightly.[14] With some help from the global economic slowdown, EU oil imports increased only 9% between 2000 and 2009. While the 2009 recession year distorted several numbers,[15] the key trend is that the Middle East is no longer the EU's main regional oil provider (down 44% from 168 million tons[16] in 2000 to 94 million in 2009). Russia now delivers most of Europe's oil (206 million tons). While the Middle East has ranked as the #2 regional supplier of oil since 2000, both Africa and Wider Europe actually supplied more oil in 2009 (119 million tons and 115 million tons, respectively).

The EU also exports oil, primarily to the U.S., Switzerland, Canada, Mexico and Nigeria. In fact overall EU oil exports grew by 14% over the course of the past decade. While exports to the EU's main oil consumer, North America, tumbled from 50 million tons to 44 million tons between 2000 and 2009, customers compensated in Wider Europe (24 million tons), Africa (19 million tons), and the Middle East (12 million tons).

Coal

Coal will remain the dominant fuel of the power sector. The IEA projects that demand for coal will grow by 20% between 2008 and 2035—or 2.3% on average per year, faster than either oil or gas. While coal is expected to remain the dominant source of electricity generation, its share is projected to decline from 41% in 2008 to 32% by 2035. The IEA projects that electricity demand will grow by 76% in this time period (3.3% average annual growth), about five times the existing capacity of the United States. But the IEA also projects that higher fossil-fuel prices, as well as increasing concerns over energy security and climate change, will

Figure 4D. EU Oil Imports in 100 Tons, 2000-2009

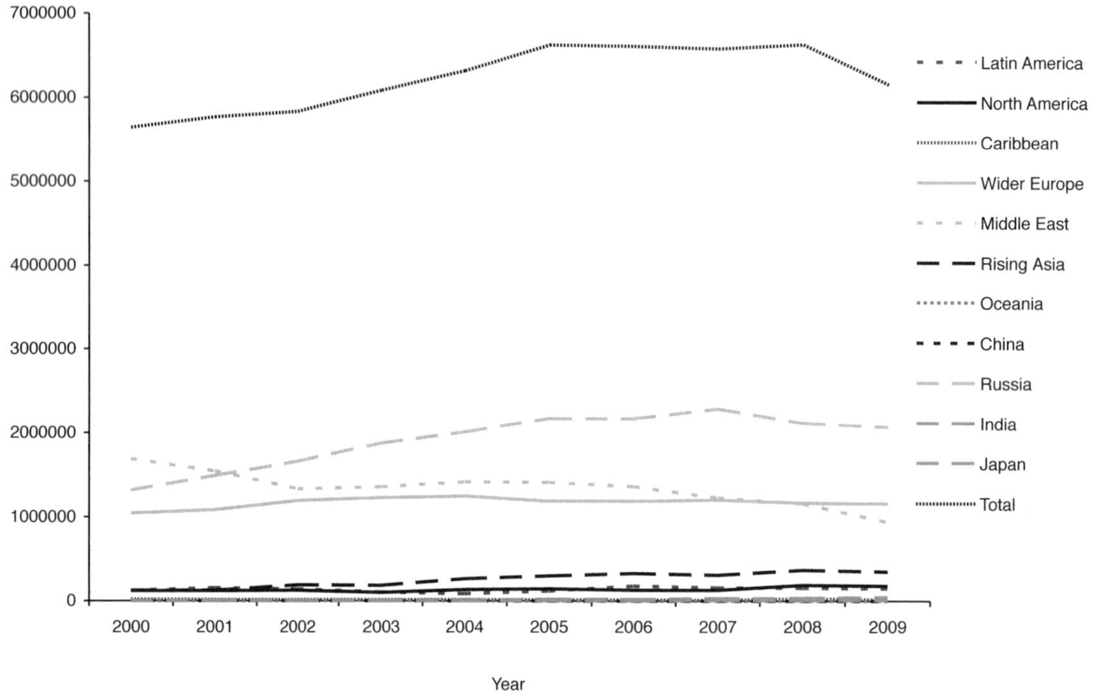

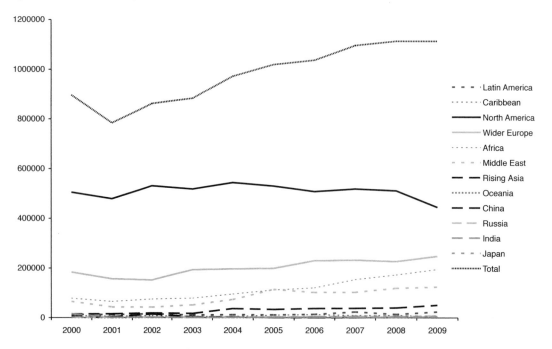

Source: Eurostat; author's calculations.

Figure 4E. EU Oil Exports in 100 Tons, 2000-2009

Source: Eurostat; author's calculations.[17]

Figure 4F. EU Coal Imports in 100 Tons, 2000-2009

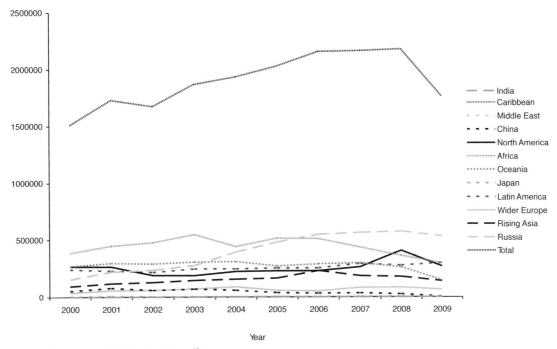

Source: Eurostat; author's calculations.[19]

Figure 4G. EU Coal Exports in 100 Tons, 2000-2009

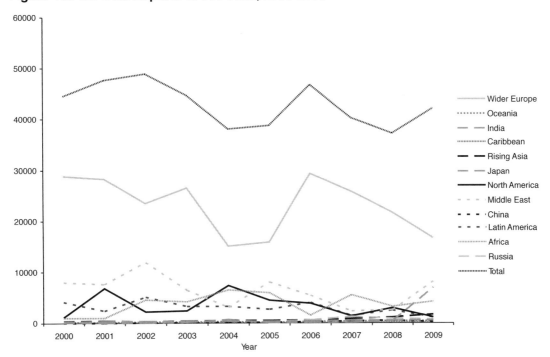

Source: Eurostat; author's calculations.

boost the share of renewables-based electricity generation from 19% in 2008 to 32% by 2030.[18]

In 2006, Russia surpassed Africa as the EU's largest regional coal supplier. In 2009, the largest regional purveyors of coal to the EU were Russia (53 million tons), Latin America (30 million), Africa (29 million) and North America (27 million). The EU has also imported 16% more coal between 2000 and 2009 (from 154 million to 176 million tons) while exporting about 6% less in 2009 than in 2000 (4.2 million vs. 4.4 million tons). This drop in exports was mostly caused by Wider Europe, the largest regional purchaser of EU coal, which imported 26% less in 2000 than in 2009 (2.2 million tons in 2009 instead of 3.0 million)

Gas

Projections for natural gas are different than for oil. To date, less than 8% of total recoverable natural gas resources have been produced (or flared), meaning that the world's remaining resources of natural gas are easily large enough to cover any conceivable rate of demand increase through to 2030 and well beyond, although the cost of developing new resources is set to rise over the long term.

Global gas demand fell by more than 3% in 2009, double the pace of decline seen for oil, and OECD Europe was the most affected. By late 2008 European demand for gas had fallen to 2004 levels. EU demand is unlikely to return to pre-recession levels until after 2013. Gas is the only fossil fuel for which EU demand is projected to be higher in 2030 than in 2008, but by only 0.4% growth per year, due to low economic growth, overall demographic stagnation and decline, and EU efficiency measures.[20]

Even though EU demand for natural gas is not expected to grow dramatically, the EU will increasingly need to secure its gas from non-EU suppliers. EU member states are already among the biggest natural gas importers, receiving about half their supplies from outside the EU. By 2030, the EU will have to import up to 80% of its consumption. Major European economies such as Germany, France and Italy, already exhibit dependency rates of this magnitude. Twelve EU member states, including Portugal and Sweden, are even wholly dependent on foreign imports of gas.[21] In future even the UK, one of the major producers of natural gas in Europe, will be purchasing more natural gas abroad than it will be producing itself.

EU natural gas imports rose 11.6% per year on average between 2000 and 2009. In 2009 Africa was the EU's largest regional source of natural gas, followed by Wider Europe and Russia, although the Middle East has considerably boosted its supplies to the EU over the course of the decade. The EU also exports small amounts of natural gas, primarily to Africa and Wider Europe.

Beyond Europe, gas demand is expected to grow by 41% between 2007 and 2030—or 1.5% a year on average, more strongly in relative terms than oil. This growth in gas consumption is forecast to occur primarily in the Middle East, India and China. China's demand is expected to grow more than six-fold between 2008 and 2035, at an annualized rate of 5.9%.[23]

Figure 4H. Ultimately Recoverable Conventional Natural Gas Resources by Region

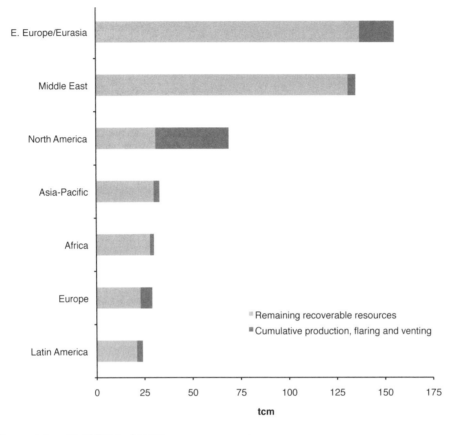

Source: International Energy Agency.

In the IEA's so-called "450 Scenario," in which governments are assumed to take strong action to cut CO2 emissions, world gas demand would grow throughout the 2020s but then decline, leading to an overall growth of 15% between 2008 and 2035 (an average annual rate of growth of 0.5%).[24]

The actual pace of demand growth is likely to depend not only on economic growth rates but on the strength of climate policy action and on new dynamics related to shale gas, which could have important repercussions for Europe.

The recent rapid development of shale gas resources in the United States and Canada has transformed the gas market outlook, both in North America and in other parts of the world. Today, shale gas is responsible for roughly 20% of total U.S. production, with expectations that it could reach 50% by 2035—an astounding change given that it represented only 1% in 2000. The development of shale gas dramatically increases estimates of American gas reserves. In 2007 the U.S. was expected to have about 30 years' worth of resources. Today the U.S. is believed to hold 100 years' worth at present usage rates. Mainly as a result of shale gas production growth, the U.S. has cut its import needs and displaced Russia as the world's largest pro-

Figure 4I. EU Gas Imports in 100 Tons, 2000-2009

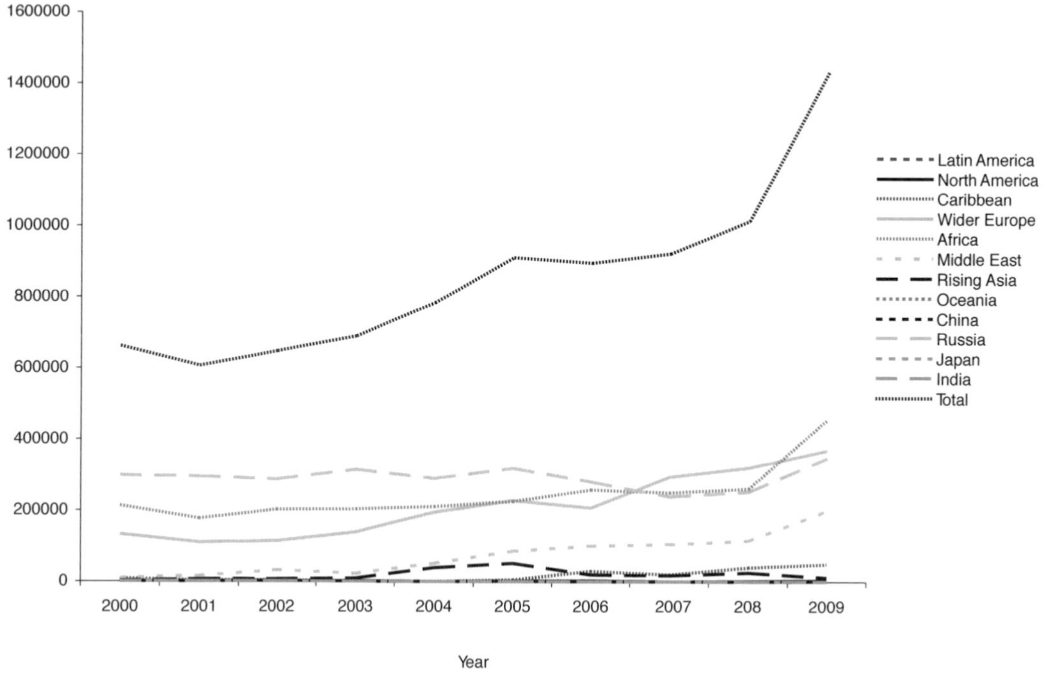

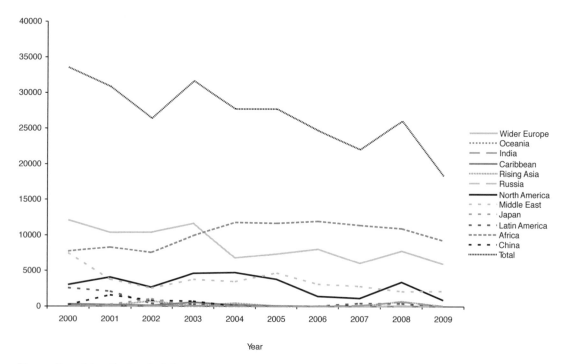

Source: Eurostat; author's calculations.[22]

Figure 4J. EU Gas Exports in 100 Tons, 2000-2009

Source: Eurostat; author's calculations

ducer of gas. It has also caused demand for liquefied natural gas to fall and has sent prices tumbling, turning the market upside down.[25]

The ripple effects of the U.S. "shale gale" are already being felt in Europe. With the U.S. market awash with natural gas and prices plummeting, LNG tankers have been re-routed to more lucrative European markets. Cheaper gas selling on the spot market, in turn, has diminished Gazprom's share of the European natural gas market. The immediate impact of North America's shale gas revolution, together with the recession's dampening impact on demand, is likely to be a glut of gas supply over the next few years and downward pressure on gas prices in Europe. Yet by 2030 additional capacity of the equivalent of 4 times Russian capacity is needed to offset declines in existing fields and to meet the increase in demand.[26]

A number of European countries are looking to their own shale gas reserves in an effort to emulate U.S. success.[27] It remains highly uncertain, however, whether the U.S. shale boom can be replicated in other parts of the world that are endowed with such resources. At first glance, the EU appears structurally well-prepared to emulate America's shale gas success story. It is home to a large and increasingly integrated gas market with relatively high prices and expectations of a steadily rising demand; it has an established pipeline infrastructure; and there are large shale gas deposits on EU territory. According to the IEA, western Europe alone may hold around 15 trillion cubic meters in shale gas, enough to supply Germany for roughly 175 years. Poland is considered to be a particularly attractive location. A study by Advanced Resources International found that Poland alone could have recoverable reserves of 3 trillion cubic meters—more than 200 years of its own consumption.

In reality, however, shale gas is likely to be developed more slowly in Europe, due to a relative dearth of geological data, capacity problems, tougher environmental regulations, local opposition in some cases, higher labor costs, and far lower political awareness or support.[28] These factors make it highly unlikely that the EU will undergo a shale gas revolution any time soon. LNG and pipeline imports will remain important for the foreseeable future. Major shale gas production in Europe is unlikely before 2020.[29]

As production of traditional natural gas declines in the Netherlands, the UK and Norway, additional supplies are likely to come from Russia, Iran and Qatar.[30] Given sanctions on Iran, only Qatar and Russia appear as viable suppliers of additional gas. This means that the EU will probably not be able to reduce its energy dependence on Russia. In fact, the European Commission itself estimates that its gas imports from Russia will climb from today's 40% to 60% (of total imports) in 2030. Such levels may not be reached due to Gazprom's problems with bringing new fields onstream and the poor performance of the Russian gas sector in general. Nevertheless, Russia's share of EU imports will remain high and is likely to increase.[31]

Russia alone will not be able to meet overall EU demand, however. In addition, seemingly annual winter spats between Moscow and Kyiv over transit flows and payment rates, together with the EU's dependency on non-transparent financial transfers in its energy trade with Russia, has raised EU concerns about reliability of supply, prompting greater interest in alternative sources. Yet lack of a common EU energy policy and weak antimonopoly enforcement of energy importers have only encouraged non-transparent state-owned energy companies to secure influence in EU member states. Rampant corruption and renationalization in

Russia of the large energy companies have hampered new investments in exploration and development and contributed to a decline in Russian oil and gas production.[32] The European Commission has proposed new initiatives to forge a more common EU energy policy, but such efforts are in their infancy and disputes among member states continue.

Nuclear

Nuclear power accounts for 12-14% of the EU's primary energy consumption. The EU imported 69% more uranium in 2009 (26,000 tons) than in 2000 (15,000 tons). Exports fell 34% from 2000 (20,433 tons) to 2009 (13,474 tons) because the EU's main buyer, Russia, only purchased 11,518 tons in 2009, down from 18,066 in 2000.

Nuclear energy faces a mixed future in the EU. In 2009 15 EU member states operated 144 reactors (about one-third of the world total), down from 177 in 1989. Dozens of additional reactors will go offline in coming years, and at least one-third of the EU's nuclear plants could be decommissioned by 2025. European public opinion remains critical of nuclear power and exhibits a strong preference for other forms of energy. Germany and Belgium have nuclear phase-out legislation, and Spain is committed to a similar course. Yet there are signs of change. In June 2010 the Swedish Parliament repealed an earlier commitment to phase out nuclear power. Finland is building a new nuclear reactor that is behind schedule and over budget, and is considering additional construction. Poland, Lithuania, Bulgaria, Hungary, Italy, the Netherlands, Slovakia are each considering new construction. The UK's nuclear plants tend to be small, inefficient and old, with most of them set to be retired by 2023 and a number replaced by new generation reactors.[33]

France is the EU's nuclear champion. 47% of the nuclear electricity in the EU is generated solely by France.[34] The nuclear industry generates about 200,000 direct and indirect jobs in France. The French company Areva is the world's largest producer of uranium, accounting for 20% of global primary uranium production and 20% of the global market share of the nuclear fuel cycle, including reactors and services. The French company EDF is the world's largest consumer of enriched uranium and the world's largest producer of nuclear electricity. EDF is AREVA's main client, and AREVA is EDF's main supplier; the French government owns 84% of EDF and 93% of Areva.[35] The French company Alstom has provided turbine generators to about 30% of the operating nuclear plants around the world.

France's 59 reactors generate about 77% of its electricity, and France has significant generating overcapacity, which it uses to export electricity to neighboring countries. France is the world's largest net exporter of electricity, and gains over €3 billion annually from these activities. Although France does not need new reactors, it is building new units at Flamanville and Penly as a means of maintaining its nuclear competence.

Reactors and fuel products and services are major French exports, and the French government has been a staunch supporter of the industry, hoping to be rewarded with a revival of interest as governments worldwide grapple with the challenges of increasing energy demand, security of supply and the need to reduce carbon emissions. The IEA projects that nuclear power will account for 8% of global energy in 2035, rising from 6% in 2008.[36] As of early 2010, the IAEA

Figure 4K. EU Uranium Imports in 100 Tons, 2000–2009

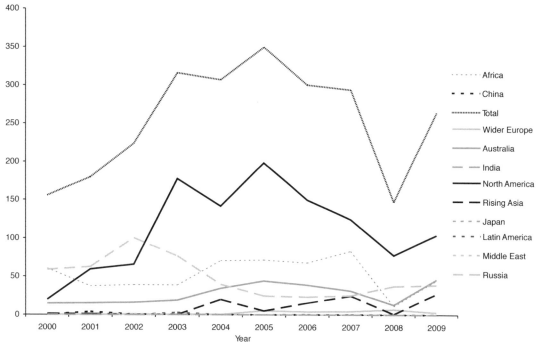

Source: Eurostat; author's calculations

Figure 4L. EU Uranium Exports in 100 Tons, 2000–2009

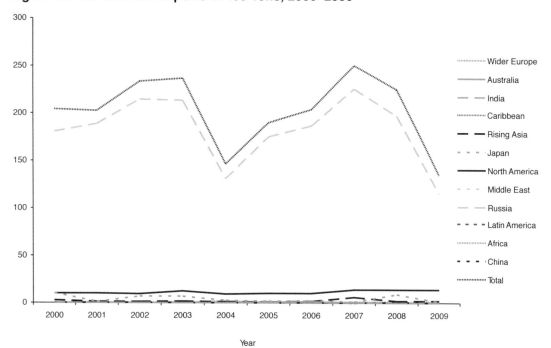

Source: Eurostat; author's calculations

identified 57 reactors under construction worldwide, and French industry sources anticipate a doubling or tripling of this rate of construction over the next 20 years. French hopes that its new-generation nuclear reactor could serve as a significant source of diplomatic and economic influence, however, have been dampened by delays, cost over-runs and foreign competition.[37]

Whereas in the past U.S. and European companies completely developed, built and supplied nuclear reactors worldwide, in future these companies could be joint venture or junior partners to companies from other parts of the world. South Korea, for example, now can now build a nuclear reactor with about 85% indigenous parts—unthinkable just ten years ago.

China has embarked on an ambitious nuclear energy program, and its sheer size and scale is transforming prospects for nuclear energy generation. Twenty years ago there was not one operating nuclear power station in China. Today 13 are in operation, 25 are under construction, and another 120 have been proposed. China is building more reactors than any other country, and its embrace of the technology drives the global industry. The International Energy Agency predicts that the increase in Chinese nuclear power generation will exceed that of the entire OECD. While in the past China has drawn on technology from France, Canada, Russia and the U.S., it is rapidly becoming self-sufficient in reactor design and construction, as well as other aspects of the nuclear fuel cycle. China has to import about half of its uranium, however, and is working to secure supplies in countries ranging from Kazakhstan and Mongolia to Namibia and Zimbabwe.[38]

Renewables and Clean Energy Technologies

Despite the predominance of fossil fuels, use of modern renewable energy—including solar, wind, biofuels, hydro, geothermal, marine energy and modern biomass—is projected to triple by 2035, and its share in total energy primary demand doubling from 7% to 14%. Clean technology solutions, including renewable energy, mobility, buildings, industrial high tech, and smart grid and other IT solutions, are expected to develop a global market potential of around €2 trillion in 2020, growing at an average 13% per annum.[39] Global private investment in renewable energy and energy efficient technologies alone is estimated to reach $450 billion annually by 2012 and at least $600 billion by 2020.[40]

Given its dependencies and looking to areas of comparative advantage, the EU is pioneering alternative energies and strategies of energy efficiency and sustainability, a field that could be a major opportunity for Europe over coming decades.[41] The EU has implemented a market-based climate change instrument, i.e. the emission trading scheme, and benefits from an electricity generation portfolio that is about 45% carbon-free. It has committed by 2020 to reduce greenhouse gas emissions to 20% below their 1990 levels; improve energy efficiency by 20%, and more than double renewables' share of energy consumption to 20%. According to a study commissioned by the European Commission, achieving the renewables target would boost EU GDP by about 0.24 % and add about 410,000 new jobs to the 1.4 million jobs already supported by the industry.[42]

Europe is in a strong position in emerging clean tech markets, thanks to the global leadership of its companies in most of the relevant industry segments and to policy makers' attention to the development of a green industry. According to the OECD, the EU accounts for the majority of worldwide PCT (Patent Cooperation Treaty) patent applications in renewable energy generation (REG), with a share of around 37%, followed by the U.S. (20%) and Japan (19%). Between 2004 and 2006 the EU accounted for about 40% of all air pollution control patents under the Patent Cooperation Treaty, compared with about 25% each for the U.S. and Japan, and with South Korea, the BRICs and South Africa together registering less than 4%. The EU lead is similar and substantial in patents for water pollution control, renewable energy and solid waste management.[43]

Within the EU, however, only Germany, Denmark and Spain exhibit above-average specialization in REG research and innovation, with five other member states—Austria, France, Italy, the Netherlands and the United Kingdom—playing a greater role. Together, these eight countries account for 92.5% of all REG patents in the EU.[44]

EU companies lead the global clean energy sector, which is growing rapidly in number of companies and size. The 2010 EU Industrial R&D Investment Scoreboard of the world's top 1400 R&D companies includes 15 companies (9 more than the year before) fully concerned with clean energy technological development. 13 of these 15 companies are based in the EU. All told, they invested more than €500 million in R&D in 2009, representing a considerable increase of 28.7% compared with the previous year.

Nonetheless, European companies are challenged by the vast investments being made in China, the expertise of competitors in Japan and the United States, and the single-minded determination of countries such as South Korea. In addition, clean-energy investments are not a zero-sum competitiveness game: increasingly, innovation is collaborative and international. Instead of encouraging the impulse to deter foreigners from participating in clean tech development, the EU should be a leader in open clean tech innovation.[45] If the EU is to lead in the global cleantech industry, EU member states must step up their game, collaborating more effectively together to provide more significant, direct and coordinated investment in clean energy R&D, manufacturing, deployment, and infrastructure.[46]

Moreover, even though governments around the world are scrambling to promote renewable energy technologies, these sectors are simply not big enough to make a significant difference to a large economy's overall growth rate. Nor is clean energy likely to be consistently cheaper than dirty sources of energy anytime soon. Barriers to the widespread commercialization of clean energy technologies include high capital costs; significant uncertainty and risk; a lack of enabling infrastructure (e.g. transmission lines, storage for solar and wind, and grid access); historically low levels of publicly funded R&D; low levels of privately funded R&D due to intellectual property concerns and spillover risks; and low to nonexistent competitive product differentiation, leaving emerging technologies to compete with well established incumbent technologies primarily on the basis of price alone. In short, clean energy is not the silver bullet to Europe's competitive challenges.[47]

Nonetheless, European leadership in such areas can provide key benefits for the European and global economy. Since emerging clean energy technologies both remain more expensive than conventional alternatives and face a variety of non-price barriers, public sector investments in clean energy will be a key factor in determining the location of clean energy invest-ments made by the private sector.[48]

Moreover, even prodigious efforts to scale up existing technologies are unlikely to keep atmospheric levels of carbon dioxide below what scientists now recognize as the point of no return. Truly transformational scientific breakthroughs are required, and given how long it takes to capitalize and deploy new technologies, such breakthroughs are needed soon, not in 2020 or 2030. The real race is to see who can become the market leader in inventing, manufac-turing, and exporting the next wave of clean technology.[49]

In terms of capital flows to clean energy between 2000-2008, the U.S. led all countries with $52.1 billion, followed by China with $41.2 billion and Germany with $36.6 billion. Together EU member states accounted for $115.7 billion. But China's share of global clean tech invest-ment is rising each year, and surpassed that of the United States for the first time in 2008.

Renewables investments in the world and in the EU were hit hard by the financial crisis and related recession in 2008-2009, although EU and member state support schemes and political determination to include clean technologies in some recovery plans helped to cushion the full impact. In 2008 the EU provided $41.7 billion (Germany $4.6 billion) in capital for clean energy, whereas China provided $16.7 billion and the U.S. provided $15.2 billion.[50] Nonethe-less, in 2010 the EU failed to reach its target of a 21% share of renewable energy sources in electricity consumption, reaching a 19% share, and missing its 5.75% target in the transport sector, reaching a 4% share.[51]

China commands an increasingly large share of global clean energy manufacturing, with the world's largest solar manufacturing capacity, a leading wind manufacturing industry, and new efforts underway to take a leading position in plug-in hybrid and electric vehicles and the advanced batteries required to power them. China is also quickly developing the capacity to construct its own nuclear power plants, and is heavily engaged in the development of carbon capture and storage technology (CCS). Finally, China has recently become a leading manufac-turer of high-speed rail technology after localizing several designs.[52]

Solar

Every year the sun generates 1.6 billion terawatt hours of energy—10,000 times the annual energy needs of the earth's human population. Solar energy has by far the greatest potential of all regenerative energies. In 2009 all of the Concentrated Solar Power (CSP) plants operating around the world produced 430 megawatts of energy, with another 500 megawatts of capacity under construction and 9000 megawatt capacity in the planning stages. Spain is the global leader, with 6 functioning CSP plants and 12 more under construction, and follows the U.S. in terms of planned capacity.[53]

The EU photovoltaic sector, although modest compared to wind, has registered impressive annual growth rates of around 40% between 2000 and 2007. Costs for manufacturing and installation have been falling steadily. Solar photovoltaic systems today are more than 60% cheaper than in the 1990s. Nonetheless, the price of solar electricity is still not on a par with conventional energy.

Figure 4M. EU Solar Imports in 1000 Euro (€), 2000–2009

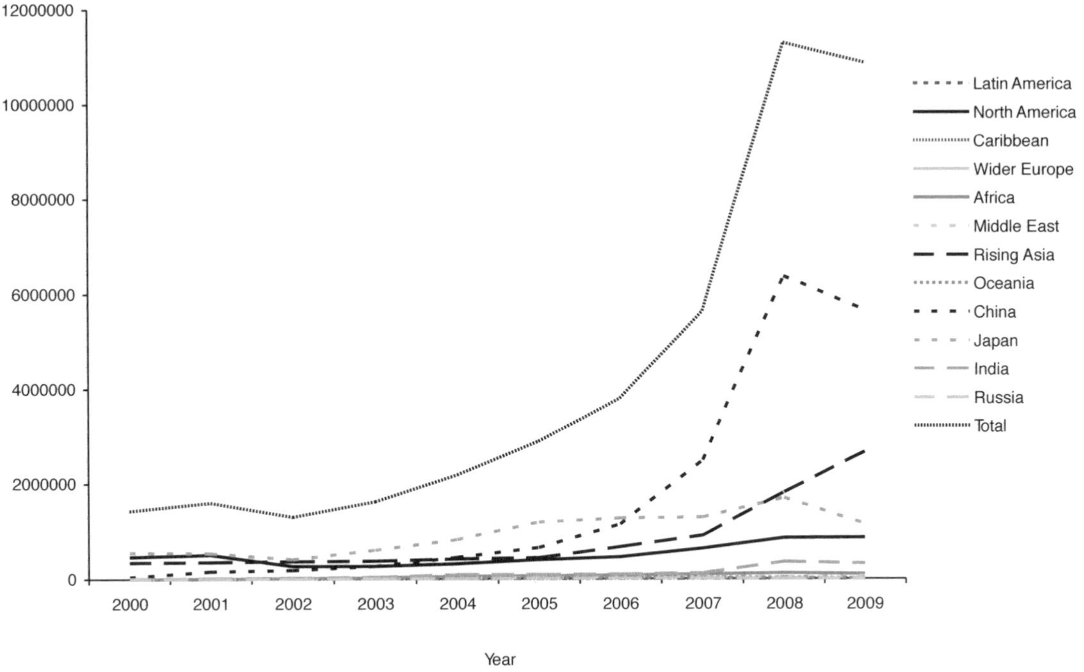

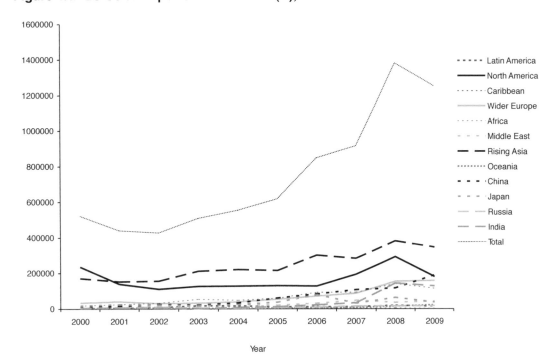

Source: Eurostat; author's calculations.[56]

Figure 4N. EU Solar Exports in 1000 Euro (€), 2000–2009

Source: Eurostat; author's calculations.

Figure 40. Transfer of Solar Photovoltaic Technologies, 1990-2006

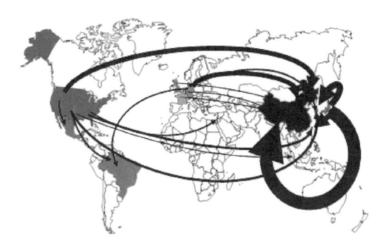

Source: OECD, Economic Globalisation Indicators, 2010, p. 149.

The solar thermal sector in the EU has also been expanding, with an annual growth rate of 17.5% since 2000. Between 2000 and 2007, installed surfaces in the EU experienced average annual growth of more than 51%. Germany has been the solar thermal leader in the EU, accounting for 39% of the cumulated capacities of thermal collectors in the EU. Germany, Spain, Italy, France and Greece account for 84% of all solar thermal installations in the EU.[54]

EU imports of solar power parts have grown substantially from €1.4 billion in 2000 to over €10 billion in 2009—a 65% average annual growth rate, and over 7 times more than EU solar exports. The EU's solar imports are powered especially by China, whose exports of solar components to the EU grew from just over €42 million in 2000 to peaking just under €6.4 billion in 2008, before slipping to €5.6 billion in 2009, but still accounting for over half of all EU solar imports. Rising Asia accounted for another €2.9 billion in EU solar imports, and Japan for an additional €1.1 billion, meaning that Asian countries account for almost all EU solar imports.

China has one-third of global solar manufacturing capacity and supplies 30% of the global solar PV market. China's solar manufacturing growth to date has been primarily driven by increasing international demand from countries like Spain, Germany, and the United States. China currently exports 98% of its manufactured PV output, and is the leading solar exporter in the world. While Europe (and the U.S.) have largely subsidized buyers of solar panels, China has subsidized solar panel manufacturers. It then exports virtually all of its panels to the EU and to the U.S., often aided by European and American consumer subsidies.[55] Domestic demand is expected to drive much of China's future growth as the government turns to more public procurement and puts in place domestic solar PV incentives to reach its domestic renewable energy targets.[56]

EU solar exports are starting from a relatively low base but grew from €521 million in 2001 to €1.38 billion in 2008—a 29% average annual growth rate. Exports took a hit during the 2009 recession, when they totaled €1.25 billion. The EU's main regional solar customer is Rising Asia, followed by China and North America. Between 2000 and 2009 EU solar exports to India jumped 36 times to €127 million; those to China rose 6 times to €189 million; those to Africa rose 5 times to €114 million; and those to Wider Europe rose almost 4 times to €158 million. Exports to North America, however, actually fell 23% from €235 million in 2000 to €179 million in 2009.

Wind Energy

Wind energy has attracted considerable investment and developed quickly since the late 1990s. Improvements in turbine efficiency combined with higher fossil fuel prices have increased wind energy's competitiveness when compared with conventional power production.[57]

Between 2000 and 2007 the installed wind energy capacity in the EU quadrupled. EU wind capacities have also become more geographically diversified and balanced. While Germany, Spain and Denmark accounted for more than 80% of the sector in 2003, their share represented around 60% in 2007, and was less than 40% in 2008. In 2008 the UK established more offshore capacities than any other member state.[58]

EU windpower imports have grown from just €468,000 in 2000 to €81 million in 2009—still relatively small, but with a high growth rate. China has become the EU's largest regional windpower parts provider, supplying over half of EU total imports, followed by Rising Asia and Latin America. Denmark's Vestas remains the world's top wind turbine manufacturer by capacity, but its largest wind energy equipment production base is located in the Chinese city of Tianjin.[59]

EU windpower exports rose more than seven-fold between 2000 (€176 million) and 2006 (€1.4 billion), but have fallen ever since. The top three exporting countries in the EU are Denmark, Germany and Spain, respectively exporting over €4 billion, €2 billion, and €1 billion in windpower parts since 2000. The EU's largest windpower clients are North America, which imported €486 million in 2009 (down from €981 million in 2006) and over €4.4 billion since 2000; the Middle East, which imported €216 million in 2009 and €592 million since 2000; and Japan, which imported only €32 million in 2009, down from €149 million the year before, but over €882 million since 2000.

Biofuels

Liquid biofuels such as ethanol and biodiesel are renewable fuels that are blended with traditional gasoline and diesel. They have the potential to become complete substitutes for petroleum products, depending on the further development and adoption of flex-fuel vehicle technology. Despite the possibilities inherent in biofuels, in 2008 they accounted for only 1.5% of total road transport fuel.

Ethanol is the liquid biofuel most widely used for transportation in the world. Global production reached 17.3 billion gallons in 2008.[61] The United States is the largest ethanol producer in the world, producing 9 billion gallons of corn-based ethanol annually. Brazil is the world's second-largest producer, with 6.4 billion gallons of sugarcane-based ethanol. The EU

Figure 4P. EU Wind Imports in 1000 Euro (€), 2000–2009

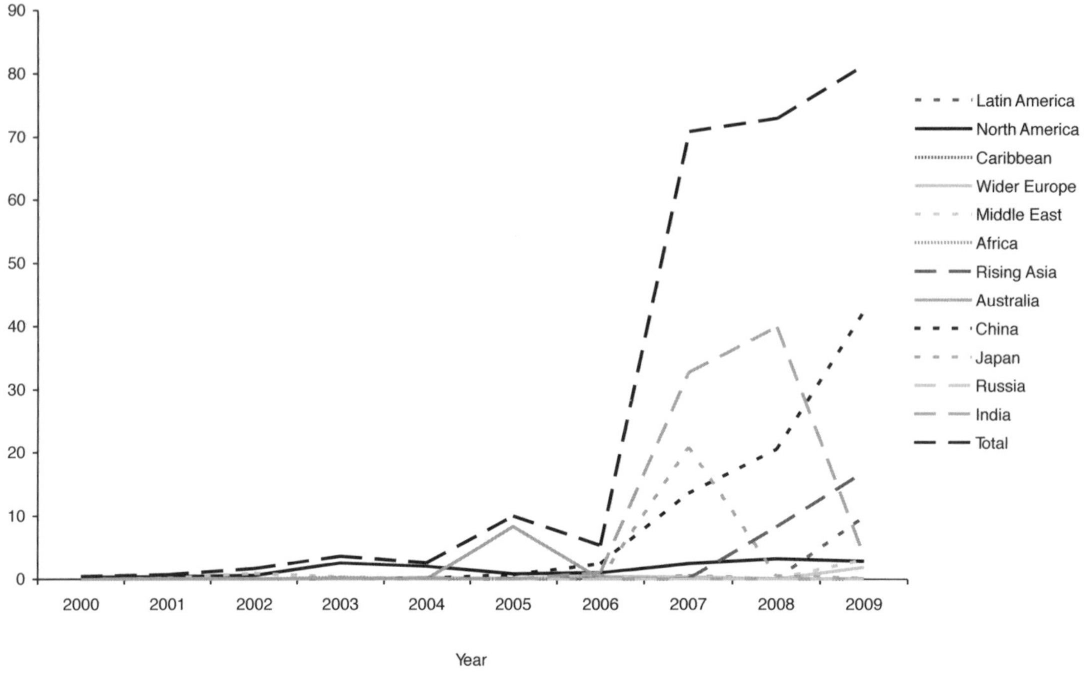

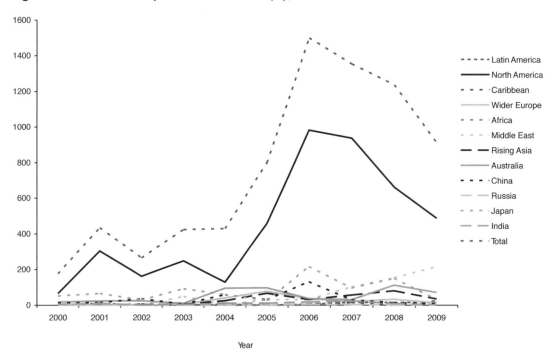

Source: Eurostat; author's calculations.[60]

Figure 4Q. EU Wind Exports in 1000 Euro (€), 2000–2009

Source: Eurostat; author's calculations

Figure 4R. Transfer of Wind Technologies, 1990-2006

Source: OECD, Economic Globalisation Indicators, 2010, p. 149.

is the third-largest producer, with 4% of the world's ethanol in 2008, while China accounted for 3% of global production. The other major ethanol producing countries include Canada, Thailand, Colombia, India, and Australia.

Biodiesel is the second most widely used liquid biofuel. With 10.3 billion gallons of capacity, total world biodiesel production was about 3.5 billion gallons in 2008. The EU is the main biodiesel producer in the world, accounting for about 95% of global production.[62] The EU's capacity in 2008 was about 5.1 billion gallons. Biodiesel constitutes about 80% of biofuels production within the EU.[63] Germany is the EU's major biodiesel producing country, accounting for about 40% of total production, followed by France and Italy.

Biofuels reflect the boom and bust cycle many alternative fuels experience during changing economic times. Production of biofuels has fallen significantly since late 2008 due to falling oil prices; weak biofuel prices, which are too low to cover feedstock and production costs; tougher credit and financing conditions; a variety of technical and regulatory uncertainties; and public concerns that greater biofuels production could result in higher food prices.[64] Due to these factors, the EU was unable to meet its 2010 target of biofuels making up an average 5.75% of transportation fuel by 2010; its goal for 2020 is 10%.

While the EU's overall biofuels exports have posted 5.3% average annual growth since 2000, they crashed after the boom years of 2001-2006. Latin America, on the other hand, continued to supply large amounts after 2007. While Brazil's exports of ethanol declined 31% in 2009 (to 2.6m tons), overall its exports have grown 28% since 2005. In 2009, Latin America provided 74% (661,362 tons) of the EU's total biofuel imports of 890,000 tons. Of that amount, Brazil shipped more than half (358,123 tons). Brazil is by far the EU's major biofuels supplier, accounting for 88% more than Rising Asia, the EU's second leading regional supplier. Wider Europe is the EU's primary biofuels customer.

Figure 4S. EU Biofuels Imports in 100 Tons, 2000–2009

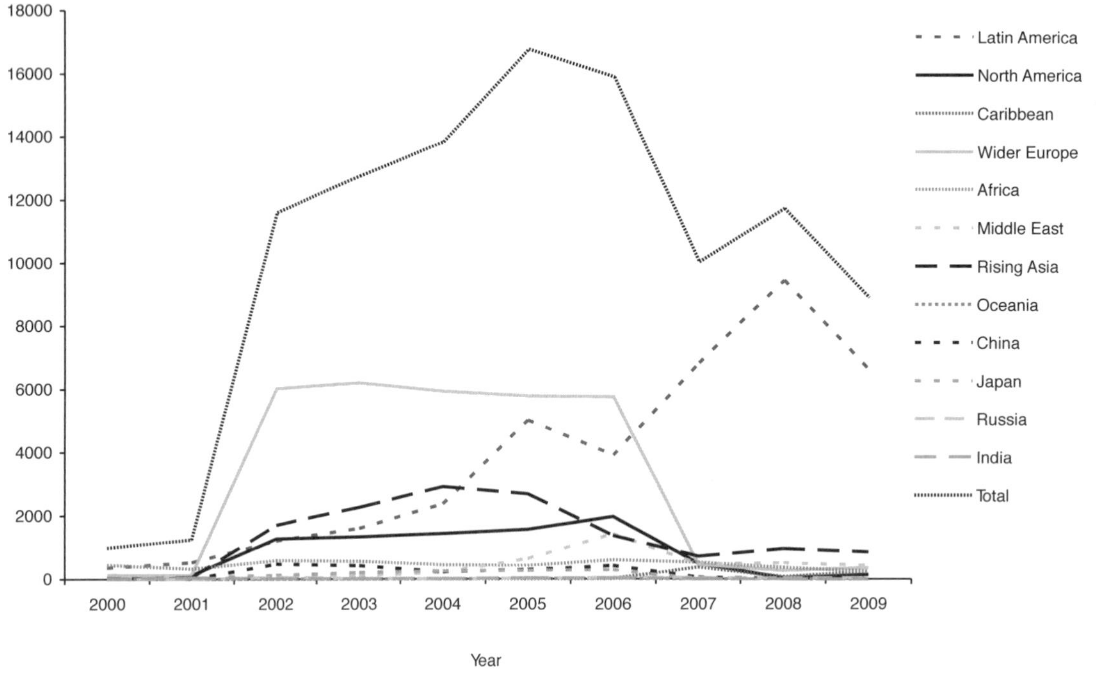

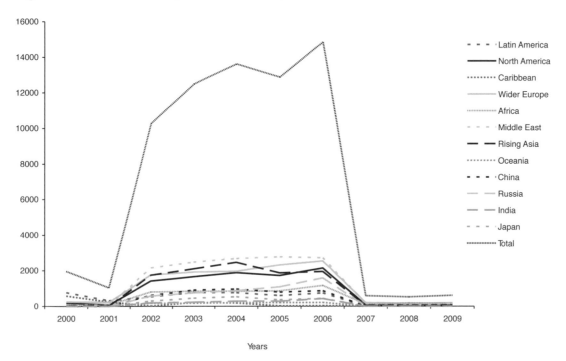

Source: Eurostat; author's calculations.[66]

Figure 4T. EU Biofuels Exports in 100 Tons, 2000–2009

Source: Eurostat; author's calculations.

While U.S. biofuel exports dropped 60% in the 2009 recession year, they had grown by 682% and 149% the previous two years. The United States surpassed the EU as a biofuels exporter in 2007 and now exports 15 times more biofuels (922,854 tons vs. 61,216 tons). This is a dramatic change, since in 2000 the U.S. exported only a fraction of amounts exported by the EU (6795 tons vs. 196,048 tons). U.S. ethanol exports benefit from domestic U.S. subsidies, and growing U.S. ethanol exports to Europe are causing some unease among European ethanol producers.

The European Union's approach to biofuels is beset with conflicting directives and objectives. On the one hand, the EU is requiring 20% of all energy to come from renewable sources and 10% of transportation fuel to come from biofuels by 2020. On the other hand, trade and non-trade barriers have prevented the EU from taking full advantage of such sources as Brazilian sugarcane-based ethanol, which produces less than half the carbon of gasoline and is far cheaper than homegrown alternatives.[67]

The EU continues to subsidize its farmers. EU government support to ethanol was $2.1 billion in 2009. It applies a Most-Favored-Nation tariff of up to €0.192 per liter—about €0.72 per gallon—on imported undenatured ethanol and 6.5% on imported ethanol-gasoline blends and biodiesel. Considering that the world price has been hovering around €0.40 per liter, EU tariffs roughly double the price of imported ethanol in the European Union.[68] As a comparison, the United States levies a 2.5% ad valorem tariff and a per unit tariff of $0.54 per gallon on ethanol. Most other biofuels producers also provide significant subsidies to domestic producers and impose tariffs on imported biofuels.

Additionally, the EU has imposed a series of anti-dumping tariffs on U.S. biofuels to counter the subsidies paid to U.S. biodiesel exporters. From March 2009 on, the EU levied an additional €68.6-198/ton tariff and a duty of €211.2-237/ton for U.S. biodiesel.[69]

The EU is also keen to ensure that the production of biofuels does not lead to a higher carbon footprint than traditional fossil fuels, for which biofuels are supposed to substitute. To ensure the carbon reduction of biofuels, the EU has also installed non-tariff measures, so-called "sustainability"standards. Such standards are intended either to limit the import of such biofuels as corn-based ethanol, which do not reduce greenhouse gases sufficiently; or the import of palm oil, the production of which leads to the destruction of carbon sinks in rain forest lands. The net result of these approaches has been to limit biofuels imports into the EU, particularly from Brazil.[70]

Environmental Goods

Over the last four years, trade in environmental goods has grown dynamically, increasing faster than total merchandise trade. Exports of environmental goods in the OECD area reached $370 billion in 2006, or 1% of OECD gross domestic product (GDP) and nearly 6% of OECD merchandise exports. In the same year, the BRICS + South Africa exported $43 billion in environmental goods, which accounted for almost 1% of their GDP and 2.7% of their total merchandise exports. BRIC exports of environmental goods have grown at an annual average rate of 35% over the past four years.

Table 4.1 Major Exporters of Environmental Goods* ($ billion)

Germany	80.6	Switzerland	8.0	India	2.4
United States	57.4	Austria	6.8	Norway	2.2
Japan	47.0	Spain	6.7	Portugal	1.6
China	29.3	Sweden	6.4	Ireland	1.5
Italy	27.5	Denmark	6.0	Australia	1.5
France	20.8	Brazil	5.3	Slovak Republic	1.2
United Kingdom	17.4	Czech Republic	5.1	Turkey	0.7
Mexico	12.9	Poland	4.4	Luxembourg	0.6
Korea	12.5	Hungary	4.2	New Zealand	0.4
Canada	11.6	South Africa	3.4	Greece	0.4
Netherlands	11.4	Finland	2.8	Iceland	0.0
Belgium	10.0	Russian Federation	2.7		

*Based on HS codes used by OECD to measure trade in "environmental goods." Definitions of "environmental goods" vary across countries, and will give different volumes of trade.
Data for 2006. Source: OECD, International Trade by Commodity Statistics database, April 2008.

Germany is the leading world exporter of environmental goods, considerably ahead of the United States, Japan and China. These four exporters together account for more than half of the total exports of environmental goods from OECD countries and the BRICS. These countries also benefit from the highest levels of public R&D budgets for environmental protection.

Nearly 60% of Germany's exports of environmental goods go to other EU member states. Other countries have more diverse export profiles and cover a wider spectrum of recipients. The United States exports mainly to Canada and Mexico (36%), to Asia (Japan, China, and Korea) and Europe (Germany, the United Kingdom and France). Most Japanese exports of environmental goods are directed to Asia (50% to China, Korea, Thailand and Singapore), then to the United States (almost 20%), followed by Germany, the United Kingdom and the Netherlands. The main recipients of China's exports are the United States, Japan (and other Asian countries such as Korea, India and Indonesia), and Germany (followed in Europe by the United Kingdom, Spain and Italy).[71]

The environmental goods exported vary from country to country, but in general more than one-quarter is comprised of equipment for wastewater treatment. This is also the fastest growing market segment, followed by air pollution control, waste management and environmental monitoring equipment.[72]

Chapter 5
People

The European Union has rich human resources; overall, its citizens are well-educated and its workforce well-trained. Yet the EU is aging, shrinking, and has become a net importer of labor. Many EU27 member states are confronted with stagnating or declining working age populations and the prospect of shrinking native labor forces.

Before World War I, Europe represented one-quarter of the world's population. By 2050, Europe is likely to account for just 6-7% of the world's population. Although 500 million live in the EU today—more than ever before—not a single EU country has replacement fertility. New EU member states have seen dramatic declines in fertility rates. India produces more babies in a week than Europe does in a year.[1]

According to medium-term population projections published by Eurostat, total population in the EU will continue to increase until 2035, when it will peak at 520 million. During the following period Eurostat expects a subsequent decline to 515 million in 2050, with all new and many old EU member states facing a marked decrease in native-born populations. The projection assumes continuing net gains from international migration on the order of 50 million people during the period 2008-2050. Without these mass net migration inflows, the EU's total population would already start to decline after 2010. By 2050 the number of people living in the EU27 would drop to 444 million.

The size of the working age population (age group 15-64) was 330 million in 2005. This group will start to shrink after 2020, reaching 328 million in 2025 and 294 million in 2050. Given that EU countries are grappling with millions unemployed, such a slowdown in the labor supply may not seem to be much of a problem. But these demographic shifts frame the possibilities for every EU member state, including their ability to sustain their welfare systems and service their public debt.

The workforce is also shifting from younger to older people at employable age. The number of younger Europeans entering the labor market (age group 15-24) is already shrinking in a number of EU member states and will decline in the EU as a whole over the next 45 years. In contrast, the age group 30-54 will continue to grow until 2020. The age group 55-65 is likely to grow until the year 2030 when the largest cohorts of the baby boom generation reach (today's) retirement age.

These trends are exacerbating mismatches in demand and supply of labor: despite relatively high numbers of unemployed, many EU member states report acute shortages in a variety of occupations. The situation is becoming so acute that a recent analysis[2] suggested that the skills shortage could cost the German economy some $27 billion a year, or 1% of GDP. And Germany is not alone.

These developments will have a profound impact on consumer trends, housing and care needs, social attitudes, defense capabilities and political priorities across the continent. The European Commission estimates that the impact of aging populations alone could reduce average potential output growth in Europe by nearly half by 2040, absent structural reforms. Voluntary population decline and demographic aging of this magnitude evoke few, if any, comparable historical parallels.[3]

Europe is the world's oldest region, on average about 10 years older than Latin America and Asia and 20 years older than Africa.[4] In 1950 40% of the EU25 population was under 25. By 2000 the figure had fallen to 30% and by 2025 it is expected to be less than a quarter. In 1950 less than 1 in every 10 Europeans was over 65. In 2000 the figure was around 1 in 6. By 2025 it will be well on the way to 1 in 4, and by 2050 1 in 3. Populations in eastern Europe are aging even faster than those in western Europe. Eurostat predicts that the population of the new member states will decline from 103.6 million in 2004 to under 100.6 million in 2015, with especially sharp drops in working age people.

The situation varies, of course, across the Union. Some countries, such as Poland, Romania, Germany and Bulgaria, face substantial projected declines, as do non-EU neighbors Russia and Ukraine. Others, such as the UK, France, Ireland, Sweden and the Netherlands, are expected to experience gains. In most cases, the projected population gains are likely to be the result of immigration.[5]

This phenomenon is not confined to Europe. Declining or stagnating fertility and increasing life expectancy are two nearly universal trends affecting the demographic future of all regions in the world.[6] Most parts of the world will witness demographic aging throughout the 21st century. Europe and Japan have already entered the stage of demographic stagnation. In China, demographic decrease will start around the year 2025. In contrast, however, populations in the EU's neighboring regions—parts of Wider Europe, Central Asia, the Middle East and North Africa will continue to grow significantly. These regions still have much higher fertility, and their populations are much younger, with a median age of 20 years or less, compared to 39 in today's Europe. The world's oldest region is bordered to its east and south by some of the world's youngest populations.

European countries can deal with their demographic challenge through a mix of policy approaches, including boosting productivity; raising the retirement age; promoting labor force participation rates of women; boosting labor force participation rates of migrants; and conducting active family policies that improve domestic fertility rates and eventually reverse current downward trends. Yet these strategies are unlikely to be sufficient without active economic migration policies. Unfortunately, even though the EU receives many immigrants, today's numbers—an estimated net inflow of some 1 million per year—are not enough to offset the trends. The EU would have to double current net immigration to halt its population decline, triple it to maintain the size of its current working-age population, and quintuple it to keep worker/elderly ratios at today's levels. To compensate fully for declining labor participation rates, the EU would have to add a net amount of 1.9 million labor migrants a year between 2005 and 2025, and 2.3 million a year between 2025 and 2050. In other words, between 2005 and 2050 the EU would need a net migration gain of 102 million people at working age (15-65).[7]

European governments and their electorates continue to display a profound ambivalence about immigration—even though most EU countries (including several new EU member states) are net immigration countries.[8] Anti-immigrant sentiment is reflected in public support for restrictive immigration and asylum policies, negative reporting on immigrants and asylum-seekers in the popular press, discrimination against resident ethnic minority groups, and racist or anti-immigrant harassment and violence. EU member states have also diverged in their approaches to integration of migrants. Some take a "multicultural" approach, implying tolerance of cultural and religious diversity, robust anti-discrimination legislation, and easy access to citizenship. Some prefer a "social citizenship" approach, offering immigrants a type of quasi-membership in the form of full social and economic rights (denizenship), but restricted access to full citizenship. Still others adopt the "republican" approach, which allows for easy access to citizenship on the condition that citizens will divest themselves of particular ethnic or religious traits in the public sphere.[9] All three approaches have come under fire in recent years.

Because labor migration is so politically sensitive, most governments turn first to measures intended to address domestic labor supply and demand. But as native European populations age and shrink, and as skills shortages become more acute, governments will increasingly be compelled to consider labor migration as a necessary vehicle to address their challenges, and to consider the effectiveness of their respective approaches to integration.[10]

Migration cannot solve all of Europe's demographic challenges. But flows of people—both within the EU and between the EU and other world regions—are critical to the EU's prosperity and its continuing competitiveness. The foreign-born are an important source of human capital for the EU. Since migrants are more mobile than native European workers, they "lubricate the wheels" of European economic change. Roughly 7% of non-EU citizens staying in the EU move homes each year, compared with 0.6% of EU citizens. Migrants are thus more than ten times more mobile than EU workers, and thus are the "oil in the machinery" for European labor markets.[11] Migrants are also consumers and thus provide work for others. They often take dangerous, dirty or low-paying jobs that native EU workers avoid. Most European economies are increasingly reliant on migrant workers to fill critical gaps in the IT sector, engineering, construction, agriculture and food processing, health care, teaching, catering and tourism, and domestic services.[12]

Skilled migrants are particularly significant for the EU. Empirical research on international migration underscores that the nature and extent of migration are important for the competitiveness of regions and countries. International flows of the highly skilled are the lifeblood of global innovation networks. Knowledge-intensive economies rely on highly qualified talent to compete and to sustain innovation. Study after study confirms that highly skilled migrants can strengthen national R&D systems; facilitate integration within international business networks; boost entrepreneurial activity; overcome skill shortages; and support regional innovation clusters ad high-tech activities.[13]

Human capital is perhaps the most crucial determinant of productivity and growth in Europe's knowledge-based economy. Highly skilled workers are vital to innovation and productivity, and thus to creating new jobs. A study on the impact of Germany's Green Card program for IT workers, for example, estimated that each high-skilled migrant created on average 2.5 new jobs.[14]

The United States offers an important comparison. Foreign-born individuals in the U.S. comprise only 12% of the population yet account for about 26% of U.S. Nobel prize recipients, 25% of the founders of venture-backed U.S. companies, 25% of new high-tech companies with more than $1 million in sales, and 24% of international patent applications from the United States.[15]

People on the Move: How Connected is the EU?

Lower transportation and communication costs have made it easier for people to move around the globe. Yet migrants account for only about 3% of world population and the world's workers. The global recession has further dampened migration, especially labor migration flows.[16] Across the OECD, permanent-type legal immigration of foreign nationals fell 6% in 2008 to about 4.4 million, the first decline after 5 years of sustained growth, and continued in 2009.[17]

Nonetheless, migration remains sizable and significant for sending and receiving countries alike. There are about 164 million migrants in the world. The largest number is in Europe—69.8 million, or about 42.6% of the total. More than half of the migrants coming to the EU in 2006 were from Wider Europe (28%) and Africa (27%), followed, in order, by Latin America (14%), North America (7%), and China (7%).

As a percentage of a region's population, however, the largest concentration is to be found in Oceania, followed by North America and then Europe. Those regions on balance attract migrants, while Latin America and Asia each lose an estimated 1 million people annually through emigration.[18]

Asian-born migrants are the largest contingent of the internationally mobile population, making up 35% of the world total. They are closely followed by European migrants, who make up 34% of highly educated individuals living outside their countries of birth, the vast majority from the EU25. They are followed by migrants from the Western Hemisphere, i.e. North America, Latin America and the Caribbean, who account for 23%. African migrants account for about 7% of the total.[19]

100 million of the overall total of 164 million migrants in the world are estimated to be are migrant workers, accounting for about 3% of the global labor force. One third of the world's migrant workers live in Europe.[20]

Most migrant workers are in their host countries legally. But the UN estimates there were roughly 20-30 million unauthorized migrants worldwide, comprising around 10-15% of the world's immigrant stock in 2004.[21]

Table 5.1. The World's Migrant Population

Geographic Area	Migrants (millions)	Percentage of Area Population
Europe	69.8	9.5
Asia	61.3	1.5
North America	50.0	14.2
Africa	19.3	1.9
Latin America	7.5	1.3
Oceania	6.0	16.8

Source: Source: United Nations, Trends in Migrant Stock: The 2008 Revision, data in digital form.

EU countries are linked to the rest of the world via five streams of human mobility. The first stems from the EU's commitment to the free flow of labor within its borders. The second involves both high- and low-skilled laborers and their families who come into the EU from outside its borders. The third includes students traveling to and from EU member states. The fourth involves EU citizens migrating to other world regions. The fifth involves refugees and asylum-seekers coming to the EU from other countries.[22]

Foreign Citizens in the EU

At the beginning of 2009, 31.9 million foreign citizens[23] lived in the European Union, of which 11.9 million were citizens of another EU member state. The remaining 20 million were citizens of countries outside the EU, in particular from Wider Europe (7.2 million), Africa (4.9 million), Asia (4.0 million) and North, South and Central America (3.3 million). Foreign citizens accounted for 6.4% of the total EU population. The proportion of foreign citizens ranged from 1% or less in Poland, Romania, Bulgaria and Slovakia to 44% in Luxembourg.

The largest numbers of foreign citizens were recorded in Germany (7.2 million), Spain (5.7 million), the United Kingdom (4 million), Italy (3.9 million) and France (3.7 million). More than 75% of the foreign citizens in the EU lived in these member states.

Among EU member states, Luxembourg has the highest percentage of foreign citizens in the population (44% of the total), followed by Latvia (18%), Cyprus and Estonia (both 16%), Spain (12%), Ireland (11%) and Austria (10%).

In 2009, 37% of the foreign citizens living in the EU were citizens of another EU member state. The largest groups were from Romania (2.0 million or 6% of the total number of foreign citizens in the EU), Poland (1.5 million or 5%), Italy (1.3 million or 4%) and Portugal (1.0 million or 3%). Among the citizens of countries outside the EU, the largest groups were from Turkey (2.4 million or 8% of the total number of foreign citizens in the EU), Morocco (1.8 million or 6%) and Albania (1.0 million or 3%). On average in 2009, foreign citizens living in the EU were significantly younger than the population of nationals (median age 34.3 years compared with 41.2 years). Among foreign citizens, those from countries outside the EU were younger than those from other EU member states (median age 33.0 years compared with 36.9 years). As of 2009, the unemployment rate of the foreign-born aged 15-24 reached 24% on average in the EU, compared to 20% in Canada and 15% in the U.S.[24]

Intra-EU Flows of People

Although the EU is committed to the free flow of labor within its borders, this process remains quite uneven. Some old member states have welcomed migrants from new EU member states, while others are delaying the phase-in of free movement of labor within the EU to their countries.[25] Over time, however, greater labor mobility will become EU reality—and even more countries are knocking on the EU door.

After the 2004 wave of EU enlargement the UK, Ireland and Sweden opened their labor markets to the new EU member states. More than a million central Europeans moved west in

Table 5.2. Foreign Citizens in the EU, 2009

	Population of foreign citizens, 2009 - Total foreign citizens		Citizens of another EU27 Member State		Citizens of countries outside the EU27	
	000s	% of total population	000s	% of total population	000s	% of total population
EU27*	31,860.3	6.4	11,944.2	2.4	19,916.2	4.0
Belgium**	971.4	9.1	659.4	6.2	312.0	2.9
Bulgaria	23.8	0.3	3.5	0.0	20.3	0.3
Czech Republic	407.5	3.9	145.8	1.4	261.7	2.5
Denmark	320.0	5.8	108.7	2.0	211.4	3.8
Germany	7,185.9	8.8	2,530.7	3.1	4,655.2	5.7
Estonia	214.4	16.0	9.6	0.7	204.8	15.3
Ireland	504.1	11.3	364.8	8.2	139.2	3.1
Greece	929.5	8.3	161.6	1.4	767.9	6.8
Spain	5,651.0	12.3	2,274.2	5.0	3,376.8	7.4
France	3,737.5	5.8	1,302.4	2.0	2,435.2	3.8
Italy	3,891.3	6.5	1,131.8	1.9	2,759.5	4.6
Cyprus	128.2	16.1	78.2	9.8	50.0	6.3
Latvia	404.0	17.9	9.4	0.4	394.6	17.5
Lithuania	41.5	1.2	2.5	0.1	39.0	1.2
Luxembourg	214.8	43.5	185.4	37.6	29.5	6.0
Hungary	186.4	1.9	109.8	1.1	76.6	0.8
Malta	18.1	4.4	8.2	2.0	9.9	2.4
Netherlands	637.1	3.9	290.4	1.8	346.7	2.1
Austria	864.4	10.3	317.0	3.8	547.4	6.6
Poland***	35.9	0.1	10.3	0.0	25.6	0.1
Portugal	443.1	4.2	84.7	0.8	358.4	3.4
Romania	31.4	0.1	6.0	0.0	25.3	0.1
Slovenia	70.6	3.5	4.2	0.2	66.4	3.3
Slovakia	52.5	1.0	32.7	0.6	19.8	0.4
Finland	142.3	2.7	51.9	1.0	90.4	1.7
Sweden	547.7	5.9	255.6	2.8	292.1	3.2
United Kingdom**	4,020.8	6.6	1,614.8	2.6	2,406.0	3.9
Iceland	24.4	7.6	19.4	6.1	5.0	1.6
Norway	302.9	6.3	165.4	3.4	137.6	2.9
Switzerland	1,669.7	21.7	1,033.6	13.4	636.1	8.3
Turkey	103.8	0.1	45.3	0.1	58.4	0.1

* Estimate
**Belgium and United Kingdom: 2008 data
***Provisional
Source: Eurostat.

search of work—the largest influx of immigrants in British, Irish or Swedish history. Yet by the end of 2008 almost half of the of the 1.4 million central European workers who had come to the United Kingdom between May 2004 and March 2009 had returned, as the British economy contracted and opportunities grew in Poland and other new member states. Likewise, after a seven-fold increase in the share of immigrants over the past decade, Spain's immigrant population suffered massive labor force dislocations in recession; flows from new EU member states Bulgaria and Romania fell by more than 60%. Thus, a good deal of recent intra-EU migration from new member states is both temporary and circular (involving several trips, sometimes on a seasonal basis); and characterized by uncertainty about the duration of stay.[26]

Table 5.3. EU Migrants To and From Other EU Countries

Country	Receiving	Sending	Net
Germany	2.5 million	692,000	+1.808 million
Spain	2.3 million	361,000	+1.939 million
UK	1.8 million	900,000	+900,000
France	1.3 million	483,000	+817,000
Belgium	659,000	203,000	+456,000
Italy	1.1 million	1.2 million	-100,000
Poland	10,000	925,000	-825,000
Portugal	85,000	911,000	-826,000
Romania	6,000	1.9 million	- 1.3 million

Note: 2009 or latest available. Source: "EU faces threat to migration principle," *Financial Times*, September 29, 2010, also based on data from Eurostat, ONS.

Evidence over the past three years indicates that this intra-EU migration wave has been a boon to sending and receiving countries alike. Yet despite all efforts at integration and at creating a single market since the early days of European integration, the EU remains a hodgepodge of national labor markets with different labor laws, labor market institutions, social security systems, tax laws, languages and formal and informal social networks. The low mobility rates between labor markets of EU member states are testimony to the lack of a single European labor market.[27] The battle between France and the European Union over Paris's treatment of Roma migrants is a particularly vivid example of the challenges to a foundational principle of the EU—the right of its 500 million citizens to live, work and study in any of the its 27 countries.

Flows of High- and Low-Skilled Labor

The second source of labor mobility involves both high- and low-skilled workers coming into the EU from outside its borders.[28] Europe used to be a net exporter of labor. Today it is a net importer. Nearly 9 million people, on a net basis, entered the EU15 between 2001 and 2005, adding 0.5% a year to the population, slightly greater than the U.S. rate of 0.4%.

Most enter and work legally in the EU. But the EU is also plagued by streams of illegal immigrants, who in recent years have been entering the EU by land, over the Greek-Turkish border, rather than by the traditional sea routes across the Mediterranean. According to the EU borders agency Frontex, 90% of illegal entries into the EU are made at the Greek-Turkish border—some 45,000 in the first half of 2010 alone. Frontex noted an eightfold rise in the second quarter from the first quarter of 2010 in the number of North Africans trying to get into the EU overland from Turkey. The heavy flow so overwhelmed local Greek authorities in October 2010 that the EU was forced to dispatch for the very first time an emergency team to secure the border.[29]

Migrants are an important source of labor in the European Union. Between 1995 and the eve of the financial crisis, migrants filled 1/3 to 2/3 of all new jobs in the EU.[30] In Italy, for example, immigrants represent one in 11 workers overall, but between 1997 and 2007 they accounted for two in three *new* Italian workers. In the United Kingdom, one in nine workers in 2007 was an immigrant, but seven in ten *new* workers were born abroad.[31] The share of immi-

Figure 5A. Migrants to the EU by Region of Origin, 2006

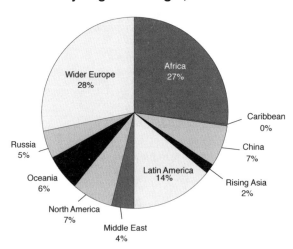

Sources: International Labor Organization; International Organization for Migration.

grants in the Spanish workforce grew eightfold from 1.1% in 1991 to 9.0% in 2007, before the recession hit home and migration slowed.[32]

Foreign-born professionals have become critical to most European economies. In most OECD countries for which data are available, the percentage of employed professionals is higher for the foreign-born than for the native-born. According to the European Labour Force Survey, 9.7% of the total tertiary-educated resident population in the EU is foreign-born, compared to 8.1% of the total resident population. The percentage of those with tertiary education in science and engineering is also higher among the foreign-born. Over 40% of new migrants into Belgium, Luxemburg, Sweden and Denmark; 35% of new migrants to France; and 30% of new migrants to the Netherlands between 1995 and 2005 had tertiary education. In many countries, migrant workers have higher qualification profiles than local-born workers.[33]

Table 5.4 Inflows of Migrants in EU 27 – by Macro Regions of Origin, 2006

1.	Wider Europe	175,660
2.	Africa	167,753
3.	Latin America	88,674
4.	North America	45,353
5.	China	43,253
6.	Oceania	38,186
7.	Russia	29,048
8.	Middle East	23,983
9.	Rising Asia	10,767
10.	Caribbean	3,036
	India	n.a.
	Japan	n.a.

Sources: International Labor Organization; International Organization for Migration.

Where do highly-skilled migrants live in the EU?

The share of the highly skilled among the resident population born outside the EU is 21.1%, while for intra-EU migrants it is 23.0%, and 17.9% for the native-born population. The foreign-born thus contribute more than proportionately to the share of highly skilled in the EU.

Highly-skilled migration flows vary considerably when it comes to individual EU member states. Around 94.2% of all highly skilled foreign-born in the EU live in old member states and only around 5.8% in new member states. There are also considerable differences when it comes to migrants from other EU countries and migrants born outside the EU. In Austria and Greece, for example, the share of the highly skilled among migrants born outside the EU (with 11.2% and 12.4% respectively) is clearly below the average for both the EU27 and the EU15, while the share of highly skilled migrants born in other EU countries is higher than average for Austria (24.5%) and only modestly below average for Greece (20.4%). By contrast, in France and the new member states the share of the highly skilled among those born in other EU countries is clearly below the average. On the other hand, the share of high-skilled migrants among those born outside the EU is relatively high in France. Former colonial or other historical ties play an important role: 34% of France's highly skilled migrants come from Africa, as do 79% of highly skilled migrants to Portugal.[34]

Italy is the only country with substantially lower shares of highly educated migrants born both outside and within the EU. The share of the highly skilled in the UK, Sweden, Luxemburg, Spain and Denmark is above average for persons born both in the EU as well as in third countries.[35]

Where do highly skilled migrants in the EU come from?

Non-EU countries are a more important source of human capital for most EU countries than migrants from within the EU. 6.6% of the total tertiary-educated resident population of the EU were born outside the EU. 2.5% were born in an EU country other than the one where they currently reside. Highly skilled non-EU-born migrants primarily come from other (non-EU) European countries (in particular Eastern Europe), South and Southeast Asia, South America, and Northern and Other Africa (with each of these groups contributing more than 0.8% to the total highly skilled population residing in the EU). Highly skilled intra-EU migrants, by contrast, are often migrants from one EU15 country to another EU15 country.

Recent migrants to the EU from Africa, Asia, and Latin America, however, are less well qualified than more established migrants from these regions, whereas recent migrants from within the EU are substantially more highly qualified than more established intra-EU migrants. The share of tertiary educated among non-EU-born residents living in the EU for less than 10 years is 20.5%, compared with 21.3% among the more established non-EU-born, due to a large influx of low-skilled seasonal and temporary workers. The share of tertiary educated among EU citizens living for less than 10 years in another EU member states is 25.9%, compared with 20.9% among intra-EU migrants resident for more than 10 years.[36]

Table 5.5. Share of EU Population Aged 15+ by Place of Birth, Duration of Stay, and Highest Completed Education, 2006/2007

Duration of stay	Skill level			Skill level		
	Low	Medium	High	Low	Medium	High
	duration of stay less than 10 years			duration of stay more than 10 years		
EU-born	25.4	48.7	25.9	42.6	36.5	20.9
of whom						
From EU-12 to EU-15	27.2	56.6	16.2	27.4	48.0	24.6
From EU-15 to EU-15	19.3	35.5	45.2	37.3	44.9	17.8
From EU-27 to EU-12	20.1	51.9	28.0	34.6	49.3	16.2
Non-EU-born	41.8	37.8	20.5	43.2	35.5	21.3
of whom						
Other Europe (including CEEC)	41.1	37.3	21.6	37.9	45.7	16.4
Turkey	64.1	29.5	(6.4)	66.2	27.4	6.5
North Africa	61.1	24.0	14.9	59.0	26.0	15.0
Other Africa	39.6	41.3	19.1	37.5	33.4	29.1
South & Central America						
Caribbean	39.7	40.7	19.6	35.3	39.8	24.8
East Asia	35.4	36.7	27.9	41.2	28.8	30.0
Near and Middle East	34.3	39.6	26.1	26.1	39.7	34.2
South and Southeast Asia	36.4	42.1	21.5	38.1	37.7	24.2
North America, Australia						
and Oceania (including other)	8.8	47.0	44.2	20.6	39.8	39.5
No answer	47.9	30.0	22.1	53.5	24.5	22.0
South and Southeast Asia	36.4	42.1	21.5	38.1	37.7	24.2
Australia and Oceania	10.2	52.0	37.9	22.5	47.0	30.5
Other	29.5	24.7	45.9	49.7	23.3	27.1
No answer	38.4	27.4	34.2	55.3	26.0	18.7

Notes: Base population aged 15+, excluding Germany and Ireland, excluding unknown highest completed education, excluding unknown duration of stay (see section 2 for details of data construction). Low-skilled = ISCED 0-2, medium-skilled = ISCED 3,4, high-skilled = ISCED 5,6. CEEC = other non EU central and eastern European countries. EEA = European Economic Area, EU-12 countries that joined the EU in 2004 and 2007, EU-15 = EU Member States before 2004, averages 2006-2007, values in brackets have a low reliability. - = data provides too few observations to be reported.
Source: EU LFS

How does the EU compare to other OECD countries ?

Overall, EU countries receive a lower share of highly skilled migrants than non-EU countries in the OECD, although they have made up some ground over the past decade due to changing immigration policies by a number of EU member states. The situation varies country by country. Ireland and the UK, for instance, receive more than 30% highly skilled migration. Luxembourg, Portugal, France and the UK all have positive net inflows of professional and technical workers and benefit from strong knowledge flows. Austria, Italy and Poland, in contrast, receive a very low share by international standards.[37]

Despite Europe's increasing intake, the United States remains the dominant destination country for highly skilled workers from developing countries. Already at the outset of the 1990s the U.S. had just over half of the world's highly skilled migrants from the developing world. The United States and Canada were the place of residence of nearly two-thirds (65%) of the world's tertiary educated foreign-born adults in 1990 and 2000. Traditional countries of immigration—the U.S., Canada, Australia and New Zealand—along with Sweden and Norway,

Table 5.6. Share of Highly-Skilled Foreign-Born among Total Foreign-Born Population in OECD Countries

European Union Country	Share	Non-EU OECD Country	Share
Ireland	41%	Canada	38%
UK	35%	Mexico	35%
Sweden	24%	New Zealand	31%
Denmark	24%	Norway	31%
Belgium	23%	Japan	30%
Luxembourg	22%	United States	26%
Spain	21%	Australia	26%
Hungary	20%	Switzerland	24%
Portugal	19%	Turkey	15%
Netherlands	19%		
Finland	19%		
France	18%	Average EU	20%
Greece	16%	Average non-EU	28%
Slovak Rep.	16%	Average major	
Germany	15%	non-EU*	30%
Czech Rep.	13%	United States	26%
Italy	12%		
Poland	12%		
Austria	11%		

Notes: Excluding individuals with unknown education level, gender or place of birth. *Major non-EU = Australia, Canada, New Zealand, United States. Source: Database on Immigrants in OECD Countries (DIOC); http://www.eurosfaire.prd.fr/7pc/doc/1268660562_european_competitiveness_report_2009_2.pdf

are the most successful countries relative to the size of their own populations in attracting highly skilled migrants.[38]

This trend is continuing with rapidly emerging countries. The U.S. remains the preferred country of residence for highly qualified foreign workers. This especially applies to BRIC migration. Except for Russians, the U.S. was the preferred location of highly educated BRIC workers, attracting 83% of highly qualified Chinese workers, 82% of Indians, and 50% of Brazilians. Among the BRICs, India was the major country of origin for highly qualified workers in the U.S., Japan, and the EU (and within the EU, mainly in the UK). On the basis of Eurostat labor surveys, BRIC skilled migrants employed in the EU grew at an annual average rate of 10% over the period 2000-2007 – mainly due to the increase in skilled migration to Spain from Brazil.

People are central to the movement of ideas and resources. They are agents of shared knowledge and of new economic and social links between the world's innovation hotspots. If the EU is going to continue to prosper as a knowledge-based economy, it must compete and win in the race for global talent. In this race, EU member states compete among themselves and with traditional countries of immigration such as the U.S., Canada and Australia. And as other global competitors move up the value chain, and as immigration and emigration barriers decrease, leading economies will vie with each other to attract and develop their shares of the world's ever more mobile talent pool. The capacity to build human capital and to attract and retain the most qualified workers is increasingly becoming the key factor for economic success. This race will determine which countries gain the most from the post-crisis recovery in global investment and services. The factors that influence the location decisions of global talent will take on ever greater significance. Europe must inspire confidence and be able to offer an attractive environment for businesses to thrive and attract and retain highly-skilled workers.

This is a competition that Europe until now has failed, particularly when it comes to attracting high-skilled migrants. Europe needs a large influx of skilled immigrants to help fill holes in the job market, maintain European living standards and the continent's economic well-being, and support its aging population. Yet Europe has become a magnet for the unskilled, receiving many poorly educated immigrants with relatively low levels of training without receiving the number of well educated, high skilled immigrants that it needs. Highly skilled foreign workers account for only 1.7% of all workers in the EU, compared with 9.9% in Australia, 7.3% in Canada and 3.5% in the United States.[39] 85% of unskilled labor goes to the EU and 5% to the U.S., whereas 55% of skilled labor goes to the U.S and only 5% to the EU.[40]

Indeed, there are serious concerns in many states about whether Europe is attractive enough to qualified workers compared with traditional immigration countries. North America and Oceania appear to be a more powerful magnets for high skilled workers, including European scientists and researchers. Europe's lack of appeal as a destination for highly skilled migrants, is a serious issue that policy makers must address.[41]

In addition, highly-skilled labor entering the EU is underutilized.[42] According to staff work done for the European Commission, the highly skilled foreign-born in the EU have a 9.3% lower probability of being employed, a 3% higher probability of being unemployed and a 5.4% higher probability of being inactive than comparable natives.

In sum, successful EU migration policy will have to be much more effective in making the EU and its member states a more attractive destination for qualified and highly motivated potential immigrants and their families. In Europe today only a small number of the newly arriving migrants are selected according to their skills and professional experience. And many ambitious immigrants are employed below their skill levels.[43] In this context, two challenges are of a pressing character: attracting qualified migrants and fostering skill upgrading in the EU. Evidence that EU countries have a lower share of highly qualified migrants than high-migration non-EU OECD economies and that the provision and quality of training varies widely in the EU signals the need for both the EU as a whole and for individual EU countries to do more.

Internationally mobile talent contributes to the creation and diffusion of knowledge, particularly tacit knowledge. To encourage this circulation of knowledge, there is much that governments can do: they can invest in public research to build absorptive capacity; facilitate the recognition of migrants' qualifications; open labor markets to foreign students for further training; ensure that the tax regime does not penalize mobile skilled workers; and focus on efforts to attract highly-skilled women migrants, who traditionally have encountered far greater difficulties with regard to immigration and integration.[44] The still-fragmented nature of EU labor markets, which make both the recognition of qualifications as well as the transparent portability of entitlements to social security systems difficult even for intra-EU migrants, is a significant impediment to attracting high-skilled migrants from abroad.

EU member states are in fact working more closely together to support legal migration and build cooperation with sending countries while tackling illegal migration. The EU's new Blue Card immigration system for highly-skilled migrants, which is based loosely on the U.S. Green Card, is a prominent example of the EU's new approach. The Blue Card, slated to go into effect in June 2011, offers a two-year renewable work permit throughout the EU to encourage highly skilled immigrants to take jobs in EU economic sectors that are suffering from skill shortages. It will not replace existing member state systems, but will provide an additional channel with a common procedure for legal migration. Although it includes a number of restrictions, and although some EU member states are opting out of the arrangement, the Blue Card appears to be a promising mechanism to make the EU more attractive to highly-skilled migrants.[45]

International Students

Over the past 15 years the number of university students studying in another country has more than doubled. Many stay on in their host country after their studies. Countries are increasingly viewing foreign students as an integral part of global knowledge flows and the leading edge of highly-skilled migration.[46]

The flow of university students to and from the EU is an important indicator of the EU's global knowledge links and its attractiveness to those who may become highly-skilled. In 2007, 2.5 million tertiary-level students were enrolled outside their country of citizenship in the OECD area, an increase of 59.3% since 2000 for an average annual growth rate of 6.9%. One out of every two tertiary-level students studying in another country went to only four coun-

Figure 5B. Distribution of Foreign Students in Tertiary Education, by Country of Destination, 2007

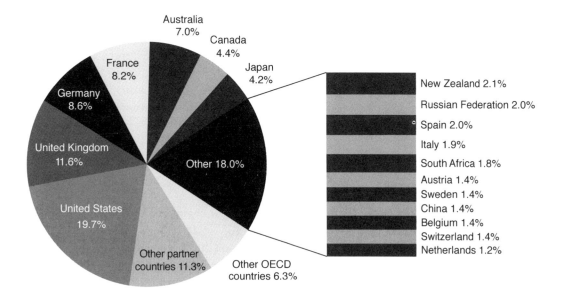

Source: OECD, Economic Globalization Indicators, 2010.

tries: the U.S. (19.7% of all foreign students worldwide); the UK (11.6%); Germany (8.6%); and France (8.2%). The U.S. share has decreased by 5% and the German share has fallen by about 1% since 2000, while those of Australia, France, Japan, New Zealand and South Africa have been growing. Russia hosts only 2% of the total, the same as Spain. China hosts 1.4% of the total—the same as Sweden or Belgium—and a lower share than at the beginning of the decade. India and Brazil host a negligible percentage of foreign tertiary-level students.[47]

Doctoral students are an important subset of tertiary-level student flows and indicator of the EU's knowledge flows. Previous research has shown that doctoral students contribute to the advancement of research in the host country during their studies and afterwards. Those who return home bring back new competences and connections with international research networks.

In absolute numbers, the United Kingdom (41,000) and France (28,000) hosted the largest foreign doctoral populations in EU member states, and ranked #2 and #3 in the world, behind the top destination, the United States (93,000).[48] The EU was the main destination of doctoral students from Russia, while the U.S. hosted the bulk of Indian, Chinese and Brazilian students. Among EU countries, the UK hosted the largest number of BRIC doctoral students, in particular from India and China.

The share of foreign students in total doctoral enrollments differs widely across EU member states. Noncitizens represent more than 40% of the doctoral population in the UK, 34.4% in France, and 20.5% in Belgium, but less than 6% in Italy and only about 3% in Poland.[49]

The OECD's 2010 annual report on international migration estimates that on average about three-quarters of international students return to their country of origin after completion of their studies, contributing to the international flow of ideas and potentially benefitting their home country due to knowledge gained abroad.

The report also calculates for the first time "stay rates" for students, converting their status from student to migrant, often facilitated by host country policies.[50] The estimated stay rate for international students studying within the OECD for all reasons is around 1 in 5 students on average. This rises to almost 1 in 3 in France and Germany. In fact, international students who stay on in France comprise almost 10% of total French immigration, the highest in the OECD. Elsewhere it ranges between less than 1% in Belgium and Austria to around 4% of total immigration in Germany.[51]

European Migration to Other World Regions

Although relatively small in comparison with the inflows of people coming to European shores, a few hundred thousand Europeans leave the EU each year for other world regions, particularly Oceania (90,174 in 2006, 33% of the total), North America (89,920 in 2006, 32% of the total) and Wider Europe (73,144 in 2006, 26% of the total). Former colonial or other historical ties play an important role. For instance, even though Australia is much closer to Asia and actively promotes policies to attract highly skilled migrants from that region, Europe is its most important source of highly skilled migrants. Outward migration is significant for some EU member states, such as Cyprus, Malta, Ireland and Portugal.[52]

Figure 5C. Migrants from the EU by Destination Region, 2006

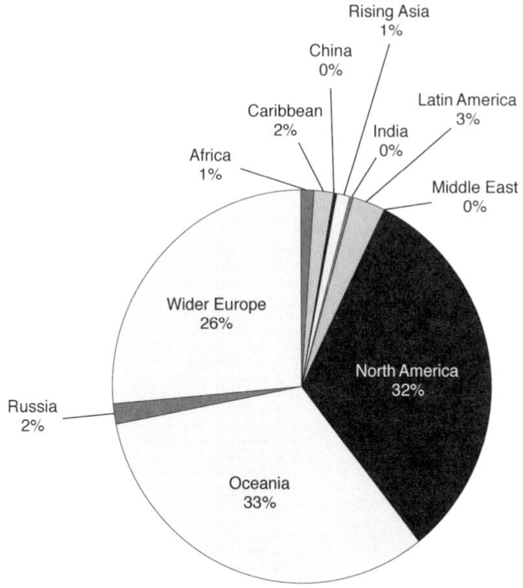

Sources: International Labor Organization; International Organization for Migration; OECD.

One of the most painful aspects of the Great Recession is the revival of emigration from countries such as Ireland. Until the 1990s Ireland traditionally lost many of its best and brightest who, facing few prospects at home, sought their fortune abroad. When the Celtic Tiger began to roar, however, the outflow dwindled. Now the Irish, particularly the young, are leaving their country again in numbers not seen in at least 20 years. In a country of 4.4 million people, the number of Irish nationals emigrating overseas jumped 50% in 2010 to nearly 28,000, and the number could double or triple in 2011. Estimates are that half of all Irish university graduates—about 150,000—will emigrate over the next five years.[53]

A number of EU countries have a notable share of highly educated migrants working abroad; the share of tertiary-educated emigrants as part of overall emigrants is substantial for

Table 5.7 Outflows of Nationals from EU 27 – by Macro Regions of Destination, 2006

Oceania	90,174
North America	89,920
Wider Europe	73,144
Latin America	7,472
Russia	5,163
Caribbean	4,940
Rising Asia	3,580
Africa	2,879
India	511
China	420
Middle East	291
Japan	n.a.

Sources: International Labor Organization; International Organization for Migration; OECD.

Table 5.8. EU Expatriates by Country of Origin

Country of birth	Emigrant population	Emigration rate(%)	Tertiary Education (%)
Austria	388,100	5.4	9.8
Belgium	357.000	4.0	5.8
Bulgaria	605,000	8.2	.....
Former Czechoslovakia	147,900	.....	.....
Czech Republic	244,100	.....	.....
Slovak Republic	362,300	.....	.....
Cyprus	147,000	18.8	24.8
Denmark	162,500	3.6	6.3
Finland	259,300	5.8	6.1
France	1,140,400	2.3	4.2
Germany	3,124,500	4.3	7.1
Greece	690,700	6.9	7.9
Hungary	334,300	3.8	8.4
Ireland	791,300	21.0	22.1
Italy	2,365,100	4.6	3.8
Luxembourg	31,900	8.3	.....
Malta	98,200	23.9	.....
Netherlands	583,400	4.3	6.2
Poland	2,118,400	6.4	12.3
Portugal	1,264,400	12.9	6.3
Romania	1,008,400	5.3	.....
Spain	759,700	2.1	2.4
Sweden	204,600	2.7	4.6
United Kingdom	3,247,500	6.4	10.3

Note: No separate data for Estonia, Latvia and Lithuania. No separate data for Slovenia; the emigrant population of the former Yugoslavia is 2,474,000.
Source: OECD.

Figure 5D. Refugees in the EU by Region of Origin, 2008

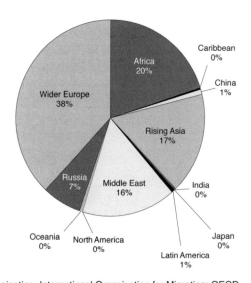

Sources: International Labor Organization; International Organization for Migration; OECD.

Table 5.9. Refugees in EU by Macro Region of Origin, 2008

Wider Europe	460,801
Africa	242,288
Rising Asia	200,388
Middle East	195,477
Russia	81,268
China	8,965
Latin America	7,652
Oceania	5,964
Caribbean	4,977
India	3,118
North America	596
Japan	160

Sources: International Labor Organization; International Organization for Migration; OECD.

Cyprus (24.8%), Ireland (22.1%), Poland (12.3%) and the UK (10.3). Some member states have instituted efforts to attract such talent back to their home country. Those who return home could accelerate the creation and strengthening of local capabilities—something that has been characterized as "brain circulation" rather than "brain drain" or "brain gain," although there is relatively little empirical research available on the results of such efforts.[54]

Refugees and Asylum-Seekers

The EU took in 1,211,635 refugees from other world regions in 2009, compared with 448,252 for North America and only 1,901 in Japan. The EU accounted for 16% of worldwide refugees at the end of 2009. More than half the refugees coming into the EU are from Wider Europe and Africa. Rising Asia and the Middle East account for another 35%. Europe took in 2½ times as many refugees from Rising Asia as did North America and more than 100 times as many as did Japan. The EU took in over 10 times more refugees than North America from the Middle East, 8 times as many from Wider Europe and Russia and twice as many from Africa. North America took in 5 times more than the EU from the Caribbean, 7 times more from China, 5 times more from India and 8 times more from Latin America.

The EU took in 238,760 asylum-seekers from other world regions in 2009, compared with 72,218 for North America and 1,380 for Japan. Over the course of the past decade, EU member states took in 2.9 million asylum-seekers, compared with 761,177 for North America and 6,714 for Japan.[55]

Chapter 6
Ideas

Global competition is not based solely on tangible assets such as energy, labor and natural resources, but also on intangible assets such as knowledge, information and innovation. Innovation turns knowledge into added value and leads to new products and services. It is a key driver of improved living standards and has emerged as the key wealth-creating asset in most industrial economies.[1] Nobel laureate economist Joseph Stiglitz argues that of all the intercontinental connections engendered by globalization, "at the top of the list is globalization of knowledge, the free flow of ideas that has followed the lowering of communication costs and the closer integration of societies. The transfer of that knowledge, which globalization has facilitated, is likely to prove one of the strongest forces for growth."[2]

OECD research and McKinsey studies indicate that firms now invest as much in intangible assets related to innovation (R&D, software, skills, organizational know-how and branding) as they invest in traditional capital such as machinery, equipment and buildings.[3] Moreover, much multifactor productivity (MFP) growth—that is, the joint productivity of capital and labor—is linked to innovation and improvements in efficiency. Estimates suggest that investment in intangible assets and MFP growth accounted for between two-thirds and three-quarters of labor productivity growth in OECD countries such as Austria, Finland, Sweden, the UK and the U.S. between 1995 and 2006. Innovation was the main driver of growth. Differences in MFP account for much of the gap between advanced and emerging economies.[4]

Leading-edge industries in advanced economies—microelectronics, telecommunications, computer software, biology, nanotechnology—rely heavily on the production and use of advanced knowledge as a key source of their value-added. Yet knowledge is also critical to many traditional sectors of the economy as well. The knowledge component of the output of manufacturing goods is estimated to have risen from 20% in the 1950s to more than 75% today.[5] According to the 2010 Global Manufacturing Competitiveness Index, talent-driven innovation remains the top driver of manufacturing competitiveness across all global regions.[6] Workers in all of these industries increasingly need to understand, process and generate advanced knowledge.

Innovation is essential to Europe's ability to recover from the economic and financial crisis and to prosper in today's highly competitive and connected global economy. Since most EU countries are knowledge economies, a substantial portion of the goods they produce, the services they provide, and the jobs they generate are tied to their ability to provide their people with good education and skills, create and commercialize new knowledge, and to tap innovation and absorb knowledge generated elsewhere. Innovation has taken on even greater importance as Europe's native population ages and shrinks, since population growth cannot fuel economic growth in Europe. Growing concerns about the unsustainable use of natural resources by a globalizing world offer further incentive to consider innovative ways to generate greater economic growth at lower levels of resource consumption. Innovation can also address societal challenges and improve quality of life.[7]

Innovation traditionally has been understood primarily in terms of technology, research and development (R&D), or creation of new products. Those aspects of innovation remain important. But other types of innovation can be equally significant. Product innovation, for instance, often has to be supplemented with innovations in a company's business model or value network to prove successful (and sustainable, as competitors can often quickly copy others' product innovations). Services innovation is also important, as service industries account for at least 75% of most European economies. Knowledge-intensive service activities play an absolutely essential role by enabling innovation and productivity growth to spread from manufacturing to services more broadly. Organizational and process innovation can also be critical to enhanced productivity and growth.[8]

Innovation rarely occurs in isolation; it is a highly interactive process across a growing and diverse network of stakeholders, institutions and users.[9] As a consequence, deriving value from innovation increasingly depends on absorbing ideas as much as creating them. Workers are called to upgrade their skills continuously, firms are compelled to upgrade their knowledge base and to generate new products, services and ways of delivering them, and countries and regions are driven to provide a setting conducive to the generation and absorption of ideas, including through information, transportation and communications infrastructure; investments in education and training; measures to welcome and integrate high-skilled talent from abroad; and efforts to facilitate connections between universities, companies and public institutions. An open knowledge economy is the key to Europe's long-term competitiveness and well-being.

Knowledge creation is still much less internationalized than the production of goods. Yet innovation is increasingly cross-border and collaborative, driven by the digitization of the economy, shortened product life cycles and business cycles, rising costs of research activities, the internationalization of research and development networks, the development of open innovation, the emergence of new and important players,[10] and the need for firms to be close to both emerging and legacy markets. The growing significance of intangible assets, especially knowledge-building skills, requires companies to harness these assets from a variety of locations. It has prompted many companies to invest abroad to gain the extra slice of knowledge that could turn into an extra slice of profit.[11] Many companies have moved from in-house, intra-company innovation models to global, collaborative models based on partnerships with other firms, universities, research institutions and other stakeholders.[12]

A good deal of media reporting and political debate focuses on "footloose firms" relocating their production facilities to low-cost locales in developing countries. This is certainly one consideration when it comes to corporate investment decisions. But a single-minded focus on cost alone ignores what is often a more significant calculus in the minds of corporate executives: in an increasingly competitive world economy, a company's "knowledge edge" may be even more important than its labor costs. Not only might an extra slice of knowledge translate into an extra slice of profit, a company's "knowledge advantage" could ultimately be the most critical element in its success. And in today's world, a company's "knowledge edge" may come as easily from across the ocean as from across town or across the country.

International cooperation in research allows firms to stay abreast of developments and tap into a large base of ideas and technology. The innovation capability of a country depends to a significant extent on the degree of cooperation between its firms and their foreign partners.[13] For these reasons, "onshored" knowledge—and the competitive networks and jobs it creates—may be as significant for any particular company—and thus the country and metropolitan area in which it is located—as domestically-sourced investments.[14] Growing global connections have meant that the knowledge base of many advanced economies—and sub-regions within countries—is no longer simply locally rooted but positioned within broader regional and inter-continental knowledge networks.[15] The OECD, which has conducted extensive research into global competitiveness, concludes that "the critical issue for the emerging economic geography of the twenty-first century is the location and spatial distribution of knowledge-assets."[16]

How connected and competitive is the EU in the world of innovation and ideas? In this chapter we assess the EU's competitive position through various indicators, particularly the European Innovation Scoreboard and the Network Readiness Index. We also look at science and technology indicators; research and development (R&D); and research rankings. We then track flows of ideas and knowledge between the EU and other world regions in five ways; through research and development flows (R&D); research cooperation; technology balance of payments; patent invention across borders; co-authorship of scientific publications across borders; and the role of cities and sub-regions as competitive knowledge economies.

Innovation Performance

The European Innovation Scoreboard (EIS) provides a comparative assessment of the innovation performance of the member states of the European Union. According to the latest assessment conducted just before the economic crisis, member states fall into four country groups based on their innovation performance across 29 indicators.

The EIS ranks Denmark, Finland, Germany, Sweden and the UK as the EU's "Innovation Leaders," with innovation performance well above that the EU average. Of these countries, Germany and Finland were improving their performance fastest while Denmark and the UK were stagnating. Austria, Belgium, Cyprus, Estonia, France, Ireland, Luxembourg, the Netherlands and Slovenia are classified as "Innovation Followers;" their innovation performance was below that of the Innovation leaders but close to or above that of the EU average. Within this group, Cyprus, Estonia and Slovenia improved strongly.

The Czech Republic, Greece, Hungary, Italy, Lithuania, Malta, Poland, Portugal, Slovakia and Spain are judged to be "Moderate Innovators," with innovation performance below the EU average. Bulgaria, Latvia and Romania are "Catching-up Countries," with innovation performance well below the EU average, although all three countries were rapidly closing their gap to the average performance level of the EU, and Bulgaria and Romania had been improving their performance the fastest of all member states. Subsequent data indicate that the economic crisis may have hurt some member states who previously had been showing good signs of progress.

EIS comparisons across the EU member states highlight three notable trends. First, there are only small differences in innovation between manufacturing and services.[17] Second, more than half of innovating firms involve users in their innovation activities. Compared to other innovation, firms involving users are more likely to introduce new products, processes or services, to perform R&D and to apply for patents. Third, internationalization and innovation performance are closely linked. This calls for more alignment between policies aimed at supporting innovation and those aimed at supporting firms' international activities.

A significant gap in persists in the EU's innovation performance relative to the United States and Japan. According to the EIS, the EU underperforms vis-a-vis the U.S. and Japan primarily in four areas: international patenting, public-private linkages, numbers of researchers, and business R&D expenditures.

The U.S. performs better than the EU in 11 indicators, while the EU performs better than the U.S. in six areas: S&E graduates, private credit, trademarks, technology balance of payments flows, medium-high and high-tech manufacturing employment, and knowledge-intensive services. While there is a clear performance gap in favor of the U.S., the U.S. innovation lead is declining, as its innovation performance has grown at an annual rate of 1.63% and that of the EU has grown at 3.17%. The EU outperforms the U.S. in growth performance in all indicators except business R&D expenditures, European Patent Office (EPO) patents, technology balance of payments flows and patents under the Patent Cooperation Treaty (PCT).[18] The EU is closing the performance gap with the U.S. in tertiary education, researchers, public R&D expenditures, venture capital, broadband subscribers, business R&D expenditures, public-private co-publications, knowledge-intensive services employment and medium-high and high-tech manufacturing exports. The EU is increasing its lead in S&E graduates, private credit, trademarks, medium-high and high-tech manufacturing employment and knowledge-intensive services exports. The U.S. is slightly improving its lead in EPO patents and PCT patents.

Japan is performing better than the EU in 12 indicators, while the EU performs better and was increasing its lead over Japan in 5 indicators: private credit, trademarks, technology balance of payments flows, knowledge-intensive services employment and knowledge-intensive services exports. The Japanese innovation lead is also decreasing, as its innovation performance has grown at 1.16% while that of the EU has grown at 3.17%. The EU outperforms Japan in growth performance in all of the indicators except business R&D expenditures and PCT patents. The EU is closing the performance gap with Japan in S&E graduates, tertiary education, researchers, public R&D expenditures, broadband subscribers, public-private co-publications, EPO patents and medium-high and high-tech manufacturing exports. Japan is improving its lead in business R&D expenditures and PCT patents.

The EU has a strong lead in innovation performance compared to each of the BRIC countries. A more detailed look at each of the BRICs, however, reveals considerable differences in relative EU strengths, weaknesses, and performance trends.

The EU's performance lead over Brazil has remained stable over the last 5 years. The EU far outperforms Brazil in all indicators except ICT expenditures and knowledge-intensive services exports. Brazil's growth performance is almost double that of the EU, however, driven in particular by performance improvements in broadband, private credit and public-private co-publications.

The EU's performance lead over Russia has slightly improved, although its lead slightly decreased during the two most recent years. The EU outperforms Russia in all indicators except tertiary education and researchers. Russia is the only BRIC country with a worse growth performance than the EU, in particular due to a sharp decline in high-tech exports. Russian performance in private credit and broadband, however, has improved much faster than that of the EU.

The EU outperforms China in all indicators except ICT expenditures and high-tech exports. The gap favoring the EU is small for private credit, but relatively large for researchers, broadband, public-private co-publications and technology balance of payments flows. Yet China's growth performance is almost 5 times higher than that of the EU and it has greatly narrowed its performance gap. China's growth is driven in particular by performance improvements in broadband, patents, trademarks and knowledge-intensive services exports. If one extrapolates China's rate of progress over the past five years, China could close the performance gap with the EU within 10 years.

India is catching up to the EU, but not in a significant way. The EU far outperforms India in all sectors except ICT expenditures and knowledge-intensive services exports. But India's growth performance is more than 5 times higher than that of the EU, driven in particular by performance improvements in broadband.

The EU must continue exploring ways to turn the strong growth performance of these BRIC countries into growth opportunities for its member states.

The European Innovation Scoreboard underscores the strong diversity that exists in regional innovation performance across the EU. All major EU countries have diverse levels of performance and relative strengths among their regions. The most heterogeneous countries are Spain, Italy and the Czech Republic, where innovation performance varies from low to medium-high.[19]

The most innovative regions are typically in the most innovative countries. Nearly all "high innovator" regions are in countries identified by the EIS as "Innovation Leaders." Similarly, all "low innovator" regions are located in countries that register below average performance. However, some regions outperform their country level. Noord-Brabant in the Netherlands, for instance, is a high innovating region located in an "Innovation Follower" country. Medium-high innovating regions in "Moderate Innovator" countries include Praha in the Czech Republic; Pais Vasco, Comunidad Foral de Navarra, Comunidad de Madrid and Cataluña in Spain; and Lombardia and Emilia-Romagna in Italy. Bucharest, Romania is a medium-low innovating region in a "Catching-up Country."[20]

Network Readiness

A second measure of relevance to the EU is Network Readiness—essentially the capacity to make use of ideas, innovation and information. Throughout this study we have underscored the importance of the EU's economically relevant connections and its ability and propensity to make use of its network capital in a globalizing world. The Network Readiness Index is one measure of the most networked economies in the world. The capacity to adopt and pioneer new technologies—among them ICT—has proven to be key for developed economies to maintain their competitive edge and support their growth potential in the long term, as well as for middle-income and developing countries to ease structural transformations in their economies and societies, increase efficiency, and leapfrog to higher development stages. ICT is crucial in promoting economic sustainability. The same is true for social and environmental sustainability: ICT has a major responsibility and role to play in this arena, both as an industry in itself and as an enabling infrastructure. More and more governments across the globe have recognized the revolutionary power of ICT as a driver of sustainable economic growth and an enabler of better living conditions for their citizens. They have increasingly put ICT in a prominent position in their general competitiveness strategies and national agendas. Given that the EIS ranked the EU behind not only the U.S. and Japan, but also China, India and Brazil in terms of ICT expenditures, the Network Readiness Index offers a closer look.

Overall Europe competes well, although the Index underscores the great diversity within the EU. 9 EU countries rank among the top 20, and Switzerland, Norway and Iceland are also in that group, together with the U.S. and Canada, Singapore, Hong Kong, Taiwan, Korea, Australia and New Zealand. Denmark, Finland, Germany, Sweden and the UK rank as both the most networked countries and as the innovation leaders on the Innovation Scoreboard.

The Nordic countries keep leveraging ICT to the fullest in their national competitiveness strategies, building on a number of enabling common factors, including an ICT-conducive market, regulatory, and infrastructure environment; a consistent focus on education as a key competitiveness lever, which resulted in top-class educational and research systems; a strong culture for innovation both at the private and public levels; and, last but not least, the central role given to ICT in the government's agenda, as an enabler of efficiency and sustained growth, coupled with a constant effort to promote ICT diffusion. As a result of the above, Nordic countries can boast extremely high ICT penetration rates and sophisticated businesses successfully competing in international markets with their high-tech and innovative products. These strengths represent solid foundations for these countries' continued competitiveness.

The EU15 economies present a more mixed picture, exhibiting a diverse set of ICT capabilities. While Sweden, Denmark, Finland, the Netherlands, Norway, Germany, the United Kingdom, Austria, France, Belgium and Ireland, among other countries, continue to be at the forefront of network readiness and are able to leverage ICT fully to enhance the competitiveness of their economies, Greece (56th) and, to a lesser extent, Italy (48th) trail behind because of a number of similar weaknesses. In particular, in both countries the market and regulatory environment does not seem to be very conducive to ICT and innovation development, with little priority given by the two governments to ICT usage and diffusion in their overall strategy (93rd and 120th for government readiness and 70th and 87th for government usage for Greece and Italy, respectively).

Although losing some ground since the previous year (down seven places), Estonia (25th) continues to lead the new EU member states with a solid network readiness performance, notwithstanding the economic downturn. Since regaining independence, Estonia has successfully leveraged ICT to transform itself into a very competitive and networked market economy in less than two decades, with top-class and widespread e-services for the benefit of its citizens.

Table 6.1. The Networked Readiness Index 2009–2010, EU Member States and Selected Countries

Country	Rank	Country	Rank	Country	Rank
Sweden	1	Malta	26	Colombia	60
Singapore	2	Malaysia	27	Brazil	61
Denmark	3	Israel	28	South Africa	62
Switzerland	4	Bahrain	29	Brunei Darussalam	63
United States	5	Qatar	30	Azerbaijan	64
Finland	6	Slovenia	31	Poland	65
Canada	7	Cyprus	32	Kazakhstan	68
Hong Kong	8	Portugal	33	Turkey	69
Netherlands	9	Spain	34	Egypt	70
Norway	10	Barbados	35	Bulgaria	71
Taiwan	11	Czech Rep.	36	Mexico	78
Iceland	12	China	37	Russian Federation	80
United Kingdom	13	Lithuania	41	Ukraine	82
Germany	14	India	43	Serbia	84
Korea, Rep.	15	Hungary	46	Pakistan	87
Australia	16	Thailand	47	Argentina	91
Luxembourg	17	Italy	48		
France	18	Costa Rica	49		
New Zealand	19	Oman	50		
Austria	20	Croatia	51		
Japan	21	Latvia	52		
Belgium	22	Vietnam	54		
United Arab Emirates	23	Slovak Rep.	55		
Ireland	24	Greece	56		
Estonia	25	Romania	59		

Source: World Economic Forum, The Global Information Technology Report 2009–2010, http://www.weforum.org/documents/GITR10/index.html.

This has been achieved thanks to a visionary leadership and a consistent focus on innovation and ICT penetration as key levers of the general competitiveness strategy. Slovenia (31st), the Czech Republic (36th), and, to a lesser extent, Lithuania (41st) follow closely, with satisfactory levels of networked readiness. Poland (65th) and Bulgaria (71st) remain the laggards in the region. In particular, Poland gained ground while Bulgaria appears to be losing ground, with significant flaws in the quality of its market (88th) and regulatory environment (104th), high ICT access costs (111th), and inadequate ICT prioritization and use by the government (98th and 61st for government readiness and usage, respectively). Poland suffers from similar weaknesses in its networked readiness landscape: although ICT usage has registered an important improvement (up 22 places), at 105th it remains disappointing, while government readiness is poorly assessed at 113th.

All other EU countries ranked among the top 50, except for Latvia (52nd), the Slovak Republic (55th), Greece (56th), and Romania (59th), all behind India (43rd); Poland (65th), behind Brazil (61st), South Africa (62nd) and Azerbaijan (64th); and Bulgaria (71st), behind Kazakhstan (68th).

In short, Europe is among the most networked regions in the world, but with some notable shortcomings, and less dynamic when compared to Asia, whose economies have progressed the most over the course of the past decade. China, Vietnam, India, Sri Lanka, Indonesia, Malaysia, and Thailand in particular have made major advances, contributing to the region's dynamism. It is important to note that Asia has many laggards as well, reflecting the diversity of this vast region.

No Latin American or Caribbean economy features in the top 20 and only four are to be found in the top 50. Most of the countries in sub-Saharan Africa trail behind the rest of the world in network readiness, with only Mauritius (53rd) and South Africa (62nd) featuring in the top half of the rankings. Indeed, although some countries improved, most of the region continues to appear in the bottom part of the rankings. By and large the Middle East continues to progress in network readiness, reflecting their increasing prioritization of ICT as a key tool for economic diversification, increased competitiveness, and modernization.

R&D Spending and R&D Connectedness

Another way to view the EU's competitive position in terms of innovation is to compare its R&D spending as a percentage of GDP with that of other major world regions.

As a percentage of GDP, most regions' spending on R&D has not moved greatly over the past ten years. Russia (average of 1.13% spending since 2000), India (0.76%), North America (1.70%), Latin America (0.34%) and Wider Europe (0.95%) spent about the same in 2000 as they did in 2008. There were, however, some exceptions to this within the regions.

Wider Europe's spending, for example, was very heterogeneous. While total spending dropped from a high of .095 % in 200 to 0.84 in 2007, these numbers were heavily distorted by the high R&D spending of Switzerland (average of 2.81 %) and Iceland (2.81). Without these two countries, the average spending would only be 0.66%. Some outliers were Ukraine and Montenegro, which with 1.0% and 1.1% have spent more than the average of this region. Montenegro's spending has risen from 0.79% in 2003 to 1.09% in 2007.

The Middle East is an even starker example of disparities within the region. As a whole the region spent an average of 1.32% of GDP on R&D. Without Israel, a country whose massive 4.49 % average spending dwarfs not only the region's, but also most other countries' spending as well, average R&D spending would only be around 0.38% of GDP.

Rising Asia's outlier was South Korea, which spent 3.21% of GDP on R&D in 2008 and posted an average spending of 2.66% since 2000. Singapore came in a close second, with 2.18% spent. Both countries raised their spending on R&D since 2000 from 2.29% to 3.21% and 1.88% to 2.51% respectively. The region's overall spending rose from 0.52% in 2000 to 1.02% in 2007. These numbers were, however, heavily inflated by Singapore and South Korea. Without these, R&D spending would only be around 0.24%.

Africa's spending rose from 0.28% in 2000 to 0.35% in 2007. The countries with the highest expenditures on R&D were Tunisia and South Africa, spending 0.72% and 0.86% respectively. While Tunisia's spending more than doubled between 2000 and 2007 (from 0.45 to 1.02), South Africa's spending increased from 0.73 to 0.93 between 2001 and 2007.

Figure 6A. R&D Spending as Percentage of GDP, 2000–2008

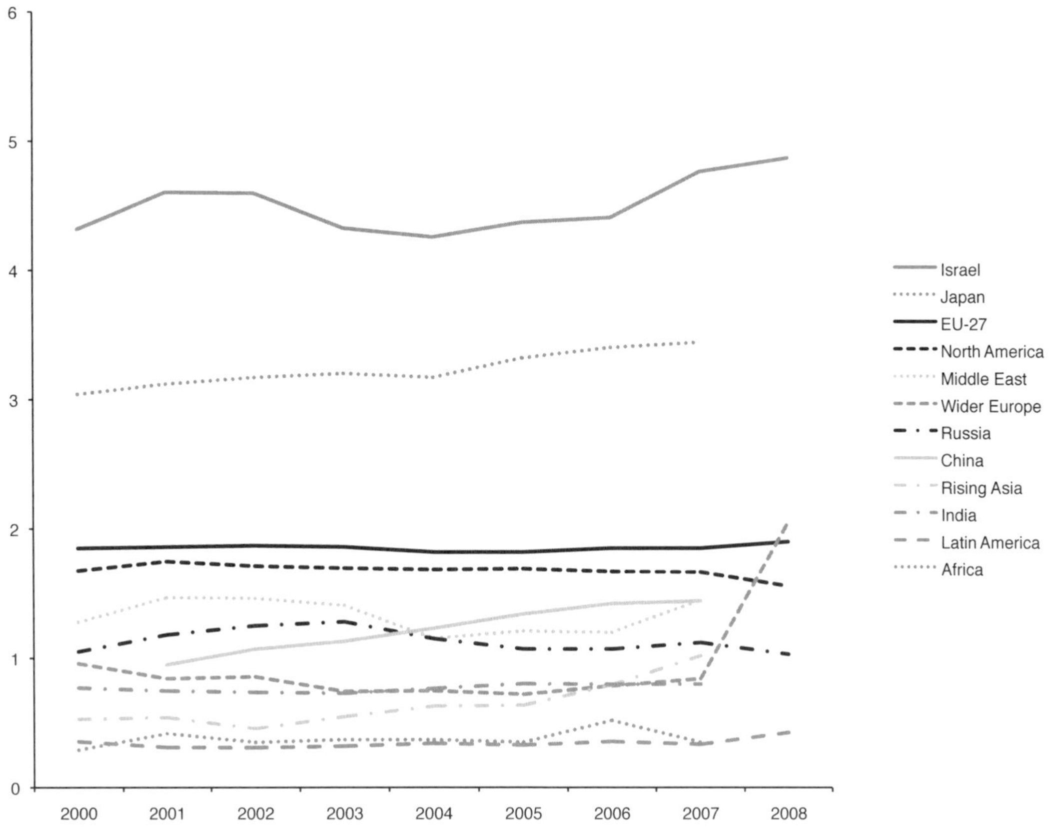

Source: Jayati Ghosh, Peter Havlik, Marcos P. Ribeiro, Waltraut Urban, "Models of BRICs' Economic Development and Challenges for EU Competitiveness," wiiw Research Report No. 359, December 2009 (Vienna: wiiw, 2009).

Japan spent an average of 3.23% on R&D since 2000 and has increased its spending from 3.04 in 2000 to 3.44 in 2007 while China's spending on R&D rose from 0.95% in 2001 to in 1.44% 2007.

Latin America's spending declined marginally from 0.35% of GDP in 2000 to 0.33% in 2007. With an average of just under 1%, Brazil spent most on R&D in this region.

Before the recession the EU had been slowly moving towards its 2020 goals of spending 3% of its GDP on R&D. While spending on GDP declined from 1.87% of GDP in 2002 to 1.82% in 2005, it remained stable in 2006 and 2007 at 1.85% and rose again to 1.9% in 2008—its highest level ever—before the recession took its toll on growth.

The clear goal behind the EU's Lisbon Strategy of 3% of GDP devoted to R&D was to catch up to U.S. levels in private R&D investments. But this clearly has not happened. The European Competitiveness Report 2010 concludes that "the EU does not invest enough in R&D, neither in absolute nor in relative terms, and a look at the sectoral distribution of R&D

Figure 6B. Gross Expenditures on R&D (GERD)

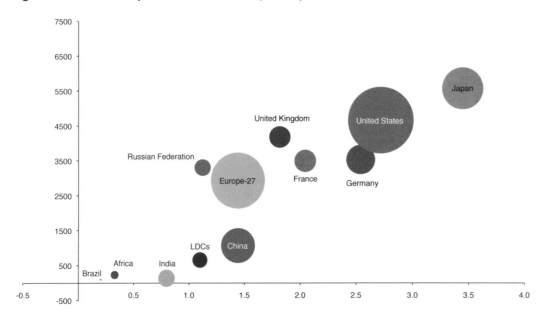

This figure pulls together three R&D indicators for 2007: the size of the dots represents the absolute size of Gross Expenditures on R&D (GERD), both public and private; the position on the horizontal axis represents the countries GERD/GDP intensity: the amount of productive resources of the country as measures through the amount of GDP devoted to R&D, both public and private; and the position on the vertical axis represents the alternative human capital R&D intensity measure: the number of researchers employed in the country as per thousands of the population. Source: UNESCO; Luc Soete, "The costs of a non-innovative Europe: the challenges ahead," September 21, 2010, available at http://ec.europa.eu/research/social-sciences/pdf/demeter-costs-non-innovative-europe_en.pdf.

Figure 6C. Business R&D Expenditures as a Percentage of GDP

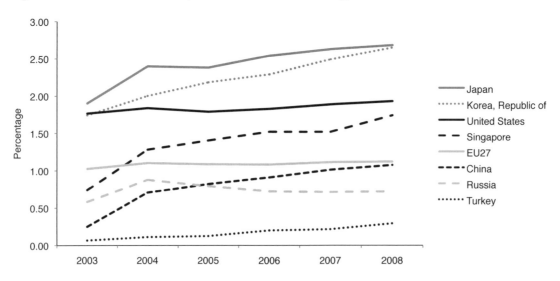

Source: OECD Main Science and Technology Indicators, 2009.

intensity in manufacturing clearly shows that it is the high-tech sectors that underperform compared to their American counterparts."[21] In addition, a review of the percentage of GDP devoted to private R&D investments by major actors over the past decade reveals not only that the EU failed utterly to catch up to the U.S., it has fallen even further behind South Korea, Singapore and Japan. Perhaps the most striking development is that China has almost caught up with the EU.

The EU still allocates a large share (32%) of its funds to preserving slow-growing, low-productivity industries such as agriculture and coal mining. Only 8% of the funds go to R&D and innovation. Europe spends substantially less on R&D than Japan and the U.S. and even lies below the OECD average. In 2008 the EU15 spent only 1.9% of GDP on private sector or government R&D, compared with around 2.7% in the U.S. Direct and indirect government funding of business R&D and tax incentives for R&D are lower in most European countries than in the U.S., Canada or South Korea. Reallocating one-third of the subsidies currently spent on agriculture to R&D would vault Europe's government-financed R&D spending as a percent of GDP to the U.S. level.

The 2010 EU Industrial R&D Investment Scoreboard presents information on the 1400 leading R&D companies in the world. It contains data drawn from the latest available companies' accounts, i.e. for fiscal year 2009.[22] Despite the global economic downturn, the world's R&D landscape has maintained its characteristic sector composition, with the U.S. dominating in high R&D intensive sectors and the EU in medium-high ones.

The most R&D intensive sectors account for 69% of total R&D by U.S. companies, 37.8% by Japanese companies and 34.9% for EU companies. EU companies account for 48% of all R&D in medium-high sectors, and for a larger share of low R&D intensive sectors compared to U.S. companies. Among the top 15 sectors, the R&D intensity of EU companies is larger than that of the U.S. and Japan in 6 sectors, including software and computers, services, technology, hardware & equipment, and automobiles and parts. Japanese companies show higher R&D intensity than the EU and the U.S. in 7 sectors, including pharmaceuticals & biotechnology, electronic and electrical equipment and chemicals. The R&D intensity of U.S. companies is higher than that of the EU and Japan in leisure goods and health care equipment and services.

The major R&D regions of the world consistently exhibit different characteristics. EU companies contribute 43.5% of total automotive R&D and 40.3% of R&D in chemicals. In these same sectors, Japanese companies contribute 36.3% and 34.4%, respectively. U.S. companies contribute a different mix: 43.2% of pharmaceuticals R&D; 48.0% of IT hardware R&D; and 74.6% of software & computer services R&D. Companies from all other countries contribute 34.1% to the electronic & electric equipment sector.

R&D is an important competitiveness factor for such leading-edge sectors as semiconductors, biotechnology and nanotechnology, which in turn have the potential to deliver hugely significant economic benefits across the entire economy, just as electricity, computers and mobile phones have done in the past. Over the next decade, annual growth rates of 30% in biotech products and 20% in nanomaterials are expected. EU companies lag behind U.S counterparts in these sectors in terms of growth, number and ranking of companies, even though

Figure 6D. R&D investment shares by sector group- US (€138bn)

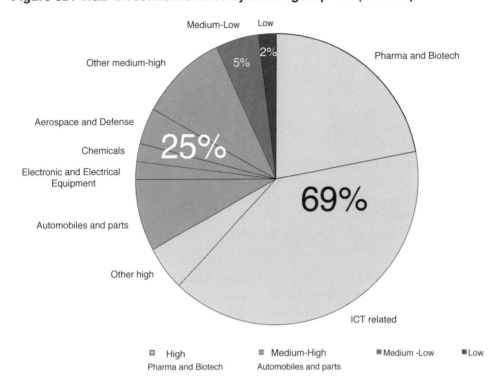

Source: The 2010 EU Industrial R&D Investment Scoreboard European Commission, JRC/DG RTD.

they outpace other regions. U.S. companies invested nearly five times more than EU companies in semiconductors, four times more in software and eight times more in biotechnology.[23]

The EU's aggregate corporate R&D intensity gap with the U.S. is due to various factors. First, EU high R&D intensity sectors are relatively much smaller than those of their U.S. counterparts. Second, the U.S. has more younger companies than the EU (54.4% vs. 17.8%). These younger U.S. firms show a higher R&D intensity than older U.S. firms (6.1% vs. 3.3%), and there are more of them engaged in leading-edge sectors of the economy than EU or Japanese firms. Younger companies based in the EU also tend to be less R&D intensive than their U.S. counterparts (4.4% vs. 11.8%); this difference alone accounts for over half of the EU-U.S. R&D intensity gap. Young firms also account for 38.6% of total U.S. R&D, whereas young firms account for only 6.2% of total EU R&D. Finally, older EU companies are also less R&D intensive than their U.S. counterparts (2.8% vs. 3.6%).

The EU compares more favorably, however, to Japan when it comes to young, innovative companies. Japan has almost no young firms among its top R&D companies (1.5%), and these young firms exhibit an even smaller R&D intensity than old ones (4.1% against 1.3%).

The outlook darkens again, however, when comparing EU R&D companies to those in other world regions; the share of young firms located in the other countries group is much

Figure 6E. R&D investment shares by sector group- EU (€123bn)

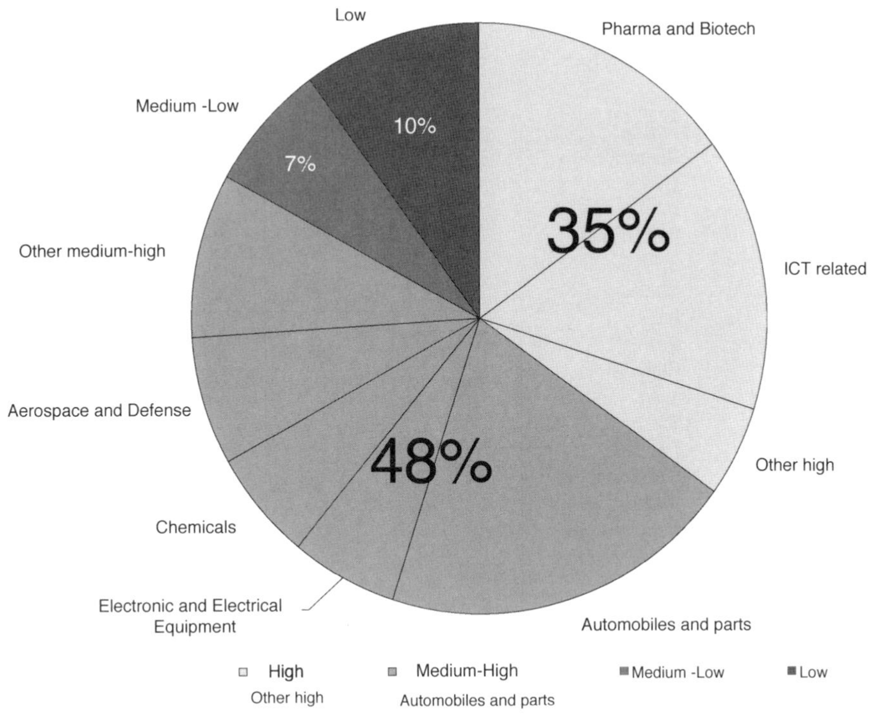

Source: The 2010 EU Industrial R&D Investment Scoreboard European Commission, JRC/DG RTD.

higher (50%) than in the EU. In addition, companies from Rising Asia and China have increased their share of high- and medium-high R&D intensive sectors. EU R&D companies will face growing competitive pressure from these new players in such medium-high R&D intensity sectors as automobiles and parts. South Korean and Japanese automotive companies have already proved themselves to be formidable competitors, and new companies from China and India are ready to follow suit.[24]

Research Rankings

An additional measure of research prowess comes from looking at the world's major research universities. Research universities are critical hubs in knowledge economies. The world's leading centers for university research are still overwhelmingly located in North America and Europe. The U.S. hosts the top four centers, but London (5th), Paris (7th), and Zurich (8th) all rank ahead of San Jose/Silicon Valley (9th). Cambridge, England is 10th, Munich 12th, Stockholm 15th, and Oxford 16th. Such clusters in North America and the EU still enjoy a commanding lead in research and knowledge-generation, indicating that efforts to upgrade research universities, attract top scientific talent, and build world-class research environments in China,

Table 6.2 Top 1400 R&D Companies in the World: Breakdown by Main World Regions

(% of total €422.2 billion R&D investments, 2009)

Country	% share
U.S.	**34.3**
EU	**30.6**
of which	
Germany	10.7
France	5.9
UK	4.5
Netherlands	2.3
Sweden	1.5
France	1.5
Italy	1.5
Denmark	0.8
Other EU	2.0
Japan	**22.0**
Other	**13.1**
of which	
Switzerland	4.4
South Korea	2.6
Taiwan	1.4
China	1.3
Canada	0.6
Other	2.8

Source: 2010 R&D Industrial Scoreboard.

India, the Middle East, and other parts of the world are likely to face significant uphill battles—provided that the EU and its member states continue to provide world-class support to their world-class research centers.[25]

The EU's Innovation Connections

R&D Flows

As companies search for new technological competences, lower research and development costs, and ways to adapt to local markets, many are collaborating with foreign partners and moving research activities abroad. This internationalization of research activities is an important driver of innovative firms and country competitiveness.[26]

Inward R&D into the European Union has become critical to Europe's competitive position. The share of foreign sources in gross domestic expenditure on R&D in overall EU15 GDP more than doubled from about 4% in 1981 to close to 9% in 2007, and for the UK the share climbed to 18%.[27]

Foreign sources are important funders of EU business-sector R&D. R&D funding from abroad represented about 10% of total EU business enterprise R&D in 2007, and more than 15% of total business R&D funding in Austria, the UK, the Slovak Republic, Hungary, and the Netherlands.[28]

Figure 6F. Funds from Abroad as Percentage of Business Enterprise R&D, 2007

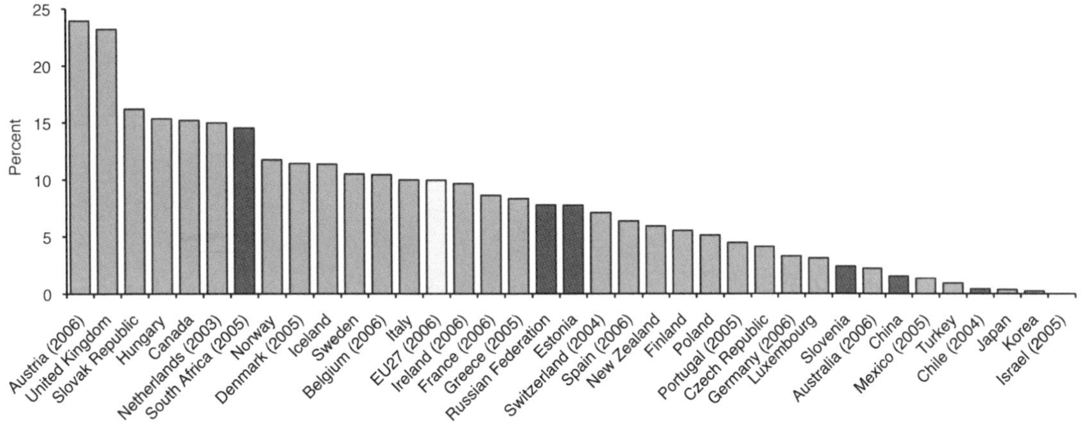

Source: OECD Economic Globalisation Indicators, 2010.

In most countries, the main providers of foreign funding are other businesses. Multinational firms play an important role in cross-border R&D investments. R&D budgets of the largest multinational companies are larger than the R&D investments of several countries. Aggregate spending by the world's top eight multinational groups in 2008 was larger than the R&D investments of all individual countries except the United States and Japan.[29]

Funding from other businesses comes largely from internal corporate transfers—from the parent company to its affiliates abroad. This form of funding accounted for over 85% of the total in Denmark, the Slovak Republic and Finland, and for more than 67% in Austria, Belgium, the Czech Republic, Norway and Sweden. However, in Slovenia, foreign R&D funding from non-affiliated enterprises accounted for more than 70% of all funds from abroad.[30]

Table 6.3. R&D Expenditure of Foreign Affiliates as a Percentage of R&D Expenditures of Enterprises

Country	Percent 2007	Percentage Change since 2001
Austria	53.3	n/a
Belgium	59.4	+2.3
Canada	35.4	+5.8
Czech Republic	54.7	+9.4
Finland	17.1	+2.9
France	19.6	- 1.9
Germany	26.2	+1.4
Hungary	66.7	+0.2
Ireland	72.4	+7.2
Italy	27.4	- 5.6
Japan	5.1	+1.7
Poland	30.7	+26.1
Slovak Republic	37.5	+18.5
Sweden	35.5	-5.2
UK	37.5	-5.3
U.S.	14.8	+1.7

Source: OECD, Activities of Foreign Affiliates database, May 2010

Between 1997 and 2007, R&D investments by foreign affiliates in the OECD area increased in value by $53 billion, taking account of purchasing power. Increases were observed in all major countries: the United States attracted $22.6 billion, Germany $8.9 billion, the United Kingdom $3.7 billion, Japan $5.1 billion, France $2.3 billion and Canada $1.9 billion. Except in Canada, increases in R&D investments by foreign affiliates were larger than the increases recorded by firms under national control. In Germany, Ireland and Sweden the R&D expenditure growth by foreign affiliates was more than 3 times that of domestic companies.[31]

The importance of foreign affiliates in national research and development (R&D) investments differs considerably across countries. In 2007, the share of foreign affiliates in business-sector R&D expenditure ranged from 5% in Japan to over 70% in Ireland. In Hungary, Belgium, the Czech Republic and Austria, which have many foreign multinationals, foreign affiliates were responsible for over half of the R&D investments.

In other countries, the contribution of foreign affiliates was more limited. This is due first to the lesser importance of foreign affiliates in such countries, but the presence of strong "indigenous" multinationals (as in Sweden) also helps explain this, since R&D activities are still often located close to the company headquarters.

In the majority of countries, foreign affiliates are characterized by higher R&D intensities than firms under national control, i.e. foreign affiliates devote a larger share of their turnover to R&D. This is because the activity of foreign affiliates in higher-technology industries is typically directly related to their proprietary knowledge. Often, foreign affiliates are concentrated in a few higher-technology sectors (*e.g.* motor vehicles in Japan and Sweden, chemicals and aerospace in France). These sectors have considerably increased their R&D spending, in contrast to firms under national control, which operate in all sectors of activity.[32]

In 2007, researchers at foreign affiliates accounted for more than half of all researchers in the manufacturing industry in Austria, the Slovak Republic, the Czech Republic, Portugal and Hungary, and for over 40% in Sweden and Estonia.[33] In fact, the number of researchers in manufacturing sector foreign affiliates was higher than in firms under national control in all countries except Finland, France, Estonia and Poland. In Germany, the number of R&D staff (and not just researchers) per thousand employees is twice as large in foreign affiliates as in national firms.[34]

The sectoral breakdown of the research and development (R&D) expenditure of foreign affiliates shows that in most countries the bulk of research is performed in the manufacturing sector. This is directly related to the fact that foreign affiliates are more active in manufacturing industries, although foreign affiliates' R&D in services accounted for half of total business-sector R&D in Portugal and Norway, and for 30% to 40% in Italy, Poland, Finland, and Canada. Foreign affiliates in the pharmaceutical industry make the largest contribution to national R&D investments, accounting for over 75% of national R&D investments in Sweden, Ireland, the Slovak Republic, the Czech Republic, Belgium and Austria. In larger countries, foreign affiliates' share is smaller and ranges between 20% and 30%. In the motor vehicles sector, foreign affiliates account for almost all R&D investments in some smaller countries (Hungary, the Czech Republic, Ireland and Belgium).[35]

Figure 6G. Geographic Origin of R&D Expenditure by Foreign-Controlled Affiliates, 1997 and 2007

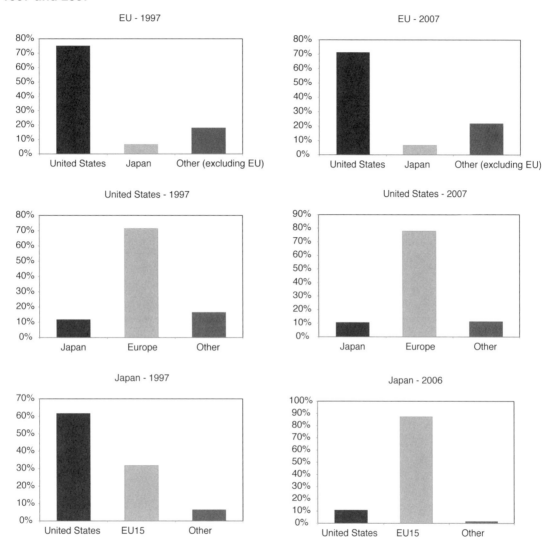

Source: OECD, Economic Globalisation Indicators, 2010.

Bilateral U.S.-EU flows in research, development and innovation are the most intense between any two international partners. For instance, the EU single attracted more than 60% of all U.S. overseas R&D expenditure between 2001 and 2007. R&D expenditure of U.S. subsidiaries in the BRICs was only one-tenth of the value of their expenditures in the EU (although it is growing fast). In 2007, U.S.-controlled affiliates accounted for 71% of all industrial R&D coming into the European Union. The United States continues to be the leading

Table 6.4. R&D Expenditure of Affiliates Abroad by Country of Destination, 2007

(Billions of current $ PPP)

Country of destination	Country of origin				
	United States	Japan	Germany	France	United Kingdom
United States	—	1,627	5,638	5,377	10,469
Japan	4,252	—	336	3,383	159
Germany	5,638	185	—	1,549	1,711
France	5,377	61	869	—	354
United Kingdom	10,469	249	528	1,037	—
Italy	359	45	275	202	225
Belgium	291	108	168	410	483
Finland	333	21	28	9	65
Norway	—	—	27	33	39
Sweden	314	34	119	60	949

Source: OECD Economic Globalisation Indicators, 2010.

R&D investor in the major European countries, including the United Kingdom (50%), Sweden (38%), Germany (36%) and France (34%).[36]

Outward R&D investment by EU firms is clearly focused on the United States. EU R&D investment in the U.S. in 2007 accounted for over three-quarters of aggregate foreign research and development (R&D) investment. The leading R&D investing country in the United States was the United Kingdom, with 26% of the R&D investment of foreign-controlled affiliates, followed by Switzerland (15%), Germany (14%), France (13%) and Japan (10%).[37]

During the last decade, Japan has attracted a large number of R&D investments. The European Union's share in Japan nearly tripled between 1997 and 2006, essentially at the expense of the United States. To a great extent, however, this trend reflects the bolstering of foreign R&D as a result of the association between Renault and Nissan.[38]

Research Cooperation

The complexity of scientific and technological innovation is leading innovators to partner to share costs, find complementary expertise, gain access to different technologies and knowledge quickly, and collaborate as part of "open" innovation networks.[39] Cross-border collaboration with foreign partners can range from a simple one-way transmission of information to highly interactive and formal arrangements. Collaboration with foreign customers and/or suppliers helps firms develop new products, processes or other innovations.[40]

EU countries mainly collaborate on innovation with other EU countries, but the dynamic of such cooperation varies widely. Less than 2% of Spanish firms collaborate with other European partners, whereas over 13% of firms in Finland, Luxembourg and Slovenia do so.

Collaboration with partners outside Europe is much less frequent, involving between 1% and 5% of firms in most European countries. The two big exceptions are the UK and Ireland, which cooperate more with the United States than with other EU partners. Innovating firms from the Nordic countries and some small European economies (Belgium, Luxembourg and

Slovenia) tend to collaborate more frequently with partners abroad than do firms from other continental EU member states.[41]

The OECD concludes that differences in international collaboration may be due to two factors: the overall innovation rate of a country, and the propensity of its firms to collaborate with foreign partners. The latter factor seems to explain most of the observed difference in European countries. For example, Spain and Slovenia have similar innovation rates but very different international collaboration rates (1.3% and 13.4%, respectively) owing to large differences in the propensity of innovative firms to engage in foreign collaboration.[42]

During 2004-2006, Japan and Korea had the least internationalized research, both in terms of domestic ownership of foreign inventions and foreign ownership of domestic inventions. In these two countries, most cross-border ownership involves a U.S. partner.

Countries such as Japan, the United States and the Netherlands seem to co-invent mostly within their borders. More than 70% of co-inventions were domestic in these three countries and Korea in 2005. Countries such as Turkey, the Slovak Republic and Canada seem more oriented toward international rather than national cooperation.

The degree of international cooperation differs significantly between small and large countries. On average, small and less developed economies engage more actively in international collaboration. This reflects their need to go beyond their small internal markets to tap better research infrastructure. Co-invention is particularly strong in Taiwan, Belgium and Switzerland, where over 40% of patents filed in the mid-2000s resulted from collaboration with at least one inventor from abroad.[43]

Among large countries, the degree of cooperation varies more. France, Germany, the United Kingdom and the United States reported international cooperation of between 11% and 24% in 2004-06. While European countries report a significant increase in international collaboration, Japan and Korea have the smallest shares of international co-invention, and less than in the mid-1990s. Brazil, China, Japan and Korea report a contraction of more than 30% in international co-invention.

In Canada, China, India, Israel, Korea, Mexico and Chinese Taipei the share of patents co-invented with the United States is at least twice as high as the share co-invented with EU countries.

Technology Balance of Payments[44]

The EU's knowledge connections to other world regions can also be assessed by its "technology balance of payments," which measures such international technology transfers as license fees, patents, purchases and royalties paid, know-how, research and technical assistance.[45] Unlike R&D expenditures, these are payments for production-ready technologies.

The European Union, which recorded a deficit in the technology balance of payments until 2001, became a net exporter of technology in 2008. This includes intra-EU flows, however, and so must be interpreted with care.

Figure 6H. Trends in Technology Flows as a Percentage of GDP by Geographical Area

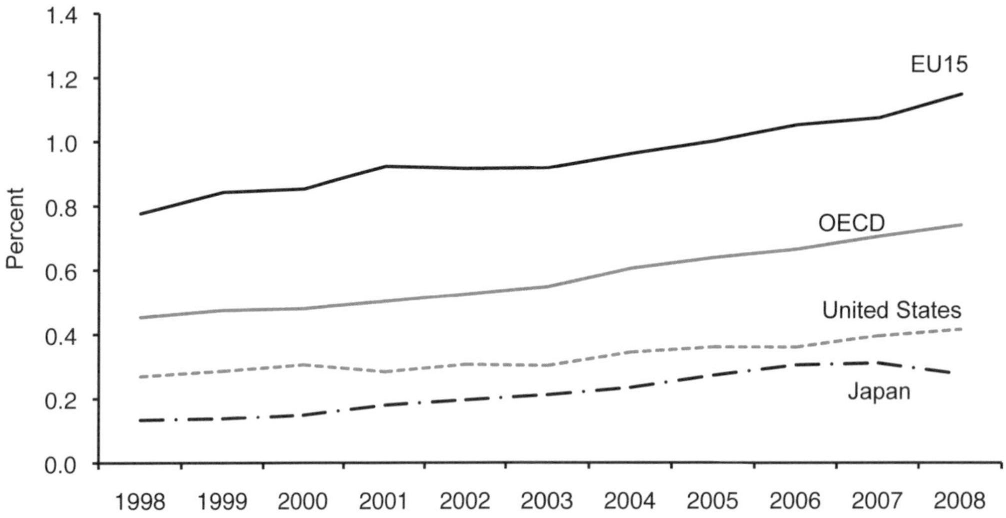

Source: OECD Economic Globalisation Indicators, 2010.

In 2008, EU member states displaying a large surplus on their technology balance of payments as a percentage of GDP were Sweden, Austria, the United Kingdom, Finland, Denmark, and the Netherlands. On the other hand, Hungary, Switzerland, Belgium and Luxembourg imported the most technology.

The magnitude of Ireland's technology flows is mainly due to the strong presence of foreign affiliates, particularly from the U.S. and the UK. The figures may also be affected by intra-firm transactions and transfer pricing.[46]

Technological development can be achieved either through a national R&D effort or the acquisition of foreign technology. Particularly in Greece, Hungary, Ireland, Poland and the Slovak Republic, expenditure on foreign technology (technological payments) is greater than expenditure for domestic business enterprise R&D.

Trade in royalties and license fees (RLF) is one component of the technology balance of payments. In 2006 the U.S. was both the main provider and a net RLF exporter. The EU, the second biggest RLF provider, was a net importer. However, with respect to the BRICs, the EU enjoyed growing surpluses, and accounted for the most RLF knowledge flows to the BRICs. Additionally, EU imports of RLF from BRIC countries have been declining, while EU exports to the BRICs have been increasing. Even though the BRICs represent a relatively small share in EU exports (4.5%), the EU has succeeded in attracting a higher proportion of the BRICs' growing demand for RLF. This has been largely due to the EU's success in attracting demand from China, which, among the BRIC countries, has been the major purchaser of EU RLF as well as the EU export destination with the highest growth rate.

Figure 6I. Technology Balance of Payments (receipts – payments) as a Percentage of GDP, 2008

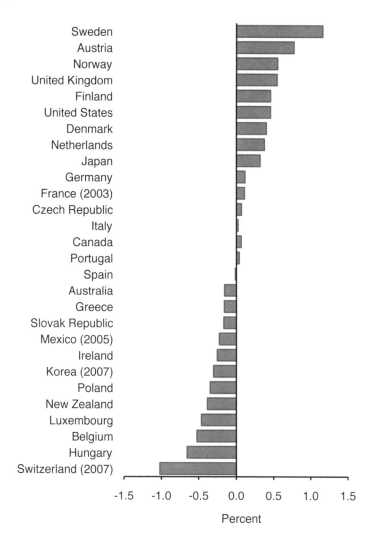

Table 6.5. Trade in Royalties and License Fees with the EU-25, 2006 ($ millions)

Partner	Exports 2006	Exports 2006 share	Exports growth rate (2003-2006)	Trade balance 2006
World	49,334	100%	12%	-16,922
EU-25	19,881	40%	10%	
BRICs	2,238	4.5%	31%	2,128
China	1,342	2.7%	33%	1,301
India	230	0.5%	23%	204
Russia	302	0.6%	29%	273

Source: Balance of Payment Statistics, *OECD Statistics on International Trade in Services 2008, Volume II*, Detailed Tables by Partner Country.

Patent Invention Across Borders

The information contained in patents makes it possible to trace the internationalization of technological activities and the circulation of knowledge among countries. Patents provide two complementary indicators of the EU's internationalization of research. The first is the share of patents filed by one country for an invention made in another country (ownership of inventions made abroad). The second is the share of inventions made in one country and patented by a foreign country (foreign ownership of domestic inventions).[47]

Europeanization of research activities is an important dynamic for many EU member states. The majority of patents owned by EU firms are also invented in the EU. Between 2004 and 2006, Luxembourg (87%) and Switzerland (63%) mainly had patents for inventions made in other countries, mainly by EU residents. In small EU countries such as Austria, Belgium, Hungary, Poland and Portugal, over 40% of inventions were filed by foreign patent applicants, mostly European companies.[48] Geographical and cultural proximity remain important factors in decisions to locate research activities abroad.

With almost 2500 foreign-owned patents, Germany and France form the most important country pair within the EU. Almost two-thirds of these patents are German and have a French applicant; the other third consists of French patents with a German applicant. The pair ranked second is Germany and the Netherlands; most of the foreign-owned patents are also German. Pair number three is comprised of Germany and Austria. Cross-border patents between old and new member states and among new member states are still rare. The exception is patenting activity between Slovakia and the Czech Republic. Germany is both the most important inventor country for the EU12 in absolute terms and also by far the most important applicant country for foreign-owned patents in the EU12. Other countries with growing relationships to the EU12 are Austria, Sweden, United Kingdom, France and Finland.[49]

EU patents originating outside the EU mostly come from the U.S., Switzerland, Canada, and Japan. When it comes to patent co-invention, the Southeast of England and the Southern and Eastern region of Ireland each share about 50% of their foreign co-inventions with regions in North America, and only about 40% with regions in Europe. Lisbon, Portugal and the western Netherlands share about 40% of their foreign co-inventions with regions in North America.[50] The dense research networks across the Atlantic are further underscored by the fact that California shared 64% of its foreign co-inventions with Europe and only 16% with other non-U.S. regions in North America in 2005. EU connections with other potential partners are far weaker: Istanbul, Turkey, the OECD metropolitan region registering the highest percentage of foreign co-patenting, shared 94% of its foreign co-inventions with North America, and only slightly more than 5% with regions in Europe. Less than 2% of Turkish firms collaboration on innovation with parties in the EU.

Internationalization of patents is still led primarily by the EU, the U.S. and Japan. The EU is the most important host country for U.S. overseas patents by far, as is the U.S. for the EU. The U.S. accounts for 60% of all overseas patents applied for by EU entities at the European Patent Office. This share is virtually unchanging over time. The U.S. is more important than the EU for Japanese overseas inventions. Other Asian countries such as China, India or Korea

Table 6.6. Regions with the Highest Number of Foreign Co-inventors by Partner Continent, 2005

	Europe	North America	Japan and Korea	Australia
Zapadne Slov.-SK	13	1	0	0
Oslo Og Aker.-NO	47	4	0	0
Alsace-FR	502	40	10	0
Wien-AT	123	18	1	2
Central Hung.-HU	56	7	3	0
Ostschweiz-CH	675	92	34	3
Attiki-GR	15	4	1	0
Lombardia-IT	124	47	0	1
Stockholm-SE	182	62	4	5
Baden-Wuertt.-DE	1080	350	73	11
Etela-Suomi-FI	153	46	14	2
Praha-CZ	19	8	0	0
Mazowieckie-PL	7	3	0	0
Vlaams Gewest-BE	419	179	14	3
Navarra-ES	17	8	0	0
California-US	606	152	141	54
West-Ned.-NL	242	132	12	1
Lisboa-PT	11	8	0	0
Kanto-JP	272	276	21	1
South East-UK	221	293	23	14
Sout. & Eas.-IR	39	56	1	5
Distrito Fed.-ME	6	10	0	1
Capital Reg.-KR	59	114	22	1
Ontario-CA	137	482	12	2
N. S. Wales.-AU	47	77	7	99
Istanbul-TR	1	15	0	0

Note: Data for Iceland, Denmark, and New Zealand are not available at the regional level. Source: OECD.

Figure 6J. Regional Average of PCT Patents with Co-inventor(s) by Location, 2005-07 (as a Percentage of all Patents)

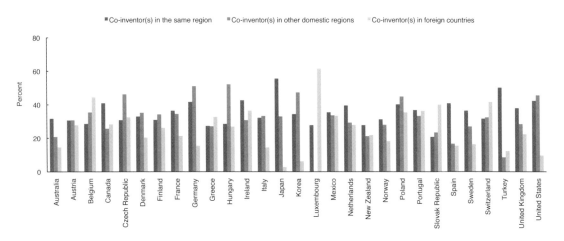

Source: OECD, REGPAT Database, January 2010.

play only a limited role as host countries of the Triad countries' overseas patents. In relative terms, the U.S. is more active than the EU as a patent partner in Asian countries.[51]

The BRIC share in total EU outward R&D and innovation is still small compared to the U.S., yet larger than that of Japan or Canada. The share of the BRICs in all patented inventions of the EU is just 1%, but rising fast, mainly because of activities in China. Russian, Indian and Brazilian shares remain marginal. Patents owned by BRICs but invented in the EU are still rare.[52] Despite this modest level of interaction, the European Competitiveness Report tentatively concludes that India and China tend to use more inventions in the United States, while Brazil and Russia are more oriented towards the EU. These differences, however, are marginal compared to the scale of the EU-U.S. relationship.

Scientific Publications

The EU accounted for slightly more than 25% of scientific publications in 2007, the highest share of any region, yet less than its share of about 28% in 1997. The United States accounted for about 18%, considerably lower than its 25% share in 1997. China boosted its share considerably over that ten-year span, registering a 12% share of scientific publications, compared with only about 2.5% in 1997. Japan's share has fallen from about 7% to 5%. India, Russia and Brazil each account for less than 3%.[53]

Co-authorship

Co-authorship of research publications provides a direct measure of collaboration in science. Research publications may have a single author or two or more co-authors. Co-authorship may involve researchers in the same institution, in the same country, or in two or more countries. These indicators help to understand how knowledge is created among researchers and how collaboration in science is changing. Collaboration among researchers in a single institution was the major form of collaborative research until the end of the 1990s. However, the percentage of single-institution co-authorship has been decreasing over the last two decades, and domestic co-authorship, i.e. collaboration by researchers of different institutions in the same country, is now the most common form of scientific collaboration.[54]

International co-authorship has been growing as fast as domestic co-authorship. In 2007, 21.9% of scientific articles involved international co-authorship—three times more than in 1985. Increases in domestic and international co-authorship point to the crucial role of interaction among researchers as a way to diversify their sources of knowledge. As a general trend, scientific knowledge production is shifting from individual to group, from single to multiple institutions, and from national to international. Researchers are increasingly networked across national and organization borders.

The degree of international collaboration varies among EU member states. Large countries tend to engage less in international collaboration. Large European countries (France, Germany and the United Kingdom) conduct more collaborative work than the United States and Asian countries. (data on natural and medical science and engineering).[55]

Figure 6K. Share of Internationally Co-authored Scientific Articles, 2007

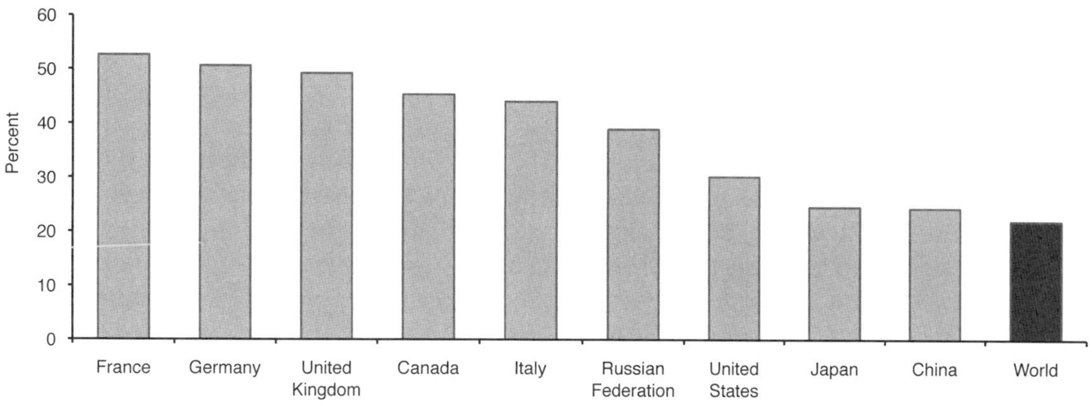

Source: OECD. As a percentage of total articles; Data are based on research articles in natural and medical sciences and engineering.

European Cities and Regions in the Global Knowledge Economy

Cities and micro-regions within countries are increasingly becoming key drivers of economic growth and competitiveness.[56] As the world's economy becomes more networked and "global," the "local" becomes more important. Globalization is simultaneously a tremendous force for geographic dispersion, because it can accelerate the diffusion of location and ownership of production across and among continents; and a powerful force for geographic concentration, because it can reward highly productive firms and workers who can capitalize on the knowledge, relationships and specialties that are often bunched spatially in key micro-regions or clusters.[57]

While the world may be getting "flatter" for routine types of activities, it actually appears to be becoming "spikier" for knowledge-intensive sectors and specialized industries the world. As many rather mundane factors become less important across regions in the global economy, those features that distinguish regions from one another become more important. In short, a company's locational footprint, and a metropolitan region's distinctive characteristics, are becoming more important, not less, for economic success in the global economy.[58] Ann Markusen has called this the paradox of "sticky places within slippery space."[59] Michael Porter explains it in this way:

> Anything that can be efficiently sourced from a distance has essentially been nullified as a competitive advantage in advanced economies. Information and relationships that can be accessed through fax and email are available to everyone. Although global sourcing mitigates disadvantages, it does not create advantages . . . paradoxically, the most enduring competitive advantages in a global economy seem to be local.[60]

Cluster strength is not only a significant indicator of competitiveness, it is also an important determinant of prosperity differences among European regions. Quantitative studies across many countries and regions offer clear evidence of a positive relationship between employment in strong clusters and economic performance. Data also suggests that companies in strong clusters receive more foreign direct investment, achieve higher levels of productivity, and reach higher levels of innovation. Evidence is also emerging that clusters are particularly strong when it comes to fostering entrepreneurship and the commercial use of knowledge, not just the creation of knowledge. More importantly, new studies also indicate that survival rates and firm growth are higher in strong clusters as well. Based on these findings, Ketels argues that cluster policies could be more effective than traditional entrepreneurship policies that have tended to create new companies but failed to trigger their growth into larger businesses.[61]

Metropolitan areas are increasingly where wealth is created and products and services are generated. Already, 75% of global added-value is produced in cities, and their inhabitants generate 9 out of 10 innovations.[62]

All of these factors indicate that a micro-region's competitiveness in the new global economy is likely to have as much to do with location *competence* as location *cost*. In the slippery space of the global economy, companies looking to invest could be looking beyond low costs to the ability of localities to offer a value-added environment.[63]

While advances in telecommunications and information technologies have made it possible for companies and individuals to source work far more widely, the geographic concentration of related resources and industries, in particular of knowledge-intensive activities, remains one of the most striking features of any nation or region, especially in the economies of Europe and the United States.

Even as multinational companies have dispersed their production to take advantage of low-cost production, they have also tended to concentrate their activities when it comes to both medium- and high-technology industries. The OECD reports that localized knowledge spillovers (due to inter-firm linkages, a versatile labor pool, strong innovation-related infrastructures, etc.) can be a tangible source of productivity gain for firms and can constitute a persuasive argument against relocation or in favor of investment.

The concentration of innovation-related assets is also striking. The ten leading regions in Europe in terms of GDP per capita account for more than one-third of all patents. Moreover, there is a very strong link between certain characteristics of regional economies and innovation. For example, the level of patenting activity is strongly correlated with GDP per capita, with students in higher education, and with employment in high-technology industries. There is also evidence of specialization across leading regions with respect to the types of patent and sectors of activity. The Eindhoven region in the southern Netherlands, for example, has attained a strong position in innovation in the semiconductor and materials engineering fields, and Stockholm, Sweden has done the same in the field of ICT innovation.[64]

The OECD has conducted extensive research into global competitiveness, and concludes that economic competitiveness should be analyzed in terms of stocks and investments in knowledge, with a firm focus on regions. And most knowledge-intensive investment activities remain heavily concentrated in micro-regions within the advanced industrialized countries, including the EU.[65] The ten leading regions in Europe in terms of GDP per capita, for instance, account for more than one-third of all patents.

Geographical proximity is becoming more important for knowledge-related activities, which are increasingly located in high agglomeration city-regions, while low-skill, routine, and low value-added activities are becoming spatially dispersed across the global economy.[66]

In general, European metro areas lag significantly behind their U.S. counterparts as competitive world knowledge regions, as well as in per capita R&D expenditures and labor productivity. U.S. cities, on the other hand, appear to be relatively less "connected" to other major world metropoles in terms of advanced producer services. This could perhaps reflect their continuing focus on the large domestic U.S. market; but it could also mean that in general many U.S. metropolitan areas are not making the kinds of international connections likely to be needed if they are to attract investment and be attractive "sticky places" in the slippery space of the global economy. The bottom line, however, is this: European cities must continually raise their game if they are to maintain their competitive positions in the 21st century.

The Most Competitive World Knowledge Regions

According to the 2008 World Knowledge Competitiveness Index, the U.S. metropolitan region of San Jose, California, the home of Silicon Valley, tops the rankings, due to its enormous investment in knowledge-intensive business development, investment in education and business R&D, high productivity and earnings. Four other U.S. cities follow. The top-ranked European city is Stockholm (6th), based on impressive rankings in business R&D spending, biotechnology and chemical sector employment, and higher education spending. The top twenty knowledge regions include 13 U.S. regions, 5 European regions, and 2 Japanese regions. Regions in Denmark, Finland, Sweden and the Netherlands all registered improvements, but London dropped 46 places to 102nd. And while European and Asian regions overall showed improvements, North American regions registered declines, including New York, Austin, Atlanta and Washington, DC.[67] Of the top 100 most competitive cities, 53 were from North America (50 from the U.S., 3 from Canada); 30 were from the EU; 9 from Japan; 4 from Wider Europe; 3 from Rising Asia; and Israel.

European Cities in the Global Information and Services Economy

Globalization and revolutionary advances in informational technology have changed the roles of cities and micro-regions in the international economy. At one level, such communities occupy a particular space at a specific place. Their physical location is an important determinant of their competitive position in the economy. At another level, however, such communities occupy a particular space within a network of interconnected places. Their competitive position can depend not only on their physical location, but the degree to which they are integral nodes in a broader web of flows of information and ideas. Saskia Sassen and Manuel Castells have identified global cities as critical nodes through which such "spaces of flows" are created and sustained.[68]

Table 6.7 World Knowledge Competitiveness Index 2008

Rank		Knowledge Competitiveness Index 2008	Rank 2005	Change in Rank 2005-08
1	San Jose-Sunnyvale-Santa Clara, US	248.3	1	0
2	Boston-Cambridge-Quincy, US	175.3	2	0
3	Hartford, US	175.1	4	1
4	Bridgeport-Stamford-Norwalk, US	174.7		
5	San Francisco-Oakland-Fremont, US	160.8	3	-2
6	Stockholm, Sweden	151.8	8	2
7	Seattle-Tacoma-Bellevue, US	151.3	5	-2
8	Providence-Fall River-Warwick, US	147.1		
9	Tokyo, Japan	147.0	22	13
10	San Diego-Carlsbad-San Marcos, US	146.1	7	-3
11	Los Angeles-Long Beach-Santa Ana, US	144.4	10	-1
12	Shiga, Japan	140.9	57	45
13	Grand Rapids, US	140.0	6	-7
14	Iceland	139.8		
15	Detroit-Warren-Livonia, US	138.1	15	0
16	West, Sweden	137.9	37	21
17	Oxnard-Thousand Oaks-Ventura, US	137.1		
18	Sacramento--Arden-Arcade--Roseville, US	133.6	11	-7
19	West, Netherlands	132.4	77	58
20	Pohjois-Suomi, Finland	132.1		
21	Minneapolis-St. Paul-Bloomington, US	131.7	13	-8
22	Portland-Vancouver-Beaverton, US	129.7	18	-4
23	Etela-Suomi, Finland	129.1	20	-3
24	Kanagawa, Japan	128.6	81	57
25	Durham, US	127.7		
26	Colorado Springs, US	124.4		
27	Singapore	123.1	78	51
28	Switzerland	122.5	44	16
29	Île de France, France	121.8	29	0
30	Toyama, Japan	120.5	80	50
31	Osaka, Japan	119.6	72	41
32	Riverside-San Bernardino-Ontario, US	119.3	16	-16
33	Philadelphia-Camden-Wilmington, US	117.7	17	-16
34	Luxembourg	116.9	58	24
35	New York-Northern New Jersey-Long Island, US	116.8	12	-23
36	Denmark	116.7	51	15
37	Tochigi, Japan	116.1	73	36
38	South, Sweden	115.2	46	8
39	Greensboro-High Point, US	113.5	40	1
40	Lansi-Suomi, Finland	112.5		
41	Washington-Arlington-Alexandria, US	112.4	23	-18
42	Austin-Round Rock, US	112.3	19	-23
43	Kyoto, Japan	111.9	96	53
44	Milwaukee-Waukesha-West Allis, US	111.2	24	-20
45	Denver-Aurora, US	110.7	14	-31
46	Chicago-Naperville-Joliet, US	109.4	28	-18
47	Brussels, Belgium	109.4	45	-2
48	Israel	109.3	86	38
49	Baltimore-Towson, US	108.9	27	-22
50	Rochester, US	108.8	9	-41
51	Shizuoka, Japan	106.8	71	20
52	Dallas-Fort Worth-Arlington, US	106.6	21	-31
53	Taiwan	106.5	99	46
54	Eastern, UK	106.1	62	8

Table 6.7. World Knowledge Competitiveness Index 2008 (continued)

Rank		Knowledge Competitiveness Index 2008	Rank 2005	Change in Rank 2005-08
55	Baden-Württemberg, Germany	106.0	54	-1
56	Aichi, Japan	105.6	75	19
57	Ostra Mellansverige, Sweden	105.3		
58	Phoenix-Mesa-Scottsdale, US	103.3	38	-20
59	Buffalo-Niagara Falls, US	102.8	25	-34
60	Virginia Beach-Norfolk-Newport News, US	102.5	48	-12
61	East Netherlands	102.1		
62	Cleveland-Elyria-Mentor, US	101.9	39	-23
63	Bayern, Germany	101.8	65	2
64	Indianapolis, US	101.7	32	-32
65	North, Netherlands	101.6	89	24
66	Raleigh-Cary, US	100.7	31	-35
67	Charlotte-Gastonia-Concord, US	100.7	41	-26
68	South, Netherlands	100.0	50	-18
69	Ulsan, Korea	100.0	113	44
70	Houston-Sugar Land-Baytown, US	99.9	26	-44
71	Richmond, US	99.9	33	-38
72	Pittsburgh, US	99.3	43	-29
73	Vlaams Gewest, Belgium	99.1	79	6
74	South East, UK	98.9	55	-19
75	Norway	98.6	52	-23
76	Ontario, Canada	98.5	66	-10
77	Hessen, Germany	97.9	67	-10
78	Columbus, US	96.0	30	-48
79	East, Austria	94.7	70	-9
80	Salt Lake City, US	94.3	34	-46
81	Akron, US	93.0		
82	Hamburg, Germany	92.4	76	-6
83	Quebec, Canada	92.2	85	2
84	Southern and Eastern, Ireland	91.2		
85	Alberta, Canada	91.0	98	13
86	Kansas City, US	90.0	42	-44
87	Centre-est, France	89.7	82	-5
88	San Antonio, US	89.4	47	-41
89	Cincinnati-Middletown, US	89.2	36	-53
90	Memphis, US	88.9	61	-29
91	St. Louis, US	88.8	49	-42
92	Nashville-Davidson--Murfreesboro, US	87.6	59	-33
93	Bremen, Germany	86.4	95	2
94	Louisville, US	86.1	53	-41
95	Atlanta-Sandy Springs-Marietta, US	85.9	35	-60
96	Lombardia, Italy	85.7	84	-12
97	West, Austria	85.2	90	-7
98	Tampa-St. Petersburg-Clearwater, US	85.1	64	-34
99	Victoria, Australia	82.9	88	-11
100	North West, Italy	82.6	101	1

Table 6.8. 20 Most Connected Cities in Advanced Producer Services, 2000 and 2008

2000			2008		
1	London	100.00	1	New York	100.00
2	New York	97.10	2	London	98.64
3	Hong Kong	73.08	3	Hong Kong	81.33
4	Tokyo	70.64	4	Paris	77.91
5	Paris	69.72	5	Singapore	74.15
6	Singapore	66.61	6	Tokyo	72.58
7	Chicago	61.18	7	Sydney	71.76
8	Milan	60.44	8	Shanghai	70.05
9	Madrid	59.23	9	Beijing	68.77
10	Los Angeles	58.75	10	Milan	67.67
11	Sydney	58.06	11	Madrid	66.42
12	Frankfurt	57.53	12	Moscow	64.24
13	Amsterdam	57.10	13	Seoul	63.54
14	Toronto	56.92	14	Brussels	63.53
15	Brussels	56.51	15	Toronto	62.29
16	Sao Paulo	54.26	16	Buenos Aires	61.21
17	San Francisco	50.43	17	Mumbai	60.24
18	Zurich	48.42	18	Kuala Lumpur	58.87
19	Taipei	48.22	19	Taipei	56.77
20	Jakarta	47.92	20	Sao Paulo	56.49
22	Buenos Aires	46.81	22	Zurich	55.83
23	Mumbai	46.81	25	Amsterdam	54.60
27	Shanghai	43.95	27	Jakarta	54.03
28	Kuala Lumpur	43.53	30	Frankfurt	52.31
29	Beijing	43.43	31	Chicago	52.20
30	Seoul	42.32	44	Los Angeles	41.77
37	Moscow	40.76	49	San Francisco	40.01

Note: Individual city connectivity scores are shown as a proportion of the most connected city, i.e. New York in 2008 =100.00).[72]

In short, the traditional national "space of places" has been supplemented by a new global "space of flows"—and cities are the critical nodes where both spaces come together. The information revolution has not only enabled a tremendous dispersion of economic activities, it has generated a need for new concentrations in services management and organization, and these functions have largely been captured by particular cities and micro-regions. In this sense the global economy may be viewed as an archipelago of interlinked city-regions that are not only linked to their traditional "hinterland" within their own region or country, but also to an increasingly important "hinterworld" of interconnected cities and regions that can be important to a particular city's prosperity.[69] Dynamic "learning regions" attuned to knowledge-driven best practice and based on interrelated business networks are more likely to attract footloose firms.[70]

The Globalization and World Cities research group devised a network model to measure the global connectivity of 307 cities across the world, and present an overview of the 20 cities with the greatest global network connectivity (GNC) in 2000 and 2008. They rank cities in terms of how interconnected they are globally in terms of "advanced producer services"—office networks of leading firms in complex, high-value decision-making functions and transactions in such areas as finance, management consultancy, accountancy, advertising and law. According to this measure, New York and London rank as the most connected global cities in advanced producer services. Although New York and London change positions, they remain at the top.[71] Hong Kong, Paris, Singapore and Tokyo follow.

Below the top six, and reflecting the rise of Asian metropoles as key nodes of the global knowledge economy, cities such as Chicago, Los Angeles and Amsterdam have slipped to such cities as Shanghai, Beijing and Seoul. In fact, it is striking that only the two North American cities of New York and Toronto were considered to be among the top 20 "most connected" cities in 2008, as opposed to 9 Asian cities. While cities such as Los Angeles, San Francisco, Miami, Chicago, St. Louis, Cologne and Düsseldorf remain well-connected, cities outside the transatlantic space, such as Shanghai, Beijing, Moscow, Seoul, and Tel Aviv, are quickening the pace of integration.

The international landscape for innovation is changing. The advanced industrial economies remain the leaders in terms of global share of R&D, but new and important players are emerging. The United States accounted for the largest share of global R&D in 2007, registering slightly more than 32%, a decline from its 37% share in 1996. The EU accounts for almost 24%, down from its 27% share in 1996. Japan accounted for 13%, down from its share of just over 15% in 1996. China has embarked on a dramatic increase in R&D expenditure, accounting for almost a third of the global increase in R&D between 2001 and 2006, as much as Japan and the EU combined, boosting its share to over 9% from only about 2%. Russia and India each account for about 2%, and Brazil for slightly more than 1%.[73]

Conclusion

Overall the European Union remains a competitive and highly connected innovation economy. It remains an important player in key enabling technologies. The European Competitiveness Report concludes that it is the world leader in advanced manufacturing technologies, holds a top position in industrial biotechnology, has been able to maintain a strong position in advanced materials and is building a strong position in photonics despite Rising Asia's strengths in this area. It has a less advantageous position in nanotechnology and micro- and nanoelectronics compared to North America, Rising Asia and Japan. In all cases competition from East Asia is growing, while North America's share in global technology output has diminished. The EU's position tends to be stronger in chemicals-related fields than in technology areas linked to electronics. Another European strength is the automotive sector, which is a key source of progress in some key enabling technologies.[74]

In terms of R&D investments, however, the EU has failed to catch up with the U.S., has fallen behind other key countries, and now could be eclipsed by China. In addition, there are great discrepancies within the Union, both among countries and among sub-regions within countries. Moreover, inadequate attention has been paid to demand-driven innovation, including social innovation; and to innovation in services, a sector of competitive strength for the EU yet one which has failed to keep pace in productivity with the U.S. and has been lagging most in reaping the benefits from Europe's large Single Market. A stronger focus is needed on user needs, demand and market opportunities and a more effective connection between innovation, research, education and job creation.[75]

Significant barriers also persist with regard to the circulation of highly-skilled individuals both within the EU and between the EU and other world regions. Fragmentation in the EU patent and a variety of organizational, human capital and cultural barriers, have hampered collaborative research and innovation activities. Finally, EU innovators are relatively less effective than the United States at taking their ideas to market, commercializing innovation so that it results in products, processes or new ways of organizing that generate jobs and growth.

All of these factors have prompted considerable concern that the EU and its member states are slipping in their efforts to promote themselves as world-class knowledge economies.[76] They require more effective cooperation among member states, and greater attention to the innovation needs and potential of sub-regions within member states, if the EU is truly to become an Innovation Union.[77,78]

The situation is serious enough that Máire Geoghegan-Quinn, the European Commissioner for Research, Innovation and Science, and European Commission Vice-President Antonio Tajani, responsible for industry and entrepreneurship, have declared a state of "innovation emergency" for the EU, arguing that without a "sea change" in the EU's innovation performance, European economies would "wither on the vine."[79]

Brent Goldfarb and Magnus Henrekson have studied the U.S.-EU commercialization gap by looking at Sweden. Even though Sweden is one of Europe's innovation leaders, the commercialization rate of academic research is low when compared with the United States. They conclude that this is due at least in partly to top-down national policies in Sweden that discourage universities from actively commercializing their knowledge and research. This situation can be found in a number of EU member states, where scholars face considerable disincentives to undertake knowledge transfer activities aimed at the commercial sector, especially the establishment of spin-off companies. Goldfarb and Henrekson argue that the EU should consider introducing a version of the U.S. Bayh-Dole Act, which in 1980 gave universities—rather than individual researchers—title to innovations established in their confines, and is widely credited with having created a more vibrant and decentralized system of knowledge transfer and commercialization while furthering the role of universities as drivers of regional business innovation.[80]

The EU's potential is great. A study by Paul Lagame[81] shows that meeting the Europe 2020 target of boosting R&D investment to 3% of GDP could create 3.7 million jobs and increase annual EU GDP by up to €795 billion by 2025. The Commission's new Innovation Union strategy sets forth a variety of approaches to tackle the key roadblocks to greater innovation across the EU and to stimulate greater innovative efforts to tackle—together with other partners—such social and global challenges as climate change, energy and food security, health and aging populations.[82] If the EU actually advanced such a strategy, it could reposition the EU favorably on the global innovation landscape. But the EU set itself related goals ten years ago, with few results. The jury is out whether EU member states understand the true nature of the innovation challenges they face, and will actually advance the type of vigorous effort needed to achieve the Innovation Union.

Maps

EU Merchandise Trade with Other World Regions in 2009

EU Exports to the World

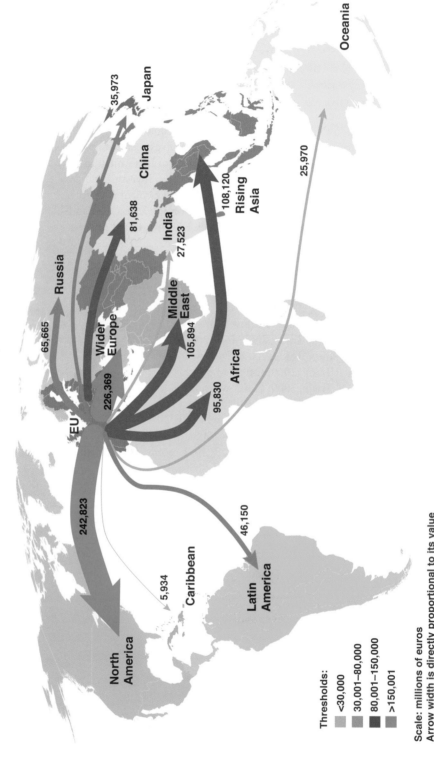

Oceania

Japan

China

35,973

Russia

81,638

India

27,523

108,120

Rising
Asia

Wider
Europe

65,665

Middle
East

226,369

105,894

Africa

EU

95,830

46,150

242,823

Caribbean

5,934

Latin
America

North
America

Thresholds:

- <30,000
- 30,001–80,000
- 80,001–150,000
- >150,001

Scale: millions of euros
Arrow width is directly proportional to its value
Data Source: EUROSTAT

EU Merchandise Trade with Other World Regions in 2009

EU Imports from the World

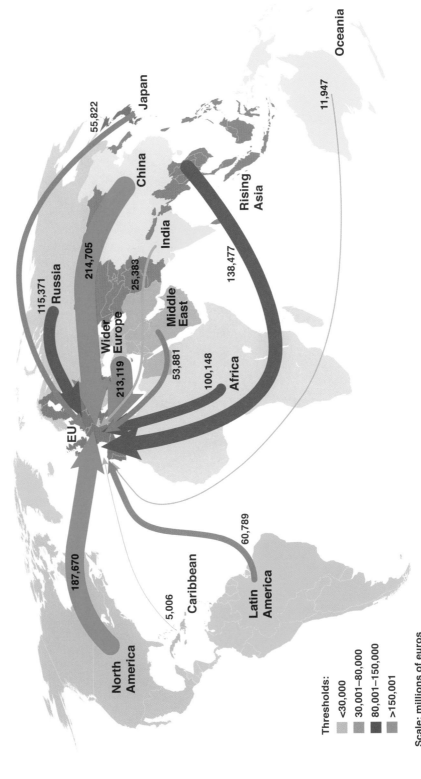

Thresholds:
- <30,000
- 30,001–80,000
- 80,001–150,000
- >150,001

Scale: millions of euros
Arrow width is directly proportional to its value
Data Source: EUROSTAT

North America 187,670
Russia 115,371
Wider Europe 214,705
Japan 55,822
China 213,119
India 25,383
Middle East 53,881
Africa 100,148
Rising Asia 138,477
Oceania 11,947
Caribbean 5,006
Latin America 60,789

EU Services Trade with Other World Regions in 2008

EU Exports to the World

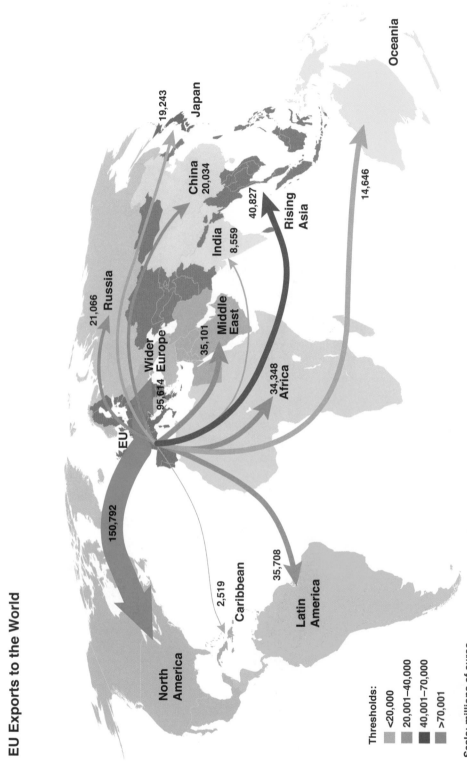

Thresholds:

<20,000

20,001–40,000

40,001–70,000

>70,001

Scale: millions of euros
Arrow width is directly proportional to its value
Data Source: EUROSTAT

EU Services Trade with Other World Regions in 2008

EU Imports from the World

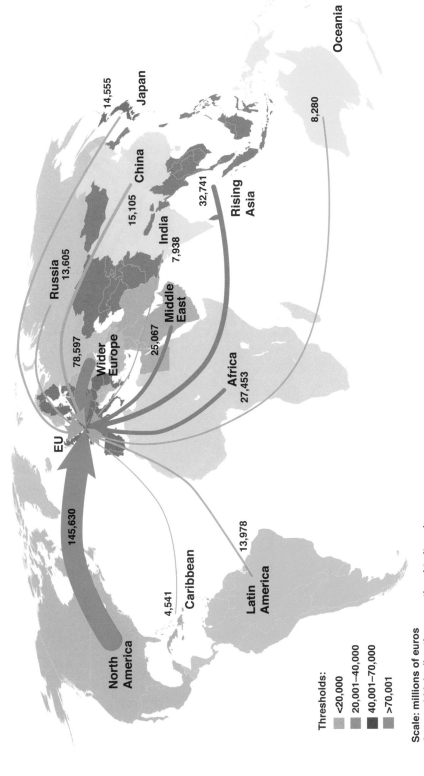

North America
145,630

Caribbean
4,541

Latin America
13,978

EU

Wider Europe
78,597

Russia
13,605

China
15,105

Japan
14,555

India
7,938

Middle East
25,067

Africa
27,453

Rising Asia
32,741

Oceania
8,280

Thresholds:
<20,000
20,001–40,000
40,001–70,000
>70,001

Scale: millions of euros
Arrow width is directly proportional to its value
Data Source: EUROSTAT

Foreign Direct Investment, 2008

EU Investment Abroad

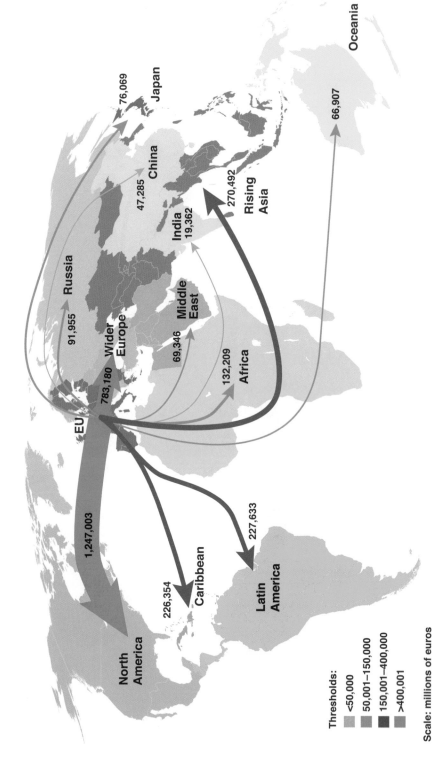

Oceania

76,069

Japan

China

47,285

66,907

Russia

India
19,362

Rising
Asia

91,955

Wider
Europe

270,492

Middle
East

69,346

783,180

132,209

Africa

EU

1,247,003

227,633

Caribbean

226,354

Latin
America

North
America

Thresholds:

<50,000

50,001–150,000

150,001–400,000

>400,001

Scale: millions of euros
Arrow width is directly proportional to its value
Data Source: Eurostat

Foreign Direct Investment, 2008

Foreign Investment in EU

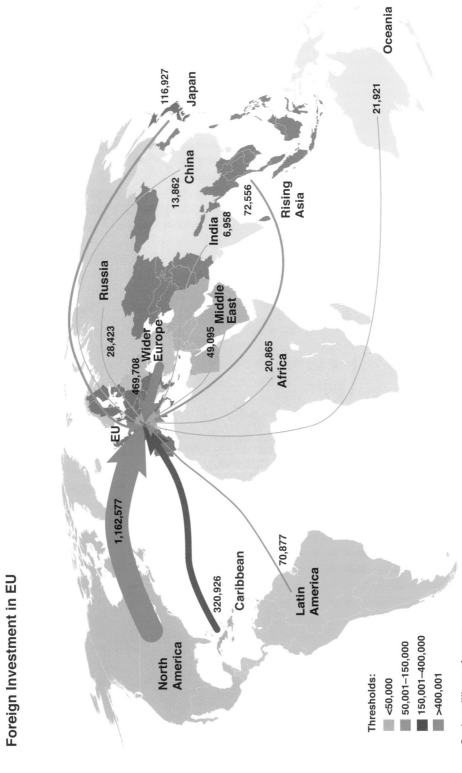

Oceania 21,921

Japan 116,927

China 13,862

Rising Asia 72,556

India 6,958

Russia 28,423

Middle East 49,095

Wider Europe 469,708

Africa 20,865

EU

North America 1,162,577

Caribbean 320,926

Latin America 70,877

Thresholds:

<50,000

50,001–150,000

150,001–400,000

>400,001

Scale: millions of euros
Arrow width is directly proportional to its value, but lowest numbers are not to scale.
Data Source: Eurostat

Total Portfolio Investment, 2008

EU Investment Abroad

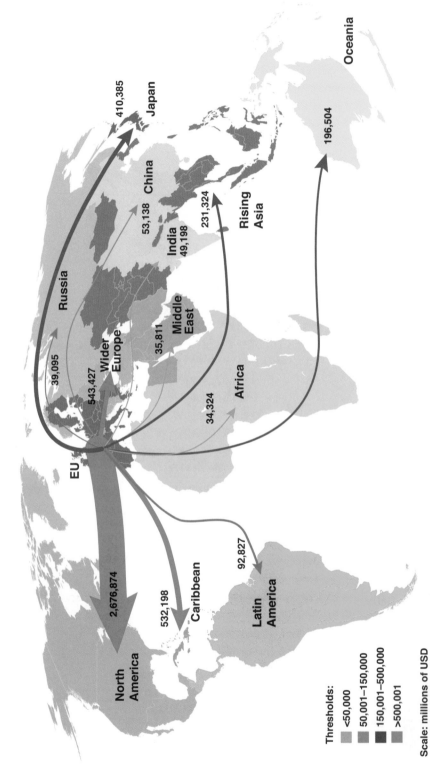

Thresholds:

- <50,000
- 50,001–150,000
- 150,001–500,000
- >500,001

Scale: millions of USD
Arrow width is directly proportional to its value, but lowest numbers are not to scale.
Data Source: Coordinated Portfolio Investment Survey, IMF

Total Portfolio Investment, 2008

Foreign Investment in EU

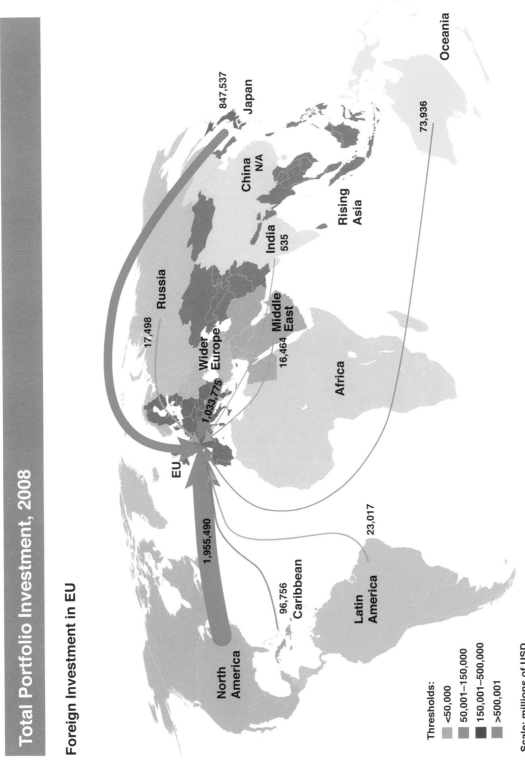

Oceania

847,537
Japan

China
N/A

Rising
Asia

India
535

Russia

17,498

Middle
East
16,464

Wider
Europe

1,033,775

Africa

EU

73,936

1,955,490

96,756
Caribbean

23,017

Latin
America

North
America

Thresholds:

<50,000
50,001–150,000
150,001–500,000
>500,001

Scale: millions of USD
Arrow width is directly proportional to its value, but lowest numbers are not to scale.
Data Source: Coordinated Portfolio Investment Survey, IMF

Portfolio Debt Investment, 2008

Foreign Investment in EU

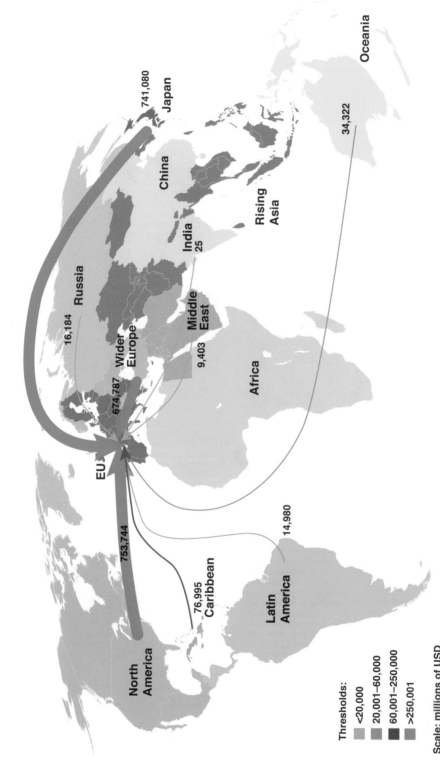

Thresholds:

- <20,000
- 20,001–60,000
- 60,001–250,000
- >250,001

Scale: millions of USD
Arrow width is directly proportional to its value, but lowest numbers are not to scale.
Data Source: Coordinated Portfolio Investment Survey, IMF

Portfolio Debt Investment, 2008

EU Investment Abroad

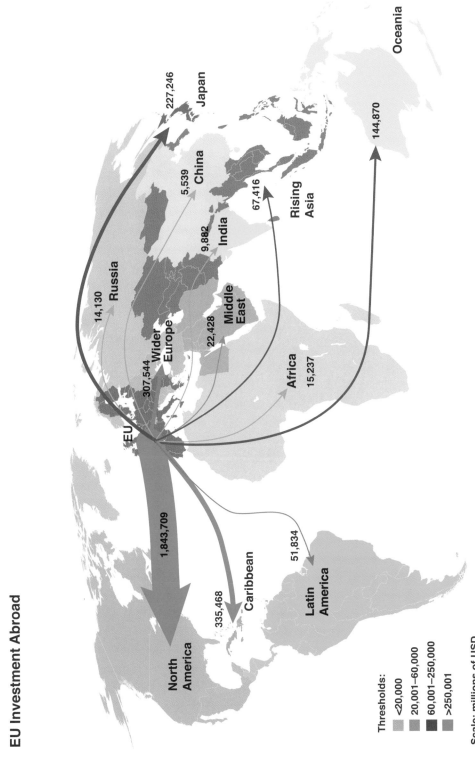

Oceania

227,246

Japan

5,539 China

67,416

9,882 India

Rising Asia

14,130 Russia

Middle East

22,428

307,544

Wider Europe

144,870

Africa

15,237

EU

1,843,709

335,468

Caribbean

51,834

Latin America

North America

Thresholds:

- <20,000
- 20,001–60,000
- 60,001–250,000
- >250,001

Scale: millions of USD
Arrow width is directly proportional to its value, but lowest numbers are not to scale.
Data Source: Coordinated Portfolio Investment Survey, IMF

Portfolio Equity Investment, 2008

Foreign Investment in EU

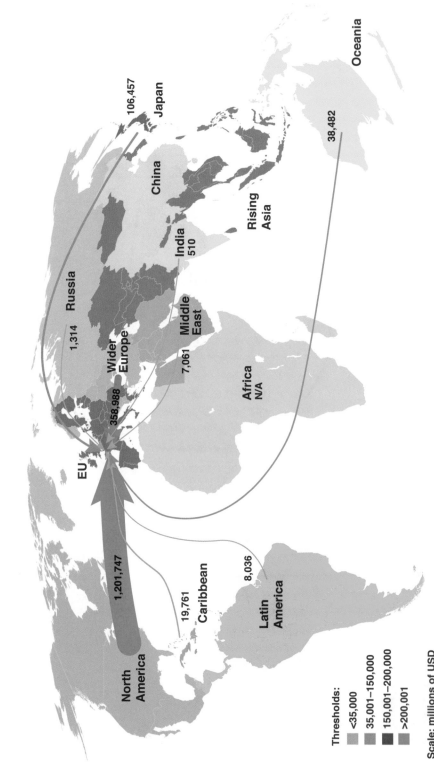

Thresholds:
- <35,000
- 35,001–150,000
- 150,001–200,000
- >200,001

Scale: millions of USD
Arrow width is directly proportional to its value, but lowest numbers are not to scale.
Data Source: Coordinated Portfolio Investment Survey, IMF

Portfolio Equity Investment, 2008

EU Investment Abroad

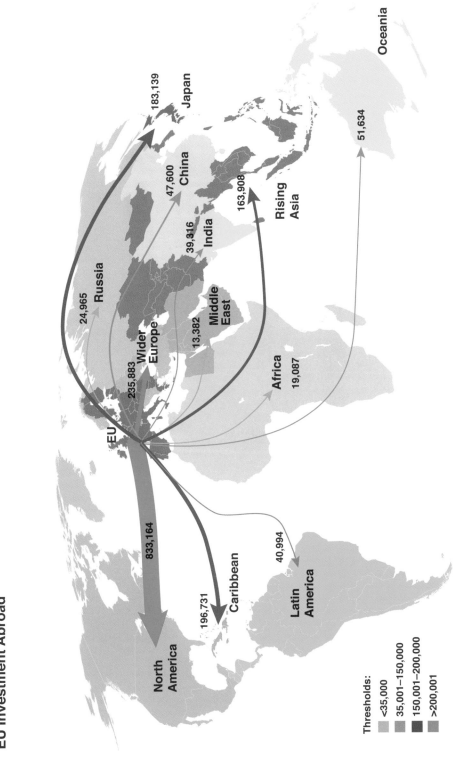

Oceania

183,139 Japan

47,600 China

39,316 India

163,908 Rising Asia

51,634

24,965 Russia

Wider Europe

Middle East

13,382

235,883

Africa 19,087

EU

833,164

196,731 Caribbean

40,994 Latin America

North America

Thresholds:

<35,000

35,001–150,000

150,001–200,000

>200,001

Scale: millions of USD
Arrow width is directly proportional to its value, but lowest numbers are not to scale.
Data Source: Coordinated Portfolio Investment Survey, IMF

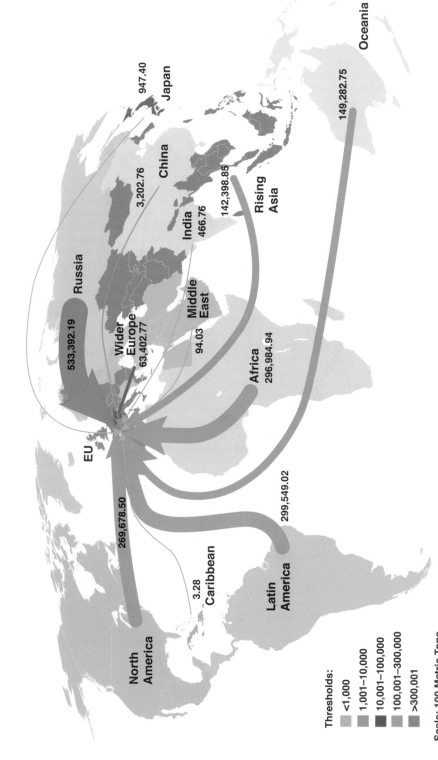

Coal Trade, 2009

Inflow to EU

Oceania

Japan   947.40

China   3,202.76

India   466.76

Russia

142,398.85   Rising Asia

149,282.75

Wider Europe   63,402.77

533,392.19

Middle East

94.03

Africa   296,984.94

EU

North America

269,678.50

Caribbean   3.28

299,549.02

Latin America

Thresholds:
<1,000
1,001–10,000
10,001–100,000
100,001–300,000
>300,001

Scale: 100 Metric Tons
Arrow width is directly proportional to its value but lower values are not to scale.
Data Source: Eurostat

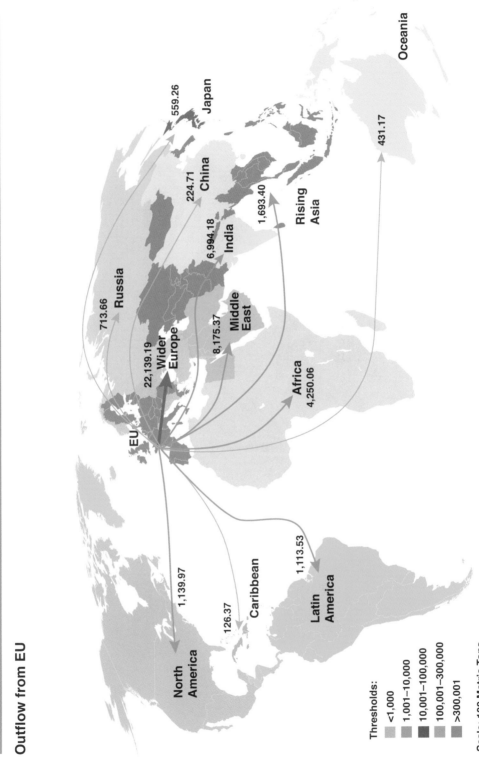

Coal Trade, 2009

Outflow from EU

Oceania

559.26

Japan

224.71

China

6,994.18

India

1,693.40

Rising
Asia

Russia

713.66

22,139.19
Wider
Europe

Middle
East

8,175.37

Africa
4,250.06

EU

North
America

1,139.97

126.37

Caribbean

1,113.53

Latin
America

431.17

Thresholds:

<1,000

1,001–10,000

10,001–100,000

100,001–300,000

>300,001

Scale: 100 Metric Tons
Arrow width is directly proportional to its value but lower values are not to scale.
Data Source: Eurostat

Uranium Trade, 2009

Inflow to EU

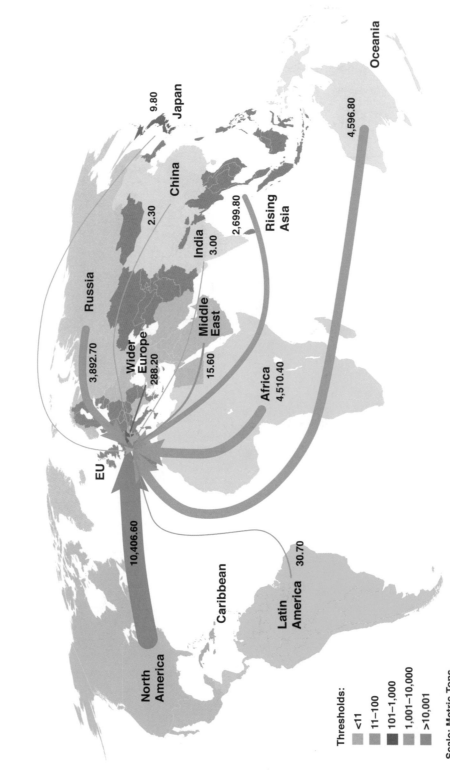

Oceania
4,596.80

Japan
9.80

China
2.30

India
3.00

Rising Asia
2,699.80

Russia
3,892.70

Middle East
15.60

Wider Europe
288.20

Africa
4,510.40

EU

Latin America
30.70

Caribbean

North America
10,406.60

Thresholds:

<11
11–100
101–1,000
1,001–10,000
>10,001

Scale: Metric Tons
Arrow width is directly proportional to its value but lower values are not to scale.
Data Source: Eurostat

Uranium Trade, 2009

Outflow from EU

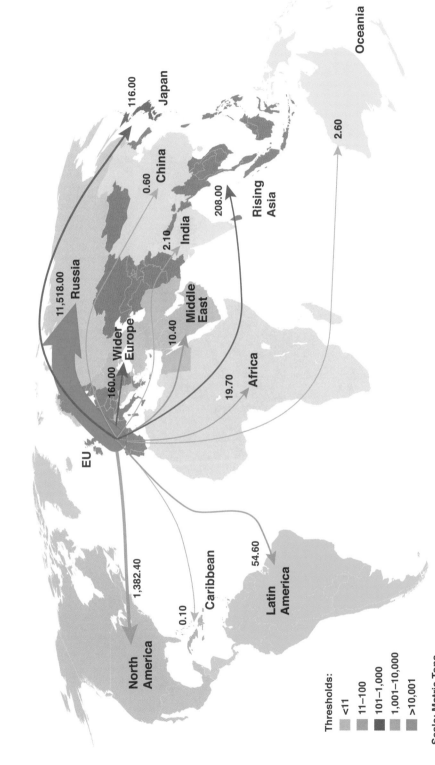

11,518.00 Russia

116.00 Japan

0.60 China

2.10 India

208.00 Rising Asia

2.60 Oceania

160.00 Wider Europe

10.40 Middle East

19.70 Africa

1,382.40 North America

0.10 Caribbean

54.60 Latin America

EU

Thresholds:
<11
11–100
101–1,000
1,001–10,000
>10,001

Scale: Metric Tons
Arrow width is directly proportional to its value but lower values are not to scale.
Data Source: Eurostat

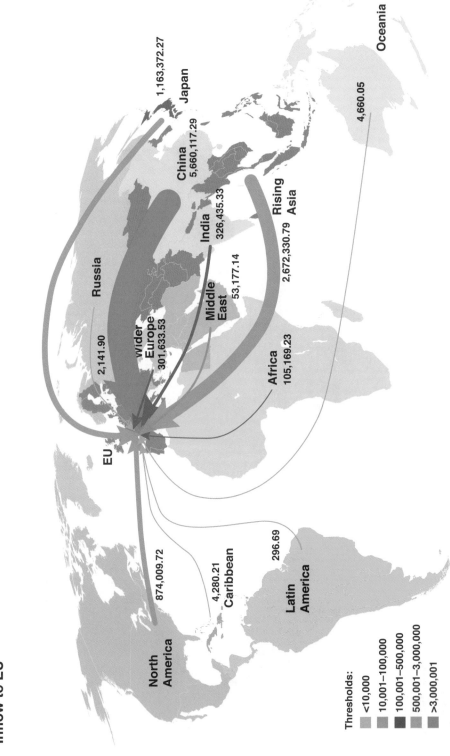

Solar Trade, 2009

Inflow to EU

1,163,372.27
Japan

China
5,660,117.29

India
326,435.33

Rising
Asia
2,672,330.79

Oceania

4,660.05

Russia

2,141.90

Wider
Europe
301,633.53

Middle
East
53,177.14

Africa
105,169.23

EU

North
America
874,009.72

Caribbean
4,280.21

Latin
America
296.69

Thresholds:
<10,000
10,001–100,000
100,001–500,000
500,001–3,000,000
>3,000,001

Scale: 1,000 euros
Arrow width is directly proportional to its value but lower values are not to scale.
Data Source: Eurostat

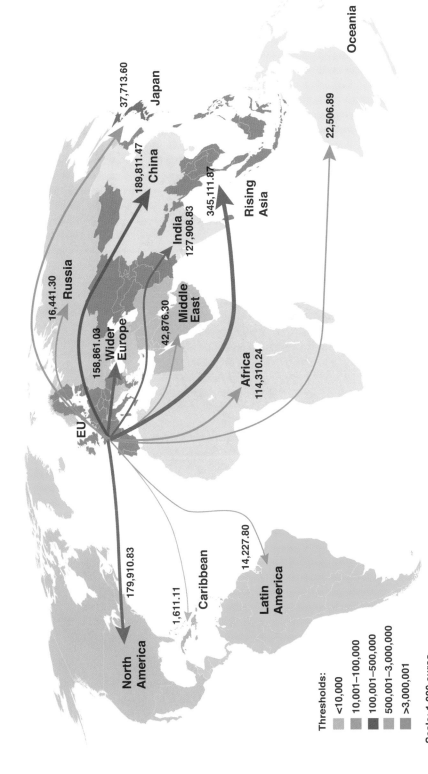

Solar Trade, 2009

Outflow from EU

Oceania
22,506.89

Japan
37,713.60

China
189,811.47

Rising Asia
345,111.87

India
127,908.83

Russia
16,441.30

Middle East
42,876.30

Wider Europe
158,861.03

Africa
114,310.24

EU

North America
179,910.83

Caribbean
1,611.11

Latin America
14,227.80

Thresholds:
- <10,000
- 10,001–100,000
- 100,001–500,000
- 500,001–3,000,000
- >3,000,001

Scale: 1,000 euros
Arrow width is directly proportional to its value but lower values are not to scale.
Data Source: Eurostat

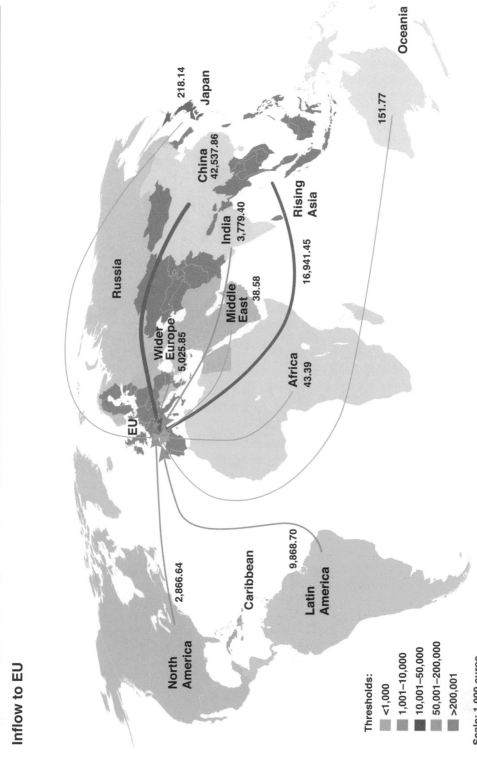

Wind Power Trade, 2009

Inflow to EU

Thresholds:

- <1,000
- 1,001–10,000
- 10,001–50,000
- 50,001–200,000
- >200,001

Scale: 1,000 euros
Arrow width is directly proportional to its value but lower values are not to scale.
Data Source: Eurostat

Oceania
151.77

Japan
218.14

China
42,537.86

Rising
Asia
16,941.45

India
3,779.40

Russia

Middle
East
38.58

Wider
Europe
5,025.85

Africa
43.39

EU

North
America
2,866.64

Caribbean

Latin
America
9,868.70

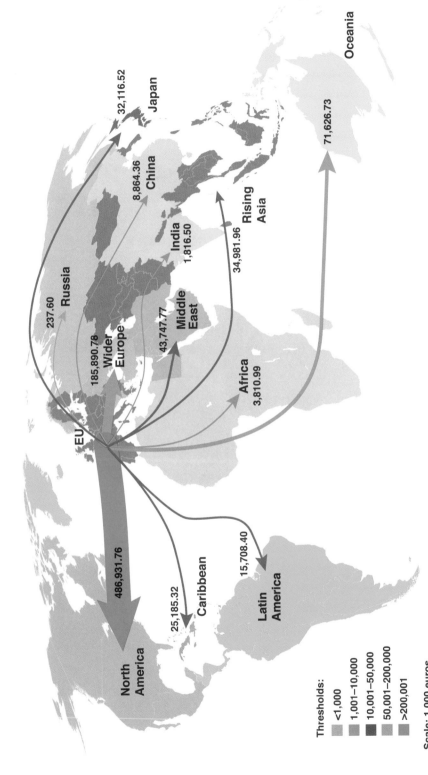

Wind Power Trade, 2009

Outflow from EU

Thresholds:
- <1,000
- 1,001–10,000
- 10,001–50,000
- 50,001–200,000
- >200,001

Scale: 1,000 euros
Arrow width is directly proportional to its value but lower values are not to scale.
Data Source: Eurostat

Oceania

Japan 32,116.52

China 8,864.36

India 1,816.50

71,626.73

Russia 237.60

Rising Asia

Wider Europe 185,890.78

Middle East 43,747.77

34,981.96

Africa 3,810.99

EU

North America 486,931.76

Caribbean 25,185.32

Latin America 15,708.40

Biofuel Trade, 2009

Inflow to EU

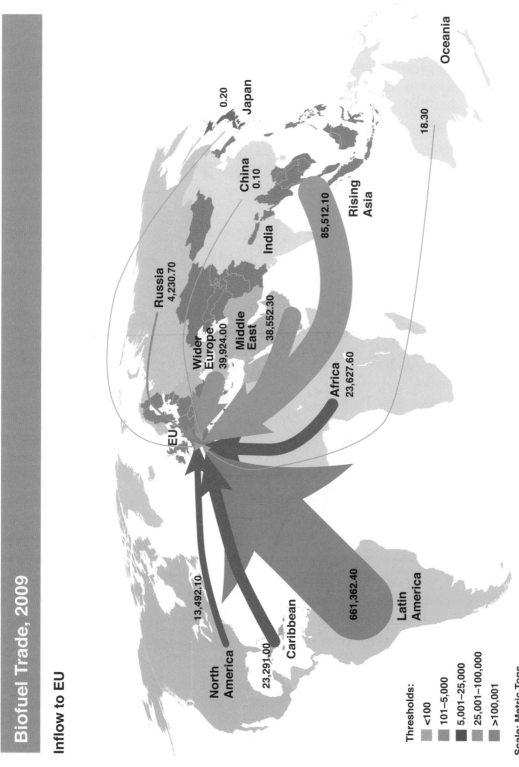

Japan
0.20

China
0.10

Rising
Asia
85,512.10

India

Russia
4,230.70

Wider
Europe
39,924.00

Middle
East
38,552.30

Africa
23,627.60

EU

Oceania

18.30

North
America
13,492.10

Caribbean
23,291.00

Latin
America
661,362.40

Thresholds:
<100
101–5,000
5,001–25,000
25,001–100,000
>100,001

Scale: Metric Tons
Arrow width is directly proportional to its value but highest and lowest values cannot be drawn to scale.
Data Source: Eurostat

Biofuel Trade, 2009

Outflow from EU

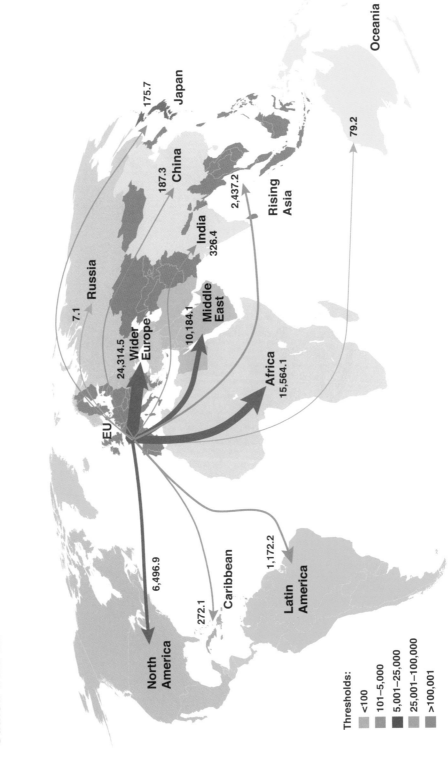

Russia 7.1
175.7 Japan
187.3 China
India 326.4
24,314.5 Wider Europe
10,184.1 Middle East
2,437.2 Rising Asia
Africa 15,564.1
79.2 Oceania
6,496.9 North America
272.1 Caribbean
1,172.2 Latin America
EU

Thresholds:
<100
101–5,000
5,001–25,000
25,001–100,000
>100,001

Scale: Metric Tons
Arrow width is directly proportional to its value but lower values are not to scale.
Data Source: Eurostat

Migrant Flows, 2006

Inflow to EU

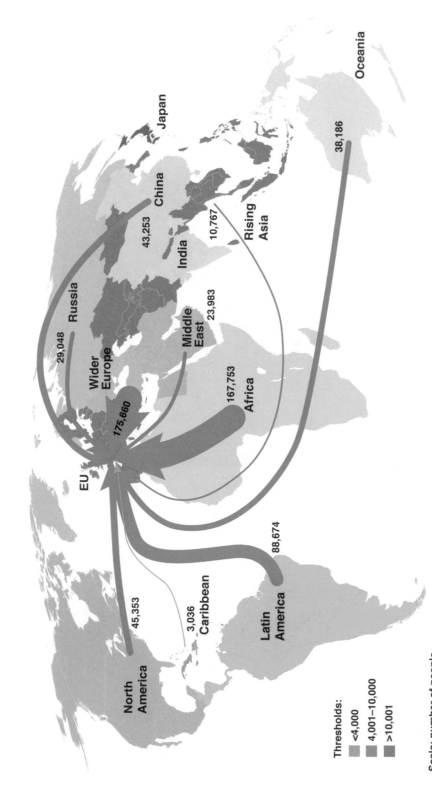

North America — 45,353

Caribbean — 3,036

Latin America — 88,674

Russia — 29,048

China — 43,253

Japan

India — 10,767

Rising Asia

Oceania — 38,186

Middle East — 23,983

Wider Europe — 175,660

Africa — 167,753

EU

Thresholds:
- <4,000
- 4,001–10,000
- >10,001

Scale: number of people
Arrow width is directly proportional to its value, but lowest numbers are not to scale.
Data Source: International Labour Organization

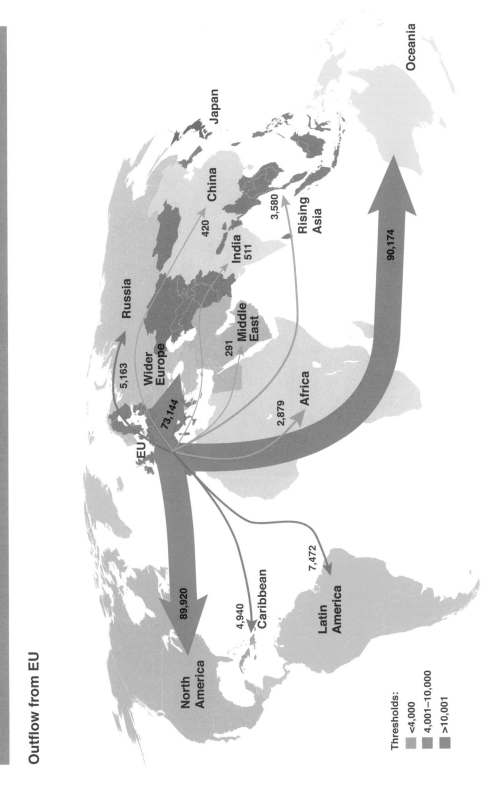

Migrant Flows, 2006

Outflow from EU

Oceania

Japan

China
420

India
511

Rising
Asia

3,580

90,174

Russia

Wider
Europe

5,163

Middle
East

291

Africa

73,144

2,879

EU

North
America

89,920

Caribbean

4,940

Latin
America

7,472

Thresholds:

<4,000
4,001–10,000
>10,001

Scale: number of people
Arrow width is directly proportional to its value, but lowest numbers are not to scale.
Data Source: International Labour Organization

Total Refugee Arrivals, 2000–2008

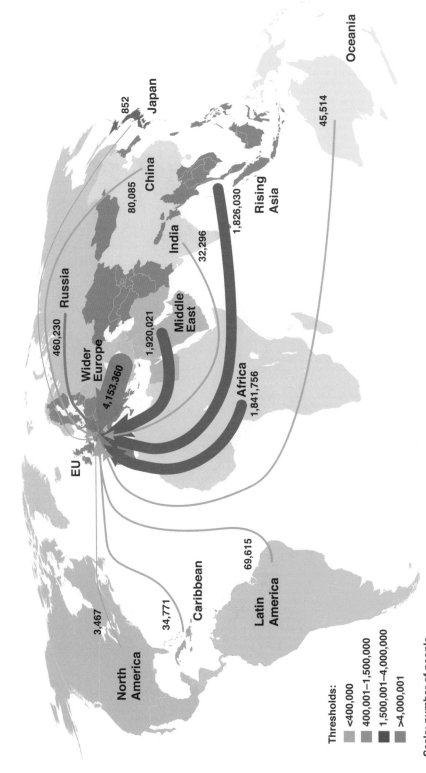

Oceania

852 Japan

China 80,085

Rising Asia 1,826,030

India 32,296

Russia 460,230

Middle East 1,920,021

Wider Europe 4,153.360

Africa 1,841,756

EU

Caribbean 34,771

North America 3.467

Latin America 69,615

Thresholds:

<400,000
400,001–1,500,000
1,500,001–4,000,000
>4,000,001

Scale: number of people
Arrow width is directly proportional to its value, but lowest numbers are not to scale.
Data Source: United Nations High Commissioner for Refugees (UNHCR)

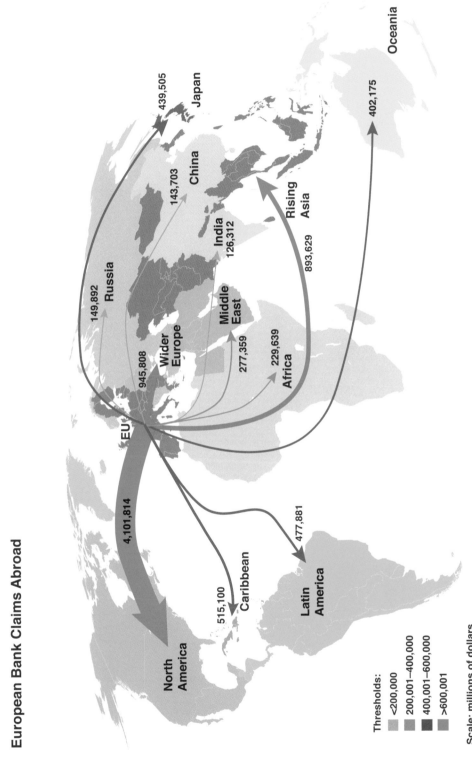

Bank Claims as of March 31, 2010

European Bank Claims Abroad

Thresholds:
<200,000
200,001–400,000
400,001–600,000
>600,001

Scale: millions of dollars
Arrow width is directly proportional to its value
Data Source: Bank for International Settlements

Section II

Partners and Competitors:
The EU and Other World Regions

How is the EU connected to other world regions? Where are European bonds with other regions thick, and where are they thin? How does the EU compare with other world regions in terms of its competitive position? Understanding Europe's interdependencies with other regions of the world is an important basis for understanding Europe's competitive strengths and weaknesses. This section looks at Europe's ties to other world regions in terms of flows of goods, services, money, energy, people, and ideas. It also compares the EU with those world regions in terms of its ability to generate goods, services, and innovation; its capacity as an investor and a financial center; and its human capital. Such comparisons allow us to gain a better understanding of the different ways in which other world regions act both as partners and competitors for the EU.

Chapter 7
The EU and North America: Deep Integration

The European Union and North America are more deeply integrated across more economically relevant areas than any other two regions of the world. It is not an exaggeration to say that Europe's continuing prosperity is more dependent on its ties to North America than to any other region of the world, including its own neighborhood. Ties are particularly thick in foreign direct investment, portfolio investment, banking claims, trade in goods and particularly services, and flows of ideas.

These deep economic bonds have been critical to European prosperity. Yet as both the EU and the United States struggle to recover from the economic and financial crisis, such ties can also amplify the challenges of slow growth. The U.S. financial system has stabilized after being pushed to the brink during the financial crisis. Yet growth remains a challenge and unemployment levels remain stubbornly high at 10%, about twice normal rates. The increase in U.S. unemployment is also roughly double that seen in the euro area, the United Kingdom, Japan, or Canada.

The U.S. needs about 2.6% growth a year to keep unemployment levels constant, and more than 3% growth to lower them. Yet the U.S. is struggling to reach these levels; the Bureau of Labor Statistics projects annual average growth of 2.4% between 2008 and 2018. Inflation-adjusted average household income today is lower than at the beginning of the last decade, and income inequality has grown. The recession cut U.S. GDP by 4.1% and destroyed 7.3 million jobs.

It will take six to seven years for the U.S. to get down to reasonable levels of private debt, and in the meantime public debt has replaced private debt as the fuel for modest growth. But this means that the U.S. government has been accumulating debt at unsustainable rates. U.S. federal debt has tripled over the past decade, from $3.5 trillion in 2000 (35% of GDP) to $9 trillion in 2010 (62% of GDP) and could reach total U.S. GDP by 2015, about the relative indebtedness of Greece and Italy today. If the government does not act to alter this trend, global capital markets are likely to do it instead. Bank credit is tight and the inventory backlog in housing continues to weigh down the economy. Low rates of resource utilization are creating deflationary pressures. The U.S. continues to be overly reliant on spending and borrowing, rather than saving, investing and competing in the global marketplace. The U.S. exhibits a lopsided pattern of strong profits and productivity growth alongside weak wage and job growth.[1]

U.S. economic challenges have consequences for Europe, given that the U.S. is the top country export destination for EU goods and services, the EU's leading source and destination of both FDI and private portfolio investment, and a key innovation partner for European economies seeking to maintain their competitive position in knowledge-based activities. The EU's deep integration with the U.S. and its North American neighbors Canada and Mexico is evident from the following comparisons.

North America was the largest destination for EU goods exports (23%) in 2009 and was the third largest source of EU goods imports (15.9%), surpassed by Wider Europe in 2006 and China in 2007.[2] EU exports of goods to North America fell 12% and EU imports of goods from North America fell 20% between 2000 and 2009. During the same time period, the EU's goods trade surplus with North America increased 35%. EU goods exports to North America peaked in 2006, at 30% more than 2009. The EU exported €242.8 billion of goods to North America; about €26 billion went to Canada (accounting for 12.5% of all Canadian goods imports); about €22 billion went to Mexico; and the bulk—about €194 billion—went to the United States.

EU goods exports to North America were about 7% more than to Wider Europe; almost 4 times more than to Russia; about 3 times more than to China (the U.S. share was 2.4 times greater than to China); 2½ times more than to Africa; 2.2 times more than to Rising Asia; almost 7 times more than to Japan; and almost 9 times more than to India. The EU exports about the same amount of goods to North America as to the entire Asia-Pacific region, with each region accounting for about 23% of EU exports. And while much attention is focused on the rise of the Asia-Pacific region, Atlantic Basin countries outside of Europe are more important customers for the EU, accounting for 36% of EU goods exports.

The EU imported €187.7 billion of goods from North America in 2009, about 87% of EU goods imports from China (the U.S. share is 70% of that coming from China) and 88% of EU goods imports from Wider Europe; 40% more than from Russia; 74% more than from Rising Asia; over 7 times than from India; over 3 times more than from Japan; almost 2 times more than from Africa. If one considered the U.S. as its own region, it would rank third as a source of EU goods imports, behind China and Wider Europe. EU goods imports from India are slightly higher than EU goods imports from Canada and almost twice those from Mexico. The Asia-Pacific region accounted for 36% of EU goods imports, compared to 29% for Atlantic Basin countries outside of Europe.

Overall, the EU appears to have withstood trade competition by emerging countries better than the United States. Whereas the EU has essentially maintained its 19% market share of world exports over a 15 year span, the U.S. lost around 6% in market shares, and now accounts for 12.5% of world market shares. While the EU registered close to a 1% gain in global market share in high-tech products between 1994 and the onset of the recession, the United States recorded an 11% loss. Between 2000 and 2007 the EU25 managed to gain market shares in "upmarket," high-quality goods, while the U.S. lost shares. Yet while the EU has maintained its overall global market share over the past 15 years, the biggest export share gains were recorded in existing markets, particularly the U.S., while market share losses were recorded in Japan and in some of the most dynamic emerging markets. The EU15's export orientation for goods still appears to be skewed to North America at a time when faster-growing emerging markets beckon.

EU-North American ties are particularly strong in trade in services.[3] North America was the largest destination for EU services exports (29%) and the largest source of EU services imports (37%) in recession year 2009 (and 32% and 39%, respectively, in 2008). EU exports of services to North America grew 3.4% per year on average between 2004 and 2008, before tumbling in 2009. EU exports of services to North America in 2009 were 31% higher than to Wider Europe; over 3.5 times more than to Rising Asia and Latin America; 4 times more than to the Middle East and to Africa; almost 5 times more than to Oceania; over 7 times more to Russia, China and Japan; almost 15 times more than to India; and 29 times more than to the Caribbean.

EU services imports from North America in 2009 were 43% more than from Wider Europe; over 4.5 times from Rising Asia; over 5 times from Africa; over 6 times from the Middle East; over 9 times more than from Oceania, China and Latin America; over 12 times more than from Japan and Russia; over 18 times more than from India; and 37 times more than from the Caribbean.

The EU has sustained or expanded its share of world trade in most broad service categories except transport services, in contrast to developments in the United States. Regarding services exports, the EU ranked number one in the world in 8 of 11 categories of services exports, and in fact boosted its position between 2005 and 2008 in communications, telecommunications, construction, computer and information services. The U.S. has the lead in three categories: royalties and license fees; personal, cultural and recreational services; and audiovisual services.

Europe registered 13% annual average growth in commercial services exports between 2000 and 2008, 1% more than the global average, 1% below that of Asia, but 5% higher than North America. The EU boosted its world market share in exports of transportation services 21.9%, largely at the expense of North America, whose share dropped dramatically from 17.1% in 2000 to 11.7% in 2008 (the U.S. share declined from 14.5% to 10.2%).

Individual EU services exporters such as the UK, Germany and France lag the U.S. when it comes to key markets such as Japan (U.S. share 56%), India (U.S. share 41.3%), and China (U.S. share 27.9%), and Rising Asia, although U.S. shares of services export markets in India, China and Rising Asia have fallen relative to EU country shares.

North America is the largest regional destination of FDI from the EU.[4] North America is also the largest regional source of foreign direct investment in the EU. The United States remains the principal country source of foreign direct investment in the EU, and the EU is the top destination of U.S. FDI around the world. EU investment in North America grew 4.8% per year on average over the course of the past decade until the recession. North America's investment in the EU grew faster, at 8.6% per year on average, in the same period.

The EU had a total of €1.247 trillion in foreign direct investment in North America in 2008, 1.7 times more than in Wider Europe; 4½ times more than in Rising Asia; 5 times more than in Latin America; over 9 times more than in Africa; over 13 times more than in Russia; 16 times more than in Japan; 18 times more than in the Middle East; over 26 times more than in China; and 65 times more than in India.

North America had a total of €1.163 trillion in foreign direct investment in the EU in 2008, nearly half of all non-EU investment into the EU, and 2½ times more than from Wider Europe; 3½ times more than from the Caribbean; 10 times more than from Japan; 16 times more than from Rising Asia and from Latin America; over 23 times more than from the Middle East; 41 times more than from Russia; 55 times more than from Africa; 83 times more than from China; and 166 times more than from India.

In 2008 U.S. FDI in the EU totaled €1.05 trillion, more than the next 20 investors combined. Corporate America's aggregate foreign assets totaled $13 trillion in 2007, and the bulk of these assets—roughly 63%—were located in Europe. U.S. corporate affiliates in Europe employ millions of European workers and are the largest source of onshored jobs throughout the EU.

50% of overall foreign portfolio investment in North America in 2008 came from the EU, and another 15% came from Japan. The EU had a total of $2.677 trillion in private portfolio investment in North America in 2008, 5 times more than in the Caribbean and in Wider Europe; 6.5 times more than in Japan; 11 times more than in Rising Asia; 28 times more than in Latin America; 50 times more than in China; 54 times more than in India; 68 times more than in Russia; 74 times more than in the Middle East; and 78 times more than in Africa.

North America had a total of $1.955 trillion in private portfolio investment in the EU in 2008, almost double that from Wider Europe 2.3 times more than from Japan; 8 times more than from Rising Asia; 20 times more than from the Caribbean; 85 times more than from Latin America; and 115 times more than from Russia.

European capital accounted for 71% of total U.S. inflows in Q1 2010. Of the global total, U.S. and EU market activity make up 65% of global banking assets; 72% in private and public debt securities outstanding and 79% of the volume of interest-rate derivatives outstanding; 58% of global stock market capitalization and 77% of the volume of equity-linked derivatives outstanding; 96% involvement in foreign exchange transactions worldwide by currency pairs; a 70% share in the volume of foreign exchange derivative transactions; and 74% of global insurance markets in terms of insurance premia collected.[5]

Even though the U.S. dollar remains the world's reserve currency, the euro has gained traction as a possible alternative since its introduction nearly a decade ago, and despite its current travails. Of total allocated global foreign exchange holdings at mid-year 2010, the euro accounted for 26.5%, compared with its 18.3% share at the end of 2000. The pound sterling also increased its share, from 2.8% to 4.2%, while the dollar's share declined from 71.1% at the end of 2000 to 62.1% at mid-year 2010. Among developing nations, demand for the euro is slightly higher—the euro accounted for 28.3% percent of allocated reserves by emerging and developing countries at mid-year 2010, compared with just 18.1% in 2000. The pound sterling also boosted its share from 2.6% to 6.3%. The dollar's share during this period declined from 74.8% to 58.4%.[6]

North America is the EU's fourth largest source of coal.[7] In 2009 North America shipped 29 million tons of coal to the EU (24 million tons of which came from the United States), less than the 53 million tons supplied by Russia, but just slightly less than that supplied by Latin America and by Africa, and almost 5 times that supplied by Wider Europe.

North America was the largest destination of EU oil in 2009. The EU sent 44 million tons of oil to North America, twice as much as the EU's number two destination, Africa. North

America sent 17 million tons of oil to the EU in 2009, less than half EU of oil deliveries to North America.

North America is the EU's largest export destination for windpower parts and its sixth largest provider. EU windpower exports to North America have fallen 50% since 2006, but since 2000 the EU has sold over €4.4 billion worth of windpower parts to North America. EU wind imports from North America grew more than eight times. The EU sold €486 million worth of windpower parts to North America and purchased €2.8 million in 2009.

North America is the EU's seventh largest biofuels provider and fourth largest client. While U.S. biofuels exports to the EU dropped by 60% in 2009, they grew six-fold in 2007 and 1.5 times again in 2008. Moreover, the United States, which used to export only a fraction of the EU's biofuels exports in 2000, has since 2007 surpassed the EU and in 2009 exported 15 times more biofuels than the EU. EU biofuel imports from North America have grown almost four-fold while EU biofuels exports to North America have fallen 64% since 2000. The EU imported 13,492 tons of biofuels from North America and sold 6,496 tons of biofuels to North America in 2009.

North America is the EU's third largest solar client and fourth largest solar provider. EU solar exports to North America fell 23% while imports surged 87% over the course of the past decade. EU solar exports to North America totaled €179 million while EU solar imports from North America totaled €874 million.

North America is the EU's number two purchaser and number one provider of uranium. It bought 39% more in 2009 than in 2000 and sold 427% more. North America bought 1,328 tons of uranium and sold 10,406 tons to the EU.

Refugees from North America accounted for less than 1% of the total refugees in the EU.[8]

Migrant flows to North America accounted for 32.3% of the total migrant flows from the EU in 2006, making it the second largest of the eleven regions for which data is available. Migrant flows from North America accounted for 7.2% of total migrant flows to the EU in 2006, making it the fourth largest of the ten regions for which data is available. Migrant flows from North America to the EU increased by 285.0% from 2000 to 2006. In 2006, the EU received 45,353 labor immigrants from North America, and had 89,920 emigrants to North America.

The EU is also more closely linked to North America than to other world regions when it comes to the flow of ideas.[9] For instance, the United States is the leading R&D investor in the EU. Although the share of U.S.-controlled affiliates in industrial R&D in the European Union declined from 75% to 71% between 1997 and 2007, it is strong in major countries such as the United Kingdom (50%), Sweden (38%), Germany (36%) and France (34%).

Outward R&D investment by EU firms is similarly focused on the United States. EU R&D investment in the U.S. in 2007 accounted for over three-quarters of aggregate foreign research and development (R&D) investment. The leading R&D investing country in the United States was the United Kingdom, with 26% of the R&D investment of foreign-controlled affiliates, followed by Switzerland (15%), Germany (14%), France (13%) and Japan (10%).

EU patents originating outside the EU mostly come from the U.S., Switzerland, Canada, and Japan. When it comes to patent co-invention, the Southeast of England and the Southern and Eastern region of Ireland each share about 50% of their foreign co-inventions with regions in North America, and only about 40% with regions in Europe. Lisbon, Portugal and the western Netherlands share about 40% of their foreign co-inventions with regions in North America. The dense research networks across the Atlantic are further underscored by the fact that California shared 64% of its foreign co-inventions with Europe and only 16% with other non-U.S. regions in North America in 2005.

A significant gap in persists in the EU's innovation performance relative to the United States. The U.S. performs better than the EU in 11 indicators, while the EU performs better than the U.S. in six areas. While there is a clear performance gap in favor of the U.S., the U.S. innovation lead is declining, as its innovation performance has grown at an annual rate of 1.63% and that of the EU has grown at 3.17%. The EU spent 1.9% of GDP on R&D in 2008, its highest level ever, and slightly more than North America (1.7%).

Most European metro areas lag significantly behind their U.S. counterparts, however, in per capita R&D expenditures, in labor productivity, and overall as competitive world knowledge regions. According to the 2008 World Knowledge Competitiveness Index, the top twenty knowledge regions include 13 U.S. regions and only 5 European regions. Of the top 100 most competitive cities, 53 were from North America (50 from the U.S., 3 from Canada); 30 were from the EU.

Convergence of European GDP per capita toward U.S. levels stopped in the early 1980s, leaving a persistent gap of close to 30%. Convergence of output per capita levels was swift during the postwar period, driven by catch-up growth, technology assimilation, product standardization, trade liberalization, and economies of scale. However, the process of convergence slowed markedly and even reversed somewhat after the 1970s. In the decade leading to the crisis, however, EU15 per capita GDP grew marginally faster than that of the United States. Faster growth in northern Europe compensated for relatively slow or stagnant growth in most of the rest of continental Europe.[10]

In addition, contrary to conventional wisdom, the EU15 created more jobs than the U.S, despite slower population growth. The McKinsey Global Institute demonstrates that between 1995 and 2008, the EU15 created 23.9 million jobs, of which only 8.7 million were related to its increase in population during this period, compared with 12.1 million due to increased participation in the labor force; 5.3 million due to lower unemployment; and 2.1 million due to shifts in age structure. In comparison, the U.S. generated 20.5 million jobs, most of which (18.8 million) accommodated a rising population, only 1.4 million due to increased participation rates, 0.3 due to lower unemployment, and 3.3 million due to shifts in age structure.[11]

McKinsey notes that the EU also compares favorably to the United States when it comes to a variety of non-growth factors that measure sustainability and quality of life dimensions such as health, education, social inclusion, security and the environment. The Environmental Performance index ranks the EU15 on average higher than the U.S., Canada and Japan. Sweden, France and Austria are all in the top ten of this global ranking.[12]

Nonetheless, the EU15's per capita GDP still lags that of the United States by about 24%—$4.5 trillion in total, or about $11,250 per inhabitant. This shortfall reflects both lower labor utilization and lower hourly productivity. The relative importance of these factors also varies considerably among EU member states. For instance, hourly productivity in Germany and France is comparable or even slightly higher than in the United States, but low hours worked by employee has resulted in lower per capita GDP than in the United States. In the UK, on the other hand, 86% of the gap is due to lower productivity. In Italy, lower productivity accounts for two-thirds of the gap and low participation accounts for the remaining third. Overall, lagging per capita GDP between northern Europe and the U.S. is due primarily to lower productivity and only marginally to other factors; continental Europe's gap is due largely to fewer hours worked per employee; and about three-quarters of southern Europe's gap is due to productivity lags and one-quarter to other factors such as lower labor participation rates.[13]

Overall, the EU15 registered 733 annual hours worked per capita in 2008, compared to 913 in the United States. The standard European response to the gap is that this reflects a choice that European societies have made to work less and enjoy more free time. About half of the difference can in fact be accounted for by less hours worked by those employed; EU15 employees work five weeks less on average than their U.S. counterparts. But the other half of the overall difference reflects an unemployment gap, a gap in female full-time work, and a participation gap by those between 55 and 64 years of age. Unemployment and lack of opportunity for females or seniors to participate more fully in the work force are not necessarily choices individuals have made. And McKinsey calculates that further reduction of unemployment and greater participation in the work force by females and seniors could close the GDP per capita gap with the U.S. by 10%.[14]

Lower productivity is the second major area contributing to the EU's lower per capita GDP when compared to the United States. In the long run, productivity is the key driver of per capita GDP growth and is critical to competitiveness. In fact, over the past 40 years all per capita GDP growth in the EU15 has come from productivity increases, while in the U.S. labor utilization rates have also made a positive difference.[15] Until the mid-1990s, the core EU countries steadily closed their productivity gap with the United Sates. Since then, however, the gap has widened again. Given the many pressures on EU growth, McKinsey finds that the EU15 would need to accelerate productivity growth by around 30% just to maintain their own past GDP growth levels—about a 0.40% increase per year over the next 20 years. The European Commission's own calculations project the need for a .16% increase per year. To achieve the U.S. rate of 2.9%, the EU15 would need incremental productivity growth of 1.3% per annum.[16] This would accelerate historic rates of productivity by two-thirds and approximate the original target of 3% per annum set out in the original Lisbon agenda.

Once again there are considerable differences within the EU. There are also notable differences depending on whether one considers labor productivity per hour worked or labor productivity per employee. In terms of labor productivity per employee, the EU15 only manage about 80% of U.S. productivity, and all regions within Europe lag U.S. levels. In terms of labor productivity per hour worked, however, continental Europe[17] has exceeded U.S. levels consistently over the past 25 years. Only with the recession has this level slipped below current U.S. levels. Southern Europe,[18] on the other hand, only managed to reach slightly more than 60%

Figure 7A. Labor Productivity per Hour Worked in 2009 US$

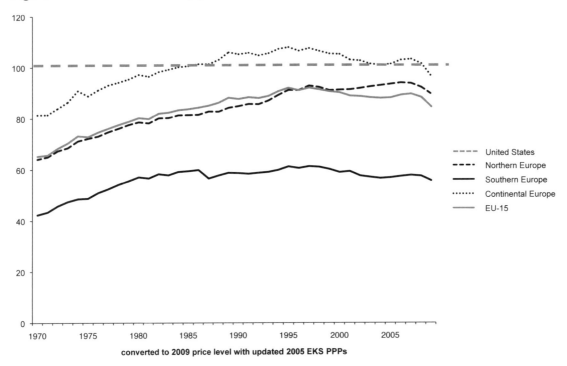

converted to 2009 price level with updated 2005 EKS PPPs

Note: Continental Europe: Germany, France, Belgium, Netherlands, Luxembourg, Switzerland and Austria
Southern Europe: Portugal, Spain, Italy, Greece, Malta, Cyprus, Turkey.
Northern Europe: Iceland, Norway, Sweden, Finland and Denmark and EU-15.
EKS stands for Elteto, Koves, Szulc and was first used by Lazlo Drechsler in the "Weighting of the index numbers in multilateral comparisons."
Source: The Conference Board.

of U.S. levels in the mid-1990s, and has been losing ground in all sectors since then. Northern Europe,[19] led by Sweden and the UK, surpassed the EU15 average in the mid-1990s and reached about 90% of U.S. levels just before the recession hit, although is fading now again.

The U.S. agriculture sector is almost twice as productive as that of the EU15, yet EU15 manufacturing and utilities have kept pace with the U.S. and contributed a full 60% of overall productivity growth. But McKinsey offers evidence that a full two-thirds of the EU15's productivity gap with the United States is in services, the sector that accounts for all net job growth in the EU.[20] There is a 43% productivity gap in business services, with significant gaps also in financial services and local services. The quickest route to faster EU productivity growth will be to further open the services sector. The IMF has calculated that if countries could reduce regulation to the average of the least restrictive of three OECD countries, annual productivity growth would rise by some 0.2% in America, 0.3% in the euro area and 0.6% in Japan. McKinsey estimates that boosting services sector productivity to the EU15 average or to European best-practice levels per sector could add 3-20% to the region's productivity.[21] The productivity gains to be achieved from moving to best practice in services would all but counter the drag on growth from the EU's shrinking and aging population.

Figure 7B. Labor Productivity per Person Employed in 2009 US$

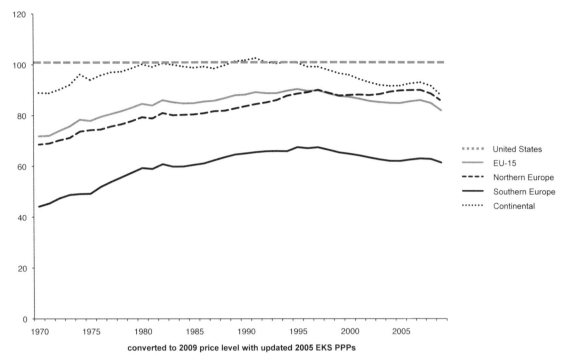

converted to 2009 price level with updated 2005 EKS PPPs

Note: Continental Europe: Germany, France, Belgium, Netherlands, Luxembourg, Switzerland and Austria
Southern Europe: Portugal, Spain, Italy, Greece, Malta, Cyprus, Turkey.
Northern Europe: Iceland, Norway, Sweden, Finland and Denmark and EU-15.
EKS stands for Elteto, Koves, Szulc and was first used by Lazlo Drechsler in the "Weighting of the index numbers in multilateral comparisons."
Source: The Conference Board.

EU member states have shown considerable reluctance to open their services markets; the EU Services Directive has limited scope. Yet as McKinsey notes, Japan offers a cautionary tale. Its services sector, unlike its world-class manufacturers, is fragmented, protected from foreign competition and heavily regulated, so it failed to capture the gains of the IT revolution. Sweden offers an encouraging tale, using its banking bust in the early 1990s to engage in some sweeping reforms, including in its services sector, and has enjoyed higher productivity growth.[22] Northern Europe has outperformed the rest of Europe with regard to productivity growth in services overall, while Continental Europe registers higher productivity than the UK and Ireland in local services and in construction.

Across the EU the productivity gap in local services with the U.S. is due to inadequate increases in multifactor productivity, which is the per capita GDP growth left over after taking account of primary inputs of capital, labor and labor quality, and intermediate inputs such as energy and services. It is a useful indicator of efficient use of such inputs, and thus also of innovation. Between 1995 and 2005 multifactor productivity in local services in the EU15 remained stagnant while it increased 2.3% a year in the U.S. and in retail and wholesale increased only 0.7% per year in the EU15 and 3.3% in the U.S.

In sum, despite the rise of rapidly developing economies, the economic ties between the EU and the U.S. remain the core of the world economy—the two economies together account for about 54% of world GDP. Their ties remain bigger, more prosperous, more tightly linked, more aligned in terms of free markets and open societies. Estimates are that a U.S.-EU zero-tariff agreement on trade in goods alone could boost annual EU GDP by up to .48% and 1.48% for the U.S.; generate welfare gains of up to $89 billion for the EU and $87 billion for the U.S.; and push EU exports to the U.S. up by 18% and U.S. exports to the EU up by 17%.[23]

A 75% reduction of services tariffs would yield almost $13.9 billion annually for the EU and $5.6 billion for the U.S.[24]

Estimates are that aligning half of relevant non-tariff barriers and regulatory differences between the EU and U.S. would push EU GDP .7% higher in 2018, an annual potential gain of €122 billion; and boost U.S. GDP .3% a year in 2018, an annual potential gain of €41 billion. An average EU household would receive an additional €12,500 over a working lifetime, and an average U.S. household would receive an additional $8,300 over a working lifetime. U.S. exports would increase by 6.1% and EU exports by 2.1%.[25]

Will the U.S. and the EU will use their current position to advance a true Transatlantic Marketplace and engage rapidly rising economies in new mechanisms of economic governance? Or will they divide their energies seeking to eke out their own marginal advantages in an emerging new order? Currently, U.S. and EU policymakers are engaged primarily in the latter, and American and European workers, consumers, and companies are poorer for it.

Canada and Mexico

EU economic ties with Canada are also significant. The EU is Canada's second largest investment partner after the U.S., and Canada is the fourth largest country investment partner for the EU. The EU is Canada's second most important trading partner, after the U.S., with a 10.5% share of its total external trade. Canada is currently the EU's 11th most important trading partner, accounting for 1.8% of the EU's total external trade in 2009.[26] The EU and Canada hope to conclude by 2012 a comprehensive trade and economic agreement that promises significant returns for both parties. Liberalizing trade in goods and services could boost EU exports to Canada by 24.3% or €17 billion and Canadian exports to the EU by 20.6% or €8.6 billion by 2014. The annual real income gain by the year 2014 would be approximately €11.6 billion for the EU (0.08% of EU GDP), and approximately €8.2 billion for Canada (0.77% of Canadian GDP). About half of the gains would come from liberalization of trade in services; more limited but still significant gains would derive from the elimination of tariffs on goods (25% of the total for the EU and 33.3% for Canada). The remaining gains are projected to result from a reduction in the trade costs of non-tariff barriers. While Canada would benefit relatively more from such an ambitious agreement (which is natural given the greater size of the EU's economy compared to Canada's), there will be notable gains to both economies.[27]

The EU signed a comprehensive free trade agreement with Mexico in 1997, with trade provisions entering into force in 2000 and 2001. The agreement has been of undoubted benefit to both parties: trade flows within the FTA have grown by over 25%, with Mexican exports to the EU growing by some 20% and EU exports to Mexico growing by close to 30%. Trade in industrial goods is fully liberalized, and agricultural products will be substantially liberalized by 2010. The FTA also foresees future negotiations on the liberalization of services trade. [28]

Chapter 8
The EU and Wider Europe:
The China Next Door?

During the past 15 years Wider Europe emerged as a key source of growth for the EU. As many of these countries embarked on high growth patterns, demand for automobiles, capital machinery, luxury goods, consumer electronics, basic materials, and other finished and unfinished goods surged, playing to the core strengths and product offerings of corporate Europe. Over the past decade, Wider Europe's growth and development has had a far greater impact on the EU than China. In fact, in 2008 my colleague Joseph Quinlan and I argued that if one looked at the EU's burgeoning periphery from North Africa across the Mediterranean up through Turkey and into eastern Europe to Russia, the EU potentially has its own China right next door.

Wider Europe was hit hard by the recession, however, clouding prospects for the region's growth. While economic growth has returned in some countries, the recovery remains sluggish and far from secure. Lower exports and a sharp drop in capital inflows ended the domestic demand boom that many countries experienced over the past decade. While the region avoided any severe banking and currency crises and is recovering, fiscal deficits remain high, credit growth and domestic demand remain weak, and the region will need to find new models of sustainable growth.

Wider Europe is a diverse region, with highly advanced countries such as Switzerland and Norway as well as some of the poorest countries on the continent. Turkey, an applicant to join the European Union, is a major economic power and energy hub in the region and is already tied to the EU through a Customs Union. The EU has particularly broad and deep ties with the region across the full range of goods and services, financial and energy flows, people and ideas. All told, Wider Europe joins North America as a key geo-economic base for the European Union. Stronger growth and demand in the region is critical to the EU's own continued prosperity and competitive standing.

Wider Europe's exports will remain heavily tied to the EU, which is the region's major market.[1] EU imports of goods from Wider Europe grew 4.7% per year on average during the past decade. Wider Europe, in turn, was the second largest regional source of EU goods imports (18%) and the second largest regional destination for EU goods exports (21%). EU exports of goods to Wider Europe grew 4.3% per year on average over the course of the past decade. In 2009, Switzerland accounted for nearly 50% of the region's exports and imports with the EU.

The EU exported €226.4 billion of goods to Wider Europe in 2009, only 93% as much as to North America, but more than twice as much as to Rising Asia and to Africa; 2.8 times more than to China; over 3 times more than to Russia, over 6 times more than to Japan; and over 8 times more than to India. Switzerland ranks as the EU's 2th largest country export market, accounting for 8.1% of EU exports in 2009, ahead of China. Turkey ranks as the EU's 5th largest export market, accounting for 5% of EU exports, behind Russia and just ahead of Norway, which ranks 6th and accounted for 3.4% of EU exports in 2009.

The EU imported €213.1 billion of goods from Wider Europe in 2009, marginally less than from China, but 12% more than from North America; over 1½ times more than from Rising Asia; almost twice as much as from Russia and from Africa; almost 4 times more than from Japan; and over 8 times more than from India. Switzerland ranks as the EU's 4th largest country supplier, accounting for 6.1% of EU imports in 2009, followed closely by Norway, the EU's 5th largest supplier, accounting for 5.7% of EU imports in 2009. Turkey ranks as the EU's 7th largest supplier, accounting for 3% of EU imports, just ahead of South Korea, Brazil and India.

Wider Europe was the second largest destination for EU services exports (19%) and the second largest source of EU services imports (17%) in recession year 2009 (compared with 20% of exports and imports in 2008).[2] EU exports of services to Wider Europe grew 8.8% per year on average and EU imports of services from Wider Europe grew 7.2% per year on average between 2004 and 2008, before falling in 2009. During the same time period, the EU's services trade surplus with Wider Europe increased 93%.

EU services exports to Wider Europe in 2009 were 69% of its services exports to North America, but 2.5 times more than to Rising Asia and to Latin America; almost 3 times more than to the Middle East and to Africa; over 3 times more than to Oceania; 5 times more than to China, Russia and Japan; 10 times more than to India; and 20 times more than to the Caribbean.

EU services imports from Wider Europe in 2009 were 57% of EU services imports from North America, but over 2.5 times more than from Rising Asia; 3 times more than from Africa; 3.5 times more than from the Middle East; over 5 times more than from Oceania, China and Latin America; 7 times more than from Japan and Russia; over 10 times more than from India; and 21 times more than from the Caribbean.

Turkey reported a stunning 11.4% expansion for the first quarter of 2010, second only to China. It is an astonishing transformation for an economy that just 10 years ago had a budget deficit of 16% of GDP and inflation of 72%.[6] Yet despite Turkey's close economic ties with the EU, the country's trade is shifting noticeably away from Europe toward its eastern neighborhood, particularly to Iraq, Egypt, Libya, and Iran. This shift is being driven primarily by the faster growth of Turkey's Middle Eastern trading partners, but also by a conscious Turkish political decision to cultivate such ties. A proposed preferential trade agreement with Iran is expected to triple bilateral trade within five years.

Wider Europe is the second largest regional destination for FDI from the EU.[3] Wider Europe is also the second largest regional source of foreign direct investment in the EU. EU FDI in Wider Europe grew 17.8% per year on average over the course of the last decade until the recession. Wider Europe's investment in the EU grew at a similar pace, 17.3% per year on average, in the same time period.

The EU had a total of €732 billion in foreign direct investment in Wider Europe in 2008, only about 60% of EU FDI in North America, but almost 3 times more than in Rising Asia; over 3 times more than in Latin America and the Caribbean; over 5 times more than in Africa; 8 times more than in Russia; over 9 times more than in Japan; over 10 times more than in the Middle East; over 15 times more than in China; and 38 times more than in India.

Figure 8A. Turkish Exports Growth 2007 to 2010

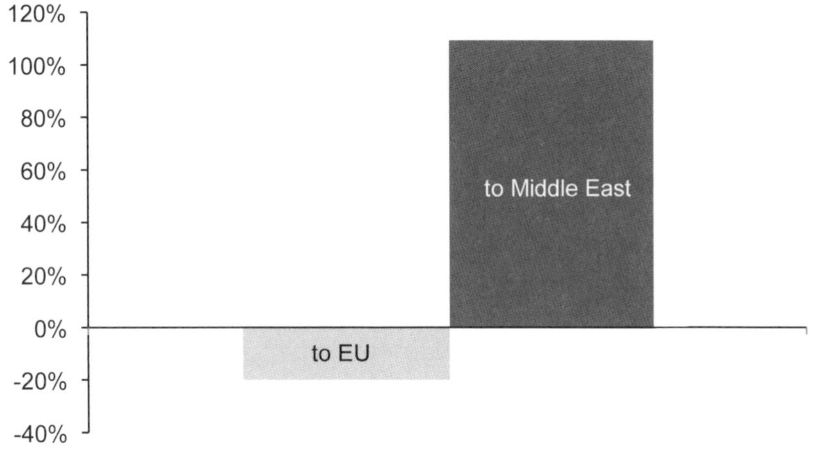

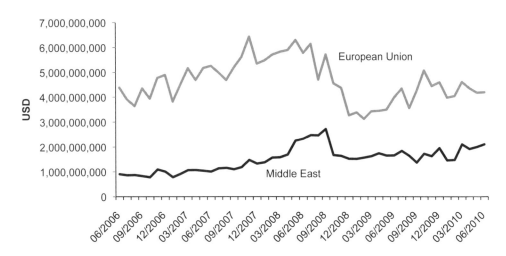

Source: Turkish Statistical Office; Council on Foreign Relations.

Figure 8B. Turkish Exports 2006 to 2010

Source: Turkish Statistical Office; Council on Foreign Relations.

Wider Europe had a total of €464 billion in foreign direct investment in the EU in 2008, only 40% of FDI coming into the EU from North America, but 69% more than from the Caribbean, 4 times more than from Japan; over 6 times more than from Rising Asia; 6½ times more than from Latin America; over 9 times more from the Middle East; over 16 times more than from Russia; 22 times more than from Africa; 33 times more than from China; and 66 times more than from India.

52% of overall foreign portfolio investment in Wider Europe came from the EU. Another 30% came from the United States, and 7% came from Japan. The EU had a total of $543 billion in private portfolio investment in Wider Europe in 2008, slightly more than in the Caribbean and 25% more than in Japan; over twice as much as in Rising Asia; almost 6 times more than in Latin America; over 10 times more than in China; 11 times more than in India; 14 times more than in Russia; 15 times more than in the Middle East; and 16 times more than in Africa.

Wider Europe had a total of $1.034 trillion in private portfolio investment in the EU in 2008, only slightly more than half that from North America, but 82% more than from Japan; 4 times more than from Rising Asia; over 10 times more than from the Caribbean; 45 times more than from Latin America; 60 times more than from Russia; and 64 times more than from the Middle East.

Wider Europe is the EU's second largest source and buyer of natural gas.[4] Wider Europe's natural gas exports to the EU grew 182% since 2000 while EU exports to the region declined by 59%. Wider Europe sent 37 million tons of natural gas to the EU and bought 629,361 tons in 2009.

Wider Europe is the second largest buyer of EU oil and the EU's third largest source of oil. Oil imports from the EU grew by 35% since 2000 while oil exports to the EU grew 10%. Wider Europe delivered 116 million tons of oil to the EU in 2009 and bought 28 million tons.

In 2009, Wider Europe was the EU's largest buyer of coal and its seventh largest source. Wider Europe's coal exports to the EU grew by 66% since 2000 while the region bought 27% less coal from the EU in 2009 than in 2000. It sent 6 million tons of coal to the EU and bought 25 million tons from the EU in 2009.

Wider Europe is the EU's sixth largest solar provider and fourth largest buyer. Wider Europe's solar exports to the EU have grown more than five-fold since 2000, and Wider Europe's solar imports from the EU have grown 3.5 times.

The region is the number one purchaser of biofuels from the EU and the number three provider. Wider Europe's biofuels exports to the EU have grown 2¼ times while biofuels imports from the EU have declined 8% since 2000. The region purchased 24,314 tons of EU biofuels in 2009 and sold 39,924 tons to the EU.

Wider Europe is the EU's second largest buyer of windpower parts, and its fourth largest provider. EU windpower sales to the region have grown almost nine-fold since 2000. Wider Europe exported €301 million to the EU and imported €158 million from the EU in 2009. The region bought €185 million worth of windpower components and sold €5 million to the EU in 2009.

Refugees from Wider Europe accounted for 39.7% of the total refugees in the EU, making it the largest contributing region of the twelve regions examined.[5] Refugee flows from Wider Europe increased by 105.1% from 2000 to 2008. From 2000 to 2008, the EU received a total of 4,153,360 refugees from Wider Europe. It received 460,801 refugees from Wider Europe in 2008.

Migrant flows from Wider Europe accounted for 28.1% of the total migrant flows to the EU in 2006, making it the largest of the ten regions for which data is available. Migrant flows to Wider Europe accounted for 26.3% of the total migrant flows from the EU in 2006, making it the third largest of the eleven regions for which data is available. Migrant flows from Wider Europe to the EU increased by 0.9% from 2000 to 2006. In 2006, the EU received 175,660 labor immigrants from Wider Europe, and had 73,144 emigrants to Wider Europe.

Chapter 9
The EU and Japan: Fading Ties?

As a highly developed economy and major global trader and investor, Japan is an important partner for the EU. Japan is the world's third largest national economy, accounting for around 1.9% of the world's population and around 9% of world GDP. Japan is a rich country: it has the greatest savings of any nation and the largest foreign currency reserves in the world (over $1000 billion in 2010).[1]

Japan's dynamic postwar growth ended in the early 1990s, after which the country entered a prolonged period of stagnation. Growth was resuming by 2003, but the recession slashed GDP by 6%. Japan continues to struggle with serious headwinds to sustained growth, including entrenched deflation and continued declines in bank lending and land prices. Large government budget deficits have boosted gross public debt to 219% of GDP in 2009, the highest in the OECD.[2] With Japan's share of the global economy falling from 14% to 8% over the past two decades, the country has entered what *The Economist* describes as a state of "gentle decline."[3]

The EU's economically relevant ties to Japan have weakened in recent decades, particularly in trade in goods and services. This not only reflects the impact of Japan's lost decade and persistent commercial barriers between the two regions, but also the fact that much intermediate trade in goods has shifted from Japan to China. Bilateral ties are still strong in terms of two-way private portfolio investments and Japanese FDI into Europe. Only a trickle of refugees or migrants flows between the two regions. Connections in the realm of innovation and ideas are stronger than between most regions, but still pale in comparison with those between the EU and North America. The EU consistently lags Japan in terms of innovation performance, but is registering better growth rates.

Japan is a major trading nation. In 2008, Japanese imports and exports of goods amounted to €504 and €500 billion respectively, representing 6.1% and 6.4 % of world flows, respectively. Historically, the trade relationship between the EU and Japan has been characterized by strong trade surpluses in favor of Japan. In recent years trade figures have become much more balanced, but Japan continues to be a country where, for specific structural features of the Japanese society and economy, doing business or investing is often particularly difficult.[4]

The EU-South Korea free trade agreement signed in October 2010 has pushed Japan to consider a similar arrangement with the EU. Such a deal could reestablish Japan's position as one of the EU's main trading partners in Asia and open Japan's rather closed market to greater EU investment. Japan has slipped behind China in EU-Asian trade, and is concerned that the EU-South Korea deal could harm its car and electronics exporters.[5]

European and Japanese companies are major exporters of goods and competitors in a range of products, particularly upmarket, manufacturing and capital-intensive goods.[6] In automotive parts, a critical sector for both partners, the EU accounted for 15.2% of world market share, compared to Japan's 13.9% share. On balance European traders have withstood competitive pressures from rapidly emerging economies better than those from Japan. Whereas the EU has essentially maintained its 19% market share of world exports over a 15 year span, Japan lost around 6%, and now accounts for 8.6% of world market share. In addition, the EU registered close to a 1% gain in global market share in high-tech products between 1994 and the onset of the recession, while Japan recorded a 13% loss.

Even though the EU and Japan are major trading powers, direct commercial ties in goods between the two are relatively weak. Between 2005 and 2009 EU goods exports to Japan declined by 6.1% a year on average, at a time when overall EU goods exports were growing. With a share of 3.3% (2009) of EU exports, Japan is the EU's seventh largest export market after the U.S., Switzerland, China, Russia, Turkey and Norway. Japan accounts for 41.5% of EU machinery and transport equipment exports; 16.8% of chemical products; and 7% of EU agricultural products.[7]

The EU exported €36 billion in goods to Japan in 2009, 25% more than to India, but only 55% of EU goods exports to Russia; 44% of those to China; 37% of those Africa; 33% of those to Rising Asia; 16% of those to Wider Europe; and 15% of those to North America.

With a 4.6% (2009) share of the EU import market, Japan is the sixth largest source of imports into the EU after China, the U.S., Russia, Switzerland and Norway. Yet EU imports of goods from Japan fell by 40% between 2000 and 2009. During the same time period, the EU's goods trade deficit with Japan decreased by 57%. Imports from Japan are mainly in the sectors of machinery and transport equipment (67.9%), miscellaneous manufactured articles (12.2%) and chemical products (8.7%).[8]

The EU imported €55.8 billion in goods from Japan in 2009, more than twice imports from India, but only 56% of those from Africa; 48% of those from Russia; 40% of those from Rising Asia; 30% of those from North America; and 26% of those from Wider Europe and China.[9]

The EU enjoys significant advantages over Japan in the area of services, with much higher market shares across every commercial sector.[10] For instance, the EU boosted its world market share in exports of transportation services between 2000 and 2008 to 21.9%, while Japan's share declined from 7.4% to 5.3%. Japan's single-minded focus on manufactured exports has come at the expense of its services sectors, which have achieved but a fraction of U.S. and EU productivity levels.[11] The two areas where Japan is a major player are construction services, where it accounts for 15.7% of the world market, compared to the EU's share of 32.9%; and royalties and license fees, where Japan's 12.5% share trails the EU's 19.3% share.

Japan is even less significant to EU services trade than it is to EU goods trade, even though the EU has a trade surplus in services with Japan. Japan ranked as the tenth largest regional destination for EU services exports in 2009, accounting for only 4% of EU services exports; and the ninth largest regional source of EU services imports, accounting for only 3% of EU services imports. Leading EU services exporters such as the UK, Germany and France lag the U.S. badly when it comes to services exports to Japan (U.S. share 56%). In fact, EU services exports to Japan actually decreased 10% between 2004 and 2009. During this same period, EU imports of services from Japan increased by 20%, resulting in a 51% decline in the EU's trade surplus in services with Japan.

EU services exports to Japan in 2009 were four times those to the Caribbean, double those to India and about the same as to China and to Russia. But they were only 2/3 those to Oceania, slightly more than half those to the Middle East and Africa, half those to Latin America and to Rising Asia, one-fifth those to Western Europe and less than one-seventh of EU services exports to North America.

EU services imports from Japan in 2009 were 3 times those from the Caribbean, slightly more than from India, and about the same as from Russia; but slightly less than from Oceania, China and Latin America, slightly more than half those from Africa, half of EU services imports from Rising Asia, about one-seventh of those from Wider Europe, and 9 times less than those from North America.

Japan is the 4th largest regional source of FDI in the EU. In 2008, 3.6% of EU inflows came from Japan. At the end of 2008, 4.5% of the stock of EU inward FDI came from Japan. Japan's investment in the EU grew over 11% on average per year over the past decade until the recession. Japan had a total of €117 billion in foreign direct investment in the EU in 2008, only 10% of that from North America, 4 times less than that from Wider Europe and almost 3 times less than from the Caribbean, but 38% more than from Rising Asia; 39% more than from Latin America; 58% more than from the Middle East; 76% more than from Russia; 82% more than from Africa; 88% more than from China; and 17 times more than from India.

Over the past few years, the EU has become the largest source of FDI into Japan.[12] At the end of 2008, 2.36% of the stock of EU outward FDI was in Japan and 1.7% of the EU outflow went to Japan. Japan is the eighth largest regional destination for EU FDI. EU investment in Japan grew 8% on average per year over the past decade until the recession, facilitated by reforms in the financial, communications and distribution sectors, as well as a small number of major mergers such as Renault/Nissan. Overall, however, foreign investment to Japan remains very low (around 4.1% of GDP) compared to the EU (36.9% of GDP).[13] The EU had a total of €76 billion in foreign direct investment in Japan in 2008, slightly more than in the Middle East; 39% more than in China; but only 83% of that in Russia; 58% of that in Africa; 34% of that in the Caribbean; one-third of that in Latin America; 28% of that in Rising Asia; 10 times less than in Wider Europe and 16 times less than in North America.

43% of overall foreign portfolio investment in Japan came from the EU. Another 41% came from the United States. The EU had a total of $410 billion in private portfolio investment in Japan in 2008, 92% more than in Africa; 91% more than in Russia and in the Middle East; 88% more than in India; 87% more than in China; 77% more than in Latin America; 56% more than in Rising Asia; but 23% less than in the Caribbean, 25% less than in Wider Europe and 6½ times less than in North America.

Japan had a total of $848 billion in private portfolio investment in the EU in 2008, 2.3 times less than from North America and 82% less than from Wider Europe, but over 3 times more than from Rising Asia; almost 9 times more than from the Caribbean; 37 times more than from Latin America; 50 times more than from Russia; 53 times more than from the Middle East; 60 times more than from China.

Over the past ten years the euro and the pound sterling have each become more desirable in terms of global foreign exchange holdings, whereas the Japanese yen's position has slipped. The euro accounted for 26.5% of total allocated global foreign exchange holdings at mid-year 2010 and the pound sterling accounted for 4.2%, while the Japanese yen's share had declined to 3.3%. The same trend is even more pronounced among developing nations: the euro accounted for 28.3% and the pound sterling for 6.3% of allocated reserves by emerging and developing countries at mid-year 2010, while the yen's share had declined to 2.4%.[14]

The EU's ties to Japan in traditional energy sources are relatively weak, as both are major net importers of energy. Both partners have a medium relationship in renewables. Japan has been the EU's second largest windpower client over the course of the past decade, although demand dropped in 2009.

Japan consistently outperforms the EU in most measures of innovation.[15] According to the European Innovation Scoreboard, Japan performs better than the EU in 12 indicators, while the EU performs better and is increasing its lead over Japan in 5 indicators. The EU also recorded 3.17% growth in innovation performance across the board, outpacing Japan's 1.16% growth rate. In addition, Japan's overall competitive performance continues to be dragged down by its macroeconomic weaknesses, with high budget deficits that have led to the buildup of one of the highest public debt levels in the world (217.6% of GDP in 2009).

Japan continues to outpace the EU in labor productivity growth. During the 1980s Japan recorded 4.1% annual average growth in labor productivity, compared to 2.5% for the countries that now comprise the euro area, and 1.8% for the UK. During the 1990s Japan's growth rate slowed to 2.5%, slightly less than the UK's 2.6% rate, but still ahead of the 1.8% euro area rate. During the past decade Japan's productivity growth rate has again slowed to 2.1% per annum, but continued to outpace the UK's 1.7% rate and the euro area's 1.2% rate.[16]

While Japan remains a formidable manufacturing and trading power, its difficulties also offer Europe a cautionary tale. Over the past twenty years Japan has lost considerable ground. In the 1980s it was heralded by many as the epicenter of world-class manufacturing. Today it faces challenges that resonate in Europe: a declining workforce, aging populations, "loss of a manufacturing culture," and failure to build a competitive services economy. The EU would do well to consider Japan's "lost decade" as it looks to its next decade.[17]

Chapter 10
The EU and China: Shaping the Future?

China's rapid economic rise since it embarked on a major transformation of its economy in 1978 is one of the most dramatic developments in today's world. The size of the Chinese economy has increased nearly twenty-fold in the last 30 years. Real GDP growth has averaged 10% annually, meaning that GDP has doubled every 7–8 years. Hundreds of millions of people have been lifted from poverty and living conditions have improved in a variety of dimensions. These improvements have occurred at a faster pace than was experienced in Europe during the Industrial Revolution or in the United States after the opening of the American West in the 19th century.[1] China roared through the recession, posting 9.1% growth in 2009 and 10% in the first half of 2010, and surpassed Japan to become the world's second largest economy.

China's rapid economic rise has had a pronounced effect on the global economy. Over the past quarter century, no other country in the world has done more to alter global trade flows, shift global foreign direct investment patterns and reconfigure global demand for commodities. But how has China's reintegration in the global economy affected Europe?

In many cases, China's influence has been contradictory or countervailing. For instance, the mainland's capacity to produce and export massive volumes of consumer goods has helped to lower the relative costs of household goods and been a brake on inflation in European countries and other developed nations. At the same time, such production has pushed up prices for basic materials like aluminum, steel, copper, bauxite, iron ore and petroleum, which are critical ingredients for China's industrialization. Similarly, while low-cost imports from China have been highly beneficial to European consumers, retailers and producers, surging Chinese imports have been blamed for job losses in some European countries. China's reintegration into the global economy has greatly expanded the global labor force over the past two decades, putting into the reach of European firms a huge new pool of skilled and unskilled labor. Not surprisingly, European multinationals have sought to leverage this resource for their operations. As we have explained elsewhere,[2] however, the actual number of jobs lost to lower cost Chinese labor has been relatively small, in part because European companies actually "nearshore" far more jobs within the larger EU than they "offshore" to China.[3]

The EU's economically relevant links to China are overwhelmingly in trade in goods, in which the EU has a large and chronic deficit. China is a far less important partner for the EU when it comes to trade in services and to foreign direct investment. Mutual investment flows are dwarfed by EU investment flows to and from the United States. Ties are modest in traditional forms of energy, but China is the EU's largest supplier of wind and solar components. Flows of Chinese refugees and migrants to the EU are modest. More students from China are coming to the EU for tertiary education, but far less than the many who study in the United States. The flow of ideas between the EU and China, as exemplified for instance by R&D investments or innovation ties, remains very weak.

China's rise is reflected in its growing share in the external trade of every major world region, where it is emerging in some sectors as a strong competitor for the EU. It accounted for nearly 12% of the external trade of other emerging Asian countries in 2008. This share, while rising rapidly, is still smaller than the share of the United States in the external trade of other Western Hemisphere countries (around 25% between 2000 and 2009) and also smaller than the share of Japan in the rest of Asia's trade (14%). Japan's share, however, has fallen to just half of its level two decades ago.

China accounts for just over 10% of Africa's external trade and just under 10% of the external trade of the Middle East. In 1980 its share of external trade in both regions was negligible. China's share in India's trade has grown from less than 1% to nearly 12%. China's share in the external trade of the Western Hemisphere rose 15-fold during 1980–2008, to nearly 8%. China became Brazil's largest country trading partner in 2009 and was set to become the biggest direct investor in Brazil in 2010. And while China's share of the EU's external trade was only 4% in 2008, that reflects a 10-fold increase between 1980 and 2008. China's share in the external trade of France, Germany, Italy, and the UK rose to 3–5% in 2008 from one-tenth that level in 1980.[4]

China is the EU's #1 goods supplier, accounting for 17.9% of EU imports in 2009. The EU also ranks as China's single most important export market, accounting for 20.4% of Chinese exports, slightly more than the United States.[5] China is only the sixth largest regional destination for EU goods exports, however, accounting for less than 8% of total EU goods exports in the world. While China has emerged as one of the fastest growing export markets for European goods and services, it starts from a relatively low base — the EU exports less to China than to Switzerland. This imbalance has generated the EU's largest trade deficit—€133 billion in 2009, down from over €169 billion in 2008.

EU goods imports from China of €214.7 billion in 2009 were slightly greater than good imports from Wider Europe of €213.1 billion and 13% greater than goods imports from North America, but 1½ times more than from Rising Asia; almost twice that of goods imports from Russia, and more than twice goods imports from Africa.

EU goods exports of €81.6 billion to China in 2009, on the other hand, were only one-third EU good exports to North America, 36% of good exports to Wider Europe; 75% of EU goods exports to Rising Asia, and slightly less than EU goods exports to Africa. Still, the EU has a 13.4% export market share in China, ahead of the United States, Japan and South Korea. EU goods exports to China have now surpassed EU goods exports to Russia, which traditionally has been the most important BRIC export market for the EU. In addition, EU goods exports to China have been growing at a 30% annual average growth rate over the course of the past decade—faster than any other goods export destination. This compares, for instance, to a 4.3% annual average growth in EU goods exports to Wider Europe.

China the consumer is not nearly as powerful as China the producer. Despite China's rapid growth and size, it remains a developing country. 150 million Chinese still live on less than €2 a day. Accounting for purchasing power, its GDP per capita in 2009 was 11% of that of the EU. Its household consumption is only around one-eighth that of the United States and has even declined as a percentage of GDP from 45% in 1997 to only 36% in 2009. China accounts for only 3% of world imports of consumer goods and for only 4% of world import growth.[6]

China's development model has been successful at generating growth, but it will inevitably run into constraints. Beijing has squeezed household income to generate additional productive capacity, via an undervalued currency, slow wage growth, and bank-based, rather than bond or equity-based forms of corporate financing—all of which amount to transfers of wealth from the household sector to exports, employment and preferred borrowers. China's growth relies too heavily on investment and external trade. Setting the economy on a more sustainable path will require greater domestic consumption. To do this, China would need to raise the value of its currency dramatically, as well as raise wages, household incomes, and interest rates. A sudden shift away from its current model, however, could send the country's exporters and employers into bankruptcy. Experts suggest that China would need 8-10 years to rebalance its economy, even if it decided to embark upon this transition. And it remains questionable whether Chinese leaders will indeed choose this path.[7]

The collapse in Chinese exports to global markets hit by the recession in fall 2008/winter 2009 was a harrowing experience, however, as tens of thousands lost their factory jobs. There is a growing realization in Beijing that China must balance its export-led growth pattern of over-investment, misallocated capital and hidden subsidies with greater domestic consumption, and has embarked on various structural reforms to effect such changes. Moreover, China has the wherewithal to make the transition. Its claim that it is poor evokes skepticism when it is sitting on $2.85 trillion in foreign reserves—an amount about the size of the German economy. Many Western economists argue that such a transition must also include a revaluation of China's currency in relation to the dollar and the euro, or that China will hit a "growth wall," in the words of NYU economist Nouriel Roubini.[8] China is the only major trading country to use capital controls to prevent its currency from rising to market levels, and its undervalued currency subsidizes Chinese exports and import substitutes.

China is unlikely to become a major global consumer overnight. It is unlikely to import more until its boosts investment in services and increases consumption, including by removing distortions that depress workers' share of income and encouraging households to save less.[9] Nonetheless, size matters, and even incremental changes in Chinese import patterns can have major implications for its trading partners. For instance, China imports just 3% of its coal, yet that accounts for about one-fifth of global seaborne trade in coal. It consumes roughly half the world's cement, a third of its steel and a quarter of its aluminum. Each year the power it adds to its electricity grid is greater than the entire generating capacity of India.[10]

China's middle class may still be small relative to the overall population, but given the huge size of China's population, its middle class currently numbers 56 million people — a consuming cohort greater than most European countries. China's middle class will swell to over 360 million people by 2030 and over time will comprise one of the largest consumer markets in the world, including for the EU. Infrastructure has dramatically improved and the country's financial services are expanding and becoming more sophisticated, making it easier for European companies to do business with potential Chinese importers.[11] And as China continues to restructure its economy and upgrade its technological capabilities, it will still absorb a large amount of investment goods, where the EU's comparative advantage is expected to continue.

Although EU exports to China are lower than their potential, China is one of the fastest growing export markets and source of global earnings for many European companies. China's emergence as the largest automobile market in the world is a vivid example of its rise as a major source of global earnings for European companies. And who is the #1 carmaker in China? Volkswagen. With 18.3% of the Chinese market—more than twice the share of Toyota, its nearest competitor—Volkswagen calls China its "second home market."[12]

Although China is likely to become a significant market for the EU, it also presents the EU with a range of challenges. For one, China's export growth rates are far exceeding those of the EU. Chinese average annual growth of exports of goods and services of 26% and imports of about 23% between 2000 and 2007, for instance far outdistance the 9-14% rates registered by almost all old EU member states. The EU19's 10% average annual growth rates in medium- and high-tech exports between 1997 and 2007 fall far behind China's 26% growth pace. If current trends continue, China will catch up and surpass the EU in a range of sectors in which the EU currently holds a large lead.

A related challenge is China's rise as a high-tech exporter and the role of European and other foreign companies in China's success. By 2007 the share of technology-driven industries in EU imports from China was already higher than in intra-EU imports. A good share of those imports come from European or other foreign firms that assemble and produce from China.

Third, European companies lose out on an estimated €20 billion a year due to China's many non-tariff barriers and regulatory discrimination, its preferential treatment of Chinese companies and indigenous technology for government procurement, its undervalued currency, its weak enforcement or implementation of existing regulations in many areas, and its lack of protections for intellectual property rights. Roughly 50% of counterfeit goods in the EU come directly from China.[13] China has failed to accede to the WTO's Government Procurement Agreement (GPA) despite repeated promises to do so over the past ten years.[14]

The impact of China's preferential procurement policies can be readily seen in the wind energy sector, where foreign companies' share of China's wind turbine market plunged from 75% in 2004 to 15% in 2009. The Spanish company Gamesa offers a case study. In 2005 the company controlled one-third of the Chinese market. But strict local content requirements led Gamesa to train local suppliers, who then used their new-found technological capacity, together with cheap land and low-interest loans from the Chinese government to undercut Gamesa with third companies. Gamesa's market share is now 3%.

The pattern has been repeated in other industries, such as desktop computers and solar panels. One report from China's State Council was straightforward in its call for the "absorption, assimilation and re-innovation of imported technologies."[15] U.S., EU and Japanese companies have been surprised to find how quickly China has taken foreign technology and converted it into a serious indigenous rapid-rail capability, which it uses to offer competing bids for contracts from Saudi Arabia to Brazil to California.[16]

Fourth, China's ravenous hunger of commodities is already generating considerable economic and political consequences. It is scouring Asia, Africa and Latin America for oil and other resources, and is not overly concerned whether the source of such materials may have problems with human rights or the rule of law, factors that sometimes hinder EU development of such ties.[17]

China is a far less important partner, and a far less important competitor, for the EU when it comes to trade in services.[18] Not only does the EU enjoy a services trade surplus with China, it roughly tripled between 2004 and 2009. Yet licensing requirements continue to exclude foreign companies from entire services sectors. Nearly ten years after China's WTO accession, and despite clear commitments to increase competition in service sectors, European companies are still denied fair market access to several of them.[19] Even though EU exports of services to China doubled between 2004 and 2009, China ranks only as the ninth largest regional destination for EU services exports (4%). EU services exports to North America, for instance, were over 7 times those to China; EU services exports to Wider Europe were 5 times those to China, and those to Latin America and Rising Asia were double those to China. Even EU services exports to Oceania were 50% more than to China. EU services exports to Russia were slightly larger than to China in 2009. Leading EU services exporters such as the UK, Germany and France lag the U.S. when it comes to China (U.S. share 27.9%).

EU imports of services from China increased by 79% between 2004 and 2009, but China was also only the seventh largest regional source of EU services imports (4%) in 2009. EU services imports from China were one-ninth of those from North America; 5 times less than from Wider Europe; half of those from Rising Asia, less than from Africa, the Middle East, and Oceania; but more than from Latin America, Japan, Russia, India and the Caribbean.

The EU's links to China are also weak in the area of foreign direct investment.[20] The EU had a total of only €47 billion in foreign direct investment in China in 2008, making China the eleventh largest foreign direct investment destination (of the twelve regions examined) for the EU. EU investment in China grew on average 23% a year during the past decade before the recession, but remains quite low in comparison with EU FDI elsewhere. China's economy is the most regulated and controlled of the world's major economies, and more than any of the BRICs. In 2008 less than 3% of EU outbound FDI went to China. EU FDI in North America was more than 26 times that in China; in Wider Europe more than 15 times; in Rising Asia almost 6 times; Caribbean and Latin America almost 5 times; in Africa almost 3 times; and in Russia twice the amount as in China. Despite this relatively low level of EU FDI, it is important to keep China's growth rates in mind. Global FDI inflows into China, for example, may only have accounted for 7% of gross world FDI inflows in 2009, but they were only 1% in 1980.[21]

China also ranks 11 out of the 12 regions in terms of FDI coming into the EU, with only €14 billion in foreign direct investment in the EU in 2008. China's investment in the EU grew 25-fold between 2000 and 2008, but remains at a relatively low level. Direct investments by Chinese companies abroad heavily favor developing over developed countries. Given China's vast reserves and financial might, its investment portfolio in Europe is negligible. It is also dwarfed by North American FDI in the EU, which is 83 times greater. Russian FDI in the EU is twice that by China. Even Africa provides more FDI in the EU than does China. Only India provides less—about ½ as much as does China. Europe accounted for only 5.8% of Chinese FDI globally, slightly more than Chinese FDI in North America but less than Chinese FDI in

Table 10.1. Chinese FDI Stock into Europe, 2003–07

(non finance part, $ millions)

	2003	2004	2005	2006	2007
Russia	61.6	123.5	465.6	929.8	1,421.5
EU	**425.8**	**553.2**	**768.0**	**1,274.5**	**2,942.1**
United Kingdom	75.2	108.5	108.0	201.9	950.3
Germany	83.6	129.2	268.4	472.0	845.4
Sweden	6.1	6.4	22.5	20.0	146.9
Spain	101.8	127.7	130.1	136.7	142.9
Netherlands	5.9	9.0	14.9	20.4	138.8
Italy	19.2	20.8	21.6	74.4	127.1
France	13.1	21.7	33.8	44.9	126.8
Poland	2.7	2.9	12.4	87.2	98.9
Hungary	5.4	5.4	2.8	53.7	78.2
Romania	29.8	31.1	39.4	65.6	72.9
Denmark	74.4	67.2	96.6	36.5	36.8
Belgium	0.4	1.6	2.3	2.7	34.0
Ireland	0.2	0.0	0.0	25.3	29.2
Czech Republic	0.3	1.1	1.4	14.7	19.6
Bulgaria	0.6	1.5	3.0	4.7	4.7

Source: MOFCOM; Françoise Nicolas, "Chinese Direct Investment in Europe: Facts and Fallacies," Chatham House Briefing Paper, June 2009.

Africa, one-third of Chinese FDI in Latin America, and less than one-tenth of Chinese FDI in Asia.[22]

While small in absolute terms, new Chinese projects surged 30% in Europe in 2009. Chinese FDI in Europe can be strategically important in certain economic sectors. For instance, in 2010 Chinese company Geely bought Volvo, the Swedish car company previously owned by Ford, for €1.5 billion. The deal was the largest acquisition of an overseas carmaker by a Chinese company and the first time China had acquired a major luxury brand.

In addition, China's recent investments in cash-strapped EU economies are giving Chinese companies important new footholds in the EU market. China has singled out Greek, Spanish and other downgraded government debt, as well as ports, highways and industries in troubled countries on Europe's eastern and southern edges.

By early 2011 China had purchased hundreds of millions of dollars in Spanish debt and pledged to buy Greek bonds once the government started selling again.[23] Chinese companies have won bids to construct highways linking central and eastern European countries to Germany and Turkey. China has provided billions of dollars in state financing for key public works projects in Greece and Italy that support Chinese state-owned companies and Chinese workers. For instance, it has created a $5 billion fund to help finance the purchase of Chinese ships by Greek shipping companies. In addition, the Chinese company Cosco won a concession in 2008 to run the two main container terminals at Piraeus port outside Athens—one of Europe's largest gateways for Chinese goods—in a deal worth €3.4 billion.[24] Cosco is also expanding the port of Naples, Italy, while HNA, a Chinese logistics, transportation and tourism group is in talks to build a giant air terminal north of Rome for cargo arriving from China. Irish authorities have opened talks with Chinese promoters to develop a 240-hectare industrial park in central Ireland where Chinese manufacturers could operate inside the EU free of quotas and costly tariffs. Irish Prime Minister Brian Cowen said that Ireland could become the "gateway" for Chinese investment into Europe.[25]

The EU accounted for 22% of overall foreign portfolio investment in China. Another 22% came from the United States, and 2% came from Japan. The EU had a total of $53 billion in private portfolio investment in China in 2008, 50 times less than in North America, 16 times less than in Japan, about one-tenth of that in the Caribbean and in Wider Europe, 3 times less than in Oceania, slightly more than half of that invested in Latin America, about the same as EU FDI in India and more than in Russia, the Middle East or Africa.

Ties are modest in traditional forms of energy, but China is the EU's largest supplier of wind and solar components and the 2nd largest buyer.[26] China has quickly become the world's largest manufacturer, and user of solar panels, and the biggest investor in renewable energy.[27] While European governments (and the U.S.) tend to subsidize solar energy consumers, China subsidizes solar energy producers. It then exports virtually all of its panels to the EU and to the U.S., often aided by European and American consumer subsidies.[28] For these reasons, European business and labor groups question whether there is a level playing field in China when it comes to renewable energy. They complain that world-class wind turbine generator producers have been shut out of China's major projects, and that no foreign producer has won a major Chinese tender since 2005.[29] In both solar and wind the EU has a significant trade deficit with China. The EU sold €189 million in solar components to China while China sold €5.6 billion to the EU in 2009, up from €42 million in 2000. The EU imported €42 million in windpower parts from China and sold €8.8 million to China in 2009.

China's quasi-monopoly on the possession of so-called "rare" earths, a group of 17 obscure—but not particularly rare—minerals needed to produce a range of products from such things as wind turbines, car batteries, fiber optics and mobile phones to hard drives, video cameras and cruise missiles, has raised concerns in the EU and elsewhere that China could use that monopoly for political purposes. China's temporary ban on rare earths exports to Japan in the wake of a political dispute between the two countries in the fall of 2010, together with overall cuts in export quotas and hikes in export taxes for 2011, have triggered the alarm bells in world capitals. Yet the reason China developed a monopoly in the first place was market-driven. During the 1980s global rare earths production shifted from the U.S. to China due to low labor costs and lower environmental standards.[30] The result: whereas the U.S. used to account for one-half of global production, China now produces 97% of all rare earths produced globally.[31] In this sense the elements in question are not so much rare as not being developed in market-based economies. The EU and other major economies will need to address the possibilities of producing such rare metals outside of China and using fewer of the minerals to begin with. The U.S. is already ramping up plans to produce once again one-half of global production, which will be more than domestic U.S. demand and thus be available to others—but the U.S. Department of Energy estimates that it could take up to 15 years to break Western dependence on Chinese supplies.[32]

Flows of Chinese refugees and migrants to the EU are modest.[33] Refugees from China accounted for 0.8% of the total refugees in the EU, making it the sixth largest contributing region of the twelve regions examined. From 2000 to 2008, the EU received a total of 80,085 refugees from China. Migrant flows to China accounted for only 0.2% of the total migrant flows from the EU in 2006. Migrant flows from China accounted for 6.9% of the total migrant flows to the EU in 2006, making it the fifth largest of the ten regions for which data is available.

More students from China are coming to the EU for tertiary education. Whereas 18,613 Chinese students were studying in the EU in 2000, by 2007 that number had increased to 117,547, of which 3,735 were Hong Kong citizens.[34] There were 12,727 European students studying in China in 2008.[35]

Nonetheless, the flow of ideas, as exemplified by R&D investments or innovation ties, remains very weak.[36] For instance, only €313 million of EU total outward stocks in China in 2006 were in R&D. Lack of protection for intellectual property rights plays an important role in this regard. The amount of EU inward stocks owned by China in R&D is meager, and in fact in 2006 was *minus* €18 million, a net *disinvestment* by China in the EU. Weak EU-China ties in innovation are part of a larger phenomenon: together the BRICs account for only 1% of EU patented inventions.[37]

Chapter 11
The EU and Rising Asia: Opportunity Knocks

Rising Asia was the fourth largest regional destination of EU goods exports (10%) and thus is currently a larger export market for the EU than China.[1] Rising Asia was also the fourth largest source of EU goods imports (11.7%) in 2009. Overall goods trade with Rising Asia has been growing only slowly over the past decade, however—EU goods exports have been growing only 1% on average per year and EU goods imports falling by an equal amount per year. This has sliced the EU's goods trade deficit with the region by 42%, and is another reflection of the shift in inter-Asian production patterns from Rising Asia and Japan to China.

The EU exported €108 billion of goods to Rising Asia in 2009, about three times more than to Japan, 40% more than to Russia and 25% more than to China; less than half than to North America and to Wider Europe; and about the same as to Africa. The EU imported €138.5 billion of goods from Rising Asia in 2009, about 65% of goods coming to the EU from Wider Europe; 74% of goods coming from North America, slightly more than goods coming from Russia and 72% more than goods coming from Africa.

Rising Asia was the third largest destination for EU services exports (8%) and the third largest source of EU services imports (8%) in 2009.[2] The EU has a services trade surplus with Rising Asia, which increased 20% between 2004 and the onset of the recession. EU services exports to Rising Asia in 2009 were about 3.5 times less than those to North America, about 2.5 times less than to Wider Europe, and about the same as to Latin America; but slightly more than to the Middle East and to Africa, about one-fourth more than to Oceania, twice as much as to Russia, China and Japan, 4 times more than to India, and 8 times more than to the Caribbean.

EU services imports from Rising Asia in 2009 were about 4.5 times less than from North America and almost 3 times less than from Wider Europe; but slightly more than from Africa, about one-fourth greater than from the Middle East, twice that from Oceania, China and Latin America, more than twice that from Japan and Russia, 4 times that from India, and 8 times that from the Caribbean.

The 2010 free trade agreement between the EU and South Korea promises to offer considerable spark to bilateral trade ties. Combined EU-Korea trade in goods was worth about €53 billion in 2009. The agreement is predicted to create about €19 billion of new exports for EU producers and about €12 billion of new exports for South Korean companies. The agreement is the largest free-trade agreement in the world since NAFTA was born in 1994. It is also the most comprehensive free trade agreement ever negotiated by the EU. Import duties are eliminated on nearly all products. Trade in services is liberalized.[3] The EU has also moved out ahead of the United States, given that the U.S. Congress has failed to approve a final trade deal struck by the Obama Administration with South Korea.

The EU is also engaged in free-trade talks with Singapore and with Malaysia, its largest and second largest trading partner in Southeast Asia, and is looking to similar talks with Vietnam and Thailand. The trade agreement with South Korea has also pushed Japan to want to move ahead with a similar accord.

The EU had a total of €270 billion in foreign direct investment in Rising Asia in 2008, making the region the third largest foreign direct investment destination (of the twelve regions examined) for the EU, albeit 4.6 times less than EU FDI in North America and 2.7 times less than EU FDI in Wider Europe, although slightly more than in Latin America and in the Caribbean, twice as much as in Africa, 3 times more than in Russia, Japan and the Middle East, and almost 6 times more than in China.[4] In 2008 the EU accounted for $13.06 billion in FDI in the ASEAN countries, a 21.9% share of all FDI in ASEAN, greater than intra-ASEAN FDI flows among ASEAN members themselves, close to double Japanese FDI in ASEAN (12%), and more than four times U.S. FDI in ASEAN (5%).

Rising Asia had a total of €73 billion in foreign direct investment in the EU in 2008, making it the fifth largest source of FDI in the EU, but again far behind others—16 times less than from North America, 6 times less than from Wider Europe, over 4 times less than from the Caribbean, and 63% of FDI from Japan. However, Rising Asia's FDI in the EU was about the same as from Latin America, 67% more than from the Middle East, 38% more than from Russia, and more than 3 times than from Africa, 5 times more than from China, and 10 times more than from India.

33% of overall foreign portfolio investment in Rising Asia came from the EU. Another 33% came from the United States, and 6% came from Japan.

The EU had a total of $231 billion in private portfolio investment in Rising Asia in 2008, only 9% of that in North America; 43% of EU portfolio investment in the Caribbean; 61% of that in Wider Europe; 56% of that in Japan; 2½ times more than in Latin America; more than 4 times that in China and in India, and about 6 times more than in Russia, the Middle East and Africa.

Rising Asia had a total of $247 billion in private portfolio investment in the EU in 2008, 13% of North American private portfolio investment in the EU; 24% of Wider European private portfolio investment in the EU; 29% of Japanese private portfolio investment; but multiple times that of any other region.

Rising Asia is a partner of medium significance to the EU in terms of traditional energy supplies, ranking as the EU's fifth largest regional source and buyer of oil; the EU's sixth largest regional source of natural gas and fifth largest buyer; and the EU's sixth largest regional source of coal and seventh largest buyer.[5]

Rising Asia is more significant in the area of renewables, ranking as the #1 purchaser of EU solar parts and second largest seller in 2009; the EU's number two provider of windpower parts and fifth largest windpower client in 2009; and the second largest source of EU biofuel imports in 2009 and fifth largest destination for EU biofuels—although imports from Rising Asia have declined 50% and exports have suffered a 99% decline since 2004, and overall totals are but a fraction of that from Brazil, the EU's major supplier. EU solar exports to Rising Asia doubled while imports grew almost 7 times over the course of the past decade. Rising Asia's windpower parts sales to the EU grew 24 times while EU sales to the region grew 7 times since 2000.

Refugees from Rising Asia accounted for 17.4% of the total refugees in the EU, making it the fourth largest contributing region of the twelve regions examined. From 2000 to 2008, the EU received about 1.83 million refugees from Rising Asia, and flows increased by 64.2% from 2000 to 2008.[6]

Migrant flows from Rising Asia to the EU increased by 10.5% from 2000 to 2006. In 2006, the EU received 10,767 labor immigrants from Rising Asia, and had 3,580 emigrants to Rising Asia. Migrant flows from Rising Asia accounted for 1.7% of the total migrant flows to the EU in 2006, making it the ninth largest of the ten regions for which data is available. Migrant flows to Rising Asia accounted for 1.3% of the total migrant flows from the EU in 2006, making it the seventh largest of the eleven regions for which data is available.

In 2009, almost 6.5 million tourists from the EU25 visited ASEAN countries, making the EU the largest source of tourists to ASEAN outside ASEAN countries themselves, and about double that from Japan or Australia and triple that from South Korea, the United States and India, and about 5 times that from Taiwan.[7]

Chapter 12
The EU and India: Surprisingly Weak Links

India has been the second-fastest growing major economy for the past few years, and weathered the financial crisis and attendant recession relatively well. The World Bank projects accelerating growth for the Indian economy—as much as 8.7% by 2012—spurred by strong domestic demand and a revival in investor confidence. Yet India remains a desperately poor country, with high rates of communicable diseases and high infant mortality. Life expectancy in India is 10 years less than in Brazil and China. Half of the population still lives in rural areas and works in agriculture. Weak physical infrastructure, restrictive labor laws and an underdeveloped manufacturing sector continue to stunt the country's potential.

India is not facing the same aging challenges as other countries, including China. By 2020 the average Indian will be 29, the average Chinese will be 37. By 2035 the population will reach 1.5 billion, with about 65% of working age, making it the world's largest labor market.[1] But it will need to both train and absorb a massive "bulge" of 240 million young people coming to working age in the next 20 years in a system not fully geared to accommodate them. It's a daunting task; close to one in three of those aged 15 to 35 is functionally illiterate, and the education system is unable to absorb such a wave of humanity.

Despite its surging prowess in a select number of services, India has essentially failed to improve significantly on most basic drivers of its competitiveness. India must boost its infrastructure, absorb and train its youth bulge, and both improve and speed up its policymaking if it is to unleash the spending power of its own billion-plus populace and sustain high growth rates for the next decade.[2]

Despite considerable attention being paid to India's dramatic growth over the past decade or so, the EU's economically relevant links to India are quite thin in most areas, including in services, which is often touted as a major area of growth for India, and where the EU and India are becoming major competitors in third markets. Flows of people and ideas are comparatively weak. On the other hand, the EU is important to India as its largest trade partner and major source of portfolio investment. India is the only BRIC country with which the EU has a trade surplus.

Over the past decade, the EU doubled its goods trade with India and boosted its goods trade balance with India by 157%. The EU is the single most important market for India, accounting for 21.1% of Indian exports and 17% of Indian imports in 2008. India has comparative advantages in marketing-driven (food processing) and in labor-intensive (textiles) industries, and its overall growth rate in goods and services has been about 7-8% higher per year than that of the EU over the course of the past decade.

India was only the 10th largest regional destination for EU goods exports, however (out of 12 regions examined), accounting for only 3% of overall EU goods exports.[3] India was also only the 10th largest regional source of EU goods imports (2.1%) in 2009. EU trade with China is 6 times greater than with India. High trade tariffs on the Indian side and EU restrictions on agriculture limit trade ties.

The EU exported €27.5 billion of goods to India in 2009, one-third as much as to China; 25% as much as to Rising Asia; 28% as much as to Africa; 76% as much as to Japan; and 42% as much as to Russia. But EU goods exports to Wider Europe were over 8 times more than to India, and EU goods exports to North America were almost 9 times more than to India.

The EU imported €25.4 billion of goods from India in 2009, 18% of goods coming from Rising Asia; 46% of goods coming from Japan; almost 4 times less than goods coming from Africa; 4½ times less than goods coming from Russia; 7 times less than goods coming from North America and 8 times less than goods coming from Wider Europe.

The EU and India are negotiating a free trade agreement that the EU expects will boost EU exports to India by up to €18 billion and triple the EU's share of India's car imports to more than 80%. By 2020 the agreement could generate an additional €5 billion for Indian exporters to the EU, 70% of which would be in textiles and leather. Yet India remains concerned about additional EU barriers to textiles and food, is resisting EU efforts to access public procurement contracts, and opposes anti-counterfeiting rules that could hurt Indian generic drug makers.[4]

Most stories about India's rise discuss India's strengths as a services economy. India's rapid development has in fact been essentially service-led and supported by services exports, which have a much higher share in GDP (8%) than in the other BRICs. India is making considerable strides in the area of computer and information services. India has become the world's top country exporter in this field. While the EU's total export market share of the top 15 economies in this field was the largest in 2007 at 22.9%, India boasted the next-largest share of 18.1%, with higher relative growth rates, and could surpass the EU's share within the decade. The EU fares better in all other services categories, however. For instance, the EU's export market share of the top 15 economies in "other business services" in 2007 was 25.3%, compared with India's 4% share. The EU's export market share of 19.8% in communications services is far greater than the 3.3% registered by India in 2007.[5]

India's direct services ties to the EU, however, are extremely weak, both as a destination for EU services exports (2%) and a source of EU services imports (2%) in 2009. Essentially, India is building its growing prowess in computers, information and communication services in third markets other than the EU, and contesting EU competitors in those third markets. Various EU regulations on services serve to limit Indian services exports to the EU.

EU services exports to India more than doubled and EU services imports from India increased by 81% between 2004 and 2009, reversing the EU's services trade balance from a deficit of €431.9 million in 2000 to a surplus of €1.3 billion in 2009. In absolute terms, however, EU-India services trade is at a very low level. Leading EU services exporters such as the UK, Germany and France lag the U.S. when it comes to the Indian market (U.S. share 41.3%).

EU services exports to India in 2009 were only larger than those to the Caribbean, but only half those to Japan, China and Russia; one-third those to Oceania; 3.5 times less than to the Middle East and to Africa; only one-fourth of those to Latin America and Rising Asia; one-tenth those to Wider Europe; and almost 15 times less those to North America.

EU services imports from India in 2009 were low, ahead of those from the Caribbean, but less than from Russia and Japan, half those from Oceania, China and Latin America, one-third of those from the Middle East, 3.5 times less than those from Africa, one-fourth those from Rising Asia, less than one-tenth those from Wider Europe, and 18 times less than those from North America.

India also ranks extremely low as a destination for EU FDI and as a source of FDI into the EU.[6] EU investment in India grew 25.7% on average per year during the past decade, until the recession, and India's investment in the EU grew 112.8% on average per year during this period. But these amounts are from miniscule levels, and even such rapid growth has barely made a ripple in the EU's overall FDI picture. The EU had a total of €19 billion in foreign direct investment in India in 2008, 40% of its FDI in China; 28% of its FDI in the Middle East; 25% of its FDI in Japan; about 20% of its FDI in Russia; 14% of its FDI in Africa; 8% of its FDI in Latin America and in the Caribbean; 7% of its FDI in Rising Asia; less than 3% of its FDI in Wider Europe; and less than 2% of its FDI in North America.

India had a total of €7 billion in foreign direct investment in the EU in 2008, only one-third of that by Africa in the EU; 25% of that by Russia; 14% of that by the Middle East; less than 10% of that by Rising Asia and Latin America; 6% of that by Japan; 2% of that by Wider Europe and from the Caribbean; and less than 1% of that by North America.

44% of the foreign portfolio investment in India came from the EU. Another 29% came from the United States, and 3% came from Japan. The EU had a total of $49 billion in private portfolio investment in India in 2008, 73% more than in the Middle East and 69% more than in Africa, 35% more than in Russia and roughly the same as in China, but only 53% of its investment in Latin America; 21% of that in Rising Asia; 12% of that in Japan; 9% of that in the Caribbean and Wider Europe; and less than 2% of that in North America. India had a total of only $1 billion in private portfolio investment in the EU in 2008.

India is likely to account for almost 20% of incremental world primary energy demand in 2006-2030, growing at about 3.9% per year, but EU-India energy ties in traditional energy sources are marginal.[7] India's solar trade with the EU has grown leaps and bounds over the course of the past decade, but from very low levels, ranking India as the EU's fifth largest solar client and provider.

The EU far outperforms India in all indicators of innovation performance except ICT expenditures and knowledge-intensive services exports, but India's innovation growth performance is more than 5 times better than that of the EU.[8] Nonetheless, the country remains saddled with inefficient, inflexible and high-surplus labor markets, a large informal sector, very low wages, low levels of general education and technical qualifications, high public debt, persistent budget deficits, high inflation, and a shortage or even lack of all types of infrastructure.

Flows of people are surprisingly weak, and primarily directed to the UK. While India is the major country of origin for highly qualified workers in the U.S., Japan, and the EU (and within the EU, mainly in the UK), 82% of highly-skilled Indian migrants go to the United States.

In 2008 the largest foreign-born population in the UK was from India (639,000).[9] Yet UK Immigration Minister Damian Green has charged that UK immigration levels are "too high." The UK government is seeking to impose a cap on immigration from non-EU nations, effective April 2011. For tertiary or advanced research qualifications, 35% of all Indian immigrants went to the UK, while 22% migrated to other EU member states. 50% of Indian immigrants with pre-primary, primary or lower secondary education migrated to the UK.

Chapter 13
The EU and Russia: Stormy Weather

The EU is by far Russia's major commercial partner, accounting for 52.3% of its overall trade turnover in 2008. It is also by far the most important investor in Russia, accounting for up to 75% of FDI stocks in Russia.[1] Russia is also of critical importance to a number of EU member states as an energy supplier, and has been of rising importance to the EU overall in terms of trade and investment. Between 2000 and 2007 Russia's economy quadrupled in size in dollar terms to about $1.2 trillion, fueled by a tripling of international oil prices. The collapse of the world economy and the speedy drop in oil prices, however, exposed not only Russia's commodity dependence but also the fact that too much money and power has been concentrated in the hands of too few. In 2009 Russia's exports plunged by more than 36% and GDP slumped by no less than 8%, more than in any G20 economy.[2]

To remain in the high-growth category over the long term, Russia must arrest its population decline, tackle endemic corruption, improve the rule of law, deal with its crumbling infrastructure, address its stunning health challenges, diversify its production away from over-reliance on the energy sector, and boost efficiency in nearly every aspect of its economy.[3]

The EU's economically relevant ties to Russia center on Russian energy flows of oil and gas. Russia holds around 6.4% of the world's oil reserves and around 25% of the world's gas reserves. It is also the world's biggest gas producer and the second biggest oil producer. A number of EU member states rely on Russian energy imports, and some are critically dependent on such flows. There is also considerable trade in capital-intensive goods. Compared to the EU's ties to other major regions, the EU's ties to Russia are relatively thin in terms of mutual portfolio flows FDI, services, people and ideas, even though the EU is Russia's largest trading partner and leading source of FDI and portfolio investment.

Russia was the seventh largest regional destination for EU goods exports (6%) and the fifth largest source of EU goods imports (9.8%) in 2009.[4] EU exports to Russia roughly tripled over the course of the past decade, but fell 37.6% between 2008 and 2009. Traditionally the EU's main export destination among the BRICs, Russia has now lost that distinction to China, although when one compares individual countries, rather than regions, Russia remains the EU's third largest country trading partner, after the United States and China, accounting for 6% of EU exports and 9.6% of its imports.

EU goods imports from Russia roughly doubled over the course of the past decade. Medium-skill industries, particularly refined petroleum, dominate EU imports from Russia. The EU has registered persistent trade deficits with Russia since 2000. The EU imported €115.3 billion of goods from Russia in 2009, slightly over half of EU goods imports from China and from Wider Europe; 83% of EU goods imports from Rising Asia; and 60% of those from North America; but over 4 times more than from India; more than twice than from Japan; and 13% more than from Africa.

The EU exported €65.5 billion in goods to Russia in 2009, more than twice those to India and to Japan; about 80% of EU goods exports to China; 68% of those to Africa; 61% of EU goods exports to Rising Asia; 29% of those to Wider Europe; and 27% of those to North America.

Russia was the eighth largest destination for EU services exports (4%) and the tenth largest source of EU services imports (3%) in 2009.[5] EU exports of services to Russia grew on average 20% per year and EU imports of services from Russia grew 7.2% per year on average between 2004 and 2008, before falling in 2009. The EU's services trade surplus with Russia increased six-fold. EU services exports to Russia in 2009 were twice those to India and similar to those to China and Japan, but less than two-thirds of those to Oceania, Africa and the Middle East, half of those to Rising Asia and Latin America, one-fifth those to Wider Europe, and about one-tenth those to North America.

EU services imports from Russia were greater than from India and similar to those from Japan; but less than from Oceania, China, and Latin America, half of those from the Middle East and Africa, less than half from Rising Asia, one-seventh from Wider Europe, and 12 times less than from North America.

Russia is the seventh largest regional destination for EU FDI and the eighth largest regional source (of the twelve regions examined) of FDI in the EU.[6] EU investment in Russia grew 11.5 times and Russia's investment in the EU grew 9.5 times over the course of the past decade until the recession, but both remain at comparatively low levels. The EU had a total of €92 billion in foreign direct investment in Russia in 2008, almost 5 times more than in India; about double that in China; a quarter more than in the Middle East; 18% more than in Japan; but only 60% of that in Africa; 40% of that in Latin America and in the Caribbean; 34% of that in Rising Asia; 8 times less than in Wider Europe; and 13 times less that in North America.

Russia had a total of €28 billion in foreign direct investment in the EU in 2008, four times that of Indian FDI in the EU and double that of Chinese FDI in the EU; and a quarter more than from Africa; but only 57% of that from the Middle East; 40% of that from Latin America; 38% of that from Rising Asia; 24% of that from Japan; 11 times less than from the Caribbean; 16 times less than from Wider Europe; and 41 times less than from North America.

The EU accounted for just over half of overall foreign portfolio investment in Russia in 2008, compared with 32% from the United States and 2% from Japan.

The EU had a total of $39 billion in private portfolio investment in Russia, 13% more than in Africa and 8% more than in the Middle East, but only 80% of its portfolio investment in India; 74% of that in China; 42% of that in Latin America; 17% of that in Rising Asia; only 9% of that in Japan; 7% of that in the Caribbean and in Wider Europe, and 1% of that in North America.

Russia had a total of $17 billion in private portfolio investment in the EU in 2008, 74% of that from Latin America and about the same as from the Middle East, but only 17% of that from the Caribbean; 7% of that from Rising Asia; 2% of that from Japan; less than 2% of that from Wider Europe, and less than 1% of that from North America.

Russia is the largest supplier of oil to the EU.[7] Russian oil deliveries to the EU rose 56% over the course of the last decade. Russia delivered 206 million tons of oil to the EU in 2009.

In addition, Russia surpassed Africa in 2006 as the EU's largest regional coal supplier. Russian coal deliveries to the EU rose 2½ times over the course of the past decade. Russia delivered 53 million tons of coal to the EU in 2009.

Russia is the EU's third largest regional provider of natural gas. Russian natural gas exports to the EU rose 16% over the course of last decade. Russia delivered 34 million tons of natural gas to the EU in 2009. The European Commission estimates that its gas imports from Russia will climb from today's 40% to 60% (of total imports) in 2030.[8] The Baltic states are already wholly dependent on Russian gas for their gas consumption needs; Slovakia and Bulgaria are each over 90% dependent; and the Czech Republic and Greece are each more than 75% dependent. Russia is also dependent on the European Union: almost 85% of its gas exports go to the EU.[9]

Russia is not a significant partner for the EU in renewables, but it is the EU's number one purchaser and number four provider of uranium.

Refugees from Russia accounted for 4.4% of the total refugees in the EU, making it the fifth largest contributing region of the twelve regions examined. Over the past decade the EU took in 237,602 more refugees from Russia than did North America. Refugee flows from Russia swelled by 168% a year on average from 2000 to 2008, as the EU received a total of 460,230 refugees.

Migrant flows from Russia accounted for 4.6% of the total migrant flows to the EU in 2006, making it the seventh largest of the ten regions for which data is available, although migrant flows from Russia decreased by 22.1% from 2000 to 2006. Migrant flows from the EU to Russia accounted for 1.9% of the total EU migrant outflows from the EU in 2006, making it the fifth largest of the eleven regions for which data is available.

The main challenge for the Russian economy in the medium and long run is whether it will succeed in replacing energy exports as the key growth driver by developing other sectors and how it will cope with its acute demographic crisis—its population is projected to decline by about 8 million in the coming decade. Raw materials are Russia's most important exports; oil alone accounts for one-third of Russian state revenues.[10] Both the oil and gas sectors are plagued by inefficiencies, monopolistic practices, and declining production capacities that will require massive investments in distant and challenging locations such as eastern Siberia and the Arctic. Other challenges include considerable restrictions on trade and foreign ownership, inadequate protection of property rights, and significant state intervention in the economy. Russia still has not joined the WTO. In addition, Russia's innovative capacity is declining; it accounts for only 1% of the international market in high technology.[11] All told, Russia's competitiveness continues to worsen, and it faces considerable hurdles in terms of keeping up with rapidly developing economies.

Chapter 14
The EU and the Middle East: Energy and People

The Middle East is a region of great disparities. It includes Israel, which has a high per capita GDP and is deeply enmeshed with the EU in a wide-ranging net of economic and other relationships; the oil-rich economies in the Gulf; and countries that are resource-scarce but rich in population, such as Morocco, Tunisia, Egypt, Jordan, Syria and Lebanon, with Iran positioned in-between. The EU is a major aid donor to countries in the region. The EU and its member states are by far the largest financial supporter of the Palestinian Territories, contributing €1 billion a year. EU aid and financial transfers to Egypt are also substantial and will amount to more than €1 billion between 2007-2013. Support to Jordan over this period will range beyond €500 million, support to Syria and Lebanon will total more than €300 million each; and transfers to Israel will total more than €15 million.[1]

The Middle East was the third largest regional destination of EU goods exports (10%) and the ninth largest regional source of EU goods imports (4.6%) in 2009.[2] The EU has run large trade surpluses in goods every year since 2000 with the Middle East, despite EU energy needs.

The Middle East was the fifth largest regional destination for EU services exports (7%) and the fifth largest regional source of EU services imports (7%) in 2008.[3] EU exports of services to the Middle East grew at an average annual pace of almost 17% between 2004 and 2008, while EU imports of services from the Middle East grew at an average annual pace of about 10%, boosting considerably the EU's services trade surplus with Middle East.

The EU exported €35 billion in services to the Middle East in 2008, 4 times more than EU services exports to India; about 2½ times more than to Oceania; about twice that to Russia and to China; about the same as to Latin America and to Africa; and 67% more than to the Caribbean; but only 86% of EU services exports to Rising Asia; 2.7 times less than EU services exports to Wider Europe; and over 4 times less than EU services exports to North America.

The EU imported €25 billion of services from the Middle East in 2008, over 5 times those from the Caribbean; 3 times those from India and Oceania; over 2 times those from Russia; about twice those from China, Japan and from Latin America; but slightly less than EU services imports from Africa; only three-fourths of EU services imports from Rising Asia; 3 times less than EU services imports from Wider Europe; and almost 6 times less than EU services imports from North America.

The Middle East is the ninth largest regional destination for FDI from the EU, and the seventh largest regional source of FDI in the EU.[4] EU FDI in the Middle East grew 27% over the course of the past decade until the recession. The Middle East's investment in the EU grew by about 34% a year on average in the same time period.

The EU had a total of €69 billion in foreign direct investment in the Middle East in 2008, almost 4 times more than its FDI in India and 32% more than in China, but slightly less than in Japan; only three-fourths of that in Russia; about half that in Africa; over 3 times less than in Latin America and in the Caribbean; 4 times less than in Rising Asia; over 10 times less than in Wider Europe; and 18 times less than in North America.

The Middle East had a total of €49 billion in foreign direct investment in the EU in 2008, 7 times that from India; 3½ times that from China; 57% more than from Africa; 43% more than from Russia; but two-thirds of that from Rising Asia, from Latin America and from the Caribbean; over 9 times less than from Wider Europe; and over 23 times less than from North America.

28% of overall foreign portfolio investment in the Middle East came from the EU. Another 40% came from the United States, and 2% came from Japan. The EU had a total of $36 billion in private portfolio investment in the Middle East in 2008, about the same as in Africa and in Russia; three-fourths of that in India; and two-thirds of that in China; but almost 3 times less than in Latin America; 9 times less than in Rising Asia, 11 times less than in Japan, almost 15 times less than in the Caribbean; 29 times less than in Wider Europe, and 74 times less than in North America.

The Middle East had a total of $16 billion in private portfolio investment in the EU in 2008, about the same as Russia but 6 times less than from the Caribbean; 15 times less than from Rising Asia; 53 times less than from Japan; 64 times less than from Wider Europe; and 122 times less than from North America.

Although the Middle East has been the EU's second largest regional source of oil since 2000, oil exports from the region to the EU have declined by 44% over the last ten years.

The Middle East was the EU's third largest regional destination for natural gas and fourth largest regional source of natural gas. Qatar is the largest country source of natural gas from the region, accounting for 13 million of the 19 million tons of natural gas supplied to the EU in 2009. Over the last ten years, EU natural gas imports from the Middle East grew more than 20 times, while EU natural gas exports to the region declined by 56%.

The Middle East was also the EU's second largest regional buyer of coal. The EU sent 23% more coal to the region since 2000. The region bought 4 million tons from the EU in 2009.

The Middle East is the EU's eighth largest regional source of solar parts and seventh largest buyer. EU solar exports to the Middle East have grown 2.3 times and EU solar imports from the Middle East have grown four-fold over the course of the past decade. The EU sold €42.9 million worth of solar products to the Middle East and imported €53.2 million from the Middle East in 2009. The EU has launched two major solar initiatives with the Middle East and North Africa that promise considerably to expand solar energy capacity for the entire region over the next decades.

The Middle East is the EU's third largest regional buyer of biofuels and fourth largest provider. EU biofuels exports to the Middle East grew 71% and EU biofuels imports grew almost 18-fold since 2000. The EU exported 10,184 tons of biofuels to the Middle East and imported 38,552 tons from the Middle East in 2009.

The Middle East is the EU's fourth largest regional windpower parts client and tenth largest provider. EU windpower purchases from the Middle East have grown 54% since 2002. The EU exported €43 million worth of windpower parts to the Middle East and imported only €38,580 from the EU in 2009.

Refugees from the Middle East accounted for 18.3% of the total refugees in the EU, making it the second largest contributing region of the twelve regions examined.[5] Refugee flows from the Middle East increased by 52.9% from 2000 to 2008. From 2000 to 2008, the EU received a total of 1,920,021 refugees from the Middle East.

Migrant flows from the Middle East accounted for 3.8% of the total migrant flows to the EU in 2006, making it the eighth largest of the ten regions for which data is available. Migrant flows from the Middle East to the EU increased over 20% on average annually from 2000 to 2006. In 2006, the EU received 23,983 labor immigrants from the Middle East.

Chapter 15
The EU and Africa:
Energy, People, and Neglected Opportunities

The EU's strongest economically relevant ties to Africa are in the areas of energy and people. Africa is an important energy supplier and destination for the EU; it also is a significant source of migrants and refugees coming to the EU. Trade in goods and services is only of medium importance to the EU, and in fact the EU share of Africa's trade has declined rather dramatically while that of Asia has grown equally dramatically. EU FDI in Africa is also of only medium importance, although larger than in some other major world regions. The flow of ideas between the EU and Africa is weak. EU R&D expenditure in Africa is negligible in all countries except South Africa. The EU is the largest provider of development assistance to Africa.

Africa boasts abundant natural resources and is home to a vast and inexpensive pool of labor, as well as a rising middle class. Yet the continent's colonial legacy is reflected in the fact that only 12% of Africa's trade takes place between African countries. Infrastructure is still largely geared to exports. Rails and roads often lead to marine ports rather than linking countries over land.[1] Many countries suffer from a weakly regulated business environment, barriers to affordable finance, rickety legal systems, poorly enforced laws, and poor power supplies.

Africa was both Europe's largest source of and export destination for natural gas and Europe's second largest source of and destination for oil in 2009.[2] In 2006, Russia surpassed Africa as the EU's largest coal supplier. Africa is growing as a partner for the EU in renewables, ranking in 2009 as the second largest export destination for EU biofuels, the fifth largest source of EU biofuels imports, sixth largest buyer of solar products and seventh largest provider.

The EU has launched an ambitious "Mediterranean Solar Plan," the goal of which is to create 20 gigawatts from renewable energies by 2020. A related private-sector "Desertec-Initiative" seeks to build a 50 gigawatt capacity by 2050. Both projects are focusing on solar energy, and both anticipate that a share of the renewable energy generated will be exported to Europe. North Africa is the target region for these initiatives.[3] Both projects face considerable hurdles, including high costs and relatively more expensive outlays than investments in other sources of energy, yet so far each is progressing with the support of the relevant parties in Europe, North Africa and the Middle East.

Refugees from Africa accounted for 17.6% of the total refugees in the EU, making it the third largest contributing region of the eleven regions examined, sending less than half of those coming from Wider Europe, slightly less than those coming from the Middle East, and slightly more than Rising Asia.[4] Refugee flows from Africa increased at an average annual rate of 8.4% between 2000 and 2008.

Africa accounted for 26.8% of the total migrant flows to the EU in 2006, making it the second largest contributing region, sending slightly less than Wider Europe, but accounting for 6 times more migrants to the EU than the Middle East. Exact figures are hard to calculate; there could be between 7 and 8 million irregular African immigrants living in the EU.

Africa was the fifth largest regional destination for EU goods exports (9%) in 2009 and the sixth largest regional source of EU goods imports (8.5%).[5] EU goods exports to Africa exceed EU goods exports to Russia, Japan and China, but EU goods imports from Africa are less than half of EU goods imports from China and slightly less than from Russia. The EU's goods trade with Africa is nearly double its trade with Latin America. EU exports to Africa were growing at about a 10% average rate before the recession.

The EU exported about one-third as many services as goods to Africa, and imported about one-fourth as many services as goods from Africa.[6] Africa was the sixth largest destination of EU services exports (7%) and the fourth largest source of EU services imports (7%) in 2009. EU services exports were also growing at more than a 10% annual clip before the recession, and the EU managed to transform its services deficit with Africa into a surplus. EU services exports to Africa in 2009 were more than 3 times those to India, almost half of those to Russia, China and Japan, slightly more than to Oceania, about the same as to the Middle East, ¼ of those to Latin America and to Rising Asia, about one-third of EU services exports to Wider Europe, and about one-fifth of those to North America. EU services imports from Africa in 2009 were more than 3 times those from India, twice those from Japan, and more than from the Middle East, Oceania, China and Latin America, but less than from Rising Asia, about one-third those from Wider Europe, and less than one-fifth those from North America.

The EU is South Africa's most important economic trade partner, accounting for over 40% of its imports and exports, as well as for 70% of foreign direct investment. Yet China has become South Africa's #1 country trading partner.

The EU accounted for €132 billion in foreign direct investment in Africa in 2008, making Africa the 6th largest regional destination for EU FDI.[7] EU investment in Africa grew at an average annual rate of 21.5% over the course of the decade until the recession. EU FDI in Africa was more than six times that in India, 2½ times that of EU FDI in China, almost twice that in Japan and the Middle East, and 1½ times that in Russia, but only half of EU FDI in Rising Asia, about 60% of that in Latin America, one-fifth of that invested in Wider Europe, and only one-tenth of the EU's FDI in North America. Africa had a total of €21 billion in foreign direct investment in the EU in 2008, making it the tenth largest regional source of foreign direct investment in the EU of the twelve regions surveyed.

The EU accounted for 41% of overall foreign portfolio investment in Africa. Another 44% came from the United States, and 5% came from Japan.

Development aid is another strong link binding the EU to Africa. The European Commission disbursed $14.7 billion in grants in 2008, and individual EU member states contributed additional funds, making the EU the largest provider of aid to Africa.[8]

Despite longstanding commercial ties with Europe, however, Africa now conducts half its trade with other developing economic regions. From 1990 through 2008, Asia's share of African trade doubled, to 28%, while Western Europe's portion shrank to 28%, from 51%.

Demand for commodities, an African strength, is growing fastest in the world's emerging economies, particularly in Asia and the Middle East.

If recent trends continue, Africa will play an increasingly important role in the global economy. By 2040, it will be home to one in five of the planet's young people, and its labor force will be bigger than China's. Africa has almost 60% of the world's uncultivated arable land and a large share of its natural resources. The rate of return on foreign investment is higher in Africa than in any other developing region. Its consumer sectors are growing two to three times faster than those in OECD countries. In 2000, roughly 59 million households on the continent earned at least $5,000 in income— a level above which roughly half of household income is spent on nonfood items. By 2014, the number of such households could reach 106 million. Africa already has more middle-class households with incomes of $20,000 or above than India.[9] Yet on balance EU companies have neglected opportunities and allowed competitors, especially from Asia, to gain important footholds on the continent—which over time could have negative repercussions as Africa continues its growth trajectory.

Chapter 16
The EU and Latin America: Commodities, Services, Energy, and People

The EU is Latin America's leading regional trade partner and largest regional source of FDI. Brazil is the EU's largest trading partner in Latin America, and the EU is Brazil's largest regional trading partner, accounting for 22.5% of Brazil's external trade. Brazil is the single biggest exporter of agricultural products to the EU, accounting for 12.4% of total EU imports in 2009 and ranks as the EU's 10th trading partner.[1] The EU's trade balance with Latin America is negative in the area of goods, but positive with respect to services. Latin America is the 3rd largest source of migrants into the EU, a relatively important supplier of coal, and Brazil is the EU's primary supplier of biofuels. Other flows are of less significance.

Latin America was the eighth largest regional destination for EU goods exports (4%) and the seventh largest source of EU goods imports (5.1%) in 2009.[2] EU exports to Latin America averaged only 1.6% annual growth over the course of the past decade, while EU imports from Latin America grew 2.9% on average annually, tripling the EU's goods trade deficit with Latin America over this period. The EU mainly imports primary products (70%) from Latin America, while it exports machinery and transport equipment (85%).

Only four countries in the region have meaningful volumes of trade with the EU: Brazil, Argentina, Chile and Colombia. A free trade agreement with Chile went into effect in 2003.[3] The European Commission and the governments of Colombia and Peru approved a comprehensive Trade Agreement in 2010, but economic ties remain at fairly low levels. The EU has also concluded negotiations with Central America[4] on an Association Agreement that includes efforts to liberalize trade. The EU is Central America's second largest trade partner after the United States with a market share of approximately 10%. Brazil is the EU's key economic partner in the region, however, accounting for 47% of EU goods exports to the region and 42% of EU goods imports from the region in 2009.

Latin America was the fourth largest regional destination for EU services exports (8%) and the eighth largest source of EU services imports (4%) in 2009.[5] EU exports of services to Latin America grew by over 17% a year on average between 2004 and 2008, while EU imports of services from Latin America grew only 3% a year on average, boosting the EU's services trade surplus with Latin America by 206% over this period.

EU exports of services to Latin America were four times those to India, twice those to Japan, China and Russia, about 75% more than to Oceania, slightly more than to the Middle East and to Africa, and about the same as to Rising Asia, but 2.5 times less than to Wider Europe and 3.5 times less than to North America.

EU imports of services from Latin America in 2009 were twice those from India, greater than from Japan and Russia, and about the same as from Oceania and China, but less than from the Middle East and Africa, about half those from Rising Asia, less than one-fifth those from Wider Europe, and over 12 times less than from North America.

The EU has neglected Latin America and is losing ground as a trade partner. In the 1960s and 1970s, the EU absorbed more than 35% of total Latin American exports. In 2009, this share dropped to 14%, while Asia surpassed the EU as an export destination. By 2014, China alone could displace the EU as a market for Latin American exports and by 2020 could account for more than 19% of Latin American exports, versus a EU share of less than 14%.[6] This has prompted renewed EU interest in relaunching negotiations on a trade agreement with the Mercosur countries of Argentina, Brazil, Paraguay and Uruguay that had collapsed in 2004 without agreement, due in particular to EU concerns that cheap Latin American commodities and agricultural produce would hurt European farmers and producers. The EU is Mercosur's most important regional market for its agricultural exports, accounting for 19.8% of total EU agricultural imports in 2009. The EU primarily exports industrial products. But Mercosur is a relatively protected market, in terms of both tariffs and non-tariff barriers. The average rate of applied tariff protection is around 13% (average bound protection is above 30%), but protection in sectors of particular interest to EU exporters is even higher (e.g. 35% for cars). For the EU, a trade deal could boost exports by around €4.5 billion per year. Mercosur is expected to benefit from a similar increase in exports to the EU.[7]

The EU is also the largest investor in Mercosur. In fact it currently has more FDI stock in Mercosur than in Russia, China and India together. Overall, Latin America is the fourth largest regional destination for FDI from the EU, and the sixth largest regional source of FDI from the EU. EU investment in Latin America grew 4% a year on average over the past decade until the recession. Latin America's investment in the EU grew a whopping 81% per year on average during this time, but from a relatively modest base.[8]

The EU had a total of €228 billion in foreign direct investment in Latin America in 2008, 12 times more than in India, almost 5 times more than in China, over 3 times more than in the Middle East and 3 times more than in Japan; almost 2½ times more than in Russia; twice that in Africa; and about the same as in the Caribbean; but only 84% of EU FDI in Rising Asia; 3 times less than EU FDI in Wider Europe and 5 times less than EU FDI in North America.

Latin America had a total of €71 billion in foreign direct investment in the EU in 2008, 10 times more than that from India; 5 times more than that from China; over 3 times more than that from Africa; 2½ times more than that from Russia; 31% more than that from the Middle East; and about the same as that from Rising Asia; but only 60% of that from Japan; 4.5 times less than from the Caribbean; 6.5 times less than from Wider Europe; 16 times less than from North America.

31% of overall foreign portfolio investment in Latin America came from the EU. Another 46% came from the United States, and 4% came from Japan. The EU had a total of $93 billion in private portfolio investment in Latin America in 2008, 29 times less than in North America; almost 6 times less than in the Caribbean and in Wider Europe; 4½ times less than in Japan; 2½ times less than in Rising Asia; but almost 3 times more than in Africa, 2½ times more than in the Middle East; more than double that in Russia; 48% more than in India; and 43% more than in China.

Latin America had a total of $23 billion in private portfolio investment in the EU in 2008, 70% more than from the Middle East and from Russia, but only 24% of that from the

Caribbean; 10 times less than from Rising Asia; 37 times less than from Japan; 45 times less than from Wider Europe, and 85 times less than from North America.

Latin America is the EU's second largest regional supplier of coal.[9] In 2009 Latin America shipped 30 million tons of coal to the EU, less than the 53 million supplied by Russia, but about the same as supplied by Africa and slightly more than from North America and 5 times that supplied by Wider Europe. Latin American coal exports to the EU grew about 2.8% a year on average during the past decade until the recession. Latin America is the EU's sixth largest regional buyer and seventh largest regional source of EU oil in 2009, with oil exports to the EU growing 2% a year on average over the past decade. Natural gas exports to the EU have grown quickly, but from a very low base.

In the area of renewables, Latin America, and specifically Brazil, is important to the EU in the realm of biofuels. In 2009, Latin America provided 74% (661,362 tons) of the EU's total biofuel imports of 890,000 tons, and exports to the EU grew 191% a year on average over the course of the last decade. Latin America was the only region to supply large amounts of biofuels to the EU after 2007; Brazil alone sends about 88% more biofuels to the EU than all of Rising Asia, the EU's second largest regional biofuels supplier. There is, however, considerable competition for the biofuels market between bioethanol producers, such as Brazil, and biodiesel manufacturers, who are located primarily in Europe. Biodiesel is the main biofuel produced in Europe, representing 80% of production, and Europe is the world's biggest producer, accounting for 95% of world output. Germany, France and Italy are the largest biodiesel producers and users. The EU's biodiesel sector has undergone very rapid growth, but is heavily dependent on state subsidies. Brazil's bioethanol trade with the EU could be far more significant if EU trade barriers in this area were reduced or eliminated. The biofuels issue is discussed in more detail in Chapter 4.

Latin America was the third largest regional provider of EU wind power parts in 2009. Sales from the region to the EU have grown 7.3 times since 2000, although are lower than imports from the region. EU windpower parts sales to Latin America have jumped over 25 times since 2000. In 2009, Latin America bought windpower parts from the EU worth €15 million and sold €9.8 million.

Refugees from Latin America accounted for 0.7% of the total refugees in the EU, making it the seventh largest contributing region of the twelve regions examined.[10] From 2000 to 2008, the EU received a total of 69,615 refugees from Latin America. Refugee flows from Latin America increased by 13.2% from 2000 to 2008.

Migrant flows from Latin America accounted for 14.2% of the total migrant flows to the EU in 2006, making it the third largest of the ten regions for which data is available. Migrant flows from the EU to Latin America accounted for 2.7% of the total migrant flows from the EU in 2006, making it the fourth largest of the eleven regions for which data is available. Migrant flows from Latin America decreased by 36.2% from 2000 to 2006. In 2006, the EU received 88,674 labor immigrants from Latin America, and had 7,472 emigrants to Latin America.

On the whole, Latin America weathered the global economic crisis better than the EU and other developed economies, and has made important strides toward sounder fiscal management, increased market efficiency, greater openness, and export diversification. Between 2002 and 2008 some 40 million Latin Americans were lifted from poverty. Democracy has been established almost everywhere.[11] At the same time, when compared with the rest of the world, the region must improve significantly in order to catch up with international best practices and fully leverage its competitiveness potential. Since 1960 it has seen the lowest growth in productivity of any region in the world, in part because about half of all economic activity takes place in the informal sector. The region is inordinately dependent on commodities; over the past decade they accounted for 52% of the region's exports, according to the World Bank. Income distribution remains the most unequal anywhere. Widespread crime and violence stunts the region's potential.

Brazil is the region's major economy, accounting for a third of Latin America's population and 40% of the region's GDP. Over the past decade it has undergone a remarkable social and economic transformation. 20 million people have been lifted out of poverty since 2003. If growth rates continue, it could be the world's fifth-largest economy by 2025, behind only China, the United States, India and Japan. It is currently following the model of a domestically oriented service-driven economy, with a relatively large private sector and foreign direct investment playing an important role. It has important comparative advantages as a producer of minerals, food and other agricultural products. In 2007, the country was the second largest recipient of FDI among emerging markets, just after China. As developed markets continue their slow-growth trajectory, however, Brazil fears a flood of foreign capital that could make its currency more expensive, impede local exports and create unsustainable asset bubbles, and so has imposed capital controls. The share of exports of goods and services in GDP is relatively small, amounting to just 12% and 1.7 % of GDP, respectively.

In 2007, the services sector had a dominant 66% share of Brazil's GDP. Industry had a share of 28% and is highly concentrated in a few competitive technology-intensive sectors, such as aerospace, biofuels and automotives (none of them very prominent on EU markets). The country is set to become a major oil exporter. Recently-discovered deepwater oilfields are estimated to put Brazil's oil reserves on a par with Russia and Kuwait. In short, the long-term prospects of the Brazilian economy look relatively bright, with solid growth rates expected. But important drawbacks include neglect of infrastructure, persistently high income inequality, a large informal sector, relatively high public indebtedness, high interest rates, significant disparities in educational quality and access, low productivity and little innovation.

Chapter 17
The EU and the Caribbean: Follow the Money

The EU's financial ties to the Caribbean are extremely strong, reflecting the region's role as an offshore financial center. The globalization of financial markets and economic activity has spawned the growth of the offshore financial services industry. Global offshore holdings now run to $5-7 trillion, five times as much as two decades ago, and make up perhaps 6-8% of worldwide wealth under management. Offshore financial centers make their living mainly by attracting overseas financial capital, and are typically in such small jurisdictions as Liechtenstein, the Channel Islands or Macau. But the Caribbean has become a real global center for the offshore financial industry. 75% of the world's hedge funds, for instance, are domiciled in the Caribbean. Places such as the Cayman Islands, Bermuda, the British Virgin Islands or the Bahamas offer political stability, low income taxes, no withholding taxes for non-residents on interest and dividend income, and bank secrecy. The Cayman Islands, a British Overseas Territory, is the world's fifth-largest banking center, with $1.4 trillion in assets, and the world's second-largest jurisdiction for so-called "captive" insurance companies, a type of limited-purpose and increasingly speculative institution. The two subprime mortgage-backed Bear Stearns funds that collapsed in 2007, precipitating the financial crisis, were incorporated in the Caymans.[1] The British Virgin Islands are home to almost 700,000 offshore companies and 2,000 hedge funds. And Bermuda, hosting over 500 hedge funds, is perhaps the richest country in the world, with a GDP per person estimated at almost $70,000.[2]

These activities make the Caribbean a major center for global financial flows, including with the EU, and particularly with the United Kingdom. The Caribbean was the EU's 3rd most important regional source of FDI in the world in 2008, accounting for €321 billion in foreign direct investment in the EU. Caribbean investment in the EU grew at an annual average of about 19% over the past decade, until the recession. Caribbean FDI in the EU in 2008 was almost 1/3 of that coming from North America and 70% of that from Wider Europe. Yet it was about 3 times more than from Japan, 4½ times more than from Latin America and 6½ times more than from the Middle East, and more than from the entire Asia-Pacific region (China, Rising Asia, India, Japan, Oceania).

The Caribbean is the fifth largest regional destination for EU FDI.[3] EU investment in the Caribbean grew on average 32% annually over the past decade, before the recession. The EU had a total of €226 billion in foreign direct investment in the Caribbean in 2008, almost 12 times more than in India, 5 times more than in China, 3 times more than in Japan and in the Middle East, 2½ times that in Russia, roughly the same as in Latin America, about 40% more than in Africa, about 90% than in Rising Asia, 31% of that in Wider Europe, and 18% of that in North America. Clearly, these investments are not ultimately destined for these markets and eventually make their way to other countries around the world.

30% of overall foreign portfolio investment in the Caribbean came from the EU. Another 30% came from the United States, and 22% came from Japan. The EU had a total of $532 billion in private portfolio investment in the Caribbean in 2008, more than in any other region except North America, which held 5 times that amount, and Wider Europe ($543 billion). EU private portfolio investment in the Caribbean was 23% more than EU portfolio investments in

Japan; almost 2½ times more than in Rising Asia; almost 6 times more than in Latin America;, over 10 times more than in China and in India; over 13 times more than in Russia and almost 15 times more than in the Middle East or in Africa.

The Caribbean had a total of $97 billion in private portfolio investment in the EU in 2008, which placed it 5th among regions, behind North America, Wider Europe, Japan and Rising Asia but far ahead of Latin America, Russia, China, India and Africa.

The Caribbean is the fourth largest regional creditor of European banks outside the EU. European banks had a total of $515 billion in claims against the Caribbean as of March 2010. These claims grew by 18% a year on average during the past decade until the recession. These claims are greater than those against any other region except North America, against which European banks had almost 8 times that amount in claims; and Wider Europe, against which European banks had almost twice that amount in claims.

The financial crisis subjected the offshore centers to considerable scrutiny, with significant pressure for more effective regulation. The competitiveness ratings of all offshore centers have declined as a result.[4]

The Caribbean offshore financial industry has intensive links in particular with the United Kingdom, itself home to 80% of Europe's hedge fund industry. Following the financial crisis, Britain wanted funds based in Commonwealth outposts such as the Caribbean, but managed in the City of London, to be able to sell throughout the EU on the strength of British regulation alone, but EU member states finally agreed on an arrangement by which funds seeking to market their products across the Single Market will need by 2013 to obtain a "passport" that includes procedures for tighter supervision and regulation. Between 2013 and 2015, EU-domiciled funds would be able to sell across Europe, although "third-country" funds—such as U.S. or Cayman Islands-based products—would not. Between 2015 and 2018 non-EU domiciled funds could obtain the EU-wide passport based on arrangements set by the Union. While the ultimate impact of these new provisions remain unclear, at least a portion of the trillion-dollar hedge fund industry is likely to move from traditional offshore financial centers, including in the Caribbean, toward jurisdictions within the EU itself, such as Ireland, Luxembourg or Cyprus.[5]

Beyond financial ties, the Caribbean has also become a growing source of natural gas for Europe. Of the 12 regions surveyed, the Caribbean represents the sixth largest source of natural gas for the EU, and Caribbean exports of natural gas to the EU have grown five-fold since 2000.[6] The region sent 4.8 million tons of natural gas to the EU in 2009, far behind major suppliers such as Africa (45 million tons), Wider Europe (37 million tons), Russia (34 million tons), Middle East (19 million tons), and Rising Asia (14 million tons).

All other links are rather weak. Of the 12 regions surveyed, the Caribbean ranks as the EU's least important trading partner. A full Economic Partnership Agreement has been initialed with the 15 Cariforum countries,[7] focusing on regional development and covering liberalization of both goods and services, with provisions on a wide range of trade-related areas—but the Caribbean accounted for 1% of EU exports and a negligible amount of EU imports.

Refugees from the Caribbean accounted for only 0.3% of the total refugees in the EU. Refugee flows from the Caribbean to the EU increased at about an 8% average annual rate from 2000 to 2008. Migrant flows from Caribbean to the EU are also miniscule, accounting for only 0.5% of total migrant flows to the EU in 2006.[8]

Chapter 18
The EU and Oceania: Distant Cousins

Oceania is among the smallest goods trade partners for the EU, accounting for only 2% of EU goods exports and just 1% of EU goods imports in 2009, and the EU maintains a trade surplus with the region. Australia and New Zealand constitute 90-95% of Oceania's goods trade with the EU. The EU exported €26 billion of goods to Oceania, about a third of EU goods exports to China, about the same as to India, and about three-quarters of EU goods exports to Japan, but only one-quarter of that to Rising Asia and 27% of that to Africa. The EU imported €12 billion of goods from Oceania in 2009, only 5% of EU goods imports from China, 8% of EU goods imports from Rising Asia; 12% of goods imports from Africa; 21% of good imports from Japan; and half of good imports from India;.[1]

Oceania is also a small services trade partner for the EU, accounting for 6% of EU services exports and 4% of EU services imports in 2009. EU exports of services to Oceania grew 11.4% per year on average while EU imports of services from Oceania grew 4.4% between 2004 and 2008, boosting the EU's services trade surplus with Oceania.[2] EU services exports to Oceania in 2009 were 3 times those to India and about two-thirds greater than to Russia, China, and Japan, but less than to the Middle East and Africa, about three-fourths of those to Latin America and Rising Asia, less than one-third those to Wider Europe, and about one-fifth those to North America.

EU services imports from Oceania in 2009 were twice those from India, more than those from Japan and Russia, and about the same as those from China and Latin America, but less than from Africa and the Middle East, about half of those from Rising Asia, one-fifth of those from Wider Europe, and one-ninth of those from North America.

Oceania's FDI links with the EU are also quite thin.[3] It is the tenth largest regional destination of EU FDI and the ninth largest regional source (of the twelve regions examined) of foreign direct investment in the EU. EU investment in Oceania grew 5.4% per year on average over the course of the past decade until the recession, but Oceania's investment in the EU grew by less than 1% per year on average during this period. The EU had a total of €67 billion in foreign direct investment in Oceania in 2008, about 72% more than in India and 30% more than in China; about the same as in the Middle East; slightly less than in Japan; one-quarter of EU FDI in Rising Asia; half as much as in Africa; and only 30% of the Caribbean or in Latin America.

Oceania had a total of €22 billion in foreign direct investment in the EU in 2008, 3 times FDI from India in the EU, about one-third more than Chinese FDI in the EU, and about the same as African FDI in the EU; but 78% less than FDI from Russia; slightly less than half from the Middle East; 31% of FDI from Latin America; 29% of FDI from Rising Asia; 19% of FDI from Japan; and 7% of FDI from the Caribbean.

36% of overall foreign portfolio investment in Oceania came from the EU. Another 30% came from the United States, and 13% came from Japan. The EU had a total of $197 billion in private portfolio investment in Oceania in 2008, 13 times less than in North America, 2.7

times less than in Wider Europe, only 37% of that in Caribbean, half of that in Japan, and 85% of that in Rising Asia; but twice that in Latin America; 3.7 times more than in China; 4 times more than in India; over 5 times more than in the Middle East and in Russia; and almost 6 times more than in Africa.

Oceania had a total of $74 billion in private portfolio investment in the EU in 2008, 3 times more than from Latin America; 4 times more than from Russia and from the Middle East; but only about three-quarters of that from the Caribbean; one-third of that from Rising Asia; 9% of that from Japan; 13 times less than from Wider Europe; and 25 times less than from North America.

Oceania is the smallest regional provider of oil to the EU, but has been the third largest overall regional provider of coal over the past decade, sending 14 million tons to the EU in 2009, although coal deliveries to the EU declined 44% over the course of the past decade.[4] Oceania is a relatively insignificant solar and biofuels partner for the EU, but is the EU's third largest windpower purchaser. EU windpower exports to Oceania grew five-fold during this period, but EU windpower exports to the region totaled only €79 million in 2009. Oceania is the EU's number two provider of uranium.

Refugees from Oceania accounted for 0.4% of the total refugees in the EU, making it the eighth largest contributing region of the twelve regions examined.[5] From 2000 to 2008, the EU received a total of 45,514 refugees from Oceania.

Migrant flows from the EU to Oceania accounted for 32.4% of the total migrant flows from the EU in 2006, making Oceania the largest recipient of EU migrants of the eleven regions for which data is available. Migrant flows from Oceania accounted for 6.1% of the total migrant flows to the EU in 2006, making it the sixth largest of the ten regions for which data is available. Migrant flows from Oceania to the EU increased by 60.7% from 2000 to 2006. In 2006, the EU received 38,186 labor immigrants from Oceania, but many more—90,174 – left Europe and emigrated to Oceania.

Section III

Europe 2020: Competitive or Complacent?

Chapter 19
Creating a Competitive Europe

This volume has concentrated on the EU's economic links and its relative standing in the world. We have compared the EU's competitive position in relation to 12 other world regions, and have "mapped" the EU's critical interdependencies with those regions in terms of goods, services, money, energy, people and ideas. This chapter offers some basic conclusions about the EU's strengths and weaknesses, and recommends 8 priorities for EU action.

The Competitive Position of Individual EU Member States

Throughout this volume we have focused on the EU as an economic entity. In many ways this is appropriate, given the common trade policy, the Single Market, and delegation of many aspects of economic life to the European Commission. But the EU consists first and foremost of its member states, and each offers strengths and faces challenges unique to its particular situation. In fact, in area after area this study has underscored the diverse reality of the European Union.

Some EU member states host companies that are highly-connected world-beating exporters and investors. They have proven to be successful in building highly-skilled, adaptable workforces and in ensuring that economic gains extend widely throughout their societies. Others struggle to boost the potential of their people. Some European countries are driving global innovation; others are catching up; and still others are competing fiercely with rapidly rising economies elsewhere. Each EU member state continues to contend in its own way with the lingering effects of the Great Recession.

The World Economic Forum's Global Competitiveness Index provides a useful tool for disaggregating these differences to better understand the strengths and weaknesses of individual EU members and the EU as a whole. Overall the EU continues to feature prominently among the most competitive regions in the world. Five EU member states rank among the 10 most competitive economies in the world and ten are among the top 20. Sweden ranked as the most competitive EU member state economy and second most competitive in the world after Switzerland. Germany followed as the 5th most competitive, followed by Finland (7th), the Netherlands (8th), Denmark (9th), the United Kingdom, (12th), France (15th), Austria (18th), Belgium (19th), and Luxembourg (20th). Norway, a major EU partner in Wider Europe, ranked 14th.

But the rankings also reveal great disparities within the EU, particularly with new member states, all of which ranked behind China. Estonia (33rd) ranked highest among the new member states. Cyprus, Spain, Portugal and Italy ranked quite low, behind Poland and the Czech Republic. Greece performed dismally, due to its severe budget deficits and debt burdens, together with weak institutions and inefficient markets. It fell 12 points to a lowly ranking of 83rd, behind Rwanda, Egypt, Namibia and Kazakhstan.

The rankings reveal different sources of strength and weakness. The Benelux and the Nordic countries, for instance, compensate for the their small size with excellent skills, sound

Table 19.1. Competitiveness Rankings of the EU 27 Member States and Selected Countries

Global Competitiveness Index

Country	Rank 2010	Rank 2009	Change 2009-2010
Switzerland	1	1	0
Sweden	**2**	**4**	**2**
Singapore	3	3	0
United States	4	2	-2
Germany	**5**	**7**	**2**
Japan	6	8	2
Finland	**7**	**6**	**-1**
Netherlands	**8**	**10**	**2**
Denmark	**9**	**5**	**-4**
Canada	10	9	-1
Hong Kong	11	11	0
United Kingdom	**12**	**13**	**1**
Taiwan	13	12	-1
Norway	14	14	0
France	**15**	**16**	**1**
Australia	16	15	-1
Qatar	17	22	5
Austria	**18**	**17**	**-1**
Belgium	**19**	**18**	**-1**
Luxembourg	**20**	**21**	**1**
Saudi Arabia	21	28	7
Korea, Rep.	22	19	-3
Israel	24	27	3
China	27	29	2
Ireland	**29**	**25**	**-4**
Chile	30	30	0
Iceland	31	26	-5
Estonia	**33**	**35**	**2**
Czech Republic	**36**	**31**	**-5**
Poland	**39**	**46**	**7**
Cyprus	**40**	**34**	**-6**
Spain	**42**	**33**	**-9**
Slovenia	**45**	**37**	**-8**
Portugal	**46**	**43**	**-3**
Lithuania	**47**	**53**	**6**
Italy	**48**	**48**	**0**
Malta	**50**	**52**	**2**
India	51	49	-2
Hungary	**52**	**58**	**6**
South Africa	54	45	-9
Brazil	58	56	-2
Slovak Republic	**60**	**47**	**-13**
Turkey	61	61	0
Romania	**67**	**64**	**-3**
Russian Federation	63	63	0
Latvia	**70**	**68**	**-2**
Bulgaria	**71**	**76**	**5**
Greece	**83**	**71**	**-12**

Note: EU member states in bold. Source: World Economic Forum: http://www.weforum.org/en/initiatives/gcp/Global%20Competitiveness%20Report/index.htm.

institutions, and, particularly in the case of the Nordic countries, a strong capacity for innovation. Some countries in the core, like France, need to focus on increasing labor participation while others, like Germany, need to tackle obstacles to service sector expansion to support domestic demand. The OECD estimates that northern European countries are well positioned to cope with the G20 world, thanks particularly to their education levels, their focus on high-tech products, their strong innovation frameworks, and their commitment to help workers adjust as jobs come and go. Most are competing less head-on with rapidly developing countries. Moreover, the export sectors of most northern European economies are geared towards fast-growing products and most have trade surpluses in services, which is likely to remain a key area of European competitiveness.[1]

Member states in the middle ground have substantially less innovation and as a whole suffer from poorer institutions than the leaders, even though their macroeconomic performance and the basic skills of their population are similar.[2] Almost half of the EU's member states ranks lower in competitiveness than China; some also rank behind Russia, India and other rapidly developing countries. In general, EU members from southern and eastern European are having a harder time coping with the new world rising because they score below average on most indicators, with their relatively poor human capital levels a major weakness. Not only do these countries tend to be competing head-on with rapidly developing nations, they also have less inherent strength to deal with the challenges.

The EU's great diversity argues against a one-size-fits-all economic strategy. Yet the EU as a whole faces many common challenges, and this study has pointed to considerable EU strengths when EU member states band together to boost trade, attract talent, or spark innovation. To the extent that individual member states are able to pool their strengths and advance common or compatible approaches, all stand to gain relatively more than if each stood alone.

Europe 2020: A "SWOT" Analysis

This study has revealed considerable EU strengths and some serious weaknesses. It has identified opportunities and warned about current and looming threats. After carefully examining Europe's connections and its competitiveness, we conclude that the EU is more competitive in some key areas than many critics are prepared to acknowledge, yet also faces more serious challenges than some policymakers are prepared to admit. Table 19.2 summarizes this analysis in terms of the EU's strengths, weaknesses, opportunities and challenges—an EU "SWOT" analysis. Let's look first at the EU's weaknesses and challenges, and then its strengths and opportunities.

Weaknesses and Challenges

The European Union is challenged on a number of fronts. Large government deficits persist despite a reviving global economy. This danger is exacerbated by the legacy of the Great Recession: in most EU member states, public debt has soared way above 60% of GDP. Restoring government debt to 60% of GDP by 2030 will require painful fiscal adjustment in many countries.

The EU is in danger of fracturing along northern, southern and eastern lines. In general most northern EU member states exhibit high education levels, strong innovation capabilities, and strengths in upmarket goods and knowledge-intensive services. Southern member states overall face challenges ranging from fiscal deficits, major debt and in some cases severe challenges of competitiveness. Eastern member states were hit hard by the crisis and are still struggling to catch up with old member states while competing head-on with rising markets elsewhere. There are some exceptions, but such varied challenges are straining European solidarity and the Union's effectiveness.

Unemployment, inactivity and poverty still blight too many European lives. Almost half of the EU's member states ranks lower in competitiveness than China; some also rank behind Russia, India and other rapidly developing countries.[3] Some EU member states still mostly rely on exports of low-tech goods that tend to encounter less dynamic world demand, hampering gains in market share, and also more intense competition from low-cost countries. The EU is still "overweight" in its trade ties to developed countries, where demand is relatively static or growing slowly, and "underweight" in its trade ties with rapidly growing developing markets.

Except for a small subset of countries, the EU's innovation performance and its productivity lags other advanced economies. The services sector remains a sleeping giant. Secondary European financial market places are losing ground to other advanced and emerging financial centers.

Aging and shrinking populations challenge European competitiveness at a time when competition has gotten tougher. They make social safety nets harder to finance just when the need for them becomes greater. Immigrant workers are crucial as the EU confronts a rapidly aging work force and an acute labor shortage of skilled and semi-skilled workers. Yet the EU has become a magnet for the unskilled, struggling to assimilate and integrate migrants into society while falling short in the global competition for talent.

The EU will continue to rely on traditional sources of energy and depend on foreign sources for over half of its energy supply, with some EU member states critically dependent on a handful of foreign sources. And the combined and ultimately unsustainable resource and energy needs of rapidly developing countries and advanced economies are adding significant pressure to Europe's energy picture.

In addition, rapidly developing countries are recording high growth rates while Western economies, including many in Europe, struggle to recover from the financial crisis. Over the next five years the EU and other advanced economies are unlikely to grow more than 3% a year while the developing world is likely to grow more than 5% a year. Mature industrial economies are losing about a percentage point a year in share of world GDP to emerging markets.[4] In a world of overall growth, simply having a smaller share of an expanding pie is not necessarily all that bad, and the developing economies are emerging quickly from a low base. But such a world is not a given. Growth rates are uneven for particular EU countries and companies, and there are still significant risks to future growth.

Despite its accomplishments, the EU remains a patchwork of jurisdictions and regulations. The Single Market has come a good way, but still has a good way to go. Integration within the

Table 19.2. Europe 2020: A SWOT Analysis

	Strengths and Opportunities	Weaknesses and Threats
Goods	*World's largest trader in goods. *Market leader in medium technology and capital intensive exports. *Top supplier of goods to developing countries. *#1 in export market share in 9 of 20 different product categories. *Maintained global export share over past 15 years. *Withstood emerging competition better than U.S. or Japan. *Strong in environmental goods *High-growth demand in European specialties	*Weak in a large number of high technology export markets *Some member states still mostly rely on exports of low-tech goods *Export gains overwhelmingly in traditional products and markets, rather than in new products or new markets. *Still "overweight" in trade ties to developed countries, and "underweight" in ties to developing markets. *Lost market share in some fast-growing emerging markets *Trade deficits with all BRICs except India *China small comparative advantage over the EU as a whole in research-intensive goods and technology-driven industries
Services	*World's largest regional trader in services. *#1 in 8 of 11 categories of services exports. *Services: all of net job growth in the EU. *Share in global services trade much higher than that of the BRICs. *EU home base is significant market for services. *In past decade EU15 almost quadrupled their services trade balance. *Services trade surplus with every world region except the Caribbean. *Well positioned to take advantage of the globalization of services. *Services account for over 70% of EU GDP but only 23% of global exports: room to grow. *Services FDI providing key access to emerging markets. *Non-EU foreign affiliates account for large share of EU services exports. *Boosting services sector productivity to the EU15 average or to EU best-practice levels per sector could add 3-20% to EU productivity.	*Failing to capitalize on Single Market in services. *Uneven capabilities: southern and central EU member states could be at competitive disadvantage *Lagging services productivity is the source of the GDP and productivity growth gap between the EU15 and the U.S. *Must harness high tech and adequately educate/train workforce. *Failing to spark services innovation. *BRICs increasing services exports faster than the EU, U.S. or Japan. *India's services firms competing hard with EU companies in third markets.
Money *Capital*	*Critical source of capital for other world regions. *Largest portfolio investor in North America, Wider Europe, Russia, India and Oceania; 2nd largest in Africa, Caribbean, Rising Asia, Japan and Middle East. *Despite woes, euro is legitimate and favorable alternative to dollar. *Euro has allowed EU to attract more of world's excess savings. *Deeper capital markets have become more globally competitive. *Capital flows within euro zone without exchange rate risk. *EU financial centers account for 10 of the 20 best performers.	*Financial crises propagate to all markets easily. *Financial crisis halted 3 decades of capital markets expansion. *Widespread concern about the volatility of capital flows. *UK and eurozone: largest declines in cross-border capital flows. *Major deficits and debts among EU member states. *EU has only 4 of the top 20 financial centers worldwide. *EU financial centers account for 8 of the 20 worst global performers. *EU secondary financial centers losing ground to other centers. *Eurozone: no common economic policy to go with common currency *Eurozone: euro crisis unnerving investors; need permanent Stability Mechanism and more effective Stability and Growth pact.

Table 19.2. Europe 2020: A SWOT Analysis (continued)

	Strengths and Opportunities	Weaknesses and Threats
Foreign Direct Investment	*Largest provider and recipient of FDI among all world regions. *Home base dynamic and significant. *55 of the 100 largest non-financial multinational corporations. *U.S. FDI in EU more than next 20 investors combined. *EU FDI inflows more than twice the amount flowing to U.S. *EU outward FDI increased five-fold in past 15 years. * EU FDI in U.S. more than next 6 investors combined. *Outward FDI boosted EU GDP by more than €20 billion between 2001-2006; EU workers increased income by almost €13 billion. *Stronger position in BRICs as investor than as exporter. *EU FDI stocks in BRICs heavily oriented to services. *FDI is main means for EU services firms to access BRIC markets. *EU companies well placed to invest in high-growth sectors of rapidly rising economies.	*Restrictions on FDI persist in many emerging markets. *EU reliant on inward investment; must remain attractive as high-talent place to invest, work and innovate.
Energy	*EU leads U.S. and Japan in energy efficiency and sustainability. *EU companies lead in high-growth global clean energy sector. *13 of world's top 15 clean energy R&D companies. *Substantial lead in patents in air and water pollution control, renewable energy and solid waste management. *Opportunities for energy efficiency and renewables worldwide. *EU can lead effort to break link between production of wealth and consumption of resources.	*The EU's overall dependence on energy imports will rise from 55% in 2008 to 70% in 2030. *All member states except Denmark are net importers of energy. *By 2030, EU will have to import up to 80% of its natural gas. Germany, France and Italy already exhibit this rate. *12 member states are 100% dependent on foreign gas imports. *The concentration of energy production in a handful of countries will grow. *EU probably not able to reduce its energy dependence on Russia. *The resource and energy needs of emerging and established economies are unsustainable. *Clean energy not big enough to make a significant difference to growth in short-term. *Clean energy not likely to be consistently cheaper than dirty sources of energy anytime soon. *Widespread commercialization of clean energy technologies faces substantial hurdles. *EU companies challenged by the clean energy investments of U.S., Japan, China, and South Korea. *EU maintains biofuels barriers on Brazil and other exporters. *Failure to secure sufficient energy supplies would be devastating.
People	*Rich human resources compared to other regions. *EU commitment to free flow of labor within its borders has been a boon to sending and receiving countries alike. *Most countries have sought to target highly skilled migrants. *EU Blue Card offers promise to attract high-skilled talent.	*The EU is aging, shrinking, and has become a net importer of labor. *Europe is the world's oldest region. *EU labor markets still fragmented. *These trends exacerbate mismatches in labor supply and demand. *Today's migration inflow of 1 million/year not enough to offset the trends.

Table 19.2. Europe 2020: A SWOT Analysis (continued)

	Strengths and Opportunities	Weaknesses and Threats
People	*EU accounted for 16% of worldwide refugees at the end of 2009.	*To compensate for declining labor participation rates, EU needs to double immigration levels. *EU has become a magnet for the unskilled. *Highly skilled foreign workers only 1.7% of all workers in the EU. Australia: 9.9%; Canada: 7.3%.; U.S.: 3.5%. *85% of unskilled labor goes to the EU and 5% to the U.S. *55% of skilled labor goes to the U.S and only 5% to the EU. *EU must be more effective in making itself a more attractive destination for qualified and highly motivated potential immigrants and their families; but anti-migrant forces rising. *EU loses skilled hundreds of thousands of skilled emigrants each year to Oceania, North America and Wider Europe.
Ideas	*Overall a competitive and highly connected innovation economy. *EU innovation leaders: Denmark, Finland, Germany, Sweden and United Kingdom. *Next tier: Austria, Belgium, Cyprus, Estonia, France, Ireland, Luxembourg, Netherlands and Slovenia. *EU performs better than U.S. in 6 of 17 innovation indicators and growth performance better in 13 of 17 indicators. *Strong innovation performance lead over the BRICs. *9 of top 20 countries in terms of Network Readiness. *EU companies: 31% of the top R&D companies. U.S.: 34%. Japan 22%. *More than 25% of scientific publications, highest share of any region. *Non-EU companies based in EU are key to EU R&D investment. *Boosting R&D investment to 3% of GDP could create 3.7 million jobs and increase annual EU GDP by up to €795 billion by 2025.	*EU innovation performance very uneven. *Moderate Innovators: Czech Republic, Greece, Hungary, Italy, Lithuania, Malta, Poland, Portugal, Slovakia, Spain. *Catching-up Countries: Bulgaria, Latvia, Romania. *Consistently fails to meet goal of 3% share of GDP for R&D; failed to catch up to the U.S.; has fallen further behind South Korea, Singapore and Japan; could be eclipsed by China. *Clear innovation performance gap in favor of the U.S. and Japan. *U.S. companies invested nearly 5 times more than EU companies in semiconductors, 4 times more in software and 8 times more in biotechnology. *Only 5 EU regions among top 20 knowledge regions. U.S.: 13. *Inadequate attention paid to demand-driven innovation; social and services innovation. *Stronger focus needed bringing ideas to market. *Significant barriers to circulation of highly-skilled individuals. *EU patent system still fragmented.

EU is far less than that within the U.S.; trade between U.S. states is two to three times higher than trade between EU member states. Decision-making is often fragmented and ineffective. The lack of a European patent means that patenting an idea in the EU is 10 times more expensive than in the United States.[5] EU member states operate under a common trade policy, but their trade orientation and performance vary considerably. In areas such as agriculture the EU remains highly protectionist. Eurozone members share a common currency without a common economic policy, and the euro crisis of 2010 has hobbled European recovery.

Of course, the EU's diversity can be one of its great strengths. An EU that could move only in lock-step would be an EU unlikely to progress at all. Yet in many ways, the European Union is still less than the sum of its parts. There is considerable discrepancy between the EU's challenges and the ability and propensity of its member states to address them together.[6]

Strengths and Opportunities

Fortunately, the EU's challenges are balanced by some notable strengths. The EU accounts for 5 of the top 10 and 10 of the top 20 most competitive nations in the world, and for 8 of the top 10 and 22 of the 30 most "economically globalized" nations in the world.[7] With only 7% of the world's population, EU GDP of about €12 trillion accounts for nearly 30% of the world's economic output. The U.S accounts for 27%, Japan for 9% and China for less than 6%.

Northern European EU member states in particular are well positioned to cope with the G20 world, thanks particularly to their education levels, their focus on high-tech and upmarket products, their strong innovation capacities, and their commitment to help workers adjust as jobs come and go. Moreover, the export sectors of most northern European economies are geared towards fast-growing products and most have trade surpluses in services.[8]

Over the past twenty years the EU has grown from 12 to 27 members and has made considerable progress toward a single internal market. Together, the creation of the Single Market and the enlargement of the EU created 2.75 million additional jobs and contributed an additional 1.85% growth between 1992 and 2009.[9] The euro shields a significant portion of intra-EU commerce from currency fluctuations. The EU is culturally rich; boasts an extraordinarily well-educated population, sophisticated product and financial markets and significant technological prowess; and is experimenting with the boldest type of supranational governance on the planet. It has at least as many wealthy consumers as the United States. Life satisfaction and happiness are higher in Europe than any other part of the world. European workers still enjoy a larger share of their countries' wealth than do U.S. workers, and most European countries have safety nets for workers that would be the envy of anxious U.S. employees. While Europe traditionally has experienced higher rates of unemployment than the United States, for many this has been more than offset by the stagnant incomes and growing income inequality that have plagued the U.S. in recent decades, and in the wake of the financial crisis the situation has reversed, with U.S. unemployment higher than in most of Europe. Life expectancy has increased and Europe could be a leader in healthy aging. Educational opportunity is expanding. Diversity has the potential to be a great source of creative strength. Successfully managed migration could help meet Europe's economic and social needs.

Europe's internal transformation has had profound external consequences. The EU is the world's largest exporting entity, largest source and destination of foreign direct investment, largest donor of foreign aid, and a critical source of capital for many other world regions. The EU is home to some of the world's most competitive companies, who are not just holding their own against global competition but have emerged or maintained their status as global leaders within their respective industries. The EU has maintained its share of world exports despite the rise of other trading powers, and is a more significant trading partner for the BRICs than either the U.S. or Japan. Rapidly emerging economies are registering high demand in the types of products in which many European exporters specialize.

In a world of continental-sized players, the EU has become an important vehicle for relatively small European countries to amplify their presence on the world stage, and to manage globalization without resorting to protectionism. EU member states together have greater ability than any of them alone would have to develop standards for globalized commerce, food and product safety, and financial transactions. Common minimum regulations in the EU have moderated potentially destructive competition among member states while allowing for national differences.[10] EU enlargement has enabled European companies to make use of a bigger Single Market to extend their production networks and thus to compete more effectively. Billions of euros in EU structural funds boost prospects for poorer regions and transition economies and make Europe as a whole more fit for global economic competition. In all these areas the EU is, and seen in Europe to be, a vehicle for European states to negotiate the terms of their deepening integration with each other and their widening interactions with the rest of the world.[11]

The EU is also a leader in clean energy and energy efficiency. It is better positioned than others to break the link between the generation of wealth and the consumption of resources. The BRICs and many other rising markets are all growing rapidly in a world economy premised on extensive use of oil and gas and intensive use of resources. Coupled with the continuing resource needs of established economies, this is untenable for a global economy of 7 billion people. Breaking this link could open the way for an entirely different patterns of consumption and competitiveness. Europe could lead the way.

None of these strengths are easily tapped, however. Instead of embracing its periphery, the EU is fearful of it. Rather than advancing low-carbon competitiveness, too many companies and politicians use it as an excuse for further protection. Rather than embracing flexicurity and related initiatives, too many hold onto false securities of the past. And rather than taking advantage of the real possibilities offered by services, European politics still portray them as low-wage and low-skill, pose false choices between services and manufacturing, and are fearful of opening up home markets to their own EU partners, much less competitors from abroad.

The 2020 Strategy: Good, But...

Given these challenges, EU leaders in 2010 set forth a strategy to turn the EU into a "smart, sustainable and inclusive economy delivering high levels of high levels of employment, productivity and social cohesion" by the year 2020. They placed three priorities at the heart of their "Europe 2020" strategy, and under each priority enumerated various "flagship" initiatives:[12]

- Smart growth—developing an economy based on knowledge and innovation;

    (i) an Innovation Union: to improve framework conditions and access to finance for research and innovation so as to strengthen the innovation chain and boost levels of investment throughout the Union.

(ii) youth on the move: to enhance the performance of education systems and to reinforce the international attractiveness of Europe's higher education.

(iii) a digital agenda for Europe: to speed up the roll-out of high-speed internet and reap the benefits of a digital single market for households and firms.

- Sustainable growth – promoting a more resource efficient, greener and more competitive economy;

  (iv) a resource-efficient Europe: to help decouple economic growth from the use of resources, by decarbonizing the economy, increasing the use of renewable sources, modernizing the transport sector and promoting energy efficiency.

  (v) an industrial policy for the globalization era: to improve the business environment, especially for small- and medium-sized enterprises, and to support the development of a strong and sustainable industrial base able to compete globally.

- Inclusive growth – fostering a high-employment economy delivering economic, social and territorial cohesion.

  (vi) an agenda for new skills and jobs: to modernize labor markets by facilitating labor mobility and the development of skills throughout the life cycle with a view to increasing labor participation and better matching labor supply and demand;

  (vii) a European platform to tackle poverty: to ensure social and territorial cohesion such that the benefits of growth and jobs are widely shared and people experiencing poverty and social exclusion are enabled to live in dignity and take an active part in society.

The EU also agreed on a number of headline targets for 2020:

- Increase the employment rate of the population aged 20-64 from the current 69% to at least 75%, including through the greater involvement of women, older workers and better integration of migrants in the work force;

- Invest 3% of GDP in R&D—the same ambitious target that it has had, and failed to achieve, for over ten years;

- Reduce greenhouse gas emissions by 20-20% compared to 1990 levels; increase the share of renewable energy sources in final EU energy consumption to 20%; and increase energy efficiency by 20%;

- Reduce the school drop-out rate to 10% from the current 15%;

- Increase the share of the population aged 30-34 having completed tertiary education from 31% to at least 40%;

- Reduce the number of Europeans living below national poverty lines by 25%, lifting over 20 million people out of poverty.

Relatedly, the Commission seeks to implement the Single Market Act, a blueprint it has offered to revitalize the Single Market by the end of 2012, the 20ᵗʰ anniversary of its birth. Its proposals, inspired by a 2010 report by former Competition Commissioner Mario Monti, include simplified accounting rules; improving small business access to public procurement contracts; boosting electronic commerce; building down barriers to intra-EU transportation; facilitating cross-border venture capital; more open and competitive pan-European procurement processes; promoting social entrepreneurship; online commerce; full implementation of the Services Directive; and streamlining recognition of professional qualifications across the Union.[13]

The overall thrust of these efforts is promising and deserves broad support. But the fatal weakness of the previous effort, the so-called Lisbon Strategy, was its inability to provide incentives or to ensure implementation by EU member states. In the end the Lisbon Strategy goals were not achieved over a ten-year period.

The Europe 2020 Strategy seeks to remedy this weakness with a number of measures. One is a so-called "European Semester," beginning in January 2011, through which national budgets are assessed by the European Commission at the draft level. Another is a macro-economic surveillance mechanism, slated to be approved in 2011, that would include an early warning mechanism to detect risks of real estate bubbles, unsustainable external imbalances, and divergences in competitiveness, and possibly include sanctions for eurozone countries unless a qualified majority of member states votes against it.[14]

While welcome, these reforms are still rather weak regarding compliance, and the related public education effort seems weak compared to the relatively massive effort needed to convince publics why key changes are needed.[15] Commission President Jose Manuel Barroso himself identified what many deem to be central to the strategy's success or failure: political will among member states. "We have to be quite honest," he has said, "there are 27 member states and if they don't want to play ball nothing will happen."[16]

The Strategy needs to be accompanied by incentives to member states to improve performance, for instance by using the EU budget as an incentive mechanism and using conditionality as a disciplining principle. Those who meet headline targets could receive additional EU funds. EU transfer rules need to be revised to better reward reformers and punish laggards; and compliance must be enforced more decisively than in the past. National reform agendas could be assessed by an independent expert group, as a way to reward good behavior and punish bad policies. EU transfers could be withheld if countries do not comply with the reform agenda. Peer review should be avoided, as pressures to weaken discipline would arise, as experienced in the past with the Stability and Growth Pact (SGP). The need to build better incentives to reform into the European governance framework is hardly new.[17] But the crisis has made changes more pressing.

Key Recommendations

The European Union and its member states have a window of opportunity to reposition themselves for the challenges of a vastly different world. Given current trendlines in such key areas as trade in goods and services, financial markets, energy dependencies, demographic changes and innovation performance, they have about decade's time to address their weaknesses and capitalize on their strengths. If they do so, Europeans are likely to prosper in the new world rising. If they do not, the resulting strains and stresses could challenge Europe's very construction.

Will the financial crisis be remembered as the moment when the EU finally cracked? Or as the spur to a more competitive Union? During the first few years of the new decade most EU member state governments will be preoccupied with recovering from the financial crisis and restoring confidence in EU and euro zone economic policy coordination. Yet even if successful, such efforts will prove inadequate to the larger challenges facing the European Union. Even as they tackle the lingering crisis, policymakers must simultaneously lay the foundation for continued European competitiveness in an increasingly interconnected world.

How can this be achieved?

There is no one-size-fits-all model. To a large extent, each member state must devise its own strategy. Different pathways can lead to success. Different circumstances call for different relative priorities. Countries in southern Europe need to focus more on regaining competitiveness, while others should promote higher labor force participation or more open service sector markets. Some common priorities do emerge, however, that underscore the importance of working better at European level. To the extent that individual member states are able to advance together along the lines below, each is likely to be strengthened as well.

Here are 8 basic priorities.

1. First things first—get the recovery right. EU leaders urgently need to fix the financial system and tackle burgeoning deficits and debt without undermining Europe's fragile return to growth. Addressing weaknesses in the financial system is essential to a strong and sustained recovery. Unfortunately, EU leaders have adopted hesitant and piecemeal approaches to the debt problems of the eurozone's weakest members, which have not helped those countries return to growth, have not reassured nervous investors, and have not protected other eurozone countries from further contagion.[18]

More fundamental efforts are needed if EU member states are to break free of the lingering economic and financial crisis. First is a permanent crisis resolution mechanism to replace the temporary European Financial Stability Facility established in 2010 to deal with the Greek crisis. EU leaders agreed to this in December 2010, but the devil is in the details. Second is the need to provide a framework that would allow eurozone members to restructure their debt if necessary.

Third are fiscal and financial reforms that actually support—and enforce—the growth and stability pact targets that have been ignored for many years. Strengthened policy coordination within the eurozone and at EU level could offer momentum to reforms. More effective bank regulation would be a start. A stronger Stability and Growth Pact is also key, with surveillance focused on the joint accomplishment of fiscal sustainability and structural reforms for growth.[19] Monitoring and enforcement of targets under a revised Pact should include more effective sticks and carrots. The sticks might involve greater penalties and European Commission oversight rules. One carrot might take the form of a "Maastricht bond," as suggested by Jacob Funk Kirkegaard, for members that successfully manage to put their government finances on a sustainable path. This "Maastricht bond" would be similar to the often suggested "eurobond," but would be open only to eurozone members that actually adhere to the Maastricht Treaty criteria of 60% maximum government debt. As Kirkegaard notes, a successful Maastricht bond, backed by credible austerity measures, could give the eurozone a scale and market depth similar to today's U.S. treasury market.[20] EU structural funds could also be directed to weaker economies who nonetheless adhere to targets under a revised Pact.

Fourth are related efforts to improve economic performance. Permanent bail-outs are not the solution to Europe's economic challenges. As Jean Pisani-Ferry notes, weaker EU member states need to regain competitiveness and resume economic growth, "not to be put inside an economic oxygen tent."[21] This will require EU leaders to convince weary voters to accept some short-term economic pain in order to build down deficits and debt and reposition their economies to compete successfully in the changing global economy.

2. Raise productivity to drive overall growth. The EU must boost its productivity if it is to deal with its demographic challenges and sustain its social welfare model.[22] Better utilization and productivity of labor would lift EU GDP substantially. McKinsey estimates that boosting services sector productivity to the EU15 average or to European best-practice levels per sector could add 3-20% to the region's productivity.[23] And simulations by the IMF and the European Commission suggest that if all EU member states were to adopt best practices by the EU's 3 best performers in labor markets and the services sector, overall EU GDP growth would rise by as much as ½ percentage point of additional annual growth annually over the next 5 years.[24] Stagnant or flagging productivity, on the other hand, will mean a period of low or no growth, which is likely to generate greater domestic and intra-EU conflicts while leaving the EU behind in a world or high-growth competitors.

Specific challenges vary across EU member states. Germany, France, and some smaller countries need to improve their utilization of labor, while many southern and eastern member states need to focus on more basic requirements, such as their institutional setting, infrastructure levels, market efficiency, technological readiness, and skill levels.[25] Yet even though each member state faces its own unique challenges, all are likely to benefit from strengthened coordination. The Europe 2020 strategy offers some useful ways forward, yet in many areas does not go far enough. Reforms could include a shift from labor to VAT taxes; reducing entry barriers in key services sectors; offering better tertiary and vocational education opportunities; promoting more effective links between business-related research and universities, allowing universities to patent output even when research has been financed through public programs (as permitted by the Bayh-Dole Act in the United States); and attracting high-skilled foreign talent. In the past, reforms have succeeded when the agenda was driven by European institutions and a common sense of purpose, but largely failed when agendas relied on peer pressure among member states alone.

3. Complete the Single Market. The Single Market is both the bedrock of European integration and the EU's most potent instrument to address the challenges and opportunities of the G20 world. The European Commission estimates that completing, deepening and making full use of the Single Market would potentially produce growth of about 4% of GDP over the next ten years. A more complete and vibrant Single Market would provide countries and companies with a stronger geo-economic base in a world of continental-sized players. It would give EU countries greater opportunities to exploit their full comparative advantage, and would give EU companies new possibilities to restructure their activities on a pan-European scale. It would much improve the EU's attractiveness as place to invest, work and study.[26]

Completing the Single Market would create jobs and boost trade, investment, productivity and growth. The EU itself is still the key market for all EU member states. Two-thirds of all EU goods and services, FDI and private portfolio investment is transferred among EU member states. Yet major opportunities go missing. Cross-border procurement, for example, accounted for only around 1.5% of all public contracts awarded in the EU in 2009. Cross-border services account for only 5% of the EU's GDP, compared with 17% for manufactured goods traded within the Single Market. Only 7% of EU consumers used the Internet to make cross-border purchases in 2008. In energy, national champions control 80-100% of domestic electricity production. A single EU energy market could lower prices for consumers and make energy supplies more secure. The ratio of intra-EU15 exports to GDP is 70% less than the ratio of intra-U.S. exports to GDP.[27]

A Digital Single Market is a related opportunity left untapped. The cost of non-digital Europe is significant: according to a recent study[28] the EU could gain 4% of GDP by stimulating the fast development of a Digital Single Market by 2020. This corresponds to a gain of almost €500 billion and means that the Digital Single Market alone could have an impact similar to the 1992 Single Market program itself.[29]

4. Awaken Europe's sleeping giant: services. The EU could make things easier for itself by playing to its strength in services — its biggest untapped source of jobs and economic growth. Services account for all net job growth in the EU. Intra-EU services trade is 35% higher today than it would be without the Single Market. Nonetheless, services account for just 20% of Europe's trade, even though they account for 70% of Europe's output.[30] Although the EU-wide Services Directive has helped forge a more coherent approach to services within the EU, it is not fully implemented, and excludes such critical areas of potential innovation and productivity growth as financial services, health, employment and social services.[31] One recent study found that if the Services Directive were fully implemented, it could deliver more than 600,000 new jobs and economic gains ranging between €60-140 billion, representing a growth potential of at least 0.6-1.5% of GDP.[32] And if services competition in the eurozone was raised to U.S. levels, the European Central Bank estimates that service sector output could be increased by 12%. Innovation, efficiency, investment and jobs could all be sparked through stronger competition, particularly in business-to-business services; easier entry requirements into professional services sectors and easier cross-border transfer of degrees and training certificates; lifting entry barriers in such network industries as energy and transportation; providing crucial enablers such as standards, education, and infrastructure in business services, tourism, and telecommunications; and facilitating European scale across member state borders. Member states such as Germany and those from northern Europe are particularly losing out on these opportunities.

The European Competitiveness Report 2010 highlights the particular importance of the "creative industries" to the EU's future prosperity. Such industries are essentially services industries. They range from information services, such as publishing or software, to such professional services as engineering, architecture, advertising and design. They account for 3.3% of total EU GDP and 3% of employment, and are among the fastest growing sectors in the EU. Overall employment in the creative industries increased by an average of 3.5% a year in 2000-2007, compared to 1.0% a year for the EU economy as a whole.[33]

A true Single Market in services would also position the EU well internationally. As discussed in Chapter 2, the EU is a world-class leader in services trade, including in exports of creative industries products and services. EU services companies are also major investors in services; in fact FDI has become the main means for EU companies to get access to high-growth emerging markets. More effective efforts to facilitate services investments, not just trade, would pay dividends to EU services companies, which still lag U.S. firms when it comes to such key markets as Japan, India, China and Rising Asia.[34]

5. Break the link between the production of wealth and the consumption of resources. The EU should lead in the transition to a low-carbon economy and promote itself as a showcase of energy efficiency and innovation. This will be neither quick nor easy. Fossil fuels are convenient, versatile, and in many cases cheaper than many renewables. But as David Buchan has noted, the EU has the capacity and the propensity to lead the great escape from fossil fuels.[35] Reducing EU energy consumption by 20% by 2020 would reduce the cost of energy imports by €100-150 billion annually, and could create a million new jobs. Under current policies, however, the EU will only reduce consumption by 10%, so the EU will miss out on at least €50 billion a year in cost savings and half a million new jobs unless stronger energy-saving approaches are put into place, including incentives to address up-front costs and efforts to heighten end-user awareness. The EU's green stimulus spending has been only half that of the U.S. and one-quarter of that provided by China. Prioritizing public funding of clean energy would send a strong signal to business and act as a catalyst for private investment.[36]

6. Innovate. Innovation drives economic growth and offers new solutions to existing challenges. It has become even more important as Europe's native population ages and shrinks, since population growth cannot fuel economic growth in Europe. The EU can—and must—offer greater opportunities to young start-ups and entrepreneurs; facilitate the mobility of workers within and across companies; invest more in R&D and higher education; boost possibilities for continuous development of skills; welcome highly-skilled migrants; introduce a unified EU patent and related litigation system; continue to build innovation clusters in sub-regions of the EU; improve access by small- and medium-sized enterprises to financial resources, simplified administrative procedures and better protection of intellectual property rights; facilitate the exchange of people, skills, technologies and ideas between large and small businesses to boost overall innovation capability; and build a more vibrant EU base of small and medium-sized companies, which are essential for growth and jobs.[37]

The EU must also turn from its traditional focus on benchmarks of innovation input such as R&D measures to a concerted focus on innovation output, and focus on user needs, demand opportunities, organizational, process and social innovation. It needs to focus more explicitly on getting ideas to market. It must recognize the collaborative and cross-border nature of innovation in today's world and actively forge and strengthen its innovation networks around the globe. The December 2010 initiative by 10 EU member states to move ahead with a unified European patent is a step in the right direction.

An effective innovation strategy must encompass both manufacturing and services. The EU needs to build on such areas of competitive advantage in high-tech manufacturing as intelligent manufacturing systems, aerospace, digital electronics and biopharmaceuticals. As emerging markets move into higher-value-added activity, ensuring that the EU maintains its advantage in those sectors will be key to keeping the EU a location of choice for innovation activity and investment. And a coherent services innovation strategy promises to extend the scope of innovation activity more widely across the Union.

The EU also needs to remain at the forefront of protecting and promoting intellectual capital. Robust protection of intellectual property drives European innovation and attracts capital to innovative and creative enterprises. It protects inventions and content and is a critical element in the fight against counterfeiting and piracy.

7. Power to the people. The EU and its member states must tap the potential of their people if they are to manage demographic challenges, sustain their social model, develop the skills needed in a knowledge-based economy, and prosper in the G20 world. In particular, the EU needs to develop a pan-European talent strategy that attracts skilled foreign labor; ensures the free movement of people among member states; facilitates better links between business and education; improves access to and harmonizes key features of the labor market; promotes higher education and training in key enabling technologies; and boosts overall skills training and re-skilling across the Union. Europe's aging population also represents a market opportunity for certain sectors, in particular healthcare, pharmaceuticals, medical and nutrition products, tourism and leisure, which should be encouraged to innovate to meet changing demand patterns.[38]

The EU also has the opportunity to demonstrate that economic strength can go hand in hand with high standards of welfare, despite intense competitive pressures. EU leaders can show that it is possible to reap globalization's benefits while making its costs bearable to those who are directly affected by rapid economic change. "Flexicurity" arrangements piloted by Denmark and other member states is one example of how Europe is doing just that.[39]

8. Become a critical hub in the G20 world. The EU is well placed to be a key hub of a multi-polar world in which new centers of economic and political power have emerged. The EU should use its network capital to make itself a focal point for the exchange of ideas, people, capital, goods, services and energy innovation in the interconnected G20 world. The more connected the EU is, the more competitive it is likely to be. The EU needs to advance on four fronts.

First, don't forget your base. That's the first rule of politics, and it should be the first rule of EU international economic policy. The Single Market is the platform for a more competitive EU in a G20 world. Better use should be made of it. "Europeanization" can be as economically profound for many EU companies and countries as "globalization," and this study has shown that Europeanization of goods, services, capital, energy, people and ideas and the competitive networks than accompany them extend beyond EU borders to encompass the EU's neighbors in Wider Europe. Before the recession the EU benefitted enormously from the dynamism of its closest neighbors. Europe's backyard can generate tremendous opportunities again—if the EU is prepared to deepen existing ties and widen its networks. If one considers the potential of Wider Europe, the EU essentially has a China right in its own backyard. Yet the popular image is of the Polish plumber and the Turkish construction worker.

Second, create an open Transatlantic Marketplace. This study underscores that potential for the EU to build an even more vibrant base through its almost organic ties to North America. No two continents are as economically fused as Europe and North America, and those bonds have tightened, not loosened, since the end of the Cold War. Together North America and the EU still comprise more than half of global GDP, are the world's and each other's most significant partners in terms of trade, investment, innovation and the norms and standards that guide global commerce. Rather than take the transatlantic partnership for granted or treat it as a "legacy" relationship rooted in the past, policymakers are called to use its considerable potential to tap new sources of innovation and growth.

The transatlantic economy is the freest in the world — but it is not free. Significant results could be achieved for smarter and more sustainable growth as well as more and well-paying jobs, from related initiatives to conclude a transatlantic zero tariff agreement; build down non-tariff measures on each shore of the North Atlantic; align legislation on "upstream" issues such as nanobiotechnology, e-health or e-mobility; and work together to establish and ensure international adherence to high level global standards in such areas as intellectual property protection, food and consumer safety and public procurement. The payoffs could be substantial: the impact of a mutual opening of the EU's Single Market and North America's vast continental market would be the equivalent of giving every European and American an entire year's extra salary over their working lifetimes.[40] Even as the U.S. and the EU push multilateral liberalization through the Doha Development Round, they should advance transatlantic market-opening initiatives in services, financial markets, telecommunications, energy, innovation policies and other areas not yet covered by multilateral agreements.

Third, leverage high-growth markets. Completing the Single Market and bolstering the EU's extended base in Wider Europe and North America would position the EU much better to face the challenges and leverage the opportunities offered by the fast-growing markets of the emerging world. EU companies must overcome the relative inertia evident in their export orientation to compete with emerging market companies in high-growth economies.

Despite the use of such terms as BRICs, this study has shown that the nature of the EU's ties to other world regions varies significantly, and each must be approached on its own terms. The EU needs to open the Chinese market to EU goods, services and investments; improve standards for trade in goods and services; and address counterfeiting and other intellectual property challenges, currency distortions and discriminatory Chinese policies. With Rising Asia it has the opportunity to build on its free trade agreement with South Korea to conclude additional pacts with others, and to press ahead with its renewables trade. The consumer markets of China and Rising Asia together will rise from 12% of world consumption prior to the economic crisis to about 32% in 2020, becoming the main driver of world growth and a key opportunity for the EU—if European companies reposition themselves and are able to export value-added goods and services to these growing consumer markets and establish affiliates to provide goods and services locally.[41]

The EU could be a major partner for Russia if Moscow would be prepared to tackle seriously its profound domestic challenges and further develop its energy infrastructure while shifting to a more balanced economy. The EU needs to strengthen its surprisingly weak links to India while bracing for tough competition in third markets from Indian services providers. And it can do more to engage Brazil through services, investment and collaboration on new energy sources.

There are some common threads in EU ties to emerging markets. Major challenges arise from weak regulatory frameworks, uneven enforcement of laws, continuing non-tariff barriers to trade and relatively low environmental and labor standards, which often discriminate against foreign companies. Prominent examples are intellectual property rights protection and its enforcement in China, labor legislation in India and Russia, and environmental regulations in both Russia and China. In addition, the strong role of the state in many emerging markets, which can be expressed in terms of preferential subsidies, tax preferences, or privileged access to bank loans or raw materials, especially for state-owned enterprises, can hamper efforts by EU companies to be competitive both home and abroad. State interference in China poses particular challenges for EU companies, in view of the export-driven character of the Chinese economy and the potential scale and scope of the Chinese domestic economy.

Fourth, don't neglect key economies. As the EU engages vigorously on these fronts, it needs to address areas in which it has allowed its economic ties to erode. Africa is perhaps the most prominent example. But Latin America has also been neglected. And Turkey is shifting its trade away from Europe.[42] EU companies have sacrificed considerable opportunities in these three markets, losing market share to rising competitors, particularly from Asia.

The rise of rapidly developing nations presents many opportunities for the EU, but also very real challenges. As this study has demonstrated, the EU still has time to reposition itself to prosper in this new world rising, if the political will is there. But time is not standing still. And in the end, history will remember not only how well leaders managed this or that crisis, but how well they positioned their countries for the future.

Four Scenarios

Europe's future economic performance depends on its ability and its propensity to leverage global growth, human talent and innovation while exploiting European strengths and consolidating public finances. These external and internal drivers define four possible scenarios for Europe's future: *Competitive Europe, Losing Steam, Europe Unhooked,* and *Europe Adrift.*[43]

Figure 19A. Europe 2020: Four Scenarios

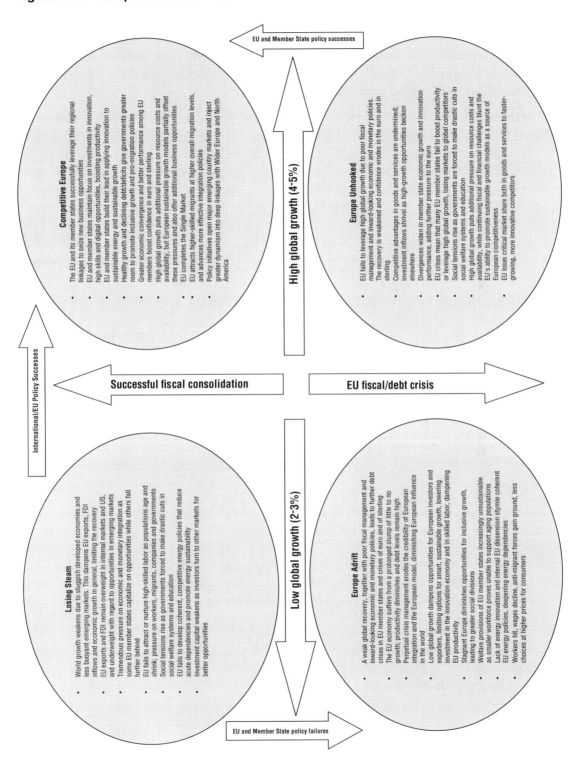

EU and Member State policy successes

Competitive Europe

- The EU and its member states successfully leverage their regional linkages to seize new business opportunities
- EU and member states maintain focus on investments in innovation, high skills and digital opportunities, boosting productivity
- EU and member states build their lead in applying innovation to sustainable energy and sustainable growth
- Healthy growth and declining debt/deficits give governments greater room to promote inclusive growth and pro-migration policies
- Greater economic convergence and better performance among EU members boost confidence in euro and sterling
- High global growth puts additional pressure on resource costs and availability, but European sustainable growth models partially offset these pressures and also offer additional business opportunities
- EU completes the Single Market
- EU attracts higher-skilled migrants at higher overall migration levels, and advances more effective integration policies
- Policy initiatives open major emerging country markets and inject greater dynamism into deep linkages with Wider Europe and North America

Europe Unhooked

- EU fails to leverage high global growth due to poor fiscal management and inward-looking economic and monetary policies. The recovery is weakened and confidence erodes in the euro and in sterling
- Competitive advantages in goods and services are undermined; investment inflows shrivel as high-growth opportunities beckon elsewhere
- Divergences widen in member state economic growth and innovation performance, adding further pressure to the euro
- EU crises mean that many EU member states fail to boost productivity or leverage high global growth, losing markets to global competitors
- Social tensions rise as governments are forced to make drastic cuts in social welfare systems and education
- High global growth puts additional pressure on resource costs and availability, while continuing fiscal and financial challenges blunt the EU's ability to promote sustainable growth models as a source of European competitiveness
- EU loses critical market share both in goods and services to faster-growing, more innovative competitors

High global growth (4-5%)

International/EU Policy Successes

Successful fiscal consolidation

EU fiscal/debt crisis

Losing Steam

- World growth weakens due to sluggish developed economies and less buoyant emerging markets. This dampens EU exports, FDI inflows and economic growth in general, limiting the recovery
- EU exports and FDI remain overweight in internal markets and US, and underweight with regard to opportunities in emerging markets
- Tremendous pressure on economic and monetary integration as some EU member states capitalize on opportunities while others fall further behind
- EU fails to attract or nurture high-skilled labor as populations age and shrink; pressure on workers, migrants, companies and governments
- Social tensions rise as governments forced to make drastic cuts in social welfare systems and education
- EU fails to develop coherent, competitive energy policies that reduce acute dependencies and promote energy sustainability
- Investment capital weakens as investors turn to other markets for better opportunities

Europe Adrift

- A weak global recovery, together with poor fiscal management and inward-looking economic and monetary policies, leads to further debt crises in EU member states and crises of euro and of sterling
- The EU economy suffers from a prolonged slump of little to no growth; productivity diminishes and debt levels remain high
- Perpetual crisis management erodes the credibility of European integration and the European model, diminishing European influence in the world
- Low global growth dampens opportunities for European investors and exporters, limiting options for smart, sustainable growth, lowering investment in the innovation economy and in skilled labor, dampening EU productivity
- Stagnant Europe diminishes opportunities for inclusive growth, leading to greater social divisions
- Welfare provisions of EU member states increasingly unsustainable as smaller workforce proves unable to support aging populations
- Lack of energy innovation and internal EU dissension stymie coherent EU energy policies, deepening energy dependencies
- Workers hit, wages decline, anti-migrant forces gain ground, less choices at higher prices for consumers

Low global growth (2-3%)

EU and Member State policy failures

Competitive Europe

If the EU is to maintain and even advance its competitive position, it must not only build on its strengths and address its weaknesses, it must bolster its capacity to leverage the dynamism of other key regions and to absorb innovation and talent from beyond its borders. In the scenario dubbed *Competitive Europe*, the EU and its member states are successful in doing these things in a high-growth global environment.

Under this scenario, the EU and its member states address their fiscal and financial problems and inject new vibrancy into their home base by improving the economic governance of the eurozone and boosting the capacity of the EU Single Market and the free flow of goods, services, money, energy, people and ideas within it. They leverage higher growth to seek greater economic convergence among EU member states at levels of high competitiveness across the board. They supplement these initiatives with efforts to infuse additional dynamism into their broader geo-economic base in Wider Europe, and to invigorate the EU's deep economic connections to North America, in particular by knocking down non-tariff barriers to transatlantic commerce, fueling greater innovation linkages, and opening up the transatlantic services economy.

These initiatives proceed in tandem with more effective efforts, both through trade and foreign direct investment, to capture greater market share in new markets, particularly in China and Rising Asia, and renewed attention to Africa and Latin America. EU firms capitalize on their advantages in services and in high-tech, upmarket and environmental goods across all markets; as well as the opportunities rapidly rising economies offer to EU medium-tech capital goods industries and those engaged in infrastructure development. Activist policies address aging and shrinking populations, boost integration levels and advance skills and training across the board. They promote innovation and knowledge-based investments, particularly in energy sustainability.

Losing Steam

Under this scenario the EU and its member states agree on ways to improve their competitiveness, but the promise dissipates due to persistently low European and global growth as the recovery from the financial crisis stutters. EU exports and FDI remain overweight in developed country markets, as opportunities falter in emerging markets. Pressure builds on economic and monetary integration as some EU member states capitalize on opportunities while others fall further behind. Social tensions rise as governments are forced to make further cuts in social welfare systems and education. The EU fails to attract or nurture high-skilled labor as populations age and shrink, adding to pressures on workers, migrants, companies and governments. Investment capital weakens as investors turn to other markets for better opportunities. Flagging investment, in turn, makes it harder for the EU to reduce acute energy dependencies and promote energy sustainability

Europe Unhooked

Under this scenario the global growth environment is good but the EU and its member states prove unable to generate the efforts needed to maintain and advance their competitiveness. The EU fails to leverage global growth, the recovery is weakened, and confidence erodes in the euro and in sterling. Faster-growing and more innovative competitors capture market share in a variety of goods and services, and investment shrivels as high-growth opportunities beckon elsewhere. Divergences widen even further between high-performing member states and thus unable to maintain their competitive position. Social tensions rise as governments forced to cut back on social welfare systems and education, and limited investment funds blunt the EU's ability to promote sustainable growth models as a source of European competitiveness.

Europe Adrift

Under this scenario there is low global and European growth and the EU and its member states fail to advance efforts to advance their competitiveness. Debt levels remain stubbornly high and further debt crises erupt in some EU member states, triggering a crisis of confidence in the euro and sterling. Continual crisis management erodes the credibility of European integration and the European model, diminishing European influence in the world, prompting intense debate about the nature and relevance of the EU itself. Innovation and productivity flag. The EU loses critical market share both in goods and services to faster-growing, more innovative competitors. Social divisions are exacerbated and the welfare state provisions of EU member states simply become unsustainable as a smaller workforce proves unable to support aging populations. The lack of energy innovation and internal EU disputes limit the possibilities for coherent EU energy policies, thus deepening energy dependencies among a greater number of EU member states. Workers suffer, wages decline, and anti-migrant forces gain ground. Consumers are confronted with less choice at higher prices.

* * *

Europeans need the European Union now as much as they did a half-century ago, but for different reasons. For fifty years, the European project was about internal reconciliation and reconstruction following the collapse of an earlier era of globalization into war and depression. It was a grand experiment in harnessing closer economic integration to build prosperity and peace. Over the past twenty years it has extended those benefits to more of the European continent than ever thought possible. Today, in a new context and with new challenges, Europeans once again have the opportunity to harness integration—to use their network capital to position themselves for the new world rising and to generate a better life, not only for themselves but for billions around the world. Whether they will use the coming decade's window to do so is likely to determine the relevance of the European project in an increasingly competitive and connected world.

Notes

Executive Summary

1. For references and further detail on points highlighted in the Executive Summary, please see the relevant chapters.

2. Remarks to the Center for Transatlantic Relations, December 10, 2010.

Introduction

1. See Richard Freeman, "The Great Doubling: The Challenge of the New Global Labor Market," August 2006, available at http://emlab.berkeley.edu/users/webfac/eichengreen/e183_sp07/great_doub.pdf.

2. Throughout this report, the term "EU" refers to all 27 member states of the European Union. The term EU15 refers to the older EU member states, including the United Kingdom, Ireland, Belgium, Luxembourg, the Netherlands, Austria, Spain, Italy, Greece, France, Germany, Portugal, Sweden, Finland, and Denmark. The term EU12 refers to the newer EU member states, including Estonia, Latvia, Lithuania, Poland, the Czech Republic, Slovakia, Hungary, Slovenia, Malta, Cyprus, Romania and Bulgaria.

3. International Monetary Fund, *Regional Outlook: Europe Building Confidence* (Washington, DC: IMF, October 2010); Barry Eichengreen and Kevin H. O'Rourke, "A tale of two depressions," http://www.voxeu.org/index.php?q=node/3421.

4. David Cameron and Fredrik Reinfeldt, "Reining in Europe's deficits is just the first step," *Financial Times*, June 17, 2010.

5. Céline Allard and Luc Everaert, et al., "Lifting Euro Area Growth: Priorities for Structural Reforms and Governance, " IMF Staff Position Note, November 22, 2010 (Washington, DC: International Monetary Fund, 2010).

6. The fall in GDP per capita was particularly sizeable in some of the new member states of the EU, particularly in the Baltic republics, ranging from -13.6% in Estonia to -17.5% in Latvia and Lithuania, but also in Hungary, Romania and Slovenia, at -6% to -9%, thus wiping out part of their previous achievements. Some older member states were also severely hit, such as Ireland and Finland, Greece, Spain and Portugal. European Commission, *European Competitiveness Report 2010* (Brussels: European Commission, 2010) p. 22; IMF, *Regional Economic Outlook: Europe Fostering Sustainability* (Washington, DC: IMF, May 2010), p. 30.

7. See Nouriel Roubini, "Irish woes should speed Europe's default plan," *Financial Times*, November 16, 2010; "Europe heads back into the storm," *Financial Times*, November 18, 2010; Philippe Legrain, "Don't blame the euro for Ireland's mess," *Financial Times*, November 18, 2010; Bruce Stokes, "What you need to know about Ireland, and what to do about it," Transatlantic Take, German Marshall Fund of the United States, November 18, 2010.

8. Anthony Faiola, "Humbled Ireland asks for bailout," *The Washington Post*, November 22, 2010.

9. Landon Thomas Jr. and James Kanter, "Europe Fears That Debt Crisis Is Ready to Spread," *The New York Times*, November 16, 2010.

10. Anders Aslund, Peter Boone, and Simon Johnson, "The Debt Problems of the European Periphery," Peterson Institute for International Economics, November 17, 2010; Simon Johnson, "Ireland Crisis Might Give China Break It Seeks," Bloomberg Opinion, November 18, 2010, http://www.bloomberg.com/news/2010-11-19/ireland-crisis-might-give-china-break-it-seeks-simon-johnson.html.

11. In December 2010 EU leaders endorsed plans for a new fund to rescue indebted eurozone countries, and proposed treaty changes to make that possible, but details remain vague. See Aslund, Boone, and Johnson, op. cit.

12. Address by Governor Patrick Honohan to the Chartered Accountants Ireland Financial Services Seminar - 23 November 2010, http://www.financialregulator.ie/press-area/speeches/Pages/AddressbyProfessorPatrickHonohanGovernoroftheCentralBankofIreland,totheCharteredAccountantsofIrelandFinancialServicesSemina.aspx.

13. http://www.bloomberg.com/news/2010-11-29/euro-region-economic-growth-will-weaken-next-year-on-budget-cuts-exports.html

14. WTO; UNCTAD; Gary Hufbauer and Kati Suominen, "Ensuring Globalization after the Great Crisis," www.voxeu.org, October 2010; http://www.bloomberg.com/news/2010-11-29/euro-region-economic-growth-will-weaken-next-year-on-budget-cuts-exports.html

15. "How to grow: A special report on the world economy," *The Economist*, October 9, 2010

16. Carmen M. Reinhart and Kenneth Rogoff, *This Time Is Different: Eight Centuries of Financial Folly* (Princeton: Princeton University Press, 2008).

17. Thomas Friedman, *The Lexus and the Olive Tree* (New York: Anchor Books, 1999).

18. A full list indicating which countries belong to which region is available in the appendix. The Middle East includes Iran and Egypt. Wider Europe includes all non-EU members from Iceland and Turkey to those bordering Russia and the Caspian Sea, including Azerbaijan and Armenia. North America includes Canada, the United States, and Mexico. Latin America includes all of mainland Central and South America. Developing Asia includes all Central, South, and East Asian countries except Japan, China and India.

19. For more on the uneven nature of globalization, see the introductory chapter by Robert O. Keohane and Joseph S. Nye, Jr., in Joseph S. Nye and John D. Donahue, eds., *Governance in a Globalizing World* (Cambridge, MA: Visions of Governance for the 21st Century), p. 11; John Dunning, *Regions, Globalization, and the Knowledge-Based Economy* (Oxford: Oxford University Press, 2002). Peter Dicken, *Global Shift: Transforming the World Economy*, 6th edition (London: Paul Chapman, 2010).

20. Giovanni Grevi, "The interpolar world: a new scenario," Occasional Paper No. 79 (Paris: European Institute for Security Studies, 2009)

21. Daniel Korski, "What kind of interpolar world?" March 30, 2010,
   http://ecfr.eu/content/entry/commentary_what_kind_of_interpolar_world_daniel_korski/

22. For some earlier efforts, see D. Held, A. McGrew, D. Goldblatt and J. Perraton, *Global Transformations: Politics, Economics and Culture* (Cambridge: Polity Press, 1999); P.J. Taylor, *World City Network: A Global Urban Analysis* (London: Routledge, 2004) A. Amin and N. Thrift, *Globalisation, Institutions, and Regional Development in Europe* (Oxford: Oxford University Press, 1993) also http://www.nesta.org.uk/library/documents/Report%2019%20-%20Globalisation%20v7.pdf.

23. Robert Huggins and Hiro Izushi, *Competing for Knowledge: Creating, Connecting, and Growing* (London: Routledge, 2009).

24. Ibid, pp. 6-7, 53-53, 61, 65

25. Dunning, *op. cit.*; NESTA, *UK global innovation – Engaging with new countries, regions and people* (London: NESTA, 2008)

26. Ibid; Huggins and Izushi, op. cit., pp. 24-25.

27. For details and references for the following summary section, please see specific chapters.

28. http://www.ecb.int/press/key/date/2008/html/sp080430_1.en.html

29. *European Competitiveness Report 2010*, op. cit., p. 17.

30. Paul Krugman, "Competitiveness: A Dangerous Obsession," *Foreign Affairs*, March/April 1994.

31. http://www.eurointelligence.com/article.581+M5c099bd850a.0.html; *European Competitiveness Report 2010*, p. 22.

32. "Expected economic benefits of the European Services Directive," Netherlands Bureau for Economic Policy Analysis (CPB), November 2007; Monti, op. cit.

Chapter 1: Goods

1. See OECD, *Economic Globalisation Indicators 2010*, pp.24-28; "Defying gravity and history," *The Economist*, August 7, 2010, p. 71; Richard Gnodde, "New actors play a vital role in the global economy," *Financial Times*, November 12, 2007, p. 11; International Monetary Fund, *World Economic Outlook*, various editions.

2. *European Competitiveness Report 2010*, op. cit., p. 73.

3. The *European Competitiveness Report 2010* demonstrates how Europe captures 55% of a Nokia phone's total value added, even though the phone was assembled both in Europe and China. When it was assembled and sold in Europe, the European share accounted for 68%. But even when it was assembled in China and sold on the U.S. market, Europe still captured as much as 51% of the value. This shows that final assembly, though

important, represents only a fraction of the overall value added of a high-tech product like a mobile phone. The value is largely detached from the physical flows of goods within the supply chain. The major parts of the value are attributed to design, R&D, brand, marketing and distribution, and management of these activities. European Commission, *European Competitiveness Report 2010*, op. cit., pp. 8; 80-82. See also OECD, op. cit.; Daniel S. Hamilton and Joseph P. Quinlan, *Globalization and Europe: Prospering in the New Whirled Order* (Washington, DC: Center for Transatlantic Relations, 2008); Martin Wolf, *Why Globalization Works* (New Haven: Yale University Press, 2004), pp. 111-112; Dicken, op. cit., p. 7; Peter Mandelson, "Europe's openness and the politics of globalisation," February 8, 2008, http://trade.ec.europa.eu/doclib/docs/2008/february/tradoc_137739.pdf. For a case study of the iPod, see G. Linden, K. Kraemer and J. Dedrick, "Who captures value in a global innovation system? The case of Apple's iPod," unpublished manuscript, Personal Computing Industry Center, UC Irvine.

4. *European Competitiveness Report 2010*, op. cit., p. 67.

5. OECD, op. cit., pp. 214-215, 226-227.

6. *European Competitiveness Report 2010*, op. cit., p. 8.

7. Filippo di Mauro, Katrin Forster, and Ana Lima, "The Global Downturn and Its Impact on Euro Area Exports and Competitiveness," Occasional Paper Series No. 119, October 2010 (Frankfurt am Main: European Central Bank, 2010).

8. http://www.wto.org/english/news_e/pres10_e/pr616_e.htm

9. "Defying gravity and history," *The Economist*, August 7, 2010, p. 71

10. OECD, op. cit., pp. 80-81; Hamilton and Quinlan, *Globalization and Europe*, op. cit.; Dicken, op. cit., p. 48.

11. At the beginning of the decade that figure was 68%. For the impact of the Irish crisis on the UK economy, see Chris Gilles and George Parker, "Dublin's problems spread to neighbor's doorstep," *Financial Times*, November 17, 2010.

12. *European Competitiveness Report 2010*, op. cit., p. 64.

13. Ibid, p. 68.

14. "The value of China's emerging middle class," *McKinsey Quarterly*, 2006 Special Edition, p. 62; Deloitte Research, "China's Consumer Market: Opportunities and Risks," 2005.

15. European Commission, Directorate General for Trade; WTO ITS 2009, http://www.wto.org/english/res_e/statis_e/its2010_e/section1_e/i09.xls and http://trade.ec.europa.eu/doclib/html/122532.htm].

16. *European Competitiveness Report 2010*, op. cit., p. 63.

17. There is considerable differentiation among individual EU member states. Ibid., p. 67.

18. Hamilton and Quinlan, *Globalization and Europe*, op. cit.

19. Eurostat.

20. *European Competitiveness Report 2009*.

21. Ibid.

22. Ibid.

23. Eurostat; Angela Cheptea, Lionel Fontagné, Soledad Zignago, "European Export Performance," Document de Travail, No. 2010 – 12, Centre d'Etudes Prospectives et d' Informations Internationales (CEPII).

24. Hamilton and Quinlan, *Globalization and Europe*, op. cit.

25. OECD.

26. OECD.

27. This percentage share is different than Eurostat figures and is based on Angela Cheptea, Lionel Fontagné, Soledad Zignago, op. cit. The authors drew on Eurostat figures but also included additional database inputs that offer greater clarity about the numbers.

28. Ibid.

29. OECD.

30. Cheptea, Fontagné and Zignago, op. cit; http://ec.europa.eu/trade/creating-opportunities/trade-topics/european-competitiveness/global-europe/.

31. Jayati Ghosh, Peter Havlik, Marcos P. Ribeiro, Waltraut Urban, "Models of BRICs' Economic Development and Challenges for EU Competitiveness," wiiw Research Report No. 359, December 2009 (Vienna: wiiw, 2009).

32. OECD, op. cit., p. 42.

33. Ghosh et. al, op. cit; Steven Schott and Jochen Möbert, "A long-term assessment of world trade," DB Research, June 30, 2010; di Mauro, Forster, op. cit.

34. OECD, op. cit., p. 150.

35. *European Competitiveness Report 2009*, p. 46; Imre Fertõ and Károly Attila Soós, "Trade Specialization in the European Union and in Postcommunist European Countries," *Eastern European Economics* May-June 2008, pp. 5-28; Dani Rodrik, "What's So Special About China's Exports?" CEPR Discussion Papers 5484, 2006.

36. "Train Makers Rail Against China's High-Speed Designs, *The Wall Street Journal*, September 28, 2010.

37. Ghosh, et. al, op. cit.; Gary P. Pisano and Willy C. Shih, "Restoring American Competitiveness," *Harvard Business Review*, July-August 2009.

38. Luc Soete, "The costs of a non-innovative Europe: the challenges ahead," September 21, 2010, available at http://ec.europa.eu/research/social-sciences/pdf/demeter-costs-non-innovative-europe_en.pdf;

39. Deloitte Touche Tohmatsu and U.S. Council on Competitiveness, *2010 Global Manufacturing Competitiveness Index*, June 2010; Daniel S. Hamilton and Joseph P. Quinlan, *Germany and Globalization* (Washington, DC: Center for Transatlantic Relations, 2009); Ross DeVol and Perry Wong, "Jobs for America: Investments and Policies for Economic Growth and Competitiveness," Milken Institute, January 26, 2010, p. 12.

40. *2010 Global Manufacturing Competitiveness Index*, op. cit.

41. Jane Corwin and Rebecca Puckett, "Japan's Manufacturing Competitiveness Strategy: Challenges for Japan, Opportunities for the United States," U.S. Department of Commerce, International Trade Administration, 2009.

42. Cheptea, Fontagné and Zignago, op. cit.; See also L. Fontagné, G. Gaulier, and S. Zignago, "Specialization across varieties and North-South competition," *Economic Policy*, 23(53), (2008), pp. 51–91.

43. Hamilton and Quinlan, op. cit.

44. Cheptea, Fontagné, Zignago, op. cit.

45. http://ec.europa.eu/trade/creating-opportunities/trade-topics/european-competitiveness/global-europe/.

46. di Mauro, Forster, Lima, op. cit.

47. OECD, op. cit., pp. 64-65.

48. *European Competitiveness Report 2009*.

Chapter 2: Services

1. In 1913 about two-thirds of the GDP in developed countries, in current prices, consisted of the production of goods; today, two-thirds of GDP in developed countries is comprised of services. See WTO; OECD, *Economic Globalisation Indicators 2010*, pp. 44-45; Wolf, op. cit.

2. Wolf, op. cit.

3. Bradford Jensen and Lori Kletzer, *Tradable Services: Understanding the Scope and Impact of Services Outsourcing* (Washington, DC: Institute for International Economics, 2005).

4. *Assessing the costs and benefits of a closer EU-Canada economic partnership: A Joint Study by the European Commission and the Government of Canada*, 2008, available at http://www.international.gc.ca/trade-agreements-accords-commerciaux/assets/pdfs/EU-CanadaJointStudy-en.pdf.

5. WTO.

6. World Trade Organization, ITS 2009, Table i.11.

7. For a closer examination of the transatlantic services economy, see Daniel S. Hamilton and Joseph P. Quinlan, eds., *Sleeping Giant: Awakening the Transatlantic Services Economy* (Washington, DC: Center for Transatlantic Relations, 2007).

8. Bureau of Economic Analysis, U.S. International Services, Cross-Border Services Exports and Imports by Type and Country, 2009.

9. B. Derudder, P.J. Taylor, P. Ni, A. De Vos, M. Hoyler, H. Hanssens, D. Bassens, J. Huang, F. Witlox and X. Yang, "Pathways of growth and decline: connectivity changes in the world city network, 2000-2008," http://www.lboro.ac.uk/gawc/rb/rb310.html.

10. *European Competitiveness Report 2009*, op. cit.

11. WTO; OECD, op. cit., pp. 44-45.

12. World Trade Organization, ITS 2009, Tables III.4, III.7, and III.10; http://trade.ec.europa.eu/doclib/docs/2008/october/tradoc_141196.pdf

13. WTO, *International Trade Statistics 2010*, Table III.2.

14. Ibid., Table III.4.

15. Ibid., Tables III.6 and III.7.

16. Ibid., Tables III.9 and III.10.

17. Ibid., Tables III.12 and III.13.

18. Ibid., Tables III.14 and III.15.

19. Ibid., Tables III.16 and III.17.

20. Ibid., Tables III.19 and III.20.

21. Ibid., Table III.23.

22. Ibid., Table III.26.

23. Ibid., Table III.31.

24. This category includes merchanting and other trade related services, operational leasing services, R & D, legal, management and public relations services; architectural, engineering and other types of services.

25. The EU is also a leader in personal, cultural and recreational services, and in audiovisual services. http://www.wto.org/english/res_e/statis_e/its2009_e/its09_trade_category_e.pdf

26. *European Competitiveness Report 2009*; *European Competitiveness Report 2010*, op. cit.

27. Charles Roxburgh, et al., *Beyond Austerity: A Path to Economic Growth and Renewal in Europe* (London: McKinsey Global Institute, 2010), p. 3.

28. Ibid, pp. 4-5; 87. "The quest for growth," *The Economist*, October 9, 2010, p. 19. Former Competition Commissioner Mario Monti has outlined initiatives in the services sectors that could strengthen the Single Market, such as improving the EU-level framework for services standardization. See Chapter 19.

Chapter 3: Money

1. Susan Lund and Charles Roxburgh, *Global capital markets: Entering a new era* (McKinsey & Company, 2009).

2. http://trade.ec.europa.eu/doclib/docs/2010/june/tradoc_146270.pdf

3. Gnodde, op. cit.

4. http://trade.ec.europa.eu/doclib/docs/2010/june/tradoc_146270.pdf.

5. OECD, *Economic Globalisation Indicators 2010*, p. 48.

6. Hamilton and Quinlan, *Globalization and Europe*, op. cit.; Hamilton and Quinlan, *The Transatlantic Economy 2010*, op. cit.

7. Based on data from Eurostat, the U.S. was the top recipient of extra-EU FDI outflows in 2008. Outflows to the U.S. totaled €121 billion, 34.8% of the extra-EU total, followed by Switzerland (9.8%), Russia (7.4%) and Singapore (4.4%). See also Daniel S. Hamilton and Joseph P. Quinlan, *The Transatlantic Economy 2011* (Washington, DC: Center for Transatlantic Relations, 2011).

8. This figure includes bank and non-bank affiliates.

9. Bureau of Economic Analysis. See also Hamilton and Quinlan, *The Transatlantic Economy 2011*, op. cit.

10. Kathryn Hauser, "Enhancing the U.S.-EU Trade Relationship: Regulatory Cooperation and Standards," Written Statement before the Subcommittee on Trade, Committee on Ways and Means, U.S. Congress, July 27, 2010.

11. Gabor Hunya and Roman Stöllinger, "Foreign Direct Investment Flows between the EU and the BRICs," The Vienna Institute for International Economic Studies, Research Report No. 358, December 2009; Eurostat.

12. *European Competitiveness Report 2009*, op. cit.

13. *European Competitiveness Report 2009*, op. cit.

14. *European Competitiveness Report 2009*, op. cit.

15. Hunya and Stöllinger, op. cit.

16. M. Frenkel, K. Funke and G. Stadtmann A Panel Analysis of Bilateral FDI Flows to Emerging Economies, *Economic Systems*, Vol. 28, (2004), pp. 281-300; Gábor Hunya, "Austrian FDI by Main Countries

and Industries," *FIW Study* No. 015 (2008); Hunya and Stöllinger, op. cit.; D. Bartlett, "Economic Trends in the BRIC Countries," April 7, 2008, http://www.thefinancedirector.com/features/feature1710/.

17. *European Competitiveness Report 2009*, op. cit.

18. Ibid.; Copenhagen Economics, "Impacts of Outward EU FDI," op. cit.

19. UNCTAD.

20. Lund and Roxburgh, op. cit.; OECD, *Economic Globalization Indicators 2010*, op. cit., p. 28.

21. http://trade.ec.europa.eu/doclib/docs/2008/october/tradoc_141196.pdf

22. OECD, *Economic Globalisation Indicators 2010*, p. 32.

23. Ibid, p. 88.

24. http://trade.ec.europa.eu/doclib/docs/2010/june/tradoc_146273.pdf; Geishecker and Görg find that outsourcing reduced the real wage for unskilled workers by up to 1.8% while it increased the real wages for skilled workers by up to 3.3%. See I. Geishecker and H. Görg, "Winners and Losers: A Micro-Level Analysis of International Outsourcing and Wages,: CEPR Discussion Paper 6484, 2007.

25. G. B. Navaretti and D. Castellani, "Investments Abroad and Performance at Home: Evidence from Italian Multinationals," CEPR Discussion Paper 4284., 2004; D. Castellani, A. Disdier and G.B. Navaretti, "How Does Investing in Cheap Labour Countries Affect Performance at Home? France and Italy, CEPR Discussion Paper 5765, 2008; C. Criscuolo and M. Leaver, "Offshore Outsourcing and Productivity," OECD and ONS, 2006; Copenhagen Economics, op. cit.

26. http://trade.ec.europa.eu/doclib/docs/2010/june/tradoc_146273.pdf

27. Ghosh et al., op. cit.

28. *European Competitiveness Report 2009*, op. cit.

29. The U.S. faces similar challenges. See Jonathan Cummings, et.al, "Growth and Competitiveness in the United States: The role of its multinational corporations" (McKinsey Global Institute, 2010)

30. OECD.

31. WTO; Hamilton and Quinlan, *Globalization and Europe*, op. cit., p. 75; http://trade.ec.europa.eu/doclib/docs/2010/june/tradoc_146270.pdf

32. Portfolio investment includes equity securities such as shares, stocks, and mutual funds; and debt securities such as bonds, Treasury bills and commercial and finance paper.

33. For an overview of capital flows then and now, see Lund and Roxburgh, op. cit.; Michael Bordo, "Globalization in Historical Perspective," *Business Economics*, January 2002; Kevin H. O'Rourke and Jeffrey G. Williamson, *Globalization and History: The Evolution of a Nineteenth-Century Atlantic Economy* (Cambridge, MA: MIT Press, 1999); Michael D. Bordo, Barry Eichengreen and Douglas A. Irwin, "Is Globalization Today Really Different from Globalization a Hundred Years Ago?" in Susan M. Collins and Robert Z. Lawrence, *Brookings Trade Forum 1999* (Washington, DC: Brookings Institution Press, 1999)

34. Much of this section is drawn from Lund and Roxburgh, op.cit.

35. Lund and Roxburgh, op. cit.

36. By 2007, the total value of global financial assets reached a peak of $194 trillion, equal to 343% of GDP. See Hamilton and Quinlan, *The Transatlantic Economy 2010*, op. cit.

37. This includes foreign direct investment (FDI), purchases and sales of foreign equities and debt securities, and cross-border lending and deposits.

38. Lund and Roxburgh, op. cit.

39. Ibid.

40. Ibid.

41. 3.5% for Japan and for Caribbean; 3.1% for Wider Europe; 2% for Rising Asia; 1% for Oceania; and less than 1% each for Latin America, Middle East, Russia, China, India and Africa.

42. Treasury International Capital (TIC) Data, U.S. Department of the Treasury. Chinese purchases are mostly foreign official accounts, whereas UK purchases are mostly private investors (retail and institutional) with accounts in London. Japan has a mix of both. Note that someone with an account in London is not necessarily British, he/she could be a French national residing in New York transacting through a London-based account. This is an unfortunate hazard of measuring cross-border flows, but does demonstrate the significance of London as a financial center.

43. and 8% in the U.S.; see Transatlantic Business Dialogue, "EU-U.S. financial markets—need for cooperation in difficult times," Transatlantic Business Dialogue (TABD), Brussels and Washington, February 2010.

44. Nicolas Veron, "Financial Newcomers Will Have Global Impact," September 2010, available at www.bruegel.org.

45. Steffen Kern, "Global financial centres after the crisis," DB Research, August 2, 2010, http://www.dbresearch.com/PROD/DBR_INTERNET_EN-PROD/PROD0000000000260736.pdf ; "International Financial Markets in the UK," International Financial Services London, May 2010, p. 5.

46. *The Global Financial Centres Index 8*, September 2010, Z/Yen Group Limited, available at http://www.zyen.com/GFCI/GFCI%208.pdf; Richard Florida, "New Global Financial Order," *Atlantic*, October 13, 2010.

47. International Financial Services (2010), op. cit., p. 5; TABD; Kern (2010), op. cit.

48. Kern, op. cit.; International Monetary Fund, "World Economic Outlook" (Washington, DC: April 2010), p. 179; City of London, "Global Financial Centres," 7, London, March 2010.

49. Patti Waldmeir, "Shanghai has some way to go to realise ambitions," *Financial Times*, October 27, 2010.

50. Kern (2010), op. cit.; Transatlantic Business Dialogue (2010), p. 9.

51. Bank for International Settlements and DB Research calculations.

52. Kern (2010), op. cit.; Transatlantic Business Dialogue (2010), p. 9.

53. Kern, op. cit.; World Federation of Exchanges and DB Research calculations; Transatlantic Business Dialogue (2010), p. 9.

54. Figure includes Hong Kong SAR. See Steffen Kern, "China's financial markets – a future global force?" Deutsche Bank Research, Frankfurt am Main, 2009, p. 22; International Financial Services (2010), p. 8; World Federation of Exchanges. For a detailed analysis of the role of U.S. and EU financial markets in the world economy, see Steffen Kern, "EU-U.S. financial market integration – work in progress," Deutsche Bank Research, Frankfurt, 2008; also TABD (2010).

55. Kern, (2010), op. cit.; Grevi, op. cit.; City of London, "Global Financial Centres," 7, London, March 2010; D. S. L. Jarvis, "Race for the money: International Financial Centres in Asia," Research Paper Series, Lee Kuan Yew School of Public Policy, June 2009; C. Leung and O. Unteroberdoerster, "Hong Kong SAR as a Financial Center for Asia: Trends and Implications," IMF Working Paper WP/08/57, International Monetary Fund, Washington, March 2008.

56. Martin Wolf, "The eurozone needs more than discipline froom Germany," *Financial Times*, December 22, 2010.

57. Patti Waldmeir, "Shanghai has some way to go to realise ambitions," *Financial Times*, October 27, 2010; Geoff Dyer, "Scramble to adjust to a new reality," *Financial Times*, October 27, 2010.

58. IMF; See also Robert Cookson and Geoff Dyer, "Yuan direction," *Financial Times*, December 14, 2010.

59. Hamilton and Quinlan, *Globalization and Europe*, op. cit; OECD, *Economic Globalisation Indicators 2010*, pp. 106-107, 111.

60. "Setting priorities for the eurozone," *Financial Times*, October 28, 2010.

Chapter 4: Energy

1. *Assessing the costs and benefits of a closer EU-Canada economic partnership: A Joint Study by the European Commission and the Government of Canada*, 2008, available at http://www.international.gc.ca/trade-agreements-accords-commerciaux/assets/pdfs/EU-CanadaJointStudy-en.pdf

2. "Towards a European strategy for the security of energy supply," Green Paper adopted by the European Commission on November 29, 2000, available at http://ec.europa.eu/energy/ green-paper-energy-supply/doc/green_paper_energy_supply_en.pdf

3. http://www.energy.eu/publications/KOAC07001ENC_002.pdf, 12, 13; International Energy Agency (IEA), *World Energy Outlook 2010*, p. 85.

4. For an overview, see World Resources Institute, *State of the World 2006* (Washington, DC: WRI, 2006).

5. IEA, *World Energy Outlook 2010*, op. cit.; Also Spencer Swartz and Shai Oster, "China Tops U.S. in Energy Use," *The Wall Street Journal*, July 18, 2010.

6. "Still Roaring," *The Economist*, January 27, 2007.

7. IEA, *World Energy Outlook 2010*, op. cit., p. 96.

8. Hamilton and Quinlan, *Globalization and Europe*, op. cit., p. 49.

9. Grevi, op. cit., p. 18; Vladimir Milov, "Russia and the West: the energy factor," Institut francais des relations internationales, Center for Strategic and International Studies, July 2008, p. 1; *Survey Energy Resources 2007*, World Energy Council, London, 2007.

10. *European Competitiveness Report 2009*, op. cit., pp. 4-6.

11. McKinsey Global Institute, *Beyond austerity*, op. cit., using 2007 data.

12. IEA, *World Energy Outlook 2009*, op. cit.; *European Competitiveness Report 2009*, op. cit.

13. China accounted for 8% of the world's oil consumption in 2007, up from 4.7% in 2000. China's growing demand accounted for 30% of global incremental demand for oil between 2000 and 2006. Ibid; IEA, *World Energy Outlook 2010*, op. cit., p. 105.

14. "Energy: Let Us Overcome Our Dependence," European Commission Green Paper, 2002. Luxembourg: Office for Official Publications of the European Communities, 2002, available at http://iter.rma.ac.be/Stufftodownload/Texts/EnergyDependenceEC.pdf

15. China, for example, exported more than twice as much oil to the EU in 2009 than the year before: 195,120 tons vs. 87,000.

16. Throughout this volume metric tons are used (1 ton = 1,000 kg).

17. Figures taken from HS Code 2707: Oils And Other Products Of The Distillation Of High Temperature Coal Tar; HS Code 2709: Petroleum Oils And Obtained From Bituminous Minerals, Crude; HS Code 2710: Petroleum Oils And Oils Obtained From Bituminous Minerals, Other Than Crude; HS Code 2712: Petroleum Jelly; Paraffin Wax, Microcrystalline Petroleum Wax, Slack Wax, Ozokerite, Lignite Wax; HS Code 2713: Petroleum Coke, Petroleum Bitumen And Other Residues Of Petroleum Oils Or Of Oils Obtained From Bitumen; HS Code 2714: Bitumen And Asphalt, Natural; Bituminous Or Oil Shale And Tar Sands; Asphaltites And Asphaltic Rocks and HS Code 2715: Bituminous Mixtures Based On Natural Asphalt, On Natural Bitumen, On Petroleum Bitum, On Mineral Tar.

18. IEA, *World Energy Outlook 2010*, op. cit., pp. 217-222.

19. Figures taken from HS Code 2701: Coal, Briquettes, Ovoids And Similar Solid Fuels Manufactured From Coal; HS Code 2702: Lignite, Whether Or Not Agglomerated, Excluding Jet, HS Code 2703; Peat (Including Peat Litter), Whether Or Not Agglomerated; HS Code 2704: Coke And Semi-Coke Of Coal, Of Lignite Or Of Peat, Whether Or Not Agglomerated; Retort Carbon; HS Code 2706: Tar Distilled From Coal, From Lignite Or From Peat, And Other Mineral Tars, Whether Or Not Dehydrate, and HS Code 2708: Pitch And Pitch Coke, Obtained From Coal Tar Or From Other Mineral Tars.

20. IEA, *Oil and Gas Medium-Term Outlook 2010*; IEA, *World Energy Outlook 2010*, op. cit., p. 183.

21. Fredrik Erixon, "Europe's energy dependency and Russia's commercial assertiveness," ECIPE Policy Brief No. 7, 2008, citing European Commission figures.

22. Figures taken from HS codes: HS 2705- coal gas, water gas, producer gas etc, ex pet gas & other gas, and HS 2711- petroleum gases & other gaseous hydrocarbons.

23. IEA, *World Energy Outlook 2010*, op, cit., p. 180.

24. Ibid., p. 180.

25. Roderick Kefferpütz, "Shale Fever: Replicating the US gas revolution in the EU?" CEPS, 2010, http://www.ceps.eu/book/shale-fever-replicating-us-gas-revolution-eu; *Fueling North America's Energy Future*, IHS CERA Special Report, IHS Cambridge Energy Research Associates, Cambridge, MA, 2010.

26. Ibid.

27. IEA, *World Energy Outlook 2009*, op cit.; IEA, *Oil and Gas Medium Term Outlook 2010*, op. cit.

28. Kefferpütz, op.cit.

29. IEA, *Oil and Gas Medium Term Outlook 2010*, op. cit., p.18; "Europe, the new frontier in shale gas rush", *Financial Times*, March 7, 2010; Andreas Korn, "Prospects for unconventional gas in Europe," Power Point Presentation, *E.On*, February 5, 2010.

30. IEA, *World Energy Outlook 2009*, op. cit.; *European Competitiveness Report 2009*, op. cit. Globally, the share of unconventional gas is projected to rise from 12% in 2007 to 15% in 2030. This projection is subject to considerable uncertainty, especially after 2020; there is potential for output to increase much more.

31. Erixon, op. cit.

32. Keith Smith, "Managing the Challenge of Russian Energy Policies: Recommendations for U.S. and EU Leadership" (Washington, DC: CSIS, November 2010); Keith Smith, "Lack of Transparency in Russian

Energy Trade: The Risks to Europe," July 2010, CSIS, http://csis.org/files/publication/100702_Smith_Lack-OfTransparency_Web.pdf; Erixon, op. cit.

33. IAEA; World Nuclear Association; Mycle Schneider, "Status and Trends of the World Nuclear Industry in 2009: Renaissance or Decline?" IICPH, Toronto, Canada, September 26, 2009; Mycle Schneider, "2008 world nuclear industry status report: Western Europe," *Bulletin of the Atomic Scientists*, September 19, 2008.

34. François Roussely, "Report Summary: Future of the French Civilian Nuclear Industry," June 16, 2010; IAEA; Schneider, "Status..." op. cit.; Schneider, "2008 ..." op. cit.

35. Geraldine Amiel, "French Nuclear Industry Faces Meltdown," *The Wall Street Journal*, May 11, 2010.

36. IEA, *World Energy Outlook 2010*, op. cit.

37. Peggy Hollinger, "Cooling ambitions," *Financial Times*, October 20, 2010.

38. Ibid; IEA, *World Energy Outlook 2010*, op. cit., p. 87.

39. IEA, *World Energy Outlook 2010*, op. cit.; *Beyond austerity*, op. cit., pp. 79-80; Michael Levi, Elizabeth C. Economy, Shannon O'Neil, and Adam Segal, "Globalizing the Energy Revolution: How to Really Win the Clean-Energy Race," *Foreign Affairs*, November/December 2010.

40. World Economic Forum, "Green Investing: Toward a Clean Energy Infrastructure" (Geneva, Switzerland: WEF, January 2009), http://www.weforum.org/pdf/climate/Green.pdf. For example, a recent opportunity estimate for China alone predicted a maximum market opportunity of $500 billion to $1 trillion by 2013. China Green Tech Initiative, "The China Greentech Report 2009" (September 10, 2009), http://www.china-greentech.com/report.

41. "Europe's energy position: markets and supply," *Market Observatory for Energy Report 2009* (Brussels: European Commission, 2009). For an overview of the competitiveness of the renewable energy sector/industry in the EU, see the recent study on the competitiveness of the EU eco-industry, prepared for the European Commission, available at http://ec.europa.eu/enterprise/newsroom/cf/itemlongdetail.cfm?item_id= 3769& tpa_id=203&lang=en. Also "Employ-RES – The impact of renewable energy policy on economic growth and employment in the European Union," available at http://ec.europa.eu/energy/renewables/studies/renew-ables_en.htm

42. "Europe's energy position,..." op. cit.

43. OECD, "Interim Report of the Green Growth Strategy: Implementing our commitment for a sustainable future Meeting of the OECD Council at Ministerial Level, 27-28 May 2010," http://www.oecd.org/dataoecd/42/46/45312720.pdf; Nesta, "UK Innovation: Engaging with new countries, regions and peoples" (London: Nesta, October 2008), available at http://www.nesta.org.uk/library/documents/Report%2019%20-%20Globalisation%20v7.pdf

44. OECD, *OECD Science, Technology and Industry Scoreboard* (Paris: Organization for Economic Cooperation and Development, 2009); OECD, *Indicators of Innovation and Transfer in Environmentally Sound Technologies: Methodological Issues* (Paris: Organization for Economic Cooperation and Development, 2009). *European Competitiveness Report 2010*, op. cit., pp. 113-115.

45. *Beyond Austerity*, op. cit., pp. 79-80; Levi, et. al, op cit.

46. Rob Atkinson, Michael Shellenberger, Ted Nordhaus, Devon Swezey, Teryn Norris, Jesse Jenkins, Leigh Ewbank, Johanna Peace and Yael Borofsky, *Rising Tigers, Sleeping Giant* (Washington, DC: Breakthrough Institute and Information Technology and Innovation Foundation, 2009)

47. "Europe's energy position,..." op. cit.

48. Stephen J. Ezell and Robert D. Atkinson, *The Good, The Bad, and The Ugly (and The Self- Destructive) of Innovation Policy: A Policymaker's Guide to Crafting Effective Innovation Policy* (Washington, DC: The Information Technology and Innovation Foundation, 2010), http://www.itif.org/files/2010-good-bad-ugly.pdf; McKinsey Global Institute, "How to compete and grow," op. cit., p. 29; Atkinson, et al., op.cit.

49. "We Can't Get There From Here," *Newsweek*, March 13, 2009, http://www.newsweek.com/2009/03/13/we-can-t-get-there-from-here.html; Atkinson, et. al; Matt Hourihan, "UN Climate Negotiations and the Race to the Top (of the Clean Energy Heap)," http://www.innovationpolicy.org/33932291

50. Deutsche Bank Climate Change Advisors, "Global Climate Change Policy Tracker: An Investor's Assessment," (New York, October 2009), http://www.dbcca.com/dbcca/EN/_media/Global_Climate_Change_Policy_Tracker_Exec_Summary.pdf; Atkinson, et al., op.cit.

51. IEA, *World Energy Outlook 2009*, op. cit.; European Commission; "Europe's energy position, ..." op. cit.

52. Ibid.; Atkinson, et al., op.cit.

53. Daniel Schäfer, "Solarthermie, Physik und Technik der Solarthermie in Afrika," *Spiegel der Forschung*, 2, December 2008, pp. 11-15, available at http://geb.uni-giessen.de/geb/volltexte/2009/6731/pdf/SdF_2008-02-11-15.pdf; See also Isabelle Werenfels and Kirsten Westphal, "Solarstrom aus Nordafrika: Rahmenbedingungen und Perspektiven," SWP-Studie, February 2010 (Berlin: Stiftung Wissenschaft und Politik, 2010).

54. "Europe's energy position,..." op. cit.

55. Keith Bradsher, "Pentagon Must 'Buy American,' Barring Chinese Solar Panels," *New York Times*, January 9, 2010.

56. Atkinson, et al., op.cit.

57. Figures taken from HS 854140: Photosensitive Semiconductor Devices, Incl. Photovoltaic Cells Whether Or Not Assembled In Modules Or Made Up Into Panels; Light Emitting Diodes (Excl. Photovoltaic Generators).

58. "Europe's energy position, ..." op. cit.

59. Ibid.

60. Atkinson, et al., op.cit.

61. Figures taken from: HS 8502.31 Wind-powered electrical generating sets.

62. Renewable Fuel Association, "*2008 World Fuel Ethanol Production*." http://www.ethanolrfa.org/industry/statistics/

63. F.O. Licht, "World Biodiesel Production Estimated 2008—Growth Continues to Slow Down," *World Ethanol & Biofuels Report*, September 23, 2008.

64. Marianne Stigset, " EU Ethanol Use to Exceed That of Biodiesel by 2020, Group Says," Bloomberg, May 23 2007.

65. Miguel Carriquiry, Fengxia Dong, Xiaodong Du, Amani Elobeid, Jacinto F. Fabiosa, Ed Chavez, and Suwen Pan, " World Market Impacts of High Biofuel Use in the European Union," *Working Paper 10-WP 508* (Ames, IA: Center for Agricultural and Rural Development, Iowa State University, July 2010); International Energy Agency (IEA), *World Energy Outlook 2009*; OECD, *Economic Assessment of Biofuel Support Policies*. Directorate for Trade and Agriculture, OECD.

66. Figures taken from HS Code 22072000 Bioethanol denatured, HS Code 22071000 Bioethanol undenatured, and HS Code 38249099 Biodiesel.

67. http://www.epa.gov/oms/renewablefuels/420f10007.htm#1

68. Some least developed countries are exempted. IEA; "Europe's energy position, ..." op. cit.; Mario Parker, "Ethanol Gains With Oil, Corn Amid Optimism on Ireland Bailout," Bloomberg, November 18, 2010.

69. "Impacts of the EU biofuel target on agricultural markets and land use: a comparative modeling assessment," available at http://ec.europa.eu/energy/renewables/consultations/doc/public_consultation_iluc/study_1_jrc_biofuel_target_iluc.pdf

70. http://ec.europa.eu/environment/etap/inaction/pdfs/apr07_algae_biofuels.pdf; http://www.bloomberg.com/news/2010-10-13/eu-may-increase-imports-of-brazilian-ethanol-adviser-forecasts.html

71. OECD.

72. OECD; 2010 EU Industrial R&D Investment Scoreboard.

Chapter 5: People

1. Carnegie Endowment, "Migration and Globalization," http://www.globalization101.org/uploads/File/Migration/migrall.pdf; Joseph Chamie, "Fewer Babies Pose Difficult Challenges for Europe," www.globalenvision.org/learn/8/1776, October 10, 2007.

2. IW Institute.

3. Chamie, op. cit.

4. Carnegie Endowment, op. cit. Chamie, op. cit.

5. Carnegie Endowment, op. cit.; Chamie, op. cit.

6. Rainer Münz, "Demographic Change, Labour Force Development and Migration in Europe—Policy Recommendations," http://www.migration-boell.de/web/migration/46_2447.asp; http://www.jonathanlaurence.net/wp-content/uploads/2009/06/transatlantic-academy-final-report-on-immigration.pdf

7. Hamilton and Quinlan, *Globalization and Europe*, op. cit. *European Competitiveness Report 2009*, op. cit.

8. It is very likely that, sooner or later, this will be the case in other new EU member states and candidate countries as well. See Münz, op. cit.

9. Christina Boswell, "Migration in Europe: A paper prepared for the Policy Analysis and Research Programme of the Global Commission on International Migration," September 2005, available at http://www.gcim.org/attachements/RS4.pdf; Commission Staff Working Document, European Competitiveness Report 2009, December 1, 2009, available at http://www.eurosfaire.prd.fr/7pc/doc/1268660562_european_competitiveness_report_2009_2.pdf

10. *European Competitiveness Report 2009*, op. cit.

11. T. Boeri, G. Hanson, and B. McCormick, *Immigration Policy and the Welfare State* (Oxford: Oxford University Press, 2002) ; P. Stalker, *The No-Nonsense Guide to International Migration* (Oxford: New Internationalist Publications, 2001), pp. 63-99; Nonneman, op. cit., p. 15.

12. Hamilton and Quinlan, *Globalization and Europe*, op. cit.

13. Wimmer AG, 2001, cited in Commission Staff Working Document, European Competitiveness Report 2009, December 1, 2009, available at http://www.eurosfaire.prd.fr/7pc/doc/1268660562_european_competitiveness_report_2009_2.pdf

14. Commission Staff Working Document, European Competitiveness Report 2009, December 1, 2009, available at http://www.eurosfaire.prd.fr/7pc/doc/1268660562_european_competitiveness_report_2009_2.pdf

15. J. Hunt and M. Gauthier-Loiselle, "How Much does Immigration boost Innovation?", NBER Working Paper 14312, (Cambridge, MA: National Bureau of Economic Research, 2008); G. Peri, "International Migrations: Some Comparisons and Lessons for the European Union," Mimeo, University of California, Davis, 2005; S. Anderson and M. Platzer, "American Made: The Impact of Immigrant Entrepreneurs and Professionals on U.S. Competitiveness," National Venture Capital Association, 2006; V. Wadhwa, A. Saxenian, B. Rissing, and G. Gereffi, "America's New Immigrant Entrepreneurs," Duke University and University of California, Berkeley, 2007; all cited in Commission Staff Working Document, European Competitiveness Report 2009, December 1, 2009, available at http://www.eurosfaire.prd.fr/7pc/doc/1268660562_european_competitiveness_report_2009_2.pdf

16. OECD, *International Migration Outlook 2010*, available at http://www.oecd.org/document/41/0,3343,en_2649_33931_45591593_1_1_1_1,00.html. See also http://www.migrationpolicy.org/transatlantic/Talent.pdf

17. "Launch of the OECD International Migration Outlook 2010: Opening remarks by Angel Gurría, OECD Secretary-General," Brussels, July 12, 2010, http://www.oecd.org/document/31/0,3343,en_21571361_44315115_45635487_1_1_1_1,00.html

18. UN. The United States accounts for less than one in 20 of the world's residents (4.5%) but is home to one-fifth (20%) of the world's migrants. See http://www.migrationpolicy.org/transatlantic/Talent.pdf

19. International Organization for Migration, *World Migration Report 2008: Managing Labor Mobility in the Evolving Global Economy*, (Geneva, Switzerland: International Organization for Migration, 2008), available at http://www.iom.int/jahia/webdav/site/myjahiasite/shared/shared/mainsite/published_docs/studies_and_reports/WMR2008/Ch1_WMR08.pdf.

20. For more, see Ibid; International Labor Organization (ILO); http://www.cedefop.europa.eu/EN/articles/15698.aspx; http://www.cedefop.europa.eu/EN/articles/4411.aspx; http://www.cedefop.europa.eu/EN/Files/8016_en.pdf; Migration Policy Institute, http://www.migrationpolicy.org/pubs/MPI-BBCreport-Sept09.pdf, p. 12; UN High Commissioner for Refugees, *2008 Global Trends: Refugees, Asylum-seekers, Returnees, Internally Displaced and Stateless Persons* (Geneva, Switzerland: UN High Commissioner for Refugees, 2009), http://www.unhcr.org/4a375c426.html; United Nations High Commissioner for Refugees, *2009 Global Trends*, http://www.unhcr.org; and Ibrahim Awad, *The Global Economic Crisis and Migrant Workers: Impact and Response* (Geneva, Switzerland: International Labor Organization, 2009), http://www.ilo.org/global/About_the_ILO/Media_and_public_information/Feature_stories/lang—en/WCMS_112537/index.htm.

21. About 11 to 12 million unauthorized migrants were estimated to reside in the United States (2008), about 618,000 in the United Kingdom (2007), and nearly 210,000 in Japan (2007).

22. http://www.nesta.org.uk/library/documents/Report%2019%20-%20Globalisation%20v7.pdf.

23. Eurostat.

24. Gurría, op. cit.

25. Austria and Germany have not yet given citizens of EU countries of 2004 enlargement free access to their labor markets. Transitional restrictions apply until May 2011. For Bulgaria and Romania many restrictions apply in EU countries until 2014.

26. See John Salt, *International Migration and the United Kingdom: Report of the United Kingdom SOPEMI Correspondent to the OECD, 2008* (London: University College London, 2008), http://www.geog.ucl.ac.uk/research/mobility-identity-and-security/migration-research-unit/pdfs/Sop08_fin.pdf; Jen Smith-Bozek, ed., *Labor Mobility in the European Union: New Members, New Challenges* (Washington, D.C.: Center for European Policy Analysis, 2007), http://www.cepa.org / publications / labormobility.pdf; Will Somerville and Madeleine Sumption, *Immigration in the United Kingdom: The Recession and Beyond* (Washington, DC: Migration Policy Institute, 2009); http://www.migrationpolicy.org/transatlantic/Talent.pdf.

27. Awad, op. cit.; Miguel Pajares, *Inmigracion y mercado de trabajo: Informe 2009* (Madrid: Minsterio de Trabajo e Inmigracion, 2009), http://extranjeros.mtas.es/es/ObservatorioPermanenteInmigracion/Publicaciones/contenido_0002.html; OECD *International Migration Outlook, Special Focus: Managing the Labour Migration Beyond the Crisis* (Paris, France: OECD, 2009). The official estimate of the size of the unauthorized migrant population was about 300,000 in early 2008.

28. Münz, op. cit.

29. Frontex. See also Stephen Fidler, "EU reinforces Greek border," *The Wall Street Journal Europe*, October 27, 2010.

30. http://www.iomjapan.org/archives/Presentation_ProfCastles.pdf.

31. The situation in similar in the United States. While immigrants represented one in six workers in the United States, they constituted one in two *new* workers in the United States. See http://www.migration-policy.org/transatlantic/Talent.pdf

32. Awad, op. cit.; IOM, op. cit.; http://www.migrationpolicy.org/transatlantic/Talent.pdf; "The Highly-Skilled as a 'Renewable Resource'," http://www.migration-boell.de/web/migration/46_2456.asp

33. As is the case for most migration data, statistics on trends concerning the mobility of the highly skilled are seriously constrained by problems of availability, access and comparability. There is, unfortunately, no international system that records highly skilled migration. See IOM, http://www.iomjapan.org/archives/Presentation_ProfCastles.pdf

34. IOM, op. cit.

35. Ibid.

36. *European Competitiveness Report 2009*, op. cit.

37. *European Competitiveness Report 2009*, op. cit.; Charles Leadbeater and James Wilsdon, *How Asian innovation can benefit us all* (London: Demos, 2007); http://www.iomjapan.org/archives/Presentation_ProfCastles.pdf; OECD, http:// masetto.sourceoecd.org/vl=4322866/cl=19/nw=1/rpsv/sti2007/b-6.htm; "The Highly-Skilled as a 'Renewable Resource'," http://www.migration-boell.de/web/migration/46_2456.asp.

38. IOM, op. cit.

39. Chamie, op. cit.; World Bank, "Global Economic Prospects. Managing the Next Wave of Globalisation," 2007; "The future of manufacturing in Europe 2015-2020: the challenge for sustainability" Case Sector Report — Basic Industrial Chemicals, Available from: http://ec.europa.eu/research/industrial_technologies / pdf/pro-futman-doc8-casestudy-basicindustrialchemicals.pdf; European Commission, "Attractive Conditions for the Admission and Residence of Highly Qualified Immigrants" (European Commission Memo 423, October 23, 2007); IOM, op.cit; Awad, op. cit; http://www.migrationpolicy.org/transatlantic/scarceskills.pdf; Walter Nonneman, "European Immigration and the Labor Market"(Migration Policy Institute/Bertelsmann Foundation, July 2007), http://www.migrationinformation.org/transatlantic/ImmigrationEULaborMarket_ 72507.pdf.

40. Former European Commission Vice President Franco Frattini, cited in "European Union seeking skilled migrants with 'Blue Card'," http://www.workpermit.com/news/2007-09-27/europe/frattini-blue-card-legislation-moving-forward.htm; Hamilton & Quinlan, *Globalization and Europe*, op. cit.

41. Jesús Alquézar Sabadie, Johanna Avato, Ummuhan Bardak, Francesco Panzica, and Natalia Popova, *Migration and Skills: The Experience of Migrant Workers from Albania, Egypt, Moldova, and Tunisia* (Washington, DC: The World Bank, 2010). See also P. Fargues, *Mediterranean Migration–2005 Report* (Florence: EUI-RSCAS, CARIM Consortium, 2005).

42. *European Competitiveness Report 2009*, op. cit.

43. Eurostat.

44. OECD, "Fostering Innovation to Strengthen Growth and Address Global and Social Challenges: Executive Summary and Key Findings," www.oecd.org/innovation/strategy; Christina Boswell, "Migration in Europe: A paper prepared for the Policy Analysis and Research Programme of the Global Commission on International Migration," September 2005, available at http://www.gcim.org/attachements/RS4.pdf; European Competitiveness Report 2009, op. cit.; European Commission 2005: "Green Paper on EU Approach to Managing Economic Migration," (Brussels: European Commission, 2004).

45. Anna Lee Saxenian, *The New Argonauts. Regional Advantage in a Global Economy* (Cambridge, MA: Harvard University Press, 2007); European Policy Brief, "INGINEUS: Impact of Networks, Globalisation, and their Interaction with EU Strategies, November 2009, available at http://ec.europa.eu/research/social-sciences/pdf/policy-briefs-ingineus_en.pdf

46. IOM, op. cit.; OECD, "Fostering Innovation to Strengthen Growth and Address Global and Social Challenges: Executive Summary and Key Findings," www.oecd.org/innovation/strategy.

47. OECD, *Economic Globalisation Indicators 2010*, p. 9.

48. Ibid., pp. 138-139.

49. Laudeline Auriol, "Careers of Doctorate Holders: Employment and Mobility Patterns," STI Working Paper 2010/4, Statistical Analysis of Science, Technology and Industry, OECD, available at http://www.oecd.org/dataoecd/46/43/44893058.pdf

50. For example Finland and Norway have amended their naturalization laws to take the years of residence as a student into account in assessing eligibility for citizenship, while Canada facilitates permanent residence for international graduates. Other rich countries allow international students to work during their studies or for a period of up to one year after graduation.

51. "The Highly-Skilled as a 'Renewable Resource'," http://www.migration-boell.de/web/migration/46_2456.asp

52. IOM, op. cit; http://www.oecd.org/document/51/0,3343,en_2649_33729_40644339_1_1_1_1,00.html.

53. Central Statistics Office of Ireland; Anthony Faiola, "Young Irish trying their luck overseas," *The Washington Post*, November 23, 2010.

54. Commission Staff Working Document, European Competitiveness Report 2009, December 1, 2009, available at http://www.eurosfaire.prd.fr/7pc/doc/1268660562_european_competitiveness_report_2009_2.pdf

55. *European Competitiveness Report 2009*, op. cit.; http://www.oecd.org/document/41/0,3343,en_2649_33931_45591593_1_1_1_1,00.html.

Chapter 6: Ideas

1. Thomas A. Stewart, *Intellectual Capital* (New York: Doubleday/Currency Publishers, 1997); Hamilton and Quinlan, *Partners in Prosperity* (Washington, DC: Center for Transatlantic Relations, 2005), p. 7; Author's own estimates. "How can Europe create jobs?" European Parliament Directorate-General for Internal Policies, Policy Department A: Economic and Scientific Policy, European Parliament's Special Committee on the Financial, Economic and Social Crisis, April 2010.

2. Joseph E. Stiglitz, "Globalization and growth in emerging markets," *Journal of Policy Modelling* 26(4), 2004, pp. 465-84.

3. OECD, "Fostering Innovation to Strengthen Growth and Address Global and Social Challenges: Executive Summary and Key Findings," www.oecd.org/innovation/strategy, p. 8; McKinsey Global Institute, "Beyond Austerity," op. cit.

4. OECD, "Fostering Innovation,..." op. cit.

5. For more, see Stewart,op. cit.; Hamilton and Quinlan, *Partners*, ... op. cit., p. 7.; Huggins and Izushi, op. cit., p. 1; W. M. Cohen and D. A. Levinthal, "Absorptive Capacity: A New Perspective on Learning and Innovation," *Administrative Science Quarterly* 35(1): 128-152, 1990. Thurow states that "today knowledge and skills stand alone as the source of comparative advantage" and "become the key ingredient in the late 20th century's location of economic activity." Lester C. Thurow, *The Future of Capitalism: How Today's Economic Forces Shape Tomorrow's World* (New York: William Morrow and Company, 1996).

6. Deloitte Touche Tohmatsu and U.S. Council on Competitiveness, *2010 Global Manufacturing Competitiveness Index*, June 2010.

7. OECD, "Fostering Innovation to Strengthen Growth and Address Global and Social Challenges: Executive Summary and Key Findings," www.oecd.org/innovation/strategy, p. 6; Ezell and Atkinson, op. cit.

8. See Soete, op. cit.; Tekes, "Seizing the White Space: Innovative Service Concepts in the United States," *Technology Review*, 205, 2007, pp. 72-74, http://www.tekes.fi/en/document/43000/innovative_service_pdf.

9. OECD, "Fostering Innovation, ..." op. cit.

10. TABD, "Accelerating the Transatlantic Innovation Economy," October 2010; European Policy Brief, "INGINEUS,..." op. cit.; J. Dunning and S.M. Lundan, "The Internationalisation of Corporate R&D: A Review of the Evidence and Some Policy Implications for Home Countries," *Review of Policy Research* 26 (1-2), 2009, pp. 13-33.

11. *European Competitiveness Report 2010*, op. cit., pp. 118-122.

12. TABD, op. cit.

13. OECD, *Science and Technology Indicators 2009*, http://www.oecdilibrary.org/content/book/sti_scoreboard-2009-en

14. Dunning, op. cit.; Suzanne Berger, *How We Compete: What Companies Around the World are Doing to Make it in Today's Global Economy* (Doubleday: New York, NY: 2005).

15. Huggins and Izushi, op. cit., p. 96.

16. See OECD, *Globalisation and Regional Economies: Can OECD Regions Compete in Global Industries?* (Paris: OECD, 2007); TABD, op. cit.

17. *European Innovation Scoreboard 2009*.

18. The Patent Cooperation Treaty (PCT) is an international treaty, administered by the World Intellectual Property Organization (WIPO), among more than 125 countries. The PCT makes it possible to seek patent protection for an invention simultaneously in each of a large number of countries by filing a single "international" patent application instead of filing several separate national or regional patent applications although the granting of patents remains under the control of the national or regional patent offices.

19. H. Hollanders, S. Tarantola and A. Loschky, "Regional Innovation Scoreboard (RIS) 2009" and H. Hollanders, S. Tarantola and A. Loschky, "Regional Innovation Scoreboard - Methodology report". Both reports are available at http://www.proinno-europe.eu/metrics.

20. INSEAD, *Global Innovation Index 2009-2010*.

21. *European Competitiveness Report 2010*, op. cit., p. 27.

22. The complete dataset containing the 2000 companies is available at: http://iri.jrc.ec.europa.eu/. There are 400 companies based in the EU and 1000 companies based elsewhere. The 1400 *Scoreboard* companies invested €402.2bn in R&D in 2009, 1.9% less than the previous year. EU companies reduced their R&D investment by 2.6%. This is roughly half of the reduction of their US counterparts (5.1%), despite showing similar drops in sales (around 10%) and a significantly higher drop in profits (13.0% vs 1.4%). Japanese companies maintained the level of R&D investment of the previous year, despite large drops in sales (around 10%) and a dramatic drop in profits (88.2%). In other areas of the world, companies increased both R&D investment and net sales. In some Asian countries, companies continued the trend of high R&D growth seen in recent years, e.g. China (40.0%), India (27.3%), Hong Kong (14.8%), South Korea (9.1%) and Taiwan (3.1%). Companies based in Switzerland also increased their R&D investment (2.5%).

23. In nanotechnologies research, Europe is also in a good position with 420 patents in 2007, compared with 465 in the United States. McKinsey Global Institute, *Beyond austerity*, op. cit., p. 80.

24. Soete, op. cit.

25. Academic Ranking of World Universities 2010, available at http://www.arwu.org/ARWU2010.jsp; Richard Florida, "Where the World's Brains Are," *Atlantic*, October 18, 2010

26. OECD, *Economic Globalisation Indicators 2010*, op. cit., p. 9. Patent data show a significant degree of internationalization of research activities. On average, over 15% of the patents filed by an OECD country in 2004-06 under the Patent Co-operation Treaty (PCT) concerned inventions made abroad. International co-authorship has also been growing fast. In 2007, 21.9% of scientific articles involved international co-authorship, a figure three times higher than in 1985. OECD, *Science, Technology and Industry Scoreboard 2009* (Paris: OECD, December 2009).

27. European Policy Brief, "INGINEUS,.." op. .cit.

28. Also Canada. In Turkey, Chile, Japan, Korea and Israel, they accounted for less than 1% of the total.

29. Among the 16 countries for which data were available, Greece and Portugal were the only ones reporting over 50% of foreign funding supplied by international organizations (in this case the European Union), a share that has been declining steadily. Spain was the only country reporting almost 10% of finance originating from other governments and foreign higher education institutions. OECD, *Economic Globalisation Indicators 2010*, op. cit., pp. 10, 120-121.

30. Ibid, pp. 118-119; OECD, *Science and Technology Indicators 2009*, op. cit.

31. OECD, *Economic Globalisation Indicators 2010*, op. cit., pp. 190-191.

32. Ibid, pp. 192-193.

33. Information on the number of researchers working for foreign affiliates in the services sector has not been available so far.

34. OECD, *Economic Globalisation Indicators 2010*, op. cit., pp. 194-195.

35. Ibid., pp. 196-197.

36. *European Competitiveness Report 2010*, op. cit., p. 9, op. cit. Foreign R&D activities that are driven primarily by knowledge-oriented reasons appear to be positively correlated with innovation performance, while foreign R&D activities driven by market- or resource-oriented reasons correlate positively with productivity. See Pietro Moncada-Paternò-Castello and Peter Voigt, eds., "D4.1 Proceedings of CONCORD 2010: *2nd European Conference on corporate R&D*. An engine for growth, a challenge for European policy. Academic Forum – Summary Report." JRC/European Commission Directorate-General for Research, 2010, available at http://iri.jrc.ec.europa.eu/concord-2010/Concord_2010_%20Summary_%20Academic_%20Forum.pdf

37. OECD, *Economic Globalisation Indicators 2010*, op. cit., pp. 196-197; OECD *Science and Technology Indicators 2009*, op. cit.

38. OECD, *Economic Globalisation Indicators 2010*, op. cit., p. 122.

39. OECD, *Science and Technology Indicators 2009*,op. cit.

40. OECD.

41. OECD, *Economic Globalisation Indicators 2010*, op. cit., pp. 124-125.

42. Ibid., p. 125.

43. OECD *Science and Technology Indicators 2009*, op. cit.

44. Trade in technology is comprised of transfer of techniques, through patents and licenses; disclosure of know-how; transfer of designs, trademarks and patterns; services with a technical content, including technical and engineering studies, as well as technical assistance; and industrial R&D.

45. OECD, *Economic Globalisation Indicators 2010*, op. cit., p. 9; OECD, *Main Science and Technology Indicators, Volume 2010/1* (Paris: OECD, 2010)

46. OECD, *Economic Globalisation Indicators 2010*, op. cit., pp. 128-129.

47. OECD. For 2004-06, both indicators show a significant degree of internationalization of research activities. On average, over 15% of the patents filed by an OECD country under the Patent Co-operation Treaty (PCT) concerned inventions made abroad. Similarly, the share of inventions owned by another country accounted for just under 15% of all OECD filings.

48. The UK is an exception among large countries, with around 37% of domestic inventions owned by foreign residents, compared to 30% in the mid-1990s. OECD, *Economic Globalisation Indicators 2010*, op. cit., pp. 124-125.

49. *European Competitiveness Report 2010*, op. cit., p. 103-110.

50. See OECD, *Regions at a Glance 2009* (Paris: OECD, 2009), p. 30.

51. *European Competitiveness Report 2010*, op. cit., pp. 118-119.

52. Ibid.

53. OECD.

54. OECD.

55. *European Competitiveness Report 2009*, op. cit. pp. 126-127; OECD, *Science and Technology Indicators 2009*, http://www.oecdilibrary.org/content/book/sti_scoreboard-2009-en.

56. See OECD, *Globalisation and Regional Economies: Can OECD Regions Compete in Global Industries?* (Paris, OECD, 2007), p. 13; *Global Location Trends: Annual Report 2009* (IBM, October 2009); OCO Insight, *A New Investment Paradigm*, 2008/2009, http://www.areadevelopment.com/article_pdf/id18985_NewInvestmentParadigm2009final.pdf; Allen J. Scott, *Regions and the World Economy: The Coming Shape of Global Production, Competition, and Political Order* (Oxford: Oxford University Press, 1998).

57. OECD, Ibid.; E.E. Leamer, "A flat world, a level playing field, a small world after all, or none of the above? A review of Thomas L. Friedman's the world is flat," *Journal of Economic Literature* (2007) XLV:83–126.

58. Leamer, Ibid.; Thomas Friedman, *The World is Flat: A Brief History of the Twenty-First Century* (New York: Farrar, Straus and Giroux, 2005), p. 11; Philip McCann, "Globalization and economic geography: the world is curved, not flat," *Cambridge Journal of Regions, Economy and Society*, 1(3): 357-370 (2008); Christian Ketels, *Clusters, Cluster Policy, and Swedish Competitiveness in the Global Economy*. Report No. 30 to Sweden's Globalisation Council (Stockholm: The Globalisation Council, 2009); Anthony J. Venables, "Shifts in economic geography and their causes," Paper prepared for the 2006 Jackson Hole Symposium, http://www.kansascityfed.org/PUBLICAT/SYMPOS/2006/pdf/venables.paper.0821.pdf; Richard Florida, "The Economic Geography of Talent," *Annals of the Association of American Geographers*, 92(4), pp. 743-755, 2002; R. Florida, K. Stolarick, and C. Mellander, "Inside the black box of regional development—human capital, the creative class and tolerance," *Journal of Economic Geography*, 2008.

59. Ann Markusen, "Sticky places in slippery space: A typology of industrial districts," *Economic Geography*, 72,3 (1996); Alan Rugman and Karl Moore, "The Myths of Globalization," *Ivey Business Journal*, September/October 2001, Vol. 66, No. 1.

60. Michael Porter, "Location, Competition, and Economic Development: Local Clusters in a Global Economy," *Economic Development Quarterly*, 14:15-34 (2000). Cited in *World Knowledge Economy Index 2008*, http://www.cforic.org/downloads.php.

61. European Commission, *Innovation Clusters in Europe: A Statistical Analysis and Overview of Current Policy Support*, PRO INNO Europe Paper No. 5, Brussels: December 2007; Michael E. Porter, "The Economic Performance of Regions," *Regional Studies*, Vol. 37 (2003), No. 6/7. Ketels, op. cit.; Gustavo Bobonis and Howard Shatz, "Agglomeration, Adjustment, and the Role of State Level Policies in the Location of Foreign Direct Investment in the United States," *Review of Economics and Statistics*, Vol. 89 (2007), 30–43; Vigdis Boasson and Alan MacPherson, "The role of geographic location in the financial and innovation performance of publicly traded pharmaceutical companies: empirical evidence from the United States, *Environment and Planning A*, Vol. 33 (2001), 1431–1444; Stuart Rosenthal and William Strange, "Agglomeration and Hours Worked," *Review of Economics and Statistics*, Vol. 90 (2008), 105–188; Luigi Guiso and Fabiano Schivardi, *What determines entrepreneurial clusters?* EUI Working Papers, ECO 2007/48 (Florence: July 2007); Edward Glaeser and Wiliam Kerr, "Local Industrial Conditions and Entrepreneurship: How much of the Spatial Distribution can we explain?" NBER Working Paper 14407 (Cambridge: October 2008); D. Audretsch and D. Dohse, "Location: A Neglected Determinant of Firm Growth, *Review of World Economics*, 143(1), 79–107 (2007); Karl Wennberg and Göran Lindqvist, "The effect of clusters on the survival and performance of new firms," *Small Business Economics*, June 2008.

62. Ernst & Young, *European Investment Report 2009*, http://www.eyeim.com/pdf/EIM%202008%20 Report%20final.pdf.

63. Dunning, op. cit., pp. 21, 29-30.

64. See OECD, op. cit., p. 11-13.

65. See Vincenzo Spiezia, "Measuring Regional Economies," OECD Statistics Brief, October 2003, No. 6; Dunning, *Regions*, op. cit.

66. Leamer, op. cit.; McCann, op. cit; http://www.oecd.org/dataoecd/49/34/40665323.pdf.

67. The Index uses 19 knowledge economy benchmarks, including employment levels in the knowledge economy, patent registrations, R&D investment by the private and public sector, education expenditure, information and communication technology, infrastructure, and access to private equity. The full report is available at http://www.cforic.org/downloads.php.

68. Saskia Sassen, *The Global City* (Princeton, NJ: Princeton University Press, 1991); Manuel Castells, *The Rise of Network Society* (Oxford: Blackwell, 1996); Manuel Castells, *Communication Power* (Oxford: Oxford University Press, 2009); P.J. Taylor, "World City Networks: Measurement, Social Organization, Global Governance, and Structural Change," http://www.lboro.ac.uk/gawc/rb/rb333.html.

69. D. Held, et al., op. cit.; L. Halbert and K. Pain, "PAR-LON - Doing Business in Knowledge-Based Services in Paris and London: A Tale of One City?" http://www.lboro.ac.uk/gawc/rb/rb307.html

70. Dunning, *Regions, Globalization*, op cit., pp. 21, 29-30.

71. Halbert and Pain, Ibid.; Taylor, op. cit.

72. B. Derudder, P.J. Taylor, P. Ni, A. De Vos, M. Hoyler, H. Hanssens, D. Bassens, J. Huang, F. Witlox and X. Yang, "Pathways of growth and decline: connectivity changes in the world city network, 2000-2008," http://www.lboro.ac.uk/gawc/rb/rb310.html. The data collection exercise was carried out in the first half of 2008 and so represents a key benchmark of the state of the world city network just before the crash of the global financial system.

73. OECD.

74. *European Competitiveness Report 2010*, op. cit., pp. 170-186.

75. "How can Europe create jobs?" European Parliament Directorate-General for Internal Policies, Policy Department A: Economic and Scientific Policy, European Parliament's Special Committee on the Financial, Economic and Social Crisis, April 2010.

76. Soete, op. cit.; S. Borrás, and B. Kahin, "Patent Reform in Europe and the US," *Science and Public Policy* 36(8), 2009.

77. See the arguments put forward by the Expert Group for DG Research on "The role of Community research policy in the knowledge based economy," December 2009; Also Soete, op. cit.

78. McKinsey Global Institute, *Beyond austerity*, op. cit., p. 5.

79. Europa press release, "The 'Innovation Union'—turning ideas into jobs, green growth and social progress," Brussels, October 6, 2010, available at http://europa.eu/rapid/pressReleasesAction.do?reference=IP/10/1288&format=HTML&aged=0&language=EN&guiLanguage=en#footnote-1

80. Huggins and Izushi, p. 150.

81. P. Zagamé, (2010) *The cost of a non-innovative Europe*, http://ec.europa.eu/research/social-sciences/policy-briefs-research-achievements_en.html .

82. Soete, op. cit.

Chapter 7: The EU and North America: Deep Integration

1. See Ben S. Bernanke, "Rebalancing the Global Recovery," November 19, 2010, available at http://www.federalreserve.gov/newsevents/speech/bernanke20101119a.htm; Terrence Checki, "Challenges Facing the U.S. Economy and Financial System," November 17, 2010, available at http://www.new-yorkfed.org/newsevents/speeches/2010/che101119.html; Roger C. Altman and Richard N. Haass, "American Profligacy and American Power: The Consequences of Fiscal Irresponsibility," *Foreign Affairs*, November/December 2010.

2. For more detail on notes and sources, see Chapter 1.

3. For more detail on notes and sources, see Chapter 2.

4. For more detail on notes and sources, see Chapter 3.

5. Transatlantic Business Dialogue (TABD), "EU-U.S. financial markets – need for cooperation in difficult times," Brussels and Washington, February 2010.

6. IMF.

7. For more detail on notes and sources, see Chapter 4.

8. International Organization for Migration; OECD. For more detail on notes and sources, see Chapter 5.

9. OECD. For more details on notes and sources, see Chapter 6.

10. International Monetary Fund, *Regional Outlook: Europe Building Confidence* (Washington, DC: IMF, October 2010); McKinsey Global Institute, *Beyond austerity*, op. cit.

11. Ibid.

12. Ibid. The Environmental Performance Index was developed by Columbia and Yale universities together with the European Commission and the World Economic Forum. The index ranks 163 countries on 25 performance indicators covering both environmental, public health and ecosystem vitality.

13. Ibid, based on data and analysis also from the Conference Board, Eurostat, Global Insight, International Monetary Fund.

14. Ibid. In this regard, considerable differences are evident within the EU. Nordic countries have boosted female participation rates so that in many cases they are higher than in the United States, and EU15 reforms have boosted participation rates by 6% over the past two decades. Some northern and continental countries have cut unemployment levels below those in the United States. And a number of countries have raised the

retirement age and introduced new initiatives to boost participation by seniors in the work force. McKinsey notes that EU countries can look to fellow EU member states to find successful initiatives in each of these areas.

15. Ibid.

16. Ibid; *2009 Ageing Report: Economic and Budgetary Projections for the EU27 Member States (2008-2060)*, European Commission, 2009.

17. Austria, Belgium, France, Germany, Luxembourg and the Netherlands.

18. Greece, Italy, Portugal and Spain.

19. Denmark, Finland, Ireland, Sweden and the UK.

20. *Beyond austerity*, op. cit.

21. Ibid; *Beyond austerity*, op. cit.; di Mauro, Forster, op. cit.

22. Ibid.; IMF; "The quest for growth," *The Economist*, October 9, 2010, p. 19.

23. Fredrik Erixon and Matthias Bauer, "A Transatlantic Zero Agreement: Estimating the Gains from Transatlantic Free Trade in Goods," ECIPE Occasional Paper No. 4/2010 (Brussels: ECIPE, 2010)

24. Koen Berden, et. al, *The Impact of Free Trade Agreements in the OECD: The Impact of an EU-US FTA, EU-Japan FTA and EU-Australia/New Zealand FTA* (Rotterdam, Ecorys, 2009).

25. Koen Berden, et. al, *Non-Tariff Measures in EU-US Trade and Investment: An Economic Analysis* (Rotterdam: Ecorys, 2009).

26. European Commission.

27. *Assessing the costs and benefits of a closer EU-Canada economic partnership: A Joint Study by the European Commission and the Government of Canada*, 2008, available at http://www.international.gc.ca/trade-agreements-accords-commerciaux/assets/pdfs/EU-CanadaJointStudy-en.pdf

28. Ibid.; European Commission, "EU launches major new trade relationship with Latin America," May 18, 2010. EU goods exports to Mexico 2009: €15.9 billion. EU goods imports from Mexico 2009: €9.9 billion. EU investment stock in the Mexico 2008: €49.0 billion.

Chapter 8: The EU and Wider Europe: The China Next Door?

1. For details, notes and sources on trade in goods, please see Chapter 1.

2. For details, notes and sources on services, please see Chapter 2.

3. For details, notes and sources on money, please see Chapter 3.

4. For details, notes and sources on energy, please see Chapter 4.

5. For details, notes and sources on movement of people, please see chapter 5.

6. Landon Thomas, "Turning East, Turkey Asserts Economic Power," *New York Times*, July 5, 2010; Council on Foreign Relations, http://www.blogs.cfr.org/geographics.

Chapter 9: The EU and Japan: Fading Ties?

1. Eva R. Sunesen, Joseph F. Francois and Martin H. Thelle, *Assessment of Barriers to Trade and Investment between the EU and Japan: Final Report* (Copenhagen: Copenhagen Economics, November 2009), available at http://trade.ec.europa.eu/doclib/docs/2010/february/tradoc_145772.pdf

2. Ibid.; Exell and Atkinson, op. cit.; William H. Lewis, "The Power of Productivity: Wealth, Poverty, and the Threat to Global Stability," Presentation to the Information Technology and Innovation Foundation, May 6, 2008, http://www.itif.org/files/LewisPresentation.pdf; Kim Jung Woo, "International Comparison of the Korean Service Industries' Productivity," Samsung Economic Research Institute, *Weekly Insight*, April 14, 2008, 10-15.

3. "Strength amid paralysis," *The Economist*, July 15, 2010.

4. Sunesen, Francois and Thelle, op. cit.

5. "Hope and hurdles for EU-Asia trade accords," *Reuters*, October 5, 2010.

6. For details, notes and sources on trade in goods, please see Chapter 1.

7. Sunesen, Francois and Thelle, op. cit.

8. Ibid.

9. Ibid.

10. For details, notes and sources on trade in services, please see Chapter 2.

11. Exell and Atkinson, op. cit.; Lewis, op. cit.; "Strength amid paralysis," op. cit.; Woo, op. cit.

12. For details, notes and sources on FDI and capital flows, please see Chapter 1.

13. Total inward FDI stocks as percentage of GDP, 2008, UNCTAD; Sunesen, Francois and Thelle, op. cit.

14. IMF. See also Chapter 3.

15. For details, notes and sources on innovation and ideas, please see Chapter 6.

16. di Mauro, Forster, op. cit.

17. See Jane Corwin and Rebecca Puckett, "Japan's Manufacturing Competitiveness Strategy: Challenges for Japan, Opportunities for the United States," U.S. Department of Commerce, International Trade Administration, 2009.

Chapter 10: The EU and China: Shaping the Future?

1. Vivek Arora and Athanasios Vamvakidis, "China's Economic Growth: International Spillovers," IMF Working Paper, July 2010, http://www.imf.org/external/pubs/ft/wp/2010/wp10165.pdf

2. Hamilton and Quinlan, *Globalization and Europe*, op. cit.

3. According to the OECD, half of Chinese exports are actually produced by foreign companies. In electrical goods the figure is 60%; in plastic products 60%; and electronics and telecoms more than 80%. In short, given the commanding role of European and other foreign affiliates in driving China's exports, "Made in China" is not what most people think. German Federal Agency for Foreign Commerce (BFAI); Wolf, op. cit.; European Commission; *China and the European Union: business issues and opportunities*, Accenture, 2005.

4. Arora and Vamvakidis, op. cit.; See also B. Eichengreen and H. Tong, "How China is Reorganizing the World Economy," *Asian Economic Policy Review* (2006) 1, pp. 73–97.

5. European Commission, DG Trade, http://trade.ec.europa.eu/doclib/docs/2006/september/tradoc_113366.pdf. For details, notes and sources on goods trade, please see Chapter 1.

6. Michael Pettis, "Chinese consumption and the Japanese 'sorpasso,'" http://www.mpettis.com; Martin Wolf, "How China must change if it is to sustain its ascent," *Financial Times*, September 22, 2010; International Monetary Fund, 2009, "Global Shifts in Demand: Making Up for Weaker Consumption in the United States," *October 2009 Asia and Pacific Regional Economic Outlook*, pp. 36–37; Council on Foreign Relations, "The Rising Chinese Consumer," http://www.cfr.org/publication/23156/rising_chinese_consumer.html

7. "Post-Crisis China and the Changing Global Order," Carnegie Endowment for International Peace, September 8, 2010.

8. http://blogs.cfr.org/geographics/2010/10/25/china-2/

9. "The quest for growth," *The Economist*, October 9, 2010, p. 19.

10. David Pilling, "How being big helps and hinders China," *Financial Times*, October 7, 2010.

11. "The Rising Chinese Consumer," op. cit.

12. Daniel Schäfer, "Strong demand from China jump-starts VW profits," *Financial Times*, October 28, 2010.

13. Christopher O' Hara, "China and the EU: Economy Prevails," Policy Brief No. 37, October 1, 2010 (Stockholm: Institute for Security and Development Policy)

14. United States Trade Representative, "National Trade Estimate Report on Foreign Trade Barriers," May 17, 2010; Ezell and Atkinson, op. cit.; Jakob Elder and Luke Georghiou, "Public procurement and innovation—Resurrecting the demand side," *Research Policy*, 36 (2007): 949-963, http://dimetic.dimeeu.org/dimetic_files/EdlerGeorghiou2007.pdf; Information Technology Industry Council, "China Policy," http://www.itic.org/index.php?src=gendocs&ref=china_policy&category=trade.

15. Cited in John Gapper, "China's crafty play on trading places," *Financial Times*, December 9, 2010.

16. Keith Bradsher, "China Sets Rules and Wins Wind Power Game," *The New York Times*, December 15, 2010; Pilling, op. cit.; Jamil Anderlini, "Pie is growing, but foreigners share is shrinking," *Financial Times*, October 27, 2010; "Train Makers Rail Against China's High-Speed Designs, *The Wall Street Journal*, September 28, 2010.

17. Pilling, op. cit.

18. For details, notes and sources on trade in services, please see Chapter 2.

19. European Chamber of Commerce in China, "European Business in China 2010/2011 Position Paper," available at http://www.europeanchamber.com.cn/images/documents/marketing_department/beijing/publications/2010/executive_summary.pdf

20. For details, notes and sources on FDI and capital flows, please see Chapter 3.

21. Arora and Vamvakidis, op. cit.

22. Nora Burghart and Vanessa Rossi, "China's Overseas Direct Investment in the UK," Chatham House Briefing Paper, December 2009.

23. Liz Alderman, "Looking for Investments, China Turns to Europe," *New York Times*, November 1, 2010.

24. Philip Inman, Terry Macalister and Richard Wachman, "Ireland at forefront of Chinese plans to conquer Europe," *The Guardian*, June 25, 2010; Helene Colliopoulou, "Greece picks up Chinese support as Wen visits," *Agence France Presse*, October 2, 2010.

25. Jijo Jacob, "Could China be the 'prince charming' for Ireland?" *International Business Times*, November 20, 2010.

26. For details, notes and sources on energy links, please see Chapter 4.

27. In 2009 clean energy investment in China totaled $34.6 billion, compared with $18.6 billion in the United States. In August 2010 Chinese officials announced that they would spend $75 billion a year on clean energy. See Juliet Eilperin, "China goes all-out to out-green the rest of the world," *The Washington Post*, September 30, 2010; John Gummer, "Europe can join hands with Beijing on emissions," *Financial Times*, October 7, 2010.

28. Keith Bradsher, "Pentagon Must 'Buy American,' Barring Chinese Solar Panels," *New York Times*, January 9, 2010.

29. European Chamber of Commerce in China, cited in Eilperin, op. cit.

30. Leslie Hoo, "China tightens its grip on the production of rare earths," Financial Times, October 7, 2010.

31. Jonathan Soble, "Japan concerned on Chinese dependence," *Financial Times*, October 7, 2010.

32. Ed Crooks, "US rare-earths concern is well-placed to profit," *Financial Times*, October 28, 2010; Keith Bradsher, "Unlocking a Grip on Rare Earths," *The New York Times*, December 15, 2010.

33. For details, notes and sources on movement of people, please see Chapter 5.

34. Eurostat Database.

35. Ministry of Education of the People's Republic of China.

36. For details, notes and sources on links in innovation and ideas, please see Chapter 6.

37. €3 million out of EU total outward stocks in Hong Kong in 2006 was in R&D, while the amount of EU inward stocks owned by Hong Kong in R&D in 2006 was €-6 million. Eurostat Database.

Chapter 11: The EU and Rising Asia: Opportunity Knocks

1. For details, notes and sources on trade in goods, please see Chapter 1.

2. For details, notes and sources on trade in services, please see Chapter 2.

3. Jonas Parello-Plesner, "Asia doesn't forget about Europe when trade is involved," European Council on Foreign Relations, October 4, 2010, http://ecfr.eu/content/entry/commentary_dont_forget_about_europe_when_trade_is_involved/. Korea faces similar challenges as Japan when it comes to the lagging productivity of its services sector, and both are far less productive than the EU when it comes to services. This has significant implications for Korea's economic prospects, given that such services as logistics, financial, consulting, engineering, and software design are important to manufacturing, and market research, business consulting, and financial services are all significant to the automobile industry. The per capita value-added of even Korea's most productive service sectors—financial and real estate services— are only 50-80% of the productivity rates of major OECD countries. Woo, op. cit.; Exell and Atkinson, op. cit.; Lewis, op. cit.

4. For details, notes and sources on FDI and capital flows, please see Chapter 3.

5. For details, notes and sources on energy, please see Chapter 4.

6. UNHCR 2008 data. The EU took in 51,136 asylum-seekers from developing East Asia in 2008. 43%, or 21,778, went to France; Germany took in 17,260, or about one-third of all those coming to the EU; and 2.5%, or 1,314 went to the UK. The United States, in contrast, took in 14,517, or 28% of the total. Japan, the Asian neighbor, only took in 1,692, or 3.3%. For details, notes and sources on movement of people, please see Chapter 5.

7. ASEAN Tourism Statistics.

Chapter 12: The EU and India: Surprisingly Weak Links

1. Amy Kazmin, "Labour to unlock," *Financial Times*, October 5, 2010.

2. "BRICs are Still on Top," *Newsweek*, December 7, 2009.

3. For details, notes and sources on trade in goods, please see Chapter 1.

4. "Hopes and hurdles,...." op. cit.

5. Less than 5% of the output of Indian ICT service firms is consumed in India by Indian firms. The lion's share is exported. The rest of the Indian economy has extremely low productivity. Ezell and Atkinson, op. cit., p. 32. For details, notes and sources on services, please see Chapter 2.

6. For details, notes and sources on FDI and capital flows, please see Chapter 3.

7. For details, notes and sources on energy, please see Chapter 4.

8. For details, notes and sources on innovation links, please see Chapter 6.

9. Migration Policy Institute, "United Kingdom: A Reluctant Country of Immigration," July 2009, http://www.migrationinformation.org/Profiles/display.cfm?ID=736; for details, notes and sources on movement of people, please see Chapter 5.

Chapter 13: The EU and Russia: Stormy Weather

1. European Commission.

2. See Anders Aslund, "Assessing Moscow's Management of the Crisis," *Moscow Times*, October 27, 2010.

3. In 2010 Transparency International ranked Russia 154th out of 178 countries in terms of corruption. See Ira Iosebashvili, "Russia ranked as more corrupt amid faltering reform efforts," *The Wall Street Journal Europe*, October 27, 2010. Also "BRICs are Still on Top," op. cit.

4. For details, notes and sources on trade in goods, please see Chapter 1.

5. For details, notes and sources on services, please see Chapter 2.

6. For details, notes and sources on FDI and capital flows, please see Chapter 3.

7. For details, notes and sources on energy, please see Chapter 4.

8. Fredrik Erixon, "Europe's energy dependency and Russia's commercial assertiveness," ECIPE Policy Brief No. 7, 2008, citing European Commission figures.

9. *Commission staff working document–Accompanying document to the Proposal for a Regulation of the European Parliament and of the Council concerning measures to safeguard security of gas supply and repealing Directive 2004/67/EC. Assessment report of directive 2004/67/EC on security of gas supply {COM(2009) 363}.* European Commission. 2009-07-16. pp. 33; 56; 63–76. http://eurlex.europa.eu/LexUriServ/LexUriServ.do?uri=SEC: 2009:0978:FIN:EN:PDF; Thomas Gomart, "EU-Russia Relations: Toward a Way Out of the Depression" (Washington, DC: CSIS, 2008).

10. Stefan Meister, "Growth without Sustainability: What the financial crisis says about Russia's economy," *DGAP Analyse*, January 2009.

11. Ibid.

Chapter 14: The EU and the Middle East: Energy, and People

1. European Commission.

2. For details, notes and sources on trade in goods, please see Chapter 1.

3. For details, notes and sources on services, please see Chapter 2.

4. For details, notes and sources on FDI and capital flows, please see Chapter 3.

5. For details, notes and sources on movement of people, please see Chapter 5.

Chapter 15: The EU and Africa: Energy, People, and Neglected Opportunities

1. "Colonial bonds hamper Africa's trade renaissance," *Financial Times*, October 22, 2010.

2. For details, notes and sources on energy, please see Chapter 4.

3. The Mediterranean Solar Plan is led by Germany, France, Italy and Spain, together with the European Solar Thermal Electricity Association (ESTELA). The Desertec Initiative is being advanced by the Desertec Foundation, a coalition of various European companies and institutions. It seeks to cover 15% of European

energy needs by 2050. See Isabelle Werenfels and Kirsten Westphal, "Solarstrom aus Nordafrika: Rahmenbe-dingungen und Perspektiven," *SWP-Studie*, Februar 2010 (Berlin: Stiftung Wissenschaft und Politik, 2010); ESTELA, *Solar Power from the Sun Belt* (Brussels, June 2009).

4. For details, notes and sources on movement of people, please see Chapter 6.

5. For details, notes and sources on trade in goods, please see Chapter 1.

6. For details, notes and sources on services, please see Chapter 2.

7. For details, notes and sources on FDI and capital flows, please see Chapter 3.

8. The World Bank committed $11.2 billion in concessional loans and grants from IDA in FY08.

9. Acha Leke, Susan Lund, Charles Roxburgh, and Arend van Wamelen, "What's driving Africa's growth," *McKinsey Quarterly*, June 2010.

Chapter 16: The EU and Latin America: Commodities, Services, Energy, and People

1. European Commission.

2. For details, notes and sources on trade in goods, please see Chapter 1.

3. *Assessing the costs and benefits of a closer EU-Canada economic partnership: A Joint Study by the European Commission and the Government of Canada*, 2008, available at http://www.international.gc.ca/trade-agreements-accords-commerciaux/assets/pdfs/EU-CanadaJointStudy-en.pdf

4. Costa Rica, Guatemala, Honduras, Nicaragua, Panamá and El Salvador.

5. For details, notes and sources on services, please see Chapter 2.

6. Osvaldo Rosales, "EU-Latin America trade relations in the new global context," Presentation, Friends of Europe, June 29. 2010, available at http://www.eclac.org/comercio/tpl/contenidos/EU_Latin_America_trade_relations_presentation.pdf

7. European Commission, DG Trade.

8. For details, notes and sources on FDI and capital flows, please see Chapter 3.

9. For details, notes and sources on energy, please see Chapter 4.

10. For details, notes and sources on movement of people, please see Chapter 5.

11. "So near and yet so far," *The Economist*, September 11, 2010.

Chapter 17: The EU and the Caribbean: Follow the Money

1. Rachel Keeler, "Tax Havens and the Financial Crisis," *Dollars & Sense*, May/June 2009, http://dollarsand-sense.org/archives/2009/0509keeler.html

2. Richard Freeman, "London's Cayman Islands: The Empire of the Hedge Funds," Global Research, March 11, 2007, http://www.globalresearch.ca/index.php?context=va&aid=5045

3. For details, notes and sources on capital flows and FDI, please see Chapter 3.

4. *The Global Financial Centres Index 8*, September 2010, Z/Yen Group Limited, available at http://www.zyen.com/GFCI/GFCI%208.pdf.

5. European Commission; Agence France Presse; Gillian Gunn Clissold, Jerome Lebleu and Louise Shelley, "Survival at What Cost? The Impact of Financial Services on Small Caribbean States," Caribbean Briefing Paper Series No. 6, November 2003.

6. For details, notes and sources on energy, please see Chapter 4.

7. Cariforum includes the Dominican Republic and the 14 members of CARICOM: Antigua and Barbuda, The Bahamas, Barbados, Belize, Dominica, Grenada, Guyana, Haiti, Jamaica, Montserrat, Saint Lucia, St. Kitts and Nevis, St. Vincent and the Grenadines, Suriname, and Trinidad and Tobago.

8. For details, notes and sources on movement of people, please see Chapter 5.

Chapter 18: The EU and Oceania: Distant Cousins

1. For details, notes and sources on trade in goods, please see Chapter 1.

2. For details, notes and sources on services, please see Chapter 2.

3. For details, notes and sources on FDI and capital goods, please see Chapter 3.

4. For details, notes and sources on energy, please see Chapter 4.

5. For details, notes and sources on movement of people, please see Chapter 5.

Notes on Terms, Data, and Sources

Throughout this report, the term "EU" refers to all 27 member states of the European Union. The term EU15 refers to the older EU member states: the United Kingdom, Ireland, Belgium, Luxembourg, the Netherlands, Austria, Spain, Italy, Greece, France, Germany, Portugal, Sweden, Finland, and Denmark. The term EU12 refers to the newer EU member states: Estonia, Latvia, Lithuania, Poland, the Czech Republic, Slovakia, Hungary, Slovenia, Malta, Cyprus, Romania and Bulgaria.

Africa: Algeria, Angola, Benin, Botswana, Burkina Faso, Burundi, Cameroon, Cape Verde, Central African Republic, Chad, Comoros, Congo, Dem. Rep. of, Congo, Rep. of, Côte d'Ivoire, Djibouti, Equatorial Guinea, Eritrea, Ethiopia, Gabon, Gambia, Ghana, Guinea, Guinea-Bissau, Kenya, Lesotho, Liberia, Libya, Madagascar, Malawi, Mali, Mauritania, Mauritius, Mayotte, Morocco, Mozambique, Namibia, Niger, Nigeria, Réunion, Rwanda, Senegal, Seychelles, Sierra Leone, Somalia, South Africa, Sudan, Swaziland, Tanzania, Tunisia, Uganda, Zambia, Zimbabwe.

Caribbean: Anguilla, Antigua and Barbuda, Aruba, Bahamas, Barbados, Bermuda, British West Indies, Cayman Islands, Cuba, Dominica, Dominican Republic, French Guiana, Grenada, Guadeloupe, Haiti, Jamaica, Martinique, Montserrat, Netherlands Antilles, Puerto Rico, São Tomé and Príncipe, St. Kitts and Nevis, St. Lucia, St. Pierre and Miquelon, St. Vincent and the Grenadines, Trinidad and Tobago, Turks and Caicos Islands, U.S. Virgin Islands.

Rising Asia: Afghanistan, Bangladesh, Bhutan, Brunei Darussalam, Cambodia, Hong Kong, Indonesia, Kazakhstan, Kyrgyzstan, Laos, Macao, Malaysia, Maldives, Mongolia, Myanmar, Nepal, North Korea, Pakistan, Palau, Philippines, Singapore, South Korea, Sri Lanka, Taiwan, Tajikistan, Thailand, Turkmenistan, Uzbekistan, Vietnam.

Latin America: Argentina, Belize, Bolivia, Brazil, Chile, Colombia, Costa Rica, Ecuador, El Salvador, Falkland Islands, Guatemala, Guyana, Honduras, Nicaragua, Panama, Paraguay, Peru, Suriname, Uruguay, Venezuela.

Middle East: Bahrain, Egypt, Iran, Iraq, Israel, Jordan, Kuwait, Lebanon, Oman, Palestinian Territories, Qatar, Saudi Arabia, Syria, Turkey, United Arab Emirates, Yemen.

North America: Canada, Mexico, United States.

Oceania: American Samoa, Australia, Christmas Island, Cocos (Keeling) Islands, Cook Islands, East Timor, Fiji, French Polynesia, Guam, Kiribati, Marshall Islands, Micronesia, Nauru, New Caledonia, New Zealand, Niue, Norfolk Island, Papua New Guinea, Pitcairn, Samoa, Solomon Islands, Togo, Tokelau, Tonga, Tuvalu, United States Minor Outlying Islands, Vanuatu, Wallis and Futuna Islands.

Wider Europe: Albania, Andorra, Armenia, Azerbaijan, Belarus, Bosnia and Herzegovina, Croatia, Faroe Islands, Georgia, Gibraltar, Greenland, Guernsey, Iceland, Isle of Man, Jersey, Liechtenstein, Macedonia, Moldova, Monaco, Montenegro, Republic of, Norway, San Marino, Serbia, Switzerland, Ukraine, Vatican.

Where possible, data is drawn from official sources: the European Commission, European governments, the U.S. Commerce Department's Bureau of Economic Analysis, the OECD, European Central Bank, the United Nations, the European Bank for Reconstruction and Development, the World Bank, and the International Monetary Fund. I have also drawn on considerable scholarly work, which has been cited. I apologize for unintended omissions or errors, and want to express my appreciation to those who have worked so hard to produce such useful data and analysis.

About the Author

Daniel S. Hamilton is the Austrian Marshall Plan Foundation Professor and Executive Director of the Center for Transatlantic Relations at the Paul H. Nitze School of Advanced International Studies (SAIS), Johns Hopkins University, named in annual surveys conducted by the University of Pennsylvania as one of the "Top 20 U.S. Go-To Think Tanks" in 2010 and one of the "Top 30 Global Go-To Think Tanks" in 2009. He also serves as Executive Director of the American Consortium for EU Studies, designated by the European Commission as the EU Center of Excellence Washington, DC. He has served as Deputy Assistant Secretary of State for Europe; U.S. Special Coordinator for Southeast European Stabilization; and as Associate Director of the U.S. Secretary of State's Policy Planning Staff. In 2008 he served as the first Robert Bosch Foundation Senior Diplomatic Fellow in the German Foreign Office. He hosted *The Washington Post/Newsweek International*'s online discussion feature *Next Europe*, and is a member of academic and advisory boards for the Robert Bosch Stiftung; the Stiftung Wissenschaft und Politik (SWP); the European-American Business Council, the Center for European Policy Analysis; the Prague Center for Transatlantic Relations; and the Council on European Studies.

Dr. Hamilton is the Coordinator of the Enabling Technologies Coalition, an international grouping of scholars, businesses, non-governmental organizations and other stakeholders that promotes research on the potential for enabling technologies to facilitate economic growth in the areas of health; low-carbon economy; education; and governance.

He has also taught graduate courses in U.S. foreign policy and U.S.-European relations at the University of Innsbruck, the Hertie School of Governance in Berlin, and the Free University of Berlin. Recent publications include *Shoulder to Shoulder: Forging a Strategic U.S.-EU Partnership* (2010); *Alliance Reborn: An Atlantic Compact for the 21st Century* (2009) by the Washington NATO Project; The *Transatlantic Economy* (annual editions, 2004-2011); *Humanitarian Assistance: Improving U.S.-European Cooperation* (2009); *France, America and the World: A New Era in Franco-American Relations?* (2009); *Germany and Globalization* (2009); *France and Globalization* (2008); *Europe and Globalization* (2008); *The Wider Black Sea Region: Strategic, Economic and Energy Perspectives* (2008); *The New Eastern Europe: Ukraine, Belarus and Moldova* (2007). *Terrorism and International Relations* (2006); *Transatlantic Homeland Security* (2005).